TOP
10
OF
EVERYTHING
2008

TOP
10
OF EVERYTHING
2008

Russell Ash

hamlyn

Contents

Produced for Hamlyn by
Palazzo Editions Ltd
15 Gay Street, Bath, BA1 2PH

Publishing director: Colin Webb
Art director: Bernard Higton
Project editor: Sonya Newland
Picture researcher: Melinda Revesz

First published in Great Britain in 2007 by
Hamlyn, a division of
Octopus Publishing Group Ltd
2–4 Heron Quays, London E14 4JP

Distributed in the United States and Canada by
Sterling Publishing Co., Inc.
387 Park Avenue South, New York
NY 10016-8810

ISBN-13: 978-0-600-61678-8
ISBN-10: 0-600-61678-9

A CIP catalogue record for this book is
available from the British Library

Printed and bound in China

10 9 8 7 6 5 4 3 2 1

The Top 10 of "Top 10 of Everything"

1. LISTMANIA

We are constantly bombarded with lists. The press and TV programs present rankings based on market research and polls, lists of the best places to live, top schools, the greatest films, the bestselling books, the worst crime rates, and so on. Ranked lists have become a way of managing what might otherwise be a daunting mass of facts and figures, putting our world into a perspective that we can readily grasp. *Top 10 of Everything* provides a unique collection of lists in a diverse array of categories that are, I hope, informative, educational, and entertaining.

2. WHY 10?

Firstly, it's a manageable number—most of us can remember 10 telephone numbers, but not, say, 100. We have 10 fingers and 10 toes, historic lists such as the 10 Commandments and modern lists of bestsellers, whether records or books, are traditionally 10s, while the decimal system is a feature of many areas of daily life. There is a magic roundedness about 10 that just doesn't apply to any other number.

3. BEST AND WORST, FIRST AND LAST

The book makes no claim to offering the "10 Best of Everything." Not only is that not its title, but nor is it its intention. *Top 10 of Everything* is a book of definitive, strictly quantifiable Top 10 lists—not anyone's favorites. The only "bests" are those that are measurably bestsellers, while "worsts" such as disasters or worst serial killers are similarly ranked by cost or the number of victims. Some lists represent the first or latest achievers in categories, from the fastest cars to the winners of major awards, high achievers in numerous world sports to the last 10 holders of the record as world's tallest building.

4. GROUND RULES

Countries are independent countries, not dependencies or overseas territories. All the lists are all-time and global unless a specific year or territory is stated. Movie lists are based on cumulative global earnings, irrespective of production or marketing budgets and, as is standard in the industry, inflation is not taken into account—which inevitably means that recent releases feature more prominently.

5. OLD AND NEW, RICHER OR POORER

Top 10 of Everything contains hundreds of Top 10s—old favorites brought up to date with the latest facts and figures, lists that change radically from year to year—such as the most-watched movies and bestselling albums—and a range of entirely new lists, such as those that focus on the emerging powers of China and India. Along with these are curiosities, from the most obese countries to the fattest US presidents, the oldest and the tallest people, the most popular first names and most watched movies across the decades, or the countries with the most people in jail. In such lists as, for example, the highest prices paid for works of art and the countries drinking the most Champagne, we can see that the rich are getting richer (even certain deceased celebrities keep on earning, proving that in the world of the dead rich it is possible to be worth more dead than alive), while some reveal the other side of the wealth divide. These lists are enhanced with a variety of features covering everything from the 100th anniversaries of the marathon race and the Scouts to the 50th anniversary of NASA.

6. WHO SAYS SO?

My sources encompass international organizations, commercial companies and research bodies, specialized publications and, especially, a network of individuals around the world who have shared their knowledge of everything from snakes and skyscrapers to ships and spiders. As ever, I gladly acknowledge their invaluable contribution (see page 255 for a full list of credits), as well as those who have been involved with the book at all stages of its development on this and the previous 18 annual editions.

7. A QUESTION OF DEFINITION

While sporting lists, for example, are definitive in that an individual or team either won or lost or broke a record, many lists in *Top 10 of Everything* present issues of definition: does a country's area include only the land or also the water, the price paid for a valuable painting at auction the buyer's premium, or the height of a tall building the spire on its roof? Where such issues arise, the standard adopted is indicated.

8. WORLD RANKING

World Internet usage recently topped one billion and, for the first time, music tracks can reach No. 1 in the chart based solely on downloads, rather than physical record sales. Such changes are reflected in Top 10 lists that are based on individual countries and those that present a worldwide ranking. If the US does not figure in a country-based list, it is generally added as an extra entry.

9. LISTLESS—THE ONES THAT GOT AWAY

Certain list themes remain elusive or downright impossible. There are those that don't get to 10—only nine actors, for example, have ever received three consecutive Oscar nominations. Then there are those where there is no way of establishing a statistical basis—we simply don't know what the most common names in the world might be. There are some where there are issues of secrecy—like the biggest robberies of all time, which may include computer theft or those from safe-deposit boxes, where the value of the contents is unknown. Finally, the 10 rarest of almost anything is an unrewarding quest: the rarest of anything is where there is only one example. Solutions to some of these imponderables may emerge in time, which is where you come in…

10. CAN I GET INVOLVED?

Yes, please—your comments, corrections, and suggestions for new lists are always welcome. Please contact me via the publishers or visit my website:

http://www.top10ofeverything.com

Russell Ash

1

THE UNIVERSE
& THE EARTH

The Universe

TOP 10 **ASTEROIDS DUE TO COME CLOSEST TO EARTH**

NAME/ DESIGNATION	DUE DATE*	DISTANCE MILES	KM
1 Aphosis	Apr 13, 2029	21,547	34,677
2 2005 YU55	Nov 8, 2011	98,998	159,322
3 2000 WO107	Dec 2, 2169	150,867	242,797
4 2000 WN5	Jun 26, 2028	155,235	249,828
5 1998 OX4	Jan 22, 2148	186,283	299,794
6 1999 AN10	Aug 7, 2027	241,684	388,954
7 1998 MZ	Nov 26, 2116	255,628	411,394
8 1997 XF11	Oct 28, 2136	256,743	413,189
9 2003 QC10	Sep 24, 2066	315,677	508,034
10 2001 GQ2	Apr 27, 2100	316,049	508,632

* Closest point to Earth

It is believed that there are up to 2,000 "Near-Earth Objects" (mostly asteroids and comets) over 0.6 miles (1 km) in diameter, and many thousands of smaller ones, that approach Earth's orbit and could potentially impact with our planet. The PHAs (Potentially Hazardous Asteroids) listed here are predicted to make the closest approaches. It is widely accepted that an asteroid impact with Earth some 65 million years ago was responsible for the extinction of the dinosaurs. However, although coming closest, the chance of Aphosis impacting with Earth or the Moon is put at 0.017 percent. Among recent visitors, asteroid 2004 XP14 approached to within 268,734 miles (432,487 km) on July 3, 2006, and we lived to tell the tale.

Canyon Diablo, Arizona
The fragments that have been recovered from the Meteor, or Barringer Crater and adjacent Canyon Diablo, from which the meteorite takes its name, represent a fraction of the total. Much of it vaporized before impact, but it may have weighed up to 330,000 tons.

TOP 10 **LARGEST METEORITES EVER FOUND**

LOCATION	ESTIMATED WEIGHT (TONS)
1 Hoba West, Grootfontein, Namibia	>66.1
2 Ahnighito ("The Tent"), Cape York, West Greenland	63.2
3 Campo del Cielo, Argentina	45.6
4 Canyon Diablo*, Arizona, USA	33.1
5 Sikhote-Alin, Russia	29.8
6 Chupaderos, Mexico	26.7
7 Bacuberito, Mexico	24.3
8 Armanty, Western Mongolia	22.0
9 Mundrabilla#, Western Australia	18.7
10 Mbosi, Tanzania	17.6

* Formed Meteor Crater; fragmented—total in public collections about 12.7 tons
# In two parts

Meteorites have been known since early times: fragments of meteorite have been found mounted in a necklace in an Egyptian pyramid and in ancient Native American burial sites. The Hoba meteorite, the largest in the world, was found on a farm in 1920. A 9 x 8 ft (2.73 x 2.43 m) slab, it consists of 82 percent iron and 16 percent nickel. "The Tent," now known by its original Inuit name, Ahnighito, was long used as a source of metals for harpoons and other tools. Along with two other large fragments, it was discovered in 1894, taken to the USA in 1897 by the American Arctic explorer Admiral Robert Peary, and is now in the Hayden Planetarium at the New York Museum of Natural History. It is the largest meteorite in the world on exhibition.

TOP 10 **GALAXIES NEAREST TO EARTH**

	GALAXY	DISCOVERED	DIAMETER (1,000 LIGHT YEARS)	APPROXIMATE DISTANCE (1,000 LIGHT YEARS)
1	Sagittarius Dwarf	1994	10	82
2	Large Magellanic Cloud	Prehist.	30	160
3	Small Magellanic Cloud	Prehist.	16	190
4	= Draco Dwarf	1954	3	205
	= Ursa Minor Dwarf	1954	2	205
6	Sculptor Dwarf	1937	3	254
7	Sextans Dwarf	1990	4	258
8	Carina Dwarf	1977	2	330
9	Fornax Dwarf	1938	6	450
10	Leo II	1950	3	660

Source: Peter Bond, Royal Astronomical Society

These, and other galaxies, are members of the so-called "Local Group," although with such vast distances "local" is clearly a relative term. As our Solar System and Earth are at the outer edge of the Milky Way, this is excluded. Over the next 100 million years, the Sagittarius Dwarf Elliptical Galaxy, our nearest neighboring galaxy, will be progressively absorbed into the Milky Way.

By and large
In astronomical terms, at a distance of 160,000 light years, the Large Magellanic Cloud is considered one of our nearest neighbors.

TOP 10 **BRIGHTEST STARS***

	STAR	CONSTELLATION	DISTANCE#	APPARENT MAGNITUDE
1	Sirius	Canis Major	8.61	−1.44
2	Canopus	Carina	312.73	−0.62
3	Arcturus	Boötes	36.39	−0.05†
4	Alpha Centauri A	Centaurus	4.40	−0.01
5	Vega	Lyra	25.31	+0.03
6	Capella	Auriga	42.21	+0.08
7	Rigel	Orion	772.91	+0.18
8	Procyon	Canis Minor	11.42	+0.40
9	Achernar	Eridanus	143.81	+0.45
10	Beta Centauri	Centaurus	525.22	+0.61

* Excluding the Sun
# From Earth in light years
† Variable

This Top 10 is based on apparent visual magnitude as viewed from Earth—the lower the number, the brighter the star, since by convention 1 was considered a star of first magnitude and 6 the faintest visible to the naked eye. On this scale, the Sun would be −26.73 and the full Moon −12.6.

TOP 10 **COMETS COMING CLOSEST TO EARTH**

	COMET	DATE*	DISTANCE MILES	DISTANCE KM
1	Comet of 1491	Feb 20, 1491	873,784	1,406,220
2	Lexell	Jul 1, 1770	1,403,633	2,258,928
3	Tempel-Tuttle	Oct 26, 1366	2,128,688	3,425,791
4	IRAS-Araki-Alcock	May 11, 1983	2,909,516	4,682,413
5	Halley	Apr 10, 1837	3,104,724	4,996,569
6	Biela	Dec 9, 1805	3,402,182	5,475,282
7	Grischow	Feb 8, 1743	3,625,276	5,834,317
8	Pons-Winnecke	Jun 26, 1927	3,662,458	5,894,156
9	Comet of 1014	Feb 24, 1014	3,783,301	6,088,633
10	La Hire	Apr 20, 1702	4,062,168	6,537,427

* Of closest approach to Earth

Space Exploration

Eyes to the skies
Sited at the summit of Mauna Kea, Hawaii, the twin Keck telescopes combine to form the most powerful on Earth.

TOP 10 LARGEST REFLECTING TELESCOPES

TELESCOPE NAME / YEAR BUILT / LOCATION	APERTURE FT	M
1 Large Binocular Telescope (2004) Mt. Graham, Arizona, USA	38.7	11.8
2 Southern African Large Telescope (2005) Sutherland, South Africa	36.1	11.0
3 Gran Telescopio Canarias (2005) La Palma, Canary Islands, Spain	34.1	10.4
4 = Keck I Telescope* (1993) Mauna Kea, Hawaii, USA	32.2	9.8
= Keck II Telescope* (1996) Mauna Kea, Hawaii, USA	32.2	9.8
6 Hobby-Eberly Telescope (1997) Mt. Fowlkes, Texas, USA	30.2	9.2
7 Subaru Telescope (1999) Mauna Kea, Hawaii, USA	27.2	8.3
8 = Antu Telescope# (1998) Cerro Paranal, Chile	26.9	8.2
= Kueyen Telescope# (1999) Cerro Paranal, Chile	26.9	8.2
= Melipal Telescope# (2000) Cerro Paranal, Chile	26.9	8.2
= Yepun Telescope# (2001) Cerro Paranal, Chile	26.9	8.2

TOP 10 MOST FREQUENTLY SEEN COMETS

	COMET	YEARS BETWEEN APPEARANCES
1	Encke 1	3.29
2	NEAT (Near Earth Asteroid Tracking) 22	4.20
3	Helfenzrieder 1	4.35
4	Catalina 3	4.42
5	LINEAR (Lincoln Near-Earth Asteroid Research) 30	4.85
6	LINEAR 46	4.86
7	= Grigg-Skjellerup 1	4.98
	= NEAT 10	4.98
9	LONEOS (Lowell Observatory Near-Earth-Object Search 6)	5.01
10	Blanpain 1	5.10

Source: NASA, Planetary Data System Small Bodies Node

The comets in the Top 10 and several others return with regularity (although with some variations), while others may not be seen again for many thousands, or even millions, of years. Encke's Comet, Earth's most frequent visitor, was named after German astronomer Johann Franz Encke (1791–1865), who calculated the period of its elliptical orbit—the second after that of Halley's Comet.

THE 10 FIRST ARTIFICIAL SATELLITES

	SATELLITE	COUNTRY	LAUNCH DATE
1	Sputnik 1	USSR	Oct 4, 1957
2	Sputnik 2	USSR	Nov 3, 1957
3	Explorer 1	USA	Feb 1, 1958
4	Vanguard 1	USA	Mar 17, 1958
5	Explorer 3	USA	Mar 26, 1958
6	Sputnik 3	USSR	May 15, 1958
7	Explorer 4	USA	Jul 26, 1958
8	SCORE	USA	Dec 18, 1958
9	Vanguard 2	USA	Feb 17, 1959
10	Discoverer 1	USA	Feb 28, 1959

Geostationary artificial satellites for use as radio relay stations were first proposed by the British science-fiction writer Arthur C. Clarke in the October 1945 issue of *Wireless World*, but it was 12 years

THE 10 FIRST BODIES TO HAVE BEEN VISITED BY SPACECRAFT

	BODY	SPACECRAFT / COUNTRY	DATE
1	Moon	Luna 1, USSR	Jan 2, 1959
2	Venus	Venera 1, USSR	May 19, 1961
3	Sun	Pioneer 5, USA	Aug 10, 1961
4	Mars	Mariner 4, USA	Jul 14, 1965
5	Jupiter	Pioneer 10, USA	Dec 3, 1973
6	Mercury	Mariner 10, USA	Mar 29, 1974
7	Saturn	Pioneer 11, USA	Sep 1, 1979
8	Comet Giacobini-Zinner	International Sun-Earth Explorer 3 (International Cometary Explorer), Europe/USA	Sep 11, 1985
9	Uranus	Voyager 2, USA	Jan 30, 1986
10	Halley's Comet	Vega 1, USSR	Mar 6, 1986

Only the first spacecraft successfully to approach or land on each body is included. Several of the bodies listed have been visited on subsequent occasions. Other bodies also visited since the first 10 include Neptune (by *Voyager 2*, USA, 1989) and asteroids Gaspra (*Galileo*, USA/Europe, 1991) and Hyakutake (*NEAR*, USA, 1996).

Venus revisited
Following the Soviet Venera probes, NASA's Pioneer Venus orbiters spent almost 14 years (1978–92) sending data from the planet.

THE 10 FIRST PLANETARY MOONS TO BE DISCOVERED

	MOON	PLANET	DISCOVERER	YEAR
1	Moon	Earth	–	Ancient
2	Io	Jupiter	Galileo Galilei (Italian)	1610
3	Europa	Jupiter	Galileo Galilei	1610
4	Ganymede	Jupiter	Galileo Galilei	1610
5	Callisto	Jupiter	Galileo Galilei	1610
6	Titan	Saturn	Christian Huygens (Dutch)	1655
7	Iapetus	Saturn	Giovanni Cassini (Italian/French)	1671
8	Rhea	Saturn	Giovanni Cassini	1672
9	Tethys	Saturn	Giovanni Cassini	1684
10	Dione	Saturn	Giovanni Cassini	1684

While Earth's Moon has been observed since ancient times, it was not until the development of the telescope that Italian astronomer Galileo Galilei (1564–1642) was able to discover (on January 7, 1610) the first moons of another planet. These, which are Jupiter's four largest, were named by German astronomer Simon Marius and are known as the Galileans. After the discoveries appearing in this list, no further moons were found until 1787, when German-born British astronomer William Herschel discovered Oberon and Titania, the largest of the 27 satellites of Uranus, followed in 1789 by Enceladus and Mimas, two further moons of Saturn.

Human Spaceflight

THE 10 **FIRST MOONWALKERS**

ASTRONAUT*	SPACECRAFT	TOTAL EVA# HR:MIN	MISSION DATES
1 Neil Armstrong	Apollo 11	2:32	Jul 16–24, 1969
2 Edwin "Buzz" Aldrin	Apollo 11	2:15	Jul 16–24, 1969
3 Charles Conrad Jr.	Apollo 12	7:45	Nov 14–24, 1969
4 Alan Bean	Apollo 12	7:45	Nov 14–24, 1969
5 Alan Shepard	Apollo 14	9:23	Jan 31–Feb 9, 1971
6 Edgar Mitchell	Apollo 14	9:23	Jan 31–Feb 9, 1971
7 David Scott	Apollo 15	19:08	Jul 26–Aug 7, 1971
8 James Irwin	Apollo 15	18:35	Jul 26–Aug 7, 1971
9 John Young	Apollo 16	20:14	Apr 16–27, 1972
10 Charles Duke Jr.	Apollo 16	20:14	Apr 16–27, 1972

* All USA—the only country to have sent men to the Moon
# Extra-Vehicular Activity—time spent out of the lunar module on the Moon's surface

Second man on the Moon
The now-iconic image of Buzz Aldrin on the surface of the Moon during the first lunar landing, July 21, 1969.

THE 10 **FIRST COUNTRIES TO HAVE ASTRONAUTS OR COSMONAUTS IN ORBIT**

COUNTRY	ASTRONAUT/COSMONAUT	DATE*
1 USSR	Yuri Gagarin	Apr 12, 1961
2 USA	John Glenn	Feb 20, 1962
3 Czechoslovakia	Vladimir Remek	Mar 2, 1978
4 Poland	Miroslaw Hermaszewski	Jun 27, 1978
5 East Germany	Sigmund Jahn	Aug 26, 1978
6 Bulgaria	Georgi Ivanov	Apr 10, 1979
7 Hungary	Bertalan Farkas	May 26, 1980
8 Vietnam	Pham Tuan	Jul 23, 1980
9 Cuba	Arnaldo T. Mendez	Sep 18, 1980
10 Mongolia	Jugderdemidiyn Gurragcha	Mar 22, 1981

* Of first orbit of a national of that country

During the first 20 years of space travel, representatives of just 10 nations entered space. All missions by non-Soviet or non-Russian and non-US citizens were as guests of one of these countries until 2003, when China conducted its first mission. Western media—but not China—have dubbed these space travelers as "taikonauts."

TOP 10 **YOUNGEST ASTRONAUTS AND COSMONAUTS***

ASTRONAUT/COSMONAUT#	FIRST FLIGHT	YEARS	AGE MONTHS	DAYS
1 Gherman Titov	Aug 6, 1961	25	10	25
2 Valentina Tereshkova	Jun 16, 1963	26	3	10
3 Boris B. Yegoro	Oct 15, 1964	26	10	19
4 Yuri Gagarin	Apr 12, 1961	27	1	3
5 Helen Sharman (UK)	May 18, 1991	27	11	19
6 Mark Shuttleworth (South Africa)	Apr 25, 2002	28	7	7
7 Dumitru Prunariu (Romania)	May 14, 1981	28	7	24
8 Valery Bykovsky	Jun 14, 1963	28	10	19
9 Salman Abdel Aziz Al-Saud (Saudi Arabia)	Jun 17, 1985	28	11	20
10 Vladimir Remek (Czechoslovakia)	Mar 2, 1978	29	5	6

* To March 31, 2007
\# Soviet unless otherwise indicated

TOP 10 **OLDEST ASTRONAUTS AND COSMONAUTS***

ASTRONAUT/COSMONAUT#	LAST FLIGHT	YEARS	AGE MONTHS	DAYS
1 John Glenn	Nov 6, 1998	77	3	19
2 Mike Melvill	Sep 29, 2004	63	9	29
3 F. Story Musgrave	Dec 7, 1996	61	3	19
4 Dennis Tito	May 6, 2001	60	8	21
5 Gregory Olsen	Oct 1, 2005	60	5	11
6 Vance D. Brand	Dec 11, 1990	59	7	2
7 Jean-Loup Chrétien (France)	Oct 6, 1997	59	1	7
8 Valey Ryumin (Russia)	Jun 12, 1998	58	9	27
9 Karl G. Henize	Aug 6, 1985	58	9	20
10 Roger K. Crouch	Jul 17, 1997	56	10	5

* Including payload specialists, space tourists, etc.; to March 31, 2007
\# US unless otherwise indicated

John Glenn, who in 1962 had been the first American astronaut to orbit Earth, re-entered space on October 29, 1998 aboard the Space Shuttle flight STS-95 *Discovery*, at the age of 77, becoming the oldest astronaut of all time by a considerable margin, and with the longest gap between missions. American businessman Dennis Tito's 2001 flight was as the first "space tourist." At 53, American astronaut Shannon Lucid holds the record as the oldest woman in space.

50 YEARS OF NASA

Up to 1958, the US space program was largely conducted as a military operation, principally by the Air Force and Navy, but on July 29 of that year President Eisenhower signed the so-called "Space Act," enabling the formation of NASA, the National Aeronautics and Space Administration, with the civilian exploration of space its principal objective. NASA came into existence on October 1, 1958. The Soviet Union had launched its *Sputnik* satellite the previous year, and the race to put a human in orbit was gaining momentum. That goal was achieved within three years of NASA's founding, with the *Mercury* program. It was followed by the *Gemini* (two-man capsules) and the *Apollo* missions that resulted in the first Moon landing in 1969, a year ahead of the target set by President Kennedy. In addition to its unmanned program, NASA has been responsible for over 115 Space Shuttle flights and has a pivotal role in the construction of the International Space Station.

NASA patches
Official NASA mission patches date from that of Gemini 5 (1965). Each includes a unique graphic device along with the designation of the mission and names of the crew members.

Elements

TOP 10 MOST COMMON ELEMENTS IN THE EARTH'S CRUST

	ELEMENT	PARTS PER MILLION*
1	Oxygen	461,000
2	Silicon	282,000
3	Aluminum	82,300
4	Iron	56,300
5	Calcium	41,500
6	Sodium	23,600
7	Magnesium	23,300
8	Potassium	20,900
9	Titanium	5,650
10	Hydrogen	1,400

* mg per kg; based on average percentages of elements in igneous rock

Source: *CRC Handbook of Chemistry and Physics* (77th ed.)

TOP 10 MOST COMMON ELEMENTS IN THE UNIVERSE

	ELEMENT	PARTS PER MILLION*
1	Hydrogen	750,000
2	Helium	230,000
3	Oxygen	10,000
4	Carbon	5,000
5	Neon	1,300
6	Iron	1,100
7	Nitrogen	1,000
8	Silicon	700
9	Magnesium	600
10	Sulfur	500

* mg per kg

TOP 10 MOST COMMON ELEMENTS IN THE OCEANS

	ELEMENT	AMOUNT (MG PER LITRE)
1	Oxygen*	857,000
2	Hydrogen*	107,800
3	Chlorine	19,870
4	Sodium	11,050
5	Magnesium	1,326
6	Sulfur	928
7	Calcium	422
8	Potassium	416
9	Bromine	67
10	Carbon	28

* Combined as water

TOP 10 MOST VALUABLE TRADED METALLIC ELEMENTS*

	ELEMENT	PRICE ($ PER KG)
1	Rhodium	176,825
2	Platinum	36,506
3	Gold	20,463
4	Ruthenium	20,174
5	Iridium	12,699
6	Osmium	12,217
7	Palladium	10,738
8	Rhenium	5,500
9	Germanium	980
10	Indium	750

* Based on 10–100 kg quantities of minimum 99.9 percent purity; excluding radioactive elements, isotopes, and rare earth elements traded in minute quantities

Source: Lipmann Walton, London Metal Bulletin, W. C. Heraeus GmbH & Co KG and www.thebulliondesk.com

TOP 10 METALLIC ELEMENTS WITH THE GREATEST RESERVES

	ELEMENT	MINIMUM ESTIMATED GLOBAL RESERVES (TONS)
1	Iron	100,000,000,000
2	Magnesium	20,000,000,000
3	Potassium	10,000,000,000
4	Aluminum	6,000,000,000
5	Manganese	3,000,000,000
6	= Chromium	1,000,000,000
	= Zirconium	1,000,000,000
8	Titanium	600,000,000
9	Barium	400,000,000
10	Copper	300,000,000

This list includes accessible reserves of commercially mined metallic elements but excludes calcium and sodium, which exist in such huge quantities that their reserves are considered "unlimited" and unquantifiable. In contrast, there are relatively small estimates of certain precious metals—gold, for example, is put at 16,500 tons. A further 500 kg of gold may be present in a cubic kilometre of seawater, but no economic method of extracting it has yet been devised.

Davy's Discoveries

By using the newly invented electric battery, British chemist Sir Humphry Davy (1778–1829) first isolated no fewer than six elements—potassium and sodium in 1807, and calcium, magnesium, strontium, and barium in 1808. He also proved chlorine to be an element in 1810. He went on to invent the Davy safety lamp.

Fiery firmament
Radiation emitted from stars within the Omega Nebula causes vast oceans of interstellar hydrogen to resemble an inferno. Some 75 percent of all matter and as much as 90 percent by number of atoms in the Universe is composed of hydrogen.

TOP 10 **LIGHTEST SOLID ELEMENTS**

ELEMENT / DISCOVERER / COUNTRY	YEAR DISCOVERED	DENSITY*
1 Lithium Johan August Arfvedson, Sweden	1817	0.533
2 Potassium Sir Humphry Davy, UK	1807	0.859
3 Sodium Sir Humphry Davy	1807	0.969
4 Calcium Sir Humphry Davy	1808	1.526
5 Rubidium Robert Wilhelm Bunsen/ Gustav Kirchhoff, Germany	1861	1.534
6 Magnesium Sir Humphry Davy	1808#	1.737
7 Phosphorus Hennig Brandt, Germany	1669	1.825
8 Beryllium Friedrich Wöhler, Germany/Antoine- Alexandré Brutus Bussy, France	1828†	1.846
9 Caesium Robert Wilhelm Bunsen/ Gustav Kirchhoff, Germany	1860	1.896
10 Sulfur	Prehist.	2.070

* Grams per cm³ at 68°F
# Recognized by Joseph Black, 1755, but not isolated
† Recognized by Nicholas Vauquelin, 1797, but not isolated

Lithium, the lightest solid element, is 42 times lighter than osmium, the heaviest. Although a metal, lithium is so soft that it can be easily cut with a knife. It is half as heavy as water, and lighter than certain types of wood. It is used in the aerospace industry to make lightweight alloys and in the air-filtration systems of spacecraft.

TOP 10 **HEAVIEST ELEMENTS**

ELEMENT / DISCOVERER / COUNTRY	YEAR DISCOVERED	DENSITY*
1 Osmium Smithson Tennant, UK	1803	22.59
2 Iridium Smithson Tennant	1803	22.56
3 Platinum Julius Caesar Scaliger#, Italy/France/ Antonio de Ulloa, Spain/ Charles Wood, UK†	1557 1735 1741	21.45
4 Rhenium Walter K. Noddack *et al*, Germany	1925	21.01
5 Neptunium Edwin Mattison McMillan/ Philip H. Abelson, USA	1940	20.47
6 Plutonium Glenn Theodore Seaborg *et al*, USA	1940	20.26
7 Gold	Prehist.	19.29
8 Tungsten Juan José and Fausto de Elhuijar, Spain	1783	19.26
9 Uranium Martin Heinrich Klaproth, Germany	1789	19.05
10 Tantalum Anders Gustav Ekeberg, Sweden	1802	16.67

* Grams per cm³ at 68°F
# Made earliest reference to
† Discovered

The two heaviest elements, the metals osmium and iridium, were discovered by British chemist Smithson Tennant (1761–1815). A 1-ft (30-cm) cube of osmium weighs 1,410 lb (640 kg)—equivalent to 10 people each weighing 141 lb (64 kg).

Waterworld

TOP 10 GREATEST* WATERFALLS

	WATERFALL	COUNTRY	AVERAGE FLOW FT³/SEC	AVERAGE FLOW M³/SEC
1	Inga	Dem. Rep. of Congo	1,500,000	42,476
2	Livingstone	Dem. Rep. of Congo	1,240,000	35,113
3	Boyoma (Stanley)	Dem. Rep. of Congo	600,000	16,990
4	Guíra	Brazil/Paraguay	491,190	13,909
5	Khône	Laos	410,000	10,783
6	Niagara (Horseshoe)	Canada/USA	212,200	6,009
7	Celilo	USA	191,215	5,415
8	Salto Pará	Venezuela	125,000	3,540
9	Paulo Afonso	Brazil	100,000	2,832
10	Iguaçu	Argentina/Brazil	61,660	1,746

* Based on volume of water

With an average flow rate of 459,090 ft³/sec (13,000 m³/sec) and a peak of 1,765,000 ft³/sec (50,000 m³/sec), the Guaíra, or Salto das Sete Quedas, between Brazil and Paraguay, once occupied second place in this list, and the Urubupungá, with a discharge rate of 97,000 ft³/sec (2,747 m³/sec) was in 6th position. Following the completion of the Itaipú dam in 1982, however, both are now "lost." At 6.7 miles (10.8 km), the Khône Falls are the widest in the world.

TOP 10 DEEPEST OCEANS AND SEAS

	SEA/OCEAN	AVERAGE DEPTH FT	AVERAGE DEPTH M
1	Pacific Ocean	12,925	3,939
2	Indian Ocean	12,598	3,840
3	Atlantic Ocean	11,730	3,575
4	Caribbean Sea, Atlantic Ocean	8,448	2,575
5	Sea of Japan, Pacific Ocean	5,468	1,666
6	Gulf of Mexico, Atlantic Ocean	5,297	1,614
7	Mediterranean Sea, Atlantic Ocean	4,926	1,501
8	Bering Sea, Pacific Ocean	4,893	1,491
9	South China Sea, Pacific Ocean	4,802	1,463
10	Black Sea, Atlantic Ocean	3,906	1,190

The deepest point in the deepest ocean is the Marianas Trench in the Pacific. In the first ever descent of the Marianas Trench, on January 23, 1960 by Jacques Piccard (Switzerland) and Donald Walsh (USA) in their 58-ft (17.7-m) bathyscaphe *Trieste 2*, a depth of 35,813 ft (10,916 m) was recorded. A more recent survey, on March 24, 1995 by Japanese unmanned probe *Kaikö*, recorded the slightly shallower depth of 35,798 ft (10,911 m). Whichever is the more precise, it is close to 6.8 miles (11 km) down, or almost 29 times the height of the Empire State Building.

TOP 10 DEEPEST FRESHWATER LAKES

	LAKE	LOCATION	GREATEST DEPTH FT	GREATEST DEPTH M
1	Baikal	Russia	5,712	1,741
2	Tanganyika	Burundi/Tanzania/Dem. Rep. of Congo/Zambia	4,826	1,471
3	Malawi	Malawi/Mozambique/Tanzania	2,316	706
4	Great Slave	Canada	2,014	614
5	Crater	Oregon, USA	1,949	594
6	Matana	Celebes, Indonesia	1,936	590
7	Toba	Sumatra, Indonesia	1,736	529
8	Hornindals	Norway	1,686	514
9	Sarezskoye (Sarez)	Tajikistan	1,657	505
10	Tahoe	California/Nevada, USA	1,643	501

TOP 10 DEEPEST DEEP-SEA TRENCHES

	TRENCH*	DEEPEST POINT FT	DEEPEST POINT M
1	Marianas	35,798	10,911
2	Tonga#	35,702	10,882
3	Philippine	34,580	10,540
4	Kuril-Kamchatka	34,449	10,500
5	Kermadec#	32,963	10,047
6	Bonin	32,789	9,994
7	New Britain	32,612	9,940
8	Izu	32,087	9,780
9	Puerto Rico	28,232	8,605
10	Yap	27,976	8,527

* With the exception of the Puerto Rico (Atlantic), all the trenches are in the Pacific
# Some authorities consider these parts of the same feature

Each of the eight deepest ocean trenches would be deep enough to submerge Mount Everest, which is 29,035 ft (8,850 m) above sea level.

TOP 10 **COUNTRIES WITH THE GREATEST AREAS OF INLAND WATER**

COUNTRY	% OF TOTAL AREA	WATER AREA SQ MILES	SQ KM
1 Canada	8.93	344,080	891,163
2 USA*	6.76	256,645	664,707
3 India	9.56	121,391	314,400
4 China	2.82	104,460	270,550
5 Sudan	5.18	50,120	129,810
6 Colombia	8.80	38,691	100,210
7 Indonesia	4.85	35,908	93,000
8 Russia	0.47	30,657	79,400
9 Dem. Rep. of Congo	3.32	30,427	77,810
10 Australia	0.90	26,610	68,920

* 50 states and District of Columbia

Source: CIA, *The World Factbook 2007*

Large areas of some countries are occupied by major rivers and lakes. Lake Victoria, for example, raises the water area of Uganda to 15.39 percent of its total. Several European countries have considerable areas of water, among them Sweden's 15,072 sq miles (39,036 sq km) and Finland's 12,185 sq miles (31,560 sq km).

Amazing Amazon
Although slightly shorter than the Nile, the Amazon basin covers a greater area—some 2.3 million sq miles (5.9 million sq km)—and discharges more water at its mouth than any other.

TOP 10 **GREATEST* RIVER SYSTEMS**

RIVER SYSTEM	CONTINENT	AVERAGE DISCHARGE AT MOUTH FT³/SEC	M³/SEC
1 Amazon	South America	7,733,912	219,000
2 Congo (Zaïre)	Africa	1,476,153	41,800
3 Yangtze (Chang Jiang)	Asia	1,126,537	31,900
4 Orinoco	South America	988,810	28,000
5 Brahmaputra (Tsangpo)	Asia	706,293	20,000
6 Yenisei-Angara	Asia	692,167	19,600
7 Río de la Plata-Paraná-Uruguay	South America	688,636	19,500
8 Mississippi-Missouri	North America	619,595	17,545
9 Lena	Asia	579,160	16,400
10 Mekong	Asia	561,503	15,900

* Based on rate of discharge at mouth

Source: River Systems of the World

Down Below

Low life
The Dead Sea is not only the lowest-lying place on Earth, but also so saline that swimmers float with ease.

TOP 10 **DEEPEST DEPRESSIONS**

DEPRESSION / LOCATION	MAXIMUM DEPTH BELOW SEA LEVEL FT	M
1 Dead Sea, Israel/Jordan	1,312	400
2 Lake Assal, Djibouti	511	156
3 Turfan Depression, China	505	154
4 Qattâra Depression, Egypt	436	133
5 Mangyshlak Peninsula, Kazakhstan	433	132
6 Danakil Depression, Ethiopia	383	117
7 Death Valley, California, USA	282	86
8 Salton Sink, California, USA	235	72
9 Zapadny Chink Ustyurta, Kazakhstan	230	70
10 Prikaspiyskaya Nizmennost', Kazakhstan/Russia	220	67

The shore of the Dead Sea is the lowest exposed ground below sea level, but the bed of the sea actually reaches 2,388 ft (728 m) below sea level, and that of Lake Baikal, Russia, attains 4,872 ft (1,485 m) below sea level. Much of Antarctica is below sea level (some as low as 8,326 ft/2,538 m)—but the land there is covered by an ice cap that averages 6,890 ft (2,100 m) in depth. The lowest points on continents outside those appearing in the Top 10 include South America's Peninsula Valdés, Argentina (131 ft/ 40 m below sea level), Europe's Caspian Sea shore (92ft/28 m), and Australia's Lake Eyre (52 ft/12 m).

TOP 10 **LONGEST CAVES**

CAVE / LOCATION / TOTAL KNOWN LENGTH MILES/KM

	Cave / Location	Miles / Km
1	Mammoth Cave System, Kentucky, USA	367 / 590.6
2	Jewel Cave, South Dakota, USA	135 / 218.2
3	Optimisticeskaja, Ukraine	134 / 215.0
4	Wind Cave, South Dakota, USA	124 / 198.8
5	Hölloch, Switzerland	120 / 193.6
6	Lechuguilla Cave, New Mexico, USA	120 / 193.4
7	Fisher Ridge System, Kentucky, USA	110 / 177.3
8	Sistema Sac Actun, Mexico	97 / 155.4
9	Siebenhengste-hohgant, Switzerland	96 / 154.0
10	Sistema Ox Bel Ha, Mexico	91 / 146.8

Going underground
The Mammoth Cave System has been explored for over 200 years and is visited by over two million people annually.

TOP 10 **COUNTRIES WITH THE LOWEST ELEVATIONS**

	COUNTRY*	HIGHEST POINT	ELEVATION FT	M
1	Maldives	Unnamed on Wilingili island in the Addu Atoll	7.8	2.4
2	Tuvalu	Unnamed	16.4	5
3	Marshall Islands	Unnamed on Likiep	32.8	10
4	The Gambia	Unnamed	173.9	53
5	Nauru	Unnamed on plateau rim	200.1	61
6	The Bahamas	Mount Alvernia on Cat Island	206.7	63
7	Vatican City	Unnamed	246.1	75
8	Kiribati	Unnamed on Banaba	265.7	81
9	Qatar	Qurayn Abu al Bawl	337.9	103
10	Singapore	Bukit Timah	544.6	166

* Excludes overseas possessions, territories, and dependencies

Source: CIA, *The World Factbook 2007*

These 10 countries are definitely off the agenda if you are planning a climbing holiday, none of them possessing a single elevation taller than a medium-sized skyscraper. Compared with these, even the Netherlands' 1,050-ft (321-m) Vaalserberg Hill makes the country's appellation as one of the "Low Countries" sound somewhat unfair. The low elevations of some countries make them vulnerable to the effects of tsunamis.

TOP 10 **DEEPEST CAVES**

The world's deepest cave is a comparatively recent discovery: in January 2001 a team of Ukrainian cave explorers in the Arabikskaja system in the western Caucasus mountains of the Georgian Republic found a branch of the Voronja or "Crow's Cave" and established that its depth far exceeded anything previously known. Progressively deeper penetrations have taken its extent to more than seven times the height of the Eiffel Tower.

	CAVE SYSTEM / LOCATION	DEPTH FT	M
10	Sistema Huautla, Mexico	4,839	1,475
9	Sistema Cheve (Cuicateco), Mexico	4,869	1,484
8	Cehi 2, Slovenia	4,928	1,502
7	Shakta Vjacheslav Pantjukhina, Georgia	4,948	1,508
6	Sarma, Georgia	5,062	1,543
5	Torca del Cerro del Cuevon/ Torca de las Saxifragas, Spain	5,213	1,589
4	Réseau Jean Bernard, France	5,256	1,602
3	Gouffre Mirolda, France	5,335	1,626
2	Lamprechtsofen Vogelschacht Weg Schacht, Austria	5,354	1,632
1	Krubera (Voronja), Georgia	7,119	2,170

On Top of the World

TOP 10 HIGHEST MOUNTAINS

MOUNTAIN / LOCATION / FIRST ASCENT / TEAM NATIONALITY	FT	M
1		
Everest, Nepal/China, May 29, 1953 British/New Zealand	29,035	8,850
2		
K2 (Chogori), Pakistan/China, Jul 31, 1954 Italian	28,251	8,611
3		
Kangchenjunga, Nepal/India, May 25, 1955 British	28,169	8,586
4		
Lhotse, Nepal/China, May 18, 1956 Swiss	27,940	8,516
5		
Makalu I, Nepal/China, May 15, 1955 French	27,838	8,485
6		
Cho Oyu, Nepal/China, Oct 19, 1954 Austrian	26,864	8,188
7		
Dhaulagiri I, Nepal, May 13, 1960 Swiss/Austrian	26,795	8,167
8		
Manaslu I (Kutang I), Nepal, May 9, 1956 Japanese	26,781	8,163
9		
Nanga Parbat (Diamir), Pakistan, Jul 3, 1953 German/Austrian	26,657	8,125
10		
Annapurna I, Nepal, Jun 3, 1950 French	26,545	8,091

* Height of principal peak; lower peaks of the same mountain are excluded

TOP 10 HIGHEST ACTIVE VOLCANOES*

VOLCANO / LOCATION	LAST ERUPTION	HEIGHT FT	M
1 Tupungato, Chile/Argentina	1986	21,555	6,570
2 Pular, Chile	1990	20,449	6,233
3 San Pedro, Chile	1960	20,161	6,145
4 Aracar, Argentina	1993	19,954	6,082
5 Guallatiri, Chile	1985	19,918	6,071
6 Tacora, Chile	1937	19,619	5,980
7 Sabancaya, Peru	2003	19,576	5,967
8 Cotopaxi, Ecuador	1942	19,393	5,911
9 Putana, Chile	1972	19,324	5,890
10 San Jose, Chile	1960	19,213	5,856

* Eruption during past 100 years

TOP 10 HIGHEST MOUNTAINS IN NORTH AMERICA

MOUNTAIN / COUNTRY	HEIGHT* FT	M
1 McKinley, Alaska, USA	20,320	6,194
2 Logan, Canada	19,545	5,959
3 Citlaltépetl (formerly Orizaba), Mexico	18,409	5,611
4 St. Elias, Alaska, USA/Canada	18,008	5,489
5 Popocatépetl, Mexico	17,887	5,452
6 Foraker, Alaska, USA	17,400	5,304
7 Ixtaccihuatl, Mexico	17,343	5,286
8 Lucania, Canada	17,147	5,226
9 King, Canada	16,971	5,173
10 Steele, Canada	16,644	5,073

* Height of principal peak; lower peaks of the same mountain are excluded

Mount McKinley was first climbed on June 7, 1913. Today, more than 600 people a year ascend the summit.

Measuring Everest

In 1852 the Great Trigonometrical Survey of India revealed that Everest (then called "Peak XV") was the world's tallest peak at 29,002 ft (8,840 m). Errors in measurement were corrected in 1955 to 29,029 ft (8,848 m) and in 1993 to 29,028 ft (8,847.7 m). In 1999 data beamed from sensors on Everest's summit to GPS (Global Positioning System) satellites established a new height of 29,035 ft (8,850 m), which geographers accept as the current "official" figure.

African heights
The world's tallest animal, the giraffe, poses against Kilimanjaro, Africa's highest mountain.

TOP 10 **HIGHEST MOUNTAINS IN AFRICA**

MOUNTAIN	COUNTRY	HEIGHT FT	M
1 Kilimanjaro	Tanganyika/Tanzania	19,340	5,895
2 Kenya	Kenya	17,058	5,199
3 Ngaliema	Uganda/Dem. Rep. of Congo	16,763	5,109
4 Duwoni	Uganda	16,062	4,896
5 Baker	Uganda	15,889	4,843
6 Emin	Dem. Rep. of Congo	15,741	4,798
7 Gessi	Uganda	15,470	4,715
8 Sella	Uganda	15,179	4,627
9 Ras Dashen	Ethiopia	15,158	4,620
10 Wasuwameso	Dem. Rep. of Congo	15,030	4,581

Kilimanjaro is the world's tallest freestanding mountain—one that is not part of a more extensive range. It was known to ancient writers such as Ptolemy as early as the 2nd century AD. It was first climbed in 1889 by Hans Meyer (Germany). Mount Kenya, also volcanic, was first scaled 10 years later by Halford Mackinder (UK).

TOP 10 **HIGHEST MOUNTAINS IN EUROPE**

MOUNTAIN	COUNTRY	HEIGHT* FT	M
1 Mont Blanc	France/Italy	15,771	4,807
2 Monte Rosa	Switzerland	15,203	4,634
3 Zumsteinspitze	Italy/Switzerland	14,970	4,564
4 Signalkuppe	Italy/Switzerland	14,941	4,555
5 Dom	Switzerland	14,911	4,545
6 Liskamm	Italy/Switzerland	14,853	4,527
7 Weisshorn	Switzerland	14,780	4,505
8 Täschorn	Switzerland	14,733	4,491
9 Matterhorn	Italy/Switzerland	14,688	4,477
10 Mont Maudit	France/Italy	14,649	4,466

* Height of principal peak; lower peaks of the same mountain are excluded

All 10 of Europe's highest mountains are in the Alps; there are, however, at least 15 mountains in the Caucasus (the mountain range that straddles Europe and Asia) that are taller than Mont Blanc. The highest of them, the west peak of Mount Elbrus, measures 18,510 ft (5,642 m).

Islands

TOP 10 MOST ISOLATED ISLANDS

ISLAND / LOCATION / ISOLATION INDEX

The United Nations' isolation index is calculated by adding together the square roots of the distances to the nearest island, group of islands, and continent. The higher the number, the more remote the island.

1 Easter Island, South Pacific 149

2 Rapa Iti, Tubuai Islands, South Pacific 130

3 Kiritimati, Line Islands, Central Pacific 129

4 Jarvis Island, Central Pacific 128

5= Kosrae, Micronesia, Pacific 126
Malden, Line Islands, Central Pacific 126
Starbuck, Line Islands, Central Pacific 126
Vostok, Line Islands, Central Pacific 126

9= Bouvet Island, South Atlantic 125
Gough Island, South Atlantic 125
Palmyra Island, Central Pacific 125

TOP 10 LARGEST ISLANDS IN THE USA

ISLAND / LOCATION	AREA SQ MILES	SQ KM
1 Hawaii, Hawaii	4,021	10,414
2 Kodiak, Alaska	3,588	9,293
3 Prince of Wales, Alaska	2,577	6,675
4 Chicagof, Alaska	2,080	5,388
5 Saint Lawrence, Alaska	1,983	5,135
6 Admiralty, Alaska	1,684	4,362
7 Nunivak, Alaska	1,625	4,209
8 Unimak, Alaska	1,590	4,119
9 Baranof, Alaska	1,569	4,065
10 Long Island, New York	1,401	3,629

TOP 10 SMALLEST ISLAND COUNTRIES

COUNTRY / LOCATION	AREA SQ MILES	SQ KM
1 Nauru, Pacific Ocean	8.2	21.2
2 Tuvalu, Pacific Ocean	10.0	26.0
3 Marshall Islands, Pacific Ocean	70.0	181.3
4 Saint Kitts and Nevis, Caribbean Sea	100.8	261.0
5 Maldives, Indian Ocean	115.1	298.0
6 Malta, Mediterranean Sea	122.0	316.0
7 Grenada, Caribbean Sea	132.8	344.0
8 Saint Vincent and the Grenadines, Caribbean Sea	150.2	389.0
9 Barbados, Caribbean Sea	166.4	431.0
10 Antigua and Barbuda, Caribbean Sea	170.9	442.6

TOP 10 **LARGEST ISLANDS**

ISLAND / LOCATION	AREA* SQ MILES	AREA* SQ KM
1 Greenland (Kalaatdlit Nunaat)	840,004	2,175,600
2 New Guinea, Papua New Guinea/Indonesia	303,381	785,753
3 Borneo, Indonesia/Malaysia/Brunei	288,869	748,168
4 Madagascar	226,917	587,713
5 Baffin Island, Canada	194,574	503,944
6 Sumatra, Indonesia	171,068	443,065
7 Honshu, Japan	87,805	227,413
8 Great Britain	84,200	218,077
9 Victoria Island, Canada	83,897	217,292
10 Ellesmere Island, Canada	75,767	196,236

* Mainlands, including areas of inland water, but excluding offshore islands

Australia is regarded as a continental land mass rather than an island, otherwise it would rank first, at 2,941,517 sq miles (7,618,493 sq km), or 35 times the size of Great Britain.

Small island
Comino, with Gozo and Malta, is one of the three inhabited islands that comprise the state of Malta. Together they form Europe's smallest island country and the smallest country in the EC.

TOP 10 **LARGEST LAKE ISLANDS**

ISLAND	LAKE / LOCATION	AREA SQ MILES	AREA SQ KM
1 Manitoulin	Huron, Ontario, Canada	1,068	2,766
2 René-Lavasseur	Manicouagan Reservoir, Quebec, Canada	780	2,020
3 Olkhon	Baikal, Russia	282	730
4 Samosir	Toba, Sumatra, Indonesia	243	630
5 Isle Royale	Superior, Michigan, USA	209	541
6 Ukerewe	Victoria, Tanzania	205	530
7 St. Joseph	Huron, Ontario, Canada	141	365
8 Drummond	Huron, Michigan, USA	134	347
9 Idjwi	Kivu, Dem. Rep. of Congo	110	285
10 Ometepe	Nicaragua, Nicaragua	107	276

Not all islands are surrounded by sea: many sizeable islands are situated in lakes. Vozrozhdeniya Island, Uzbekistan, previously second in this list with an area of approximately 900 sq miles (2,300 sq km), has grown as the Aral Sea contracts, and has now linked up with the surrounding land to become a peninsula. There are even larger islands in freshwater river outlets, including Marajó, in the mouth of the Amazon, Brazil (18,533 sq miles/ 48,000 sq km), and Bananal, in the River Araguaia, Brazil (7,722 sq miles/20,000 sq km).

Extreme World Weather

TOP 10 **COLDEST PLACES**

	LOCATION*	LOWEST RECORDED TEMPERATURE	
		°F	°C
1	Vostok#, Antarctica	−128.6	−89.2
2	Sovietskaya#, Antarctica	−124.1	−86.7
3	Oymyakon, Russia	−96.2	−71.2
4	Verkhoyansk, Russia	−93.6	−69.8
5	Northice#, Greenland	−87.0	−66.0
6	Eismitte#, Greenland	−85.0	−64.9
7 =	Snag, Yukon, Canada	−81.4	−63.0
=	Bulunkul Lake, Tajikistan	−81.4	−63.0
9	Mayo, Yukon, Canada	−80.0	−62.2
10	Prospect Creek, Alaska, USA	−79.8	−62.1

* Maximum of two places per country listed
\# Present or former scientific research base

Source: Philip Eden/Roland Bert

Vostok, a Russian research station, recorded the lowest temperature on Earth on July 21, 1983, and, though unofficial, an even colder one of −132°F (−91°C) in 1997. It is situated at an altitude of 11,220 ft (3,420 m) and is susceptible to high-speed katabatic (downhill) winds that can reach up to 200 mph (322 km/h).

Cold comfort
The Siberian village of Oymyakon recorded the lowest temperature in the Northern Hemisphere and of any inhabited place on Earth.

TOP 10 **PLACES WITH THE MOST RAINY DAYS**

LOCATION* / RAINY DAYS PER ANNUM#

* Maximum of two places per country listed
\# Averaged over a long period of years

Source: Philip Eden

1 Waialeale, Hawaii, USA 335
2 Marion Island, South Africa 312
3 Pohnpei, Federated States of Micronesia 311
4 Andagoya, Colombia 306
5 Macquarie Island, Australia 299
6 Gough Island, Tristan da Cunha group, South Atlantic 291
7 Palau, Federated States of Micronesia 286
8 Heard Island, Australia 279
9 Camp Jacob, Guadeloupe 274
10 Atu Nau, Alaska, USA 268

TOP 10 **HOTTEST PLACES**

	LOCATION*	HIGHEST TEMPERATURE °F	°C
1	Al'Aziziyah, Libya	136.4	58.0
2	Greenland Ranch, Death Valley, USA	134.0	56.7
3	= Ghudamis, Libya	131.0	55.0
	= Kebili, Tunisia	131.0	55.0
5	Tombouctou, Mali	130.1	54.5
6	= Araouane, Mali	130.0	54.4
	= Mammoth Tank#, California, USA	130.0	54.4
8	Tirat Tavi, Israel	129.0	54.0
9	Ahwaz, Iran	128.3	53.5
10	Agha Jari, Iran	128.0	53.3

* Maximum of two places per country listed
\# Former weather station

Source: Philip Eden/Roland Bert

Dead hot
Death Valley, California, and the Western Hemisphere's record highest temperature was measured at the ironically named Greenland Ranch (now Furnace Creek) weather station on July 10, 1913.

TOP 10 **SUNNIEST PLACES***

	LOCATION#	% OF MAXIMUM POSSIBLE	AVERAGE ANNUAL HOURS SUNSHINE
1	Yuma, Arizona, USA	91	4,127
2	Phoenix, Arizona, USA	90	4,041
3	Wadi Halfa, Sudan	89	3,964
4	Bordj Omar Driss, Algeria	88	3,899
5	Keetmanshoop, Namibia	88	3,876
6	Aoulef, Algeria	86	3,784
7	Upington, South Africa	86	3,766
8	Atbara, Sudan	85	3,739
9	Mariental, Namibia	84	3,707
10	Bilma, Niger	84	3,699

* Highest yearly sunshine total, averaged over a long period of years
\# Maximum of two places per country listed

Source: Philip Eden

TOP 10 **PLACES WITH THE FEWEST RAINY DAYS**

	LOCATION*	NO. OF RAINY DAYS#
1	Arica, Chile	1 day every 6 years
2	Asyût, Egypt	1 day every 5 years
3	Dakhla Oasis, Egypt	1 day every 4 years
4	Al'Kufrah, Libya	1 day every 2 years
5	= Bender Qaasim, Somalia	1 day per year
	= Wadi Halfa, Sudan	1 day per year
7	Iquique, Chile	2 days per year
8	= Dongola, Sudan	3 days per year
	= Faya-Largeau, Chad	3 days per year
	= Masirah Island, Oman	3 days per year

* Maximum of two places per country listed
\# Lowest number of days with rain per year, averaged over a long period of years

Source: Philip Eden

Natural Disasters

Sri Lankan tragedy
Although less severely affected than Indonesia, over 30,000 people died in Sri Lanka, with great damage to coastal property as a result of the 2004 tsunami.

THE 10 MOST EXPENSIVE TYPES OF DISASTER*

TYPE OF DISASTER / ESTIMATED DAMAGE 1900–2005 ($)

1 Wind storms 499,554,558,000

2 Floods 353,338,772,000

3 Earthquakes 305,890,593,000

4 Droughts 63,602,469,000

5 Extreme temperatures 62,715,997,000

6 Forest/scrub fires 34,804,550,000

7 Industrial accidents 28,094,717,000

8 Tsunamis 7,767,077,000

9 Avalanches/landslides 4,850,232,000

10 Volcanoes 3,808,546,000

* Includes natural and non-natural

Source: EM-DAT, CRED, University of Louvain, Belgium

THE 10 WORST FLOODS

	LOCATION	DATE	ESTIMATED NO. KILLED
1	Huang He River, China	Aug 1931	3,700,000
2	Huang He River, China	Spring 1887	1,500,000
3	Holland	Nov 1, 1530	400,000
4	Kaifong, China	1642	300,000
5	Henan, China	Sep–Nov 1939	>200,000
6	Bengal, India	1876	200,000
7	Yangtze River, China	Aug–Sep 1931	140,000
8	Holland	1646	110,000
9	North Vietnam	Aug 30, 1971	>100,000
10 =	Friesland, Holland	1228	100,000
=	Dort, Holland	Apr 16, 1421	100,000
=	Canton, China	Jun 12, 1915	100,000
=	Yangtze River, China	Sep 1911	100,000

Records of floods caused by China's Huang He, or Yellow River, date back to 2297 BC. Since then, it has flooded at least 1,500 times, inundating entire towns and villages, causing millions of deaths, and giving it the apt nickname of "China's Sorrow."

THE 10 WORST TSUNAMIS

	LOCATIONS AFFECTED	DATE	ESTIMATED NO. KILLED
1	Southeast Asia	Dec 26, 2004	>186,983
2	Krakatoa, Sumatra/Java*	Aug 27, 1883	36,380
3	Sanriku, Japan	Jun 15, 1896	28,000
4	Agadir, Morocco#	Feb 29, 1960	12,000
5	Lisbon, Portugal	Nov 1, 1755	10,000
6	Papua New Guinea	Jul 18, 1998	8,000
7	Chile/Pacific islands/Japan	May 22, 1960	5,700
8	Philippines	Aug 17, 1976	5,000
9	Hyuga to Izu, Japan	Oct 28, 1707	4,900
10	Sanriku, Japan	Mar 3, 1933	3,000

* Combined effect of volcanic eruption and tsunamis
# Combined effect of earthquake and tsunamis

Tsunamis (from the Japanese *tsu*, port and *nami*, wave), are powerful waves caused by undersea disturbances such as earthquakes and volcanic eruptions. Tsunamis can be so intense that they frequently cross oceans, devastating islands and coastal regions in their paths. Triggered by a massive undersea earthquake in the Indian Ocean, the 2004 tsunami was exceptionally destructive. It destroyed coastal settlements in low-lying areas of Indonesia, Sri Lanka, Thailand, and other countries, resulting in loss of life on an unprecedented scale.

THE 10 **WORST AVALANCHES AND LANDSLIDES***

	LOCATION	INCIDENT	DATE	ESTIMATED NO. KILLED
1	Alps, Italy	Avalanche	Oct 218 BC	18,000
2	Yungay, Peru	Landslide	May 31, 1970	17,500
3	Italian Alps	Avalanche	Dec 13, 1916	10,000
4	Huarás, Peru	Avalanche	Dec 13, 1941	5,000
5	Nevada Huascaran, Peru	Avalanche	Jan 10, 1962	3,500
6	Chiavenna, Italy	Landslide	Sep 4, 1618	2,427
7	Plurs, Switzerland	Avalanche	Sep 4, 1618	1,496
8	Goldau Valley, Switzerland	Landslide	Sep 2, 1806	800
9	Medellin, Colombia	Landslide	Sep 27, 1987	683
10	Chungar, Peru	Avalanche	Mar 19, 1971	600

* Excluding those where most deaths resulted from flooding, earthquakes, volcanoes, etc., associated with landslides

This list is headed by the catastrophe that befell Carthaginian troops under Hannibal as they descended the Alps, probably in the region of the Col de la Traversette, a pass between France and Italy, when 18,000 men, 2,000 horses, and a number of elephants fell victim to a series of avalanches on a single day.

THE 10 **WORST EARTHQUAKES**

	LOCATION	DATE	ESTIMATED NO. KILLED
1	Near East/Mediterranean	May 20, 1202	1,100,000
2	Shenshi, China	Feb 2, 1556	820,000
3	Calcutta, India	Oct 11, 1737	300,000
4	Antioch, Syria	May 20, 526	250,000
5	Tang-shan, China	Jul 28, 1976	242,419
6	Nan-Shan, China	May 22, 1927	200,000
7	Yeddo, Japan	Dec 30, 1703	190,000
8	Kansu, China	Dec 16, 1920	180,000
9	Messina, Italy	Dec 28, 1908	160,000
10	Tokyo/Yokohama, Japan	Sep 1, 1923	142,807

There are some discrepancies between the "official" death tolls in many of the world's worst earthquakes and the estimates of other authorities: a figure of 750,000 is sometimes quoted for the Tang-shan earthquake of 1976. Several other earthquakes in China and Turkey resulted in deaths of 100,000 or more. In recent times, the Armenian earthquake of December 7, 1988, and that which struck northwest Iran on June 21, 1990, resulted in the deaths of more than 55,000 (official estimate 28,854) and 50,000 respectively. For comparison, the earthquakes that destroyed San Francisco on April 18, 1906 killed between 500 and 1,000.

100 YEARS AGO: THE MESSINA EARTHQUAKE

Two cataclysmic natural disasters occurred in 1908. The first, known as the Tunguska Event, took place on June 30, when a meteorite or asteroid exploded above Siberia, flattening 60 million trees in an area of 830 square miles (2,150 square km)—but the forest was so sparsely inhabited that no human loss of life was recorded.

In contrast, the death toll in the second disaster was huge, when, early in the morning of December 28, 1908, a series of earthquakes struck Messina, Sicily—Italy's eighth-largest city. Within minutes, 80,000 of its 147,000 inhabitants were killed, along with 25,000 of the 34,000 in Reggio di Calabria. Some 25 towns and villages within a radius of 120 miles (193 km) were completely destroyed. A 50-ft (15-m) 500 mph (800 km/h) tsunami struck coastal towns, water mains burst, and fires raged as gas mains fractured, causing yet more destruction. At least 160,000 and possibly as many as 250,000 died in the region, making it Europe's worst earthquake of modern times.

Messina had suffered a tsunami in 1169 and a severe earthquake in 1783, in which 60,000 had been killed. The buildings had been poorly reconstructed and in this second event virtually every structure, including the city's theaters, hotels, churches, and its magnificent cathedral, were reduced to rubble, burying thousands beneath them. The prison walls collapsed, allowing 750 prisoners to escape. They and survivors looted, fought for food, and rioted until Russian and British warships arrived to restore law and order and provide assistance in one of the biggest relief operations ever undertaken.

Above: Aftershock
Rescuers tend to the wounded and homeless of Messina amid the devastation caused by the earthquake of 1908.

2

LIFE ON EARTH

Extinct & Endangered

TOP 10 **LONGEST DINOSAURS EVER DISCOVERED**

NAME	ESTIMATED WEIGHT (TONS)	ESTIMATED LENGTH (FT)
1 Argentinosaurus huinculensis	88–110	115–148

An Argentinean farmer discovered a 6 ft (1.8 m) bone in 1988. It was the shinbone of a previously unknown dinosaur, which was named Argentinosaurus.

2 Seismosaurus	55–88	108

A skeleton of this colossal planteater was excavated in 1985 near Albuquerque, New Mexico, and given a name that means "earth-shaking lizard."

3 Sauroposeidon	55–66	98

From vertebrae discovered in 1994, it has been estimated that this creature was probably the tallest ever to walk on Earth, able to extend its neck to 60 ft (18 m).

4 = Giraffatitan brancai	Uncertain	82–98

This lightly built but long dinosaur was found in Tanzania and named by Gregory S. Paul in 1988.

= Paralititan stromeri	77	82–98

Remains discovered in 2001 suggest that this was a planteater. Its name, "Stromer's tidal giant," commemorates geologist Ernst Stromer von Reichenbach.

6 Supersaurus vivianae	55	79–98

The remains of Supersaurus were found in Colorado in 1972. Some scientists have suggested a length of up to 138 ft (42 m).

7 Andesaurus delgadoi	14	59–98

Found in Argentina and named in 1991 by Calvo and José Bonaparte, its vertebrae alone measure 2 ft (0.6 m).

8 Diplodocus	11–20	89

A relative lightweight in the dinosaur world, Diplodocus was also probably one of the most stupid dinosaurs, having the smallest brain in relation to its body size.

9 Barosaurus	44	66–89

Barosaurus ("heavy lizard") has been found in North America and Africa, thus proving the existence of a land link in Jurassic times (205–140 million years ago).

10 Brachiosaurus	33–88	85

Its name means "arm lizard." The mounted skeleton in the Humboldt Museum, Berlin, is the largest in the world.

TOP 10 **SMALLEST DINOSAURS**

	DINOSAUR	MAXIMUM SIZE IN	CM
1	Micropachycephalosaurus	20	50
2	= Saltopus	23	60
	= Yandangornis	23	60
4	Microraptor	30	77
5	Lesothosaurus	35	90
	= Nanosaurus	35	90
7	Bambiraptor	36	91
	= Sinosauropteryx	36	91
9	Wannanosaurus	39	99
10	Procompsognathus	47	120

Discovered in Argentina, Mussaurus (meaning "mouse lizard") is the smallest complete dinosaur skeleton found, but all known specimens are of infants and measure just 7 to 15 in (18 to 37 cm); adults may have attained 118 in (300 cm). The partial remains of a Microraptor ("little plunderer") found in China and measuring 16 in (40 cm) may be those of an adult.

Dead as a dodo
Discovered by European travelers in 1507, the dodo's name comes from the Portuguese for "stupid."

TOP 10 TIMELINE: LAST SEEN ALIVE

These are the years when some notable creatures became extinct, especially as a result of human intervention. In the case of those that occurred in captivity, the precise date can be stated.

1627
Aurochs
Extensively hunted, the last of these large oxen died in the Jaktorow Forest in Poland.

1649
Aepyornis
Also known as the "Elephant bird," this wingless bird was a native of Madagascar.

1681
Dodo
The last of these flightless birds was observed on Mauritius by Benjamin Harry.

1768
Steller's sea cow
This large marine mammal, named after its 1741 discoverer, was hunted to extinction.

1844
Great auk
The last surviving pair was killed on Eldey island for Icelandic collector Carl Siemsen.

THE 10 **COUNTRIES WITH THE MOST THREATENED ANIMAL SPECIES***

	COUNTRY	MAMMALS	BIRDS	REPTILES	AMPHIBIANS	FISH	INVERTEBRATES	TOTAL
1	USA	41	79	27	53	159	576	935
2	Australia	64	65	39	47	85	283	583
3	Mexico	74	62	21	204	109	40	510
4	Indonesia	146	121	28	39	105	31	470
5	Colombia	38	88	16	217	28	2	389
6	China	84	88	34	91	59	6	362
7	Ecuador	34	76	11	165	14	48	348
8	Brazil	73	124	22	28	58	34	339
9	India	89	82	26	68	35	22	322
10	South Africa	28	38	20	21	58	141	306

* Identified by the IUCN as Critically Endangered, Endangered, or Vulnerable

Source: International Union for Conservation of Nature, *2006 Redlist of Threatened Species*

THE 10 **MOST THREATENED SPECIES OF ANIMAL**

	TYPE	NO. EVALUATED	NO. THREATENED*
1	Amphibians	5,918	1,811
2	Birds	9,934	1,206
3	Mammals	4,864	1,093
4	Actinopterygii (bony fish)	2,351	1,058
5	Gastropods (snails, etc.)	1,951	880
6	Insects	1,192	623
7	Crustaceans	537	459
8	Reptiles	664	341
9	Chondrichthyes (sharks, etc.)	547	110
10	Bivalves (clams, etc.)	212	95
	Total (including classes not in Top 10)	28,270	7,723

* Identified by the IUCN as Critically Endangered, Endangered, or Vulnerable

Source: International Union for Conservation of Nature, *2006 Redlist of Threatened Species*

In many instances, the IUCN has evaluated a very small proportion of the total known species—for example, some 950,000 species of insect have been described, but only 1,192 have been evaluated, of which 623 are regarded as threatened.

Last of the quaggas
After being hunted for meat and leather, the last known quagga died in an Amsterdam zoo.

1875
Tarpan
The last pure-bred tarpan, a European wild horse, died in a Moscow zoo.

1883
Quagga
Found in South Africa, this zebra-like creature, became extinct in the wild by 1883.

1914
Passenger pigeon
Once seen in vast flocks, the last specimen died in Cincinnati Zoo on September 1, 1914.

1932
Heath hen
The grouse-like prairie chicken was extensively hunted in New England.

1936
Tasmanian wolf
Also known as the thylacine, the last specimen died in captivity.

Mammals

TOP 10 SMALLEST PRIMATES

PRIMATE* / SCIENTIFIC NAME	WEIGHT#	
	OZ	G
1 Pygmy mouse lemur (*Microcebus myoxinus*)	1.0	30
2 Hairy-eared dwarf lemur (*Allocebus trichotis*)	2.4–3.5	70–100
3 Tarsius pumilus	2.8–5.8	80–165
4 Lesser bush baby (*Galago moholi*)	4.9–8.1	140–230
5 Greater dwarf lemur (*Cheirogaleus major*)	6.2–21.1	177–600
6 Buffy-headed marmoset (*Callithrix flaviceps*)	8.1–15.9	230–453
7 Cotton-top tamarin (*Saguinus oedipus*)	9.1–13.4	260–380
8 Golden potto (*Arctocebus calabarensis*)	9.3–16.4	266–465
9 Golden-rumped lion tamarin (*Leontopithecus chrysopygus*)	10.5–24.6	300–700
10 Callimico goeldii	13.8–30.3	393–860

* Lightest species per genus
# Weights range across male and female; ranked by lightest

TOP 10 HEAVIEST PRIMATES

PRIMATE* / SCIENTIFIC NAME	AVERAGE WEIGHT RANGE#	
	LB	KG
1 Gorilla (*Gorilla gorilla gorilla*)	297–606	135–275
2 Man (*Homo sapiens*)	100–200	45–90
3 Orangutan (*Pongo pygmaeus*)	66–198	30–90
4 Chimpanzee (*Pan troglodytes*)	90–110	40–50
5 Hamadryas baboon (*Papio hamadryas*)	44–99	20–45
6 Japanese (snow) monkey (*Macaca fuscata*)	22–66	10–30
7 Mandrill (*Mandrillus sphinx*)	24–55	11–25
8 Proboscis monkey (*Nasalis lavatus*)	17–50	8–23
9 Gelada baboon (*Theropithecus gelada*)	26–46	12–21
10 Hanuman langur (*Semnopithecus entellus*)	20–44	9–20

* Heaviest species per genus
# Weights range across male and female

TOP 10 HEAVIEST TERRESTRIAL MAMMALS

MAMMAL* / SCIENTIFIC NAME / LENGTH FT/M / WEIGHT LB/KG

The list excludes domesticated cattle and horses. It also avoids comparing close kin such as the African and Indian elephants, highlighting instead the sumo stars within distinctive large mammal groups such as the bears, deer, big cats, primates, and bovines (ox-like mammals). The elephant is 357,000 times as heavy as smallest mammal, the pygmy shrew.

African elephant
(*Loxodonta africana*)
24.6 / 7.5   16,534 / 7,500

Hippopotamus
(*Hippopotamus amphibius*)
16.4 / 5.0   9,920 / 4,500

White rhinoceros
(*Ceratotherium simum*)
13.7 / 4.2   7,937 / 3,600

Giraffe
(*Giraffa camelopardalis*)
15.4 / 4.7   4,255 / 1,930

* Heaviest species per genus

TOP 10 **FASTEST MAMMALS**

	MAMMAL* / SCIENTIFIC NAME	MAXIMUM RECORDED SPEED MPH	KM/H
1	Cheetah (*Acinonyx jubatus*)	71	114
2	Pronghorn antelope (*Antilocapra americana*)	57	95
3	= Blue wildebeest (brindled gnu) (*Connochaetes taurinus*)	50	80
	= Lion (*Panthera leo*)	50	80
	= Springbok (*Antidorcas marsupialis*)	50	80
6	= Brown hare (*Lepus capensis*)	48	77
	= Red fox (*Vulpes vulpes*)	48	77
8	= Grant's gazelle (*Gazella granti*)	47	76
	= Thomson's gazelle (*Gazella thomsonii*)	47	76
10	Horse (*Equus caballus*)	45	72

* Of those species for which data available

The cat's away
Cheetahs are the speediest mammals over short distances.

TOP 10 **LIGHTEST TERRESTRIAL MAMMALS**

	MAMMAL* / SCIENTIFIC NAME	LENGTH# IN	MM	WEIGHT† OZ	G
1	Pygmy shrew (*Sorex hoyi*)	1.8–3.9	46–100	0.07–0.63	2.1–18
2	Pygmy shrew (*Suncus etruscus*)	1.4–1.9	35–48	0.22	2.5
3	African pygmy mouse (*Mus minutoides*)	1.8–3.2	45–82	0.09–0.42	2.5–12.0
4	Desert shrew (*Notiosorex crawfordi*)	1.9–2.7	48–69	0.1–0.17	3.0–5.0
5	Forest musk shrew (*Sylvisorex species*)	1.8–3.9	45–100	0.1–0.42	3.0–12.0
6	White-toothed shrew (*Crocidura suaveolens*)	1.6–3.9	40–100	0.1–0.46	3.0–13.0
7	Asiatic shrew (*Soriculus salenskii*)	1.7–3.9	44–99	0.17–0.21	5.0–6.0
8	Delany's swamp mouse (*Delanymys brooksi*)	1.9–2.5	50–63	0.18–0.23	5.2–6.5
9	Birch mouse (*Sicista species*)	1.9–3.5	50–90	0.21–0.49	6.0–14
10	Pygmy mouse (*Baiomys species*)	1.9–3.2	50–81	0.24–0.59	7.0–8.0

* Lightest species per genus, excluding bats
\# Some jerboas are smaller, but no precise weights have yet been recorded
† Ranked by lightest in range

TOP 10 **COUNTRIES WITH THE MOST MAMMAL SPECIES**

	COUNTRY	MAMMAL SPECIES
1	Indonesia	667
2	Brazil	578
3	Mexico	544
4	China	502
5	USA	468
6	Colombia	467
7	Peru	441
8	Dem. Rep. of Congo	430
9	India	422
10	Kenya	407

Source: EarthTrends/World Conservation Monitoring Centre of the United Nations Environment Programme (UNEP-WCMC)

American buffalo
(*Bison bison*)
11.4 / 3.5
2,205 / 1,000

Moose
(*Alces alces*)
10.1 / 3.1
1,820 / 825

Grizzly bear
(*Ursus arctos*)
9.8 / 3.0
1,720 / 780

Arabian camel
(dromedary)
(*Camelus dromedarius*)
11.3 / 3.45
1,521 / 690

Siberian tiger
(*Panthera tigris altaica*)
10.8 / 3.3
793 / 360

Gorilla
(*Gorilla gorilla gorilla*)
6.5 / 2.0
606 / 275

Birds

TOP 10 FASTEST BIRDS

BIRD / SCIENTIFIC NAME	MAXIMUM RECORDED SPEED	
	MPH	KM/H
1 Common eider (*Somateria mollissima*)	47	76
2 Bewick's swan (*Cygnus columbianus*)	44	72
3 =Barnacle goose (*Branta leucopsis*)	42	68
=Common crane (*Grus grus*)	42	68
5 Mallard (*Anas platyrhynchos*)	40	65
6 =Red-throated loon (*Gavia stellata*)	38	61
=Wood pigeon (*Columba palumbus*)	38	61
8 Oystercatcher (*Haematopus ostralegus*)	36	58
9 =Ring-necked pheasant (*Phasianus colchichus*)	33	54
=White-fronted goose (*Anser albifrons*)	33	54

Source: Chris Mead

TOP 10 HEAVIEST FLIGHTED BIRDS

BIRD / SCIENTIFIC NAME*	WEIGHT		
	LB	OZ	KG
1 Mute swan (*Cygnus olor*)	49	6	22.50
2 Kori bustard (*Ardeotis kori*)	41	8	19.00
3 =Andean condor (*Vultur gryphus*)	33	1	15.00
=Great white pelican (*Pelecanus onocrotalus*)	33	1	15.00
5 Eurasian black vulture (*Aegypius monachus*)	27	5	12.50
6 Sarus crane (*Grus antigone*)	26	9	12.24
7 Himalayan griffon (vulture) (*Gyps himalayensis*)	26	5	12.00
8 Wandering albatross (*Diomedea exulans*)	24	9	11.30
9 Steller's sea eagle (*Haliaeetus pelagicus*)	19	8	9.00
10 Marabou stork (*Leptoptilos crumeniferus*)	19	6	8.90

* By species
Source: Chris Mead

TOP 10 HEAVIEST FLIGHTLESS BIRDS

BIRD / SCIENTIFIC NAME*	WEIGHT		
	LB	OZ	KG
1 Ostrich (male) (*Struthio camelus*)	343	9	156.0
2 Northern cassowary (*Casuarius unappendiculatus*)	127	9	58.0
3 Emu (female) (*Dromaius novaehollandiae*)	121	6	55.0
4 Emperor penguin (female) (*Aptenodytes forsteri*)	101	4	46.0
5 Greater rhea (*Rhea americana*)	55	2	25.0
6 Flightless steamer# (duck) (*Tachyeres brachypterus*)	13	7	6.2
7 Flightless cormorant (*Nannopterum harrisi*)	9	15	4.5
8 Kiwi (female) (*Apteryx haastii*)	8	4	3.8
9 Takahe (rail) (*Porphyrio mantelli*)	7	2	3.2
10 Kakapo (parrot) (*Strigops habroptilus*)	7	1	3.2

* By species
# The flightless steamer is 33 in (84 cm) long, but does not stand upright

Source: Chris Mead

The flightless great auk, extinct since 1844, weighed about 17 lb 6 oz (8 kg) and stood about 35.4 in (90 cm) high. Other flightless birds were much bigger. The two heaviest, at almost 1,102 lb 5 oz (500 kg), were the elephant bird (*Aepyornis maximus*) that became extinct from Madagascar 350 years ago, and the emu-like *Dromornis stirtoni* from Australia. The tallest, but more lightly built, was the biggest of the moas of New Zealand, *Dinornis maximus*, that became extinct when the Maoris colonized the country, but prior to European settlement; there is thus no account of any living moa, and all evidence is based on discoveries of bones.

Earthbound athlete
Despite its size, the ostrich is capable of running faster—as much as 40 mph (65 km/h)—than the air speeds of many of its flighted cousins.

TOP 10 **LONGEST BIRD MIGRATIONS**

1 Pectoral sandpiper (*Calidris melanotos*) 11,806 / 19,000*

2 Wheatear (*Oenanthe oenanthe*) 11,184 / 18,000

3 Slender-billed shearwater (*Puffinus tenuirostris*) 10,874 / 17,500*

4 Ruff (*Philomachus pugnax*) 10,314 / 16,600

5 Willow warbler (*Phylloscopus trochilus*) 10,128 / 16,300

6 Arctic tern (*Sterna paradisaea*) 10,066 / 16,200

7 Parasitic Jaeger (*Stercorarius parasiticus*) 9,693 / 15,600

8 Swainson's hawk (*Buteo swainsoni*) 9,445 / 15,200

9 Knot (*Calidris canutus*) 9,320 / 15,000

10 Barn swallow (*Hirundo rustica*) 9,258 / 14,900

* Thought to be only half of the path taken during a whole year

Source: Chris Mead

This list is of the likely extremes for a normal migrant, not one that has become lost and wandered into new territory. All migrant birds fly far longer than is indicated by the direct route. Many species fly all year, except when they come to land to breed, or, in the case of seabirds such as the albatross, to rest on the sea.

TOP 10 **LARGEST OWLS**

OWL* / SCIENTIFIC NAME	WINGSPAN		WEIGHT		
	IN	CM	LB	OZ	KG
1 Eurasian eagle-owl (*Bubo bubo*)	29	75	9	4	4.20
2 Verraux's eagle-owl (*Bubo lacteus*)	26	65	6	14	3.11
3 Snowy owl (*Bubo scandiacus*)	28	70	6	8	2.95
4 Great horned owl (*Bubo virginianus*)	24	60	5	8	2.50
5 Pel's fishing-owl (*Scotopelia peli*)	25	63	5	2	2.32
6 Pharaoh eagle-owl (*Bubo ascalaphus*)	20	50	5	1	2.30
7 Cape eagle-owl (*Bubo capensis*)	23	58	3	15	1.80
8 Great grey owl (*Strix nebulosa*)	27	69	3	12	1.70
9 Powerful owl (*Ninox strenua*)	24	60	3	5	1.50
10 Ural owl (*Strix uralensis*)	24	62	2	14	1.30

* Some owls closely related to these species may be of similar size; most measurements are from female owls as they are usually larger

Source: Chris Mead

Eagle-eyed hunter
The Eurasian eagle owl is a formidable predator, capable of preying on mammals as large as fox and deer.

Reptiles & Amphibians

THE 10 MOST VENOMOUS REPTILES AND AMPHIBIANS

	CREATURE*	TOXIN	FATAL AMOUNT (MG)#
1	Indian cobra	Peak V	0.009
2	Mamba	Toxin 1	0.02
3	Brown snake	Texilotoxin	0.05
4 =	Inland taipan	Paradotoxin	0.10
=	Mamba	Dendrotoxin	0.10
6	Taipan	Taipoxin	0.11
7 =	Indian cobra	Peak X	0.12
=	Poison arrow frog	Batrachotoxin	0.12
9	Indian cobra	Peak 1X	0.17
10	Krait	Bungarotoxin	0.50

* Excluding bacteria
# Quantity required to kill an average-sized human adult

The venom of these creatures is almost unbelievably powerful: mambas have a mortality rate approaching 100 percent—1 mg (the approximate weight of a banknote) of mamba Toxin 1 would be sufficient to kill 50 people. Deadly poisons such as strychnine (35 mg), and cyanide (700 mg), seem relatively innocuous in comparison.

Friendly dragon
The bearded dragon, one of Australia's numerous native reptile species, has become popular worldwide as a pet.

TOP 10 LONGEST SNAKES

SNAKE / SCIENTIFIC NAME	MAXIMUM LENGTH FT	M
1 Reticulated (royal) **python** (*Python regius*)	35	10.7
2 Anaconda (*Eunectes murinus*)	28	8.5
3 Indian python (*Python molurus molurus*)	25	7.6
4 Diamond python (*Morelia spilota spilota*)	21	6.4
5 King cobra (*Opiophagus hannah*)	19	5.8
6 Boa constrictor (*Boa constrictor*)	16	4.9
7 Bushmaster (*Lachesis muta*)	12	3.7
8 Giant brown snake (*Oxyuranus scutellatus*)	11	3.4
9 Diamondback rattlesnake (*Crotalus atrox*)	9	2.7
10 Indigo or gopher snake (*Drymarchon corais*)	8	2.4

Although the South American anaconda is sometimes claimed to be the longest snake, and reports of monsters up to 120 ft (36.5 m) have been published, none has never been authenticated—despite offers of substantial rewards for material evidence.

TOP 10 COUNTRIES WITH THE MOST REPTILE SPECIES

COUNTRY / REPTILE SPECIES

1	Australia 880		**6**	Colombia 518
2	Mexico 837		**7**	China 424
3	Indonesia 749		**8**	Ecuador 419
4	Brazil 651		**9**	Malaysia 388
5	India 521		**10**	Madagascar 383
				USA 360

Source: World Conservation Monitoring Centre of the United Nations Environment Programme (UNEP-WCMC)

TOP 10 **HEAVIEST TURTLES**

TURTLE / SCIENTIFIC NAME	MAXIMUM WEIGHT	
	LB	KG
1 Pacific leatherback turtle (*Dermochelys coriacea*)*	704.4	1,552
2 Atlantic leatherback turtle (*Dermochelys coriacea*)*	463.0	1,018
3 Green sea turtle (*Chelonia mydas*)	355.3	783
4 Loggerhead turtle (*Caretta caretta*)	257.8	568
5 Alligator snapping turtle (*Macroclemys temmincki*)#	100.0	220
6 Flatback (sea) turtle (*Natator depressus*)	78.2	171
7 Hawksbill (sea) turtle (*Eretmochelys imbricata*)	62.7	138
8 Kemps Ridley turtle (*Lepidochelys kempi*)	60.5	133
9 Olive Ridley turtle (*Lepidochelys olivacea*)	49.9	110
10 Common snapping turtle (*Chelydra serpentina*)#	38.5	85

* One species, differing in size according to where they live
# Freshwater species

Source: Lucy T. Verma

The sizes and the longevity of turtles and tortoises are hotly debated by zoologists and there are many claims of even larger specimens among the 265 species of *Chelonia* (turtles and tortoises). All living examples would be dwarfed in size by prehistoric monster turtles such as *Stupendemys geographicus*, which measured up to 10 ft (3 m) in length and weighed over 4,497 lb (2,040 kg).

TOP 10 **COUNTRIES WITH THE MOST AMPHIBIAN SPECIES**

COUNTRY / AMPHIBIAN SPECIES

1 Brazil 695

2 Colombia 623

3 Ecuador 428

4 Peru 361

5 Mexico 358

6 China 340

7 Venezuela 288

8 = Indonesia 285

   = USA 285

10 Papua New Guinea 253

Source: World Conservation Monitoring Centre of the United Nations Environment Programme (UNEP-WCMC)

The world total of amphibian species (frogs toads, newts, salamanders, and caecilians) is put at 6,074, so representatives of over 11 percent of them are found in Brazil. In contrast, there are countries such as Jordan, and islands including Barbados, Cyprus, and Malta, that have just one native amphibian species.

Pacific leatherback
Numbers of Pacific leatherbacks, the largest of all turtles, have declined in recent years and the species is considered endangered.

Sea Creatures

TOP 10 **FASTEST FISH**

FISH / SCIENTIFIC NAME / MAXIMUM RECORDED SPEED MPH / KM/H

1 Sailfish (*Istiophorus platypterus*) 69 / 112

2 Striped marlin (*Tetrapturus audax*) 50 / 80

3 Wahoo (peto, jack mackerel)
(*Acanthocybium solandri*) 48 / 77

4 Southern bluefin tuna (*Thunnus maccoyii*) 47 / 76

5 Yellowfin tuna (*Thunnus albacares*) 46 / 74

6 Blue shark (*Prionace glauca*) 43 / 69

7 = Bonefish (*Albula vulpes*) 40 / 64
= Swordfish (*Xiphias gladius*) 40 / 64

9 Tarpon (ox-eye herring)
(*Megalops cyprinoides*) 35 / 56

10 Tiger shark (*Galeocerdo cuvier*) 33 / 53

Source: Lucy T. Verma

Flying fish are excluded: they have a top speed in the water of only 23 mph (37 km/h), but airborne they can reach 35 mph (56 km/h). Many sharks qualify for the list, but only two are listed here to prevent the Top 10 becoming overly shark-infested. Just in case you thought it was safe to go back in the water, the great white shark (of *Jaws* fame), the largest of all predatory fish, cruises at just 2 mph (3.2 km/h) but can manage bursts of 30 mph (48 km/h).

TOP 10 **HEAVIEST SHARKS**

SHARK / SCIENTIFIC NAME	MAXIMUM WEIGHT LB	KG
1 Whale shark (*Rhincodon typus*)	67,240	30,500
2 Basking shark (*Cetorhinus maximus*)	20,410	9,258
3 Great white shark (*Carcharodon carcharias*)	7,731	3,507
4 Greenland shark (*Somniosus microcephalus*)	2,224	1,009
5 Tiger shark (*Galeocerdo cuvieri*)	2,043	927
6 Great hammerhead shark (*Sphyrna mokarran*)	1,889	857
7 Six-gill shark (*Hexanchus griseus*)	1,327	602
8 Grey nurse shark (*Carcharias taurus*)	1,243	564
9 Mako shark (*Isurus oxyrinchus*)	1,221	554
10 Thresher shark (*Alopias vulpinus*)	1,097	498

Source: Lucy T. Verma

As well as specimens that have been caught, estimates have been made of beached examples, but such is the notoriety of sharks that many accounts of their size are exaggerated, and this list should be taken as an approximate ranking based on the best available evidence.

TOP 10 **LONGEST-LIVED MARINE MAMMALS***

MARINE MAMMAL / SCIENTIFIC NAME	LIFESPAN (YEARS)
1 Bowhead whale (*Balaena mysticetus*)	200
2 Dugong (*Dugong dugon*)	60
3 Bottlenose dolphin (*Tursiops truncatus*)	48
4 Grey seal (*Halichoerus grypus*)	46
5 = Beluga whale (*Delphinapterus leucas*)	30
= Californian sea lion (*Zalophus californianus*)	30
= Walrus (*Odobenus rosmarus*)	30
8 Canadian otter (*Lontra canadensis*)	21
9 Polar bear (*Ursus maritimus*)	20
10 Harbour porpoise (*Phocoena phocoena*)	8

* Longest-lived of each genus listed

Source: Lucy T. Verma

Tail of a whale
Found exclusively in Arctic waters and second only to the blue whale in size, there are believed to be fewer than 10,000 bowhead whales worldwide, and it is considered as under threat of extinction.

TOP 10 COUNTRIES WITH THE MOST FISH SPECIES

COUNTRY	FISH SPECIES
1 India	5,749
2 Indonesia	4,080
3 Australia	1,489
4 USA	1,101
5 Japan	1,007
6 Philippines	952
7 Papua New Guinea	858
8 Taiwan	816
9 Mexico	674
10 Palau	631

Source: World Conservation Monitoring Centre (WCMC)

Left: Tropical totals
The warm waters of the tropics are host to the world's most diverse fish populations.

TOP 10 HEAVIEST MARINE MAMMALS

MAMMAL / SCIENTIFIC NAME	LENGTH FT	M	WEIGHT (TONS)
1 Blue whale (*Balaenoptera musculus*)	110.0	33.5	151.0
2 Bowhead whale (Greenland right) (*Balaena mysticetus*)	65.0	20.0	94.8
3 Northern right whale (black right) (*Balaena glacialis*)	60.0	18.6	85.6
4 Fin whale (common rorqual) (*Balaenoptera physalus*)	82.0	25.0	69.9
5 Sperm whale (*Physeter catodon*)	59.0	18.0	48.2
6 Grey whale (*Eschrichtius robustus*)	46.0	14.0	38.5
7 Humpback whale (*Megaptera novaeangliae*)	49.2	15.0	38.1
8 Sei whale (*Balaenoptera borealis*)	60.0	18.5	32.4
9 Bryde's whale (*Balaenoptera edeni*)	47.9	14.6	22.0
10 Baird's whale (*Berardius bairdii*)	18.0	5.5	13.3

Source: Lucy T. Verma

Probably the largest animal that ever lived, the blue whale dwarfs even the other whales listed here, all but one of which far outweigh the biggest land animal, the elephant. The elephant seal, with a weight of 3.9 tons, is the largest marine mammal that is not a whale.

Insects & Spiders

TOP 10 **FASTEST INSECT FLYERS**

SPECIES* / SCIENTIFIC NAME	MAXIMUM RECORDED SPEED	
	MPH	KM/H
1 Hawkmoth (*Sphingidae*)	33.3	53.6
2 = Deer bot fly (*Cephenemyia pratti*)	30.0	48.0
= West Indian butterfly (*Nymphalidae prepona*)	30.0	48.0
4 Deer bot fly (*Chrysops*)	25.0	40.0
5 West Indian butterfly (*Hesperiidae species*)	18.6	30.0
6 Lesser Emperor dragonfly (*Anax parthenope*)	17.8	28.6
7 = Dragonfly (*Aeschna*)	15.6	25.2
= Hornet (*Vespa*)	15.6	25.2
9 = Honey bee (*Apis millefera*)	13.9	22.4
= Horsefly (*Tabanus bovinus*)	13.9	22.4

* Of those for which data available

Few accurate assessments of insect flying speeds have ever been attempted, and this Top 10 represents only the results of the handful of scientific studies that are widely recognized by entomologists. Some experts have also suggested that the male horsefly (*Hybomitra linei wrighti*) is capable of traveling at 90 mph (145 km/h) when in pursuit of a female, while there are exceptional one-off examples such as that of a dragonfly allegedly recorded in 1917 by Dr. Robert J. Tilyard as flying at a speed of 61 mph (98 km/h). Many so-called records are clearly flawed, however. For example, Charles Townsend estimated the flying speed of the deer bot fly at an unbelievable 818 mph (1,317 km/h). If true, it would have broken the sound barrier!

Buzzing along
Various species of hawkmoth have been claimed to achieve exceptional wingbeat and flying speeds.

TOP 10 **LARGEST MOTHS**

MOTH / SCIENTIFIC NAME	WINGSPAN	
	IN	MM
1 Atlas moth (*Attacus atlas*)	11.8	300
2 Owlet moth (*Thysania agrippina*)*	11.4	290
3 Haematopis grataria	10.2	260
4 Hercules emperor moth (*Coscinocera hercules*)	8.3	210
5 Malagasy silk moth (*Argema mitraei*)	7.1	180
6 Eacles imperialis	6.9	175
7 = Common emperor moth (*Bunaea alcinoe*)	6.3	160
= Giant peacock moth (*Saturnia pyri*)	6.3	160
9 Gray moth (*Brahmaea wallichii*)	6.1	155
10 = Black witch (*Ascalapha odorata*)	5.9	150
= Regal moth (*Citheronia regalis*)	5.9	150
= Polyphemus moth (*Antheraea polyphemus*)	5.9	150

* Exceptional specimen measured at 12.2 in (308 mm)

TOP 10 **SMALLEST BUTTERFLIES**

BUTTERFLY / SCIENTIFIC NAME	AVERAGE WINGSPAN	
	IN	MM
1 Dwarf blue (*Brephidium barberae*)	0.55	14
2 Western pygmy blue (*Brephidium exilis*)	0.62	15
3 Western square-dotted blue (*Euphilotes battoides*)	0.66	17
4 Pallid dotted-blue (*Euphilotes pallescens*)	0.70	18
5 = Bernardino dotted-blue (*Euphilotes bernardino*)	0.74	19
= Cyna blue (*Zizula cyna*)	0.74	19
= Intermediate dotted-blue (*Euphilotes intermedia*)	0.74	19
= Little metalmark (*Calephelis virginiensis*)	0.74	19
= Rita dotted-blue (*Euphilotes rita*)	0.74	19
= Small dotted-blue (*Philotiella speciosa*)	0.74	19
= Telea hairstreak (*Chlorostrymon teleai*)	0.74	19

TOP 10 **LARGEST BUTTERFLIES**

BUTTERFLY / SCIENTIFIC NAME	APPROX. WINGSPAN	
	IN	MM
1 Queen Alexandra's birdwing (*Ornithoptera alexandrae*)	11.0	280
2 African giant swallowtail (*Papilio antimachus*)	9.1	230
3 Goliath birdwing (*Ornithoptera goliath*)	8.3	210
4 = Buru opalescent birdwing (*Troides prattorum*)	7.9	200
= (Birdwing) Trogonoptera trojana	7.9	200
= (Birdwing) Troides hypolitus	7.9	200
7 = Chimaera birdwing (*Ornithoptera chimaera*)	7.5	190
= Ornithoptera lydius	7.5	190
= Troides magellanus	7.5	190
= Troides miranda	7.5	190

TOP 10 **DEADLIEST SPIDERS**

SPIDER / SCIENTIFIC NAME / RANGE

1 Banana spider (*Phonenutria nigriventer*)
Central and South America

2 Sydney funnel web (*Atrax robustus*) Australia

3 Wolf spider (*Lycosa raptoria/ erythrognatha*)
Central and South America

4 Black widow
(*Latrodectus species*) Widespread

5 Violin spider/Recluse spider
(*Loxesceles reclusa*) Widespread

6 Sac spider (*Cheiracanthium punctorium*)· Central Europe

7 Tarantula (*Eurypelma rubropilosum*) Neotropics

8 Tarantula (*Acanthoscurria atrox*) Neotropics

9 Tarantula (*Lasiodora klugi*) Neotropics

10 Tarantula (*Pamphobeteus species*) Neotropics

The list ranks spiders according to their "lethal potential"—their venom yield divided by their venom potency. The banana spider, for example, yields 6 mg of venom, with 1 mg the estimated lethal dose in humans. However, few spiders are capable of killing people—there were just 14 recorded deaths caused by black widows in the USA in the whole of the 19th century—since their venom yield is relatively low compared with that of the most dangerous snakes. The tarantula, for example, produces 1.5 mg of venom, but the lethal dose for an adult human is 12 mg. Anecdotal evidence suggests that the Thailand and Sumatran black bird-eaters may be equally dangerous, but insufficient data are available.

Furry jumper
The family of jumping spiders contains the most known species, comprising some 13 percent of all known spiders. They are found worldwide, with one even reported high on Mount Everest.

TOP 10 **SPIDER FAMILIES**

FAMILY / SCIENTIFIC NAME	FAMILIES
1 Jumping spiders (*Salticidae*)	4,869
2 Money spiders (*Linyphiidae*)	4,179
3 Orb-web weavers (*Araneidae*)	2,815
4 Wolf spiders (*Lycosidae*)	2,261
5 Tangle-web spiders (*Theridiidae*)	2,201
6 Crab spiders (*Thomisidae*)	2,024
7 Mouse spiders (*Gnaphosidae*)	1,957
8 Grass spiders (*Tetragnathidae*)	986
9 Huntsman spiders (*Sparassidae*)	985
10 Tarantulas and **bird-eating spiders** (*Theraphosidae*)	873
Total (including those not in Top 10)	*37,776*

Pets

Chinese whistlers
The total number of birds and other pets in China has escalated by 20 percent in the past five years.

TOP 10 **PET-OWNING COUNTRIES***

COUNTRY	PETS
1 USA	344,334,000
2 China	307,116,400
3 Japan	81,181,000
4 Germany	76,642,000
5 Brazil	69,344,000
6 France	66,235,000
7 Italy	60,052,000
8 Russia	56,900,000
9 UK	47,700,000
10 Philippines	28,674,400
World total	*1,532,585,800*

* Countries for which data available

Source: Euromonitor

The considerable recent rise in pet ownership worldwide has been explained by such social phenomena as the desire for companionship in smaller families and increasingly urban dwellers.

TOP 10 **PET BIRD POPULATIONS**

COUNTRY	ESTIMATED PET BIRD POPULATION (2005)
1 China	75,328,200
2 Japan	19,500,000
3 Brazil	18,105,000
4 USA	15,870,000
5 Italy	12,980,000
6 Turkey	10,437,000
7 Spain	7,900,000
8 Australia	7,850,000
9 France	6,590,000
10 Germany	4,100,000

Source: Euromonitor

The ease with which caged birds can be kept, especially in crowded urban settings, and the pleasure of their singing, have contributed to their centuries-long popularity as pets.

TOP 10 **PET REPTILE POPULATIONS**

COUNTRY / ESTIMATED PET REPTILE POPULATION (2005)

1 USA 18,371,000

2 China 4,682,100

3 UK 2,010,000

4 France 1,500,000

5 Italy 1,400,000

6 Russia 600,000

7 Spain 234,000

8 Australia 215,000

9 Canada 196,000

10 Thailand 195,000

Source: Euromonitor

TOP 10 **PET FISH POPULATIONS**

COUNTRY / ESTIMATED PET FISH POPULATION (2005)

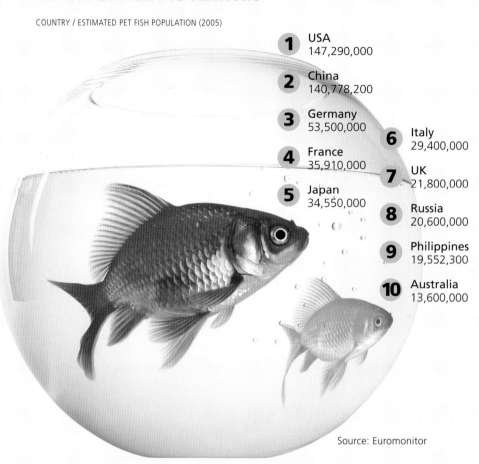

1 USA
147,290,000

2 China
140,778,200

3 Germany
53,500,000

4 France
35,910,000

5 Japan
34,550,000

6 Italy
29,400,000

7 UK
21,800,000

8 Russia
20,600,000

9 Philippines
19,552,300

10 Australia
13,600,000

Source: Euromonitor

TOP 10 **PET DOG POPULATIONS**

COUNTRY / ESTIMATED PET DOG POPULATION (2005)

1 USA 63,010,000

2 Brazil 31,408,300

3 China 26,153,600

4 Mexico 16,581,800

5 Japan 12,780,000

6 Russia 11,200,000

7 France 8,495,000

8 Philippines 7,690,000

9 Thailand 7,440,000

10 South Africa 7,300,000

Source: Euromonitor

Oldest Pet
Adwayita, an Aldabra Giant
Tortoise that died at the
Alipore Zoo, Kolkata (Calcutta)
on March 23, 2006, was
claimed to have been the pet
of Robert Clive (1725–74),
known as "Clive of India."
If true, it could have been
as much as 250 years old.

TOP 10 **PET CAT POPULATIONS**

COUNTRY / ESTIMATED PET CAT POPULATION (2005)

1 USA 81,420,000

2 China 58,180,100

3 Russia 17,100,000

4 Brazil 12,234,000

5 Japan 11,500,000

6 France 9,960,000

7 UK 9,200,000

8 Germany 7,600,000

9 Ukraine 7,470,000

10 Italy 7,430,000

Source: Euromonitor

Livestock

TOP 10 **TYPES OF LIVESTOCK**

	ANIMAL	WORLD STOCKS (2005)
1	Chickens	16,695,877,000
2	Cattle	1,372,250,974
3	Sheep	1,079,005,851
4	Ducks	1,044,736,450
5	Pigs	960,847,340
6	Goats	808,903,601
7	Rabbits	535,379,620
8	Geese	301,905,920
9	Turkeys	276,821,650
10	Buffaloes	173,921,455

Source: Food and Agriculture Organization of the United Nations

The 23,249,649,861 animals accounted for by the Top 10 outnumber the world's human population by almost four to one. The world chicken population is more than double the human population, while the world's cattle population outnumbers the population of China. There are almost as many pigs in the world as the entire population of India, nearly enough turkeys for every citizen of the USA to have one each for Thanksgiving, and—though just outside the Top 10—sufficient horses for every inhabitant of the UK to go riding.

TOP 10 **CATTLE COUNTRIES**

	COUNTRY	CATTLE (2005)
1	Brazil	207,000,000
2	India	185,000,000
3	China	115,229,500
4	USA	95,848,000
5	Argentina	50,768,000
6	Ethiopia	38,500,000
7	Sudan	38,325,000
8	Mexico	31,800,000
9	Australia	27,730,000
10	Colombia	25,000,000
	World total	*1,372,250,974*

Source: Food and Agriculture Organization of the United Nations

Since the 1960s, growing and increasingly wealthy populations have raised the demand for milk and meat, prompting an increase in the world's cattle populations: the world total has risen by over 45 percent since 1961, while that of China has more than doubled. India, which long held first place in this list, was overtaken by Brazil in 2003, prompting concern that the latter's increase was linked to severe deforestation to provide grazing lands.

TOP 10 **PIG COUNTRIES**

	COUNTRY	PIGS (2005)
1	China	488,809,978
2	USA	60,644,500
3	Brazil	33,200,000
4	Vietnam	27,000,000
5	Germany	26,858,000
6	Spain	25,250,000
7	Poland	18,112,380
8	France	15,020,198
9	Canada	14,675,000
10	Mexico	14,625,199
	World total	*960,847,340*

Source: Food and Agricultural Organization of the United Nations

The distribution of the world's pig population is determined by cultural, religious, and dietary factors—few pigs are found in African and Islamic countries, for example—with the result that there is a disproportionate concentration of pigs in those countries that do not have such prohibitions. Denmark, in 12th place, is the country in which the pig population (13,466,283) most outnumbers the human population (5,450,661).

TOP 10 **BEEHIVE COUNTRIES**

COUNTRY / BEEHIVES (2005)

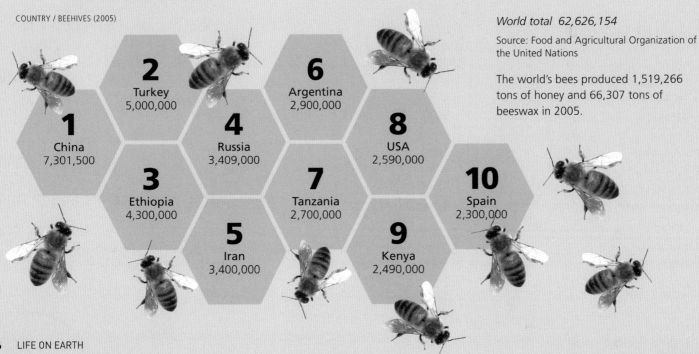

1 China 7,301,500
2 Turkey 5,000,000
3 Ethiopia 4,300,000
4 Russia 3,409,000
5 Iran 3,400,000
6 Argentina 2,900,000
7 Tanzania 2,700,000
8 USA 2,590,000
9 Kenya 2,490,000
10 Spain 2,300,000

World total 62,626,154

Source: Food and Agricultural Organization of the United Nations

The world's bees produced 1,519,266 tons of honey and 66,307 tons of beeswax in 2005.

Horses for courses
Mongolia figures in few Top 10 lists, but is noted for its presence among the world's leading horse-owners. The horse figures prominently in Mongolian culture, with cross-country horseracing a major part of national festivals.

TOP 10 **HORSE COUNTRIES**

COUNTRY	HORSES (2005)
1 China	7,641,320
2 Mexico	6,260,000
3 Brazil	5,700,000
4 USA	5,300,000
5 Argentina	3,655,000
6 Colombia	2,750,000
7 Mongolia	2,005,300
8 Russia	1,505,000
9 Ethiopia	1,500,000
10 Kazakhstan	1,120,000
World total	*54,701,074*

Source: Food and Agricultural Organization of the United Nations

TOP 10 **GOAT COUNTRIES**

COUNTRY	GOATS (2005)
1 China	195,758,954
2 India	120,000,000
3 Pakistan	56,700,000
4 Sudan	42,000,000
5 Bangladesh	36,900,000
6 Nigeria	28,000,000
7 Iran	26,500,000
8 Indonesia	13,182,100
9 Somalia	12,700,000
10 Tanzania	12,550,000
USA	*2,522,500*
World total	*808,903,601*

Source: Food and Agriculture Organization of the United Nations

The goat is one of the most widspread domesticated animals, its resilience to diseases and adaptability to harsh conditions making it suited to environments that are unsuitable for other livestock.

TOP 10 **SHEEP COUNTRIES**

COUNTRY	SHEEP (2005)
1 China	170,882,215
2 Australia	102,700,000
3 India	62,500,000
4 Iran	54,000,000
5 Sudan	48,000,000
6 New Zealand	39,928,000
7 UK	35,253,048
8 South Africa	25,316,424
9 Turkey	25,201,156
10 Pakistan	24,900,000
USA	*6,135,000*
World total	*1,079,005,851*

Source: Food and Agriculture Organization of the United Nations

This is one of the few world lists in which the UK ranks considerably higher than the USA. The 1900 census put the USA's sheep stocks at an all-time level of over 61 million, since when they have been in decline.

Living off the Land

TOP 10 **CEREAL CROPS**

CROP	PRODUCTION 2005 (TONS)
1 Maize	773,454,537
2 Wheat	639,977,761
3 Rice (paddy)	681,714,110
4 Barley	153,269,713
5 Sorghum	64,692,679
6 Millet	31,481,518
7 Oats	26,404,488
8 Rye	17,102,587
9 Triticale (wheat/rye hybrid)	14,881,006
10 Mixed grain	5,336,635
Total of all cereals (including those not in Top 10)	*2,468,515,787*

Source: Food and Agriculture Organization of the United Nations

TOP 10 **CEREAL-PRODUCING COUNTRIES**

COUNTRY	PRODUCTION 2005 (TONS)
1 China	471,363,127
2 USA	404,014,239
3 India	260,049,566
4 Russia	84,238,630
5 Indonesia	72,750,671
6 France	70,691,061
7 Brazil	61,425,483
8 Canada	55,515,263
9 Germany	50,700,808
10 Bangladesh	45,840,718
World total	*2,468,515,787*

Source: Food and Agriculture Organization of the United Nations

Rice bowl
China's production of rice is 207 million tons annually, 30 percent of the world total.

TOP 10 **NON-FOOD CROPS**

CROP	PRODUCTION 2005 (TONS)
1 Cotton	75,285,114
2 Rubber	10,057,036
3 Coffee	8,575,425
4 Tobacco	7,235,590
5 Tea	3,787,740
6 Jute	3,154,795
7 Linseed	3,087,824
8 Castor beans	1,536,415
9 Coir	1,051,925
10 Flax	978,000

Source: Food and Agriculture Organization of the United Nations

TOP 10 **FRUIT-PRODUCING COUNTRIES**

COUNTRY / PRODUCTION* 2005 (TONS)

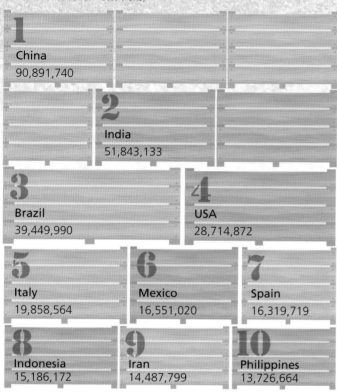

1 China
90,891,740

2 India
51,843,133

3 Brazil
39,449,990

4 USA
28,714,872

5 Italy
19,858,564

6 Mexico
16,551,020

7 Spain
16,319,719

8 Indonesia
15,186,172

9 Iran
14,487,799

10 Philippines
13,726,664

World total 556,630,398

* Excluding melons

Source: Food and Agriculture Organization of the United Nations

TOP 10 **NUT-PRODUCING COUNTRIES**

	COUNTRY	PRODUCTION 2005 (TONS)
1	Mexico	104,885
2	Indonesia	99,208
3	Ethiopia	82,673
4	China	49,604
5	Australia	43,541
6=	Azerbaijan	30,865
	Russia	30,865
8	Guatemala	26,455
9	Thailand	25,353
10	Portugal	23,149
	World total	835,343

Source: Food and Agriculture Organization of the United Nations

TOP 10 **VEGETABLE-PRODUCING COUNTRIES**

	COUNTRY	PRODUCTION* 2005 (TONS)
1	China	479,531,954
2	India	88,767,476
3	USA	40,720,608
4	Turkey	27,993,318
5	Egypt	17,819,305
6	Russia	17,795,714
7	Italy	17,652,362
8	Iran	14,875,691
9	Spain	13,928,004
10	South Korea	13,404,216
	World total	972,736,868

* Including watermelons; only vegetables grown for human consumption, excluding crops from private gardens

Source: Food and Agriculture Organization of the United Nations

TOP 10 **VEGETABLE CROPS**

	CROP*	PRODUCTION 2005 (TONS)
1	Sugar cane	1,423,839,990
2	Potatoes	356,159,998
3	Sugar beets	265,639,716
4	Soybeans	236,277,439
5	Sweet potatoes	142,630,604
6	Cabbages	77,069,809
7	Onions (dry)	63,272,974
8	Cucumbers/pickles	46,117,229
9	Yams	43,934,771
10	Eggplants	33,595,996
	Total of all vegetables (including those not in Top 10)	972,736,868

* Excluding cereals; including only vegetables grown for human and animal consumption

Source: Food and Agriculture Organization of the United Nations

TOP 10 **NUT CROPS**

CROP / PRODUCTION 2005 (TONS)

1 Groundnuts (in shell)
39,534,824

2 Cashew nuts
2,576,496

3 Almonds
1,817,619

4 Walnuts
1,722,710

5 Chestnuts
1,240,099

6 Areca nuts (betel)
801,849

7 Filberts
777,371

8 Karite nuts (sheanuts)
763,902

9 Tung nuts
580,424

10 Pistachios
539,261

World total 835,343

Source: Food and Agriculture Organization of the United Nations

Trees

TOP 10 COUNTRIES WITH THE LARGEST AREAS OF FOREST

	COUNTRY	SQ MILES	% OF TOTAL	SQ KM
1	Russia	3,122,756	47.9	8,087,900
2	Brazil	1,844,402	57.2	4,776,980
3	Canada	1,197,434	33.6	3,101,340
4	USA	1,170,233	33.1	3,030,890
5	China	761,741	21.2	1,972,900
6	Australia	631,964	21.3	1,636,780
7	Dem. Rep. of Congo	515,871	58.9	1,336,100
8	Indonesia	341,681	48.8	884,950
9	Peru	265,414	53.7	687,420
10	India	261,395	22.8	677,010
	World total	*15,258,855*	*30.3*	*39,520,250*

Source: Food and Agriculture Organization of the United Nations, *Global Forest Resources Assessment 2005*

TOP 10 DEFORESTING COUNTRIES*

	COUNTRY	ANNUAL FOREST LOSS 2000–05 SQ MILES	SQ KM
1	Brazil	11,980	31,030
2	Indonesia	7,223	18,710
3	Sudan	2,274	5,890
4	Myanmar	1,799	4,660
5	Zambia	1,718	4,450
6	Tanzania	1,590	4,120
7	Nigeria	1,583	4,100
8	Dem. Rep. of Congo	1,231	3,190
9	Zimbabwe	1,208	3,130
10	Venezuela	1,111	2,880
	World total	*28,251*	*73,170*

* Countries for which data available

Source: Food and Agriculture Organization of the United Nations, *Global Forest Resources Assessment 2005*

Some 16,413 sq miles (42,510 sq km) of forest were lost in South America each year between 2000 and 2005, 15,598 sq miles (40,400 sq km) in Africa, and 14,826 sq miles (38,400 sq km) in Asia. The total global loss during the period was 169,506 sq miles (439,020 sq km).

TOP 10 TIMBER-PRODUCING COUNTRIES

COUNTRY / WOOD PRODUCTION* 2005 / FT³/M³

* Roundwood and fuel

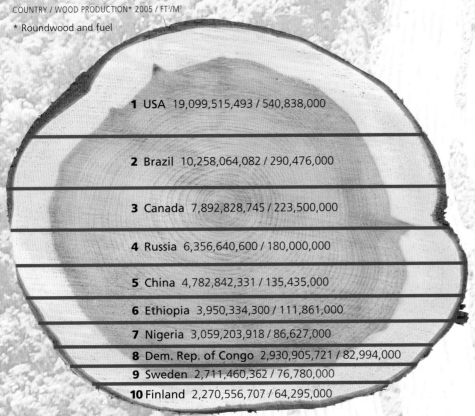

1 USA 19,099,515,493 / 540,838,000

2 Brazil 10,258,064,082 / 290,476,000

3 Canada 7,892,828,745 / 223,500,000

4 Russia 6,356,640,600 / 180,000,000

5 China 4,782,842,331 / 135,435,000

6 Ethiopia 3,950,334,300 / 111,861,000

7 Nigeria 3,059,203,918 / 86,627,000

8 Dem. Rep. of Congo 2,930,905,721 / 82,994,000

9 Sweden 2,711,460,362 / 76,780,000

10 Finland 2,270,556,707 / 64,295,000

Source: Food and Agriculture Organization of the United Nations, *Global Forest Resources Assessment 2005*

TOP 10 REFORESTING COUNTRIES*

	COUNTRY	ANNUAL FOREST GAIN 2000–05 SQ MILES	SQ KM
1	China	15,629	40,480
2	Spain	1,142	2,960
3	Vietnam	930	2,410
4	USA	613	1,590
5	Italy	409	1,060
6	Chile	220	570
7	Cuba	216	560
8	Bulgaria	193	500
9	France	158	410
10	Portugal	154	400

* Countries for which data available

Source: Food and Agriculture Organization of the United Nations, *Global Forest Resources Assessment 2005*

Trees top
Suriname has a greater proportion of forest areas than any other country. Its 6,178 square mile (16,000 square km) Central Suriname Nature Reserve, an unspoilt tropical rainforest, was designated a UNESCO World Heritage Site in 2000.

TOP 10 **MOST FORESTED COUNTRIES**

COUNTRY	AREA		%
	SQ MILES	SQ KM	FOREST COVER
1 Suriname	57,050	147,760	94.7
2 French Guiana	31,131	80,630	91.9
3 Micronesia	243	630	90.6
4 American Samoa	69	180	89.4
5 Seychelles	154	400	88.9
6 Palau	154	400	87.6
7 Gabon	84,074	217,750	84.5
8 Pitcairn	15	40	83.3
9 Turks and Caicos Islands	131	340	80.0
10 Solomon Islands	8,386	21,720	77.6
USA	*1,170,233*	*3,030,890*	*33.1*
World total	*15,258,855*	*39,520,250*	*30.3*

Source: Food and Agriculture Organization of the United Nations, *Global Forest Resources Assessment 2005*

These are the 10 countries with the greatest area of forest and woodland as a percentage of their total land area. Although deforestation in tropical countries remains an environmental concern, recent research has indicated that reforestation is also taking place and the "forest identity" in 22 of the world's 50 most-forested countries has actually increased during the past 15 years.

TOP 10 **TALLEST TREES IN THE USA**

SPECIES* / LOCATION	HEIGHT	
	FT	M
1 Coast redwood (*Sequoia sempervirens*) Jedediah Smith Redwoods State Park, CA	321	97.8
2 Coast Douglas-fir (*Pseudotsuga menziesii var menziesii*) Jedediah Smith Redwoods State Park, CA	301	91.7
3 Giant sequoia (*Sequoiadendron giganteum*) Sequoia National Park, CA	274	83.5
4 Noble fir (*Abies procera*) Mt. St. Helens National Monument, WA	272	82.9
5 Grand fir (*Abies grandis*) Redwood National Park, CA	257	78.3
6 Western hemlock (*Tsuga heterophylla*) Olympic National Park, WA	241	73.5
7 Port Orford cedar (*Chamaecyparis lawsoniana*) Siskiyou National Forest, OR	229	69.8
8 Ponderosa pine (*Pinus ponderosa var. ponderosa*) Plumas County, CA	227	69.2
9 Pacific silver fir (*Abies amabilis*) Olympic National Park, WA	218	66.4
10 California white fir (*Abies concolor var. lowiana*) Yosemite National Park, CA	217	66.1

* Tallest example of each species only

Recent research in California's Humboldt Redwoods State Park has shown that the maximum height of a tree cannot exceed 427 ft (130 m), since gravity and friction prevent water from being drawn up a greater distance, so foliage at the top would be unable to thrive.

3

THE HUMAN WORLD

The Human Body

TOP 10 **MOST COMMON ELEMENTS IN THE HUMAN BODY**

	ELEMENT	AVERAGE ADULT TOTAL OZ	G
1	Oxygen*	1,517	43,000
2	Carbon	564	16,000
3	Hydrogen*	247	7,000
4	Nitrogen	63	1,800
5	Calcium	42	1,200
6	Phosphorus	28	780
7	Sulfur	5	140
8	Potassium	4–5	110–140
9	Sodium	4	100
10	Chlorine	3	95

* Mostly combined as water

The Top 10 elements account for more than 99 percent of the total, the balance comprising minute quantities of metallic elements including iron, zinc, tin, and aluminum.

TOP 10 **LARGEST HUMAN ORGANS**

	ORGAN		AVERAGE WEIGHT OZ	G
1	Skin		384.0	10,886
2	Liver		55.0	1,560
3	Brain	male	49.7	1,408
		female	44.6	1,263
4	Lungs	right	20.5	580
		left	18.0	510
		total	38.5	1,090
5	Heart	male	11.1	315
		female	9.3	265
6	Kidneys	right	4.9	140
		left	5.3	150
		total	10.2	290
7	Spleen		6.0	170
8	Pancreas		3.5	98
9	Thyroid		1.2	35
10	Prostate	male only	0.7	20

This list is based on average immediate post-mortem weights. The skin heads the list, at 16 percent of a body's total weight, an average of 24 lb (10.9 kg).

TOP 10 **LONGEST BONES IN THE HUMAN BODY**

BONE / AVERAGE LENGTH IN/CM

Sternum
(breastbone)
6.69 / 17.00

7th rib
9.45 / 24.00

8th rib
9.06 / 23.00

Humerus
(upper arm)
14.35 / 36.46

Radius
(outer lower arm)
10.40 / 26.42

Ulna
(inner lower arm)
11.10 / 28.20

Innominate bone
(hipbone—half pelvis)
7.28 / 18.50

Femur
(thighbone—upper leg)
19.88 / 50.50

Fibula
(outer lower leg)
15.94 / 40.50

Tibia
(shinbone—inner lower leg)
16.94 / 43.03

These are average dimensions of the bones of an adult male measured from their extremities (ribs are curved and the pelvis measurement is taken diagonally). The same bones in the female skeleton are usually 6 to 13 percent smaller, with the exception of the sternum, which is virtually identical.

TOP 10 **OLDEST PEOPLE**

	NAME / COUNTRY	BORN	DIED	YEARS	AGE MONTHS	DAYS
1	Jeanne Calment (France)	Feb 21, 1875	Aug 4, 1997	122	5	14
2	Sarah Knauss (USA)	Sep 24, 1880	Dec 30, 1999	119	3	6
3	Lucy Hannah (USA)	Jul 16, 1875	Mar 21, 1993	117	8	5
4	Marie-Louise Meilleur (Canada)	Aug 29, 1880	Apr 16, 1998	117	7	18
5	María Capovilla (Ecuador)	Sep 14, 1889	Aug 27, 2006	116	11	13
6	Tane Ikai (Japan)	Jan 18, 1879	Jul 12, 1995	116	5	24
7	Elizabeth Bolden (USA)	Aug 15, 1890	Dec 11, 2006	116	3	26
8	Maggie Barnes (USA)	Mar 6, 1882	Jan 19, 1998	115	10	13
9	Charlotte Hughes (UK)	Aug 1, 1877	Mar 17, 1993	115	7	16
10	Christian Mortensen* (Denmark/USA)	Aug 16, 1882	Apr 25, 1998	115	7	9

* Oldest male—all others female

This list is based on the longevity of supercentenarians (those aged over 110) for whom there is undisputed evidence of their birth date. It thus excludes alleged oldest man Shigechiyo Izumi (Japan), as there is doubt as to whether he was born in 1865 or 1880, and Carrie C. White (USA), whose 1874 birth date cannot be verified, as well as earlier claims like that of Thomas Parr (UK), said to have been 152 at his death in 1635.

TOP 10 **TALLEST PEOPLE**

	NAME / DATES / COUNTRY	FT	HEIGHT IN	M	CM
1	Robert Pershing Wadlow (1918–40) USA	8	11.1	2	72
2	John William Rogan (1868–1905) USA	8	9.8	2	68
3	John Aasen (1887–1938) USA	8	9.7	2	67
4	John F. Carroll (1932–69) USA	8	7.6	2	64
5	Al Tomaini (1918–62) USA	8	4.4	2	55
6	Trijntje Keever* (1616–33) Netherlands	8	3.3	2	54
7	Edouard Beaupré (1881–1904) Canada	8	2.5	2	50
8	= Bernard Coyne (1897–1921) USA	8	1.2	2	49
	= Don Koehler (1925–81) USA	8	1.2	2	49
10	= Jeng Jinlian* (1964–82) China	8	1.1	2	48
	= Väinö Myllyrinne (1909–63) Finland	8	1.1	2	48

* Female—all others male

Made to measure
Measured shortly before his death at the age of 22, Robert Wadlow still holds the record as the world's tallest person.

Health & Healthcare

TOP 10 MOST COMMON REASONS FOR VISITS TO A PHYSICIAN IN THE USA

REASON FOR VISIT* / VISITS (2003)

1	General medical examination 59,938,000		**6**	Gynaecological examination 15,553,000
2	Cough 28,759,000		**7**	Knee symptoms 15,501,000
3	Routine prenatal examination 24,457,000		**8**	Back symptoms 15,023,000
4	Postoperative visit 24,202,000		**9**	Vision dysfunctions 13,568,000
5	Throat symptoms 23,314,000		**10**	Stomach pains, cramps, and spasms 13,429,000

* Excluding nonspecific and progress visits

Source: National Center for Health Statistics

TOP 10 COUNTRIES WITH THE MOST DENTISTS

	COUNTRY	DENTISTS PER 1,000
1	USA	1.63
2	Jordan	1.29
3	= Estonia	1.28
	= Finland	1.28
5	Lebanon	1.21
6	= Israel	1.17
	= Seychelles	1.17
8	Uruguay	1.16
9	Greece	1.13
10	Brazil	1.11

Source: World Health Organization, *The World Health Report 2006*

TOP 10 COUNTRIES WITH THE MOST NURSES

	COUNTRY	NURSES PER 1,000
1	San Marino	95.48
2	Ireland	15.20
3	Norway	14.84
4	Finland	14.33
5	Netherlands	13.73
6	Iceland	13.63
7	UK	12.12
8	Belarus	11.63
9	Switzerland	10.75
10	Denmark	10.36
	USA	9.37

Source: World Health Organization, *The World Health Report 2006*

TOP 10 COUNTRIES WITH THE MOST DOCTORS

COUNTRY / DOCTORS PER 1,000

1	San Marino	47.35
2	Cuba	5.91
3	Monaco	5.81
4	St. Lucia	5.17
5	Belarus	4.55
6	Belgium	4.49
7	Estonia	4.48
8	Greece	4.38
9	Russia	4.25
10	Italy	4.20
	USA	*2.56*

Source: World Health Organization, *The World Health Report 2006*

THE 10 MOST UNDERNOURISHED COUNTRIES

	COUNTRY	% OF POPULATION UNDERNOURISHED 2000–03*
1	Eritrea	73
2	Dem. Rep. of Congo	72
3	Burundi	67
4	Comoros	62
5	Tajikistan	61
6	Sierra Leone	50
7 =	Haiti	47
=	Zambia	47
9	Ethiopia	46
10 =	Central African Republic	45
=	Mozambique	45
=	Zimbabwe	45

* Food intake that is insufficient to meet dietary requirements continuously

Source: United Nations, *Human Development Report 2006*

TOP 10 MOST OBESE COUNTRIES

		% OF OBESE ADULTS*	
	COUNTRY	MEN	WOMEN
1	Nauru	80.2	78.6
2	Tonga	46.6	70.3
3	Samoa	32.9	63.0
4	Jordan#	32.7	59.8
5	Nieue	15.0	46.0
6	Qatar	34.6	45.3
7	French Polynesia	36.3	44.3
8	Saudi Arabia	26.4	44.0
9	Palestine	23.9	42.5
10	United Arab Emirates	25.9	39.9
	USA	27.7	34.0

* Ranked by percentage of obese women (those with a BMI greater than 30) in those countries and latest year for which data available
# Urban population only

Source: International Obesity Task Force (IOTF)

TOP 10 COSMETIC-SURGERY PROCEDURES PERFORMED IN THE USA

	PROCEDURE	NO. PERFORMED (2006)
1	Liposuction	403,604
2	Breast augmentation	383,886
3	Cosmetic eyelid surgery	209,999
4	Nose reshaping	141,912
5	Tummy tuck	172,457
6	Breast reduction (women)	145,822
7	Facelift	138,245
8	Breast lift	125,896
9	Forehead lift	54,149
10	Breast reduction (men)	23,670

Source: American Society for Aesthetic Plastic Surgery

Face facts
Over 11 million cosmetic-surgery procedures a year, at a cost of over $8 billion, are undertaken in the USA alone.

In 2006, 1,922,788 and 9,533,980 nonsurgical procedures were performed in the USA. The latter category included 3,181,592 botox injections—a remarkable 4,883 percent increase over the 65,157 recorded in 1997. The total cost was put at $7,632,270,642 for surgical and $4,542,014,327 nonsurgical, a total of $12,174,284,969. Following extensive publicity of unsatisfactory lip-augmentation procedures, the number plummeted by 83 percent from the 50,237 performed in 2005.

Birth & Life Expectancy

TOP 10 YEARS WITH MOST BIRTHS IN THE USA

	YEAR	BIRTHS
1	1957	4,308,000
2	1961	4,268,000
3	1960	4,258,000
4	1958	4,255,000
5	1959	4,245,000
6	1956	4,218,000
7	1962	4,167,000
8	1990	4,158,000
9	2004	4,116,000
10	1991	4,111,000

The total number of births in the USA first exceeded three million in 1921, but then remained below this figure throughout the 1920s and 1930s until 1943, when it hit a new peak of 3,104,000. The first year in which it topped four million was 1954, with 1957 remaining the all-time peak. A postwar low of 3,137,000 was experienced in 1973, but by 2000 the figure once again exceeded the four million mark and has been maintained into the 21st century.

TOP 10 COUNTRIES WITH THE HIGHEST BIRTH RATES

COUNTRY	ESTIMATED BIRTH RATE (LIVE BIRTHS PER 1,000, 2008)
1 Niger	49.62
2 Mali	49.38
3 Uganda	48.15
4 Afghanistan	45.82
5 Sierra Leone	45.07
6 Burkina Faso	44.93
7 Chad	44.88
8 Angola	44.09
9 Somalia	44.08
10 Dem. Rep. of Congo	42.96
USA	*14.18*
World average	*20.00*

Source: US Census Bureau, International Data Base

The countries with the highest birth rates are among the poorest countries in the world. In these countries, people often deliberately have large families so that the children can help earn income for the family when they are older. The 10 countries with the highest birth rates therefore corresponds very closely with the list of countries with the highest fertility rates—the average number of children born to each woman in the country.

TOP 10 COUNTRIES WITH THE MOST BIRTHS

COUNTRY	ESTIMATED BIRTHS (2008)
1 India	25,508,469
2 China	18,234,912
3 Nigeria	5,528,564
4 Pakistan	4,900,375
5 Indonesia	4,569,738
6 Bangladesh	4,431,364
7 USA	4,308,233
8 Brazil	3,078,214
9 Ethiopia	2,879,751
10 Dem. Rep. of Congo	2,861,321
World	*133,975,284*

Source: US Census Bureau, International Data Base

THE 10 COUNTRIES WITH THE LOWEST BIRTH RATES

COUNTRY	ESTIMATED BIRTH RATE (LIVE BIRTHS PER 1,000, 2008)
1 Germany	8.18
2 Andorra	8.23
3 Italy	8.36
4 Austria	8.66
5 Bosnia and Herzegovina	8.82
6 Czech Republic	8.89
7 = Singapore	8.99
= Slovenia	8.99
9 Lithuania	9.00
10 Japan	9.07

Source: US Census Bureau, International Data Base

Although not independent countries, several places record similarly low rates, among them Hong Kong (7.37) and Guernsey (8.57).

TOP 10 **COUNTRIES WITH THE HIGHEST LIFE EXPECTANCY**

	COUNTRY	LIFE EXPECTANCY AT BIRTH (2008)
1	Andorra	83.53
2	Singapore	81.89
3	San Marino	81.88
4	Japan	81.44
5	= Sweden	80.74
	= Switzerland	80.74
7	Australia	80.73
8	Iceland	80.55
9	Canada	80.46
10	Italy	80.07
	USA	*78.14*
	World average	*66.10*

Source: US Census Bureau, International Data Base

Several other territories, including Hong Kong, the Cayman Islands, Gibraltar, and Guernsey, all have life expectancies of more than 80 years.

THE 10 **COUNTRIES WITH THE LOWEST LIFE EXPECTANCY**

	COUNTRY	LIFE EXPECTANCY AT BIRTH (2008)
1	Swaziland	31.99
2	Botswana	33.83
3	Lesotho	34.61
4	Angola	37.92
5	Zambia	38.59
6	Zimbabwe	39.73
8	Mozambique	41.04
9	Liberia	41.17
10	South Africa	42.37

Source: US Census Bureau, International Data Base

Life span
Diet, medical, and other factors have resulted in a progressive increase in life expectancy in Japan: over half those born since 2000 are expected to live beyond 90.

Quality of Life

Best and worst
Despite the efforts of governments and international agencies, the graphic contrast between countries where most people are healthy, wealthy, and well-educated and those where they are not—as here, in Norway (left) and Niger (below)—is one of the biggest challenges of the 21st century.

TOP 10 **MOST LIVABLE COUNTRIES**

COUNTRY / HDI RANK (2003)

 1 Norway 0.963

 2 Iceland 0.956

 3 Australia 0.955

 4 = Canada 0.949
= Luxembourg 0.949
= Sweden 0.949

 7 Switzerland 0.947

 8 Ireland 0.946

 9 Belgium 0.945

 10 USA 0.944

Source: United Nations, *Human Development Report 2005*

The UN Human Development Index ranks countries by their quality of life. Criteria for the ranking include life expectancy, adult literacy, school enrolment, educational attainment, and per capita GDP.

THE 10 **LEAST LIVABLE COUNTRIES**

COUNTRY / HDI RANK (2003)

 1 Niger 0.281

 2 Sierra Leone 0.298

 3 Burkina Faso 0.317

 4 Mali 0.333

 5 Chad 0.341

 6 Guinea Bissau 0.348

 7 Central African Republic 0.355

 8 Ethiopia 0.367

 9 Burundi 0.378

 10 Mozambique 0.379

Source: United Nations, *Human Development Report 2005*

TOP 10 **MOST LIVABLE STATES IN THE USA**

STATE / RATING

1 New Hampshire 35.84

2 Minnesota 34.68

3 Iowa 32.39

4 Vermont 31.89

5 New Jersey 31.30

6 Wyoming 31.16

7 Massachusetts 31.14

8 Virginia 30.84

9 Nebraska 30.70

10 Connecticut 30.61

Source: Morgan Quitno Press, *State Rankings 2006*

A state's "livability rating" is ranked in 44 categories. The scale is 1 to 50, the higher the number the better the state's overall ranking.

Molasses in Massachusetts
One of the worst places to live in the USA in 1919 was Boston, Massachusetts. On January 15, a tank containing 2.3 million gallons of molasses burst and a wave of the viscous liquid poured through the streets, killing 21 people and injuring 150. The sticky residue and smell lingered in the city for many years.

THE 10 **LEAST LIVABLE STATES IN THE USA**

STATE / RATING

1 Louisiana 15.00

2 Mississippi 15.43

3 Arkansas 18.45

4 Kentucky 18.66

5 South Carolina 19.11

6 Tennessee 19.41

7 West Virginia 19.57

8 Oklahoma 19.67

9 = New Mexico 20.30

    = Texas 20.30

Source: Morgan Quitno Press, *State Rankings 2006*

TOP 10 **MOST CORRUPT COUNTRIES**

	COUNTRY	RATING
1	= Bangladesh	1.7
	= Chad	1.7
3	= Haiti	1.8
	= Myanmar	1.8
	= Turkmenistan	1.8
6	= Côte d'Ivoire	1.9
	= Equatorial Guinea	1.9
	= Nigeria	1.9
9	Angola	2.0
10	= Dem. Rep. of Congo	2.1
	= Kenya	2.1
	= Pakistan	2.1
	= Paraguay	2.1
	= Somalia	2.1
	= Sudan	2.1
	= Tajikistan	2.1

THE 10 **LEAST CORRUPT COUNTRIES**

	COUNTRY	RATING
1	Iceland	9.7
2	= Finland	9.6
	= New Zealand	9.6
4	Denmark	9.5
5	Singapore	9.4
6	Sweden	9.2
7	Switzerland	9.1
8	Norway	8.9
9	Australia	8.8
10	Austria	8.7
	USA	*7.6*

Source: Transparency International, *Corruption Perceptions Index 2005*

The Corruption Perceptions Index ranks countries by how likely they are to accept bribes, as perceived by the general public, business people, and risk analysts. They are ranked on a scale of 0–10, the higher the score, the "cleaner," or less corrupt the country. A total of 159 countries were covered by the latest survey.

First Names First

TOP 10 **FIRST NAMES IN THE USA, 1900s**

BOYS		GIRLS
John	1	Mary
William	2	Helen
James	3	Margaret
George	4	Anna
Charles	5	Ruth
Robert	6	Elizabeth
Joseph	7	Dorothy
Frank	8	Marie
Edward	9	Florence
Thomas	10	Mildred

Based on the most popular names of boys (1,467,664 births) and girls (3,105,534 births) during the decade.

TOP 10 **FIRST NAMES IN THE USA, 1910s**

BOYS		GIRLS
John	1	Mary
William	2	Helen
James	3	Dorothy
Robert	4	Margaret
Joseph	5	Ruth
George	6	Mildred
Charles	7	Anna
Edward	8	Elizabeth
Frank	9	Frances
Thomas	10	Virginia

Source: Social Security Administration

Based on the most popular names of boys (6,949,059 births) and girls (8,502,959 births) during the decade.

TOP 10 **FIRST NAMES IN THE USA, 1920s**

BOYS		GIRLS
Robert	1	Mary
John	2	Dorothy
James	3	Helen
William	4	Betty
Charles	5	Margaret
George	6	Ruth
Joseph	7	Virginia
Richard	8	Doris
Edward	9	Mildred
Donald	10	Frances

Based on the most popular names of boys (11,365,663 births) and girls (12,396,631 births) during the decade.

TOP 10 **FIRST NAMES IN THE USA, 1930s**

BOYS		GIRLS
Robert	1	Mary
James	2	Betty
John	3	Barbara
William	4	Shirley
Richard	5	Patricia
Charles	6	Dorothy
Donald	7	Joan
George	8	Margaret
Thomas	9	Nancy
Joseph	10	Helen

Based on the most popular names of boys (10,838,935 births) and girls (11,040,785 births) during the decade.

TOP 10 **FIRST NAMES IN THE USA, 1940s**

BOYS		GIRLS
James	1	Mary
Robert	2	Linda
John	3	Barbara
William	4	Patricia
Richard	5	Carol
David	6	Sandra
Charles	7	Nancy
Thomas	8	Judith
Michael	9	Sharon
Ronald	10	Judith

Based on the most popular names of boys (15,125,934 births) and girls (14,884,155 births) during the decade.

TOP 10 **FIRST NAMES IN THE USA, 1950s**

BOYS		GIRLS
James	1	Mary
Michael	2	Linda
Robert	3	Patricia
John	4	Susan
David	5	Deborah
William	6	Barbara
Richard	7	Debra
Thomas	8	Karen
Mark	9	Nancy
Charles	10	Donna

Based on the most popular names of boys (20,489,548 births) and girls (19,723,422 births) during the decade.

TOP 10 FIRST NAMES IN THE USA, 1960s

1960

BOYS		GIRLS
Michael	1	Lisa
David	2	Mary
John	3	Susan
James	4	Karen
Robert	5	Kimberly
Mark	6	Patricia
William	7	Linda
Richard	8	Donna
Thomas	9	Michelle
Jeffrey	10	Cynthia

Based on the most popular names of boys (19,601,516 births) and girls (18,893,668 births) during the decade.

TOP 10 FIRST NAMES IN THE USA, 1970s

1970

BOYS		GIRLS
Michael	1	Jennifer
Christopher	2	Amy
Jason	3	Melissa
David	4	Michelle
James	5	Kimberly
John	6	Lisa
Robert	7	Angela
Brian	8	Heather
William	9	Stephanie
Matthew	10	Nicole

Based on the most popular names of boys (17,080,756 births) and girls (16,449,682 births) during the decade.

TOP 10 FIRST NAMES IN THE USA, 1980s

1980

BOYS		GIRLS
Michael	1	Jessica
Christopher	2	Jennifer
Matthew	3	Amanda
Joshua	4	Ashley
David	5	Sarah
James	6	Stephanie
Daniel	7	Melissa
Robert	8	Nicole
John	9	Elizabeth
Joseph	10	Heather

Based on the most popular names of boys (19,203,301 births) and girls (18,431,842 births) during the decade.

TOP 10 FIRST NAMES IN THE USA, 1990s

1990

BOYS		GIRLS
Michael	1	Jessica
Christopher	2	Ashley
Matthew	3	Emily
Joshua	4	Sarah
Jacob	5	Samantha
Nicholas	6	Amanda
Andrew	7	Brittany
Daniel	8	Elizabeth
Tyler	9	Taylor
Joseph	10	Megan

Based on the most popular names of boys (20,524,632 births) and girls (19,620,525 births) during the decade.

TOP 10 FIRST NAMES IN THE USA, 2000s

2000

BOYS		GIRLS
Jacob	1	Emily
Michael	2	Madison
Joshua	3	Hannah
Matthew	4	Emma
Andrew	5	Ashley
Christopher	6	Abigail
Joseph	7	Alexis
Daniel	8	Olivia
Nicholas	9	Samantha
Ethan	10	Sara

Source: Social Security Administration

Based on the most popular names of boys (12,485,039 births) and girls (11,929,533 births) during the decade to February 2006.

You Called Him What?

British and American Puritans of the late 16th and early 17th centuries abandoned first names they considered "heathen" in favor of those with biblical associations, baptizing their children with names that included Be-faithful, Small-hope, Praise-god, Kill-sin, Thankful, Search-the-scriptures, Hope-on-high, Increase, and Weep-not.

Marriage & Divorce

COUNTRY	% OF 15–19-YEAR-OLD GIRLS WHO HAVE EVER BEEN MARRIED*
1 Dem. Rep. of Congo	74.2
2 Congo	55.0
3 Afghanistan	53.7
4 Bangladesh	51.3
5 Uganda	49.8
6 Mali	49.7
7 Guinea	49.0
8 Chad	48.6
9 Mozambique	47.1
10 Senegal	43.8
USA	3.9

* In latest year for which data available

Source: United Nations

Young love
A teenage bride and groom celebrate their marriage in traditional Afghan style by exchanging a sweet drink. The world average age for marriage is 27.8.

TOP 10 **MONTHS FOR MARRIAGES IN THE USA**

MONTH / MARRIAGES (2005)

1 August 235,000

2 July 228,000

3 June 227,000

4 September 222,000

5 October 206,000

6 May 186,000

7 November 176,000

8 April 163,000

9 December 158,000

10 March 156,000

Source: National Center for Health Statistics

Estimates are for 2005 from a US total of some 2,230,000—a decrease of 49,000 compared with the previous year. January was at No. 11 with 138,000, and February the least popular month with 135,000 marriages.

TOP 10 **COUNTRIES WITH THE HIGHEST PROPORTION OF TEENAGE HUSBANDS**

COUNTRY	% OF 15–19-YEAR-OLD BOYS WHO HAVE EVER BEEN MARRIED*
1 Iraq	14.9
2 Nepal	13.5
3 Congo	11.8
4 Uganda	11.4
5 Central African Republic	8.1
6 India	9.5
7 Afghanistan	9.2
8 Guinea	8.2
9 Guatemala	7.8
10 Columbia	7.7
USA	1.3

* In latest year for which data available

Source: United Nations

TOP 10 COUNTRIES WHERE MOST WOMEN MARRY

COUNTRY	% OF WOMEN MARRIED BY AGE 50*
1 = Comoros	100.0
= Gambia	100.0
= Ghana	100.0
= Nauru	100.0
5 Chad	99.9
6 = China	99.8
= Guinea	99.8
= Mali	99.8
= Papua New Guinea	99.8
10 Benin	99.7
USA	*93.9*

* In latest year for which data available

Source: United Nations

Marriage in these countries can be considered only marginally above the norm, contrasting with a relatively small number where almost half the female population opts never to marry.

TOP 10 COUNTRIES WHERE MOST MEN MARRY

COUNTRY	% OF MEN MARRIED BY AGE 50*
1 = Chad	100.0
= Gambia	100.0
3 Guinea	99.7
4 = Mali	99.6
= Niger	99.6
6 = Bangladesh	99.3
= Mozambique	99.3
8 Cameroon	99.2
9 Nepal	99.1
10 = Central African Republic	99.0
= Eritrea	99.0
= Tajikistan	99.0
USA	*91.9*

* In latest year for which data available

Source: United Nations

THE 10 COUNTRIES WITH THE LOWEST DIVORCE RATES

COUNTRY	DIVORCE RATE PER 1,000*
1 Guatemala	0.12
2 Belize	0.17
3 Mongolia	0.28
4 Libya	0.32
5 Georgia	0.40
6 Chile	0.42
7 St. Vincent and the Grenadines	0.43
8 Jamaica	0.44
9 Armenia	0.47
10 Turkey	0.49

* In those countries/latest year for which data available

Source: United Nations

The countries that figure among those with the lowest rates represent a range of cultures and religions that either condone or condemn divorce to varying extents, thus affecting its prevalence or otherwise. In some countries, legal and other obstacles make divorce difficult or costly, while in certain societies, such as Jamaica, where the marriage rate is also low, partners often separate without the formality of divorce.

TOP 10 COUNTRIES WITH THE HIGHEST DIVORCE RATES

COUNTRY	DIVORCE RATE PER 1,000*
1 Russia	5.30
2 Aruba	5.27
3 USA	4.19
4 Ukraine	3.79
5 Belarus	3.77
6 Moldova	3.50
7 Cuba	3.16
8 Czech Republic	3.11
9 = Lithuania	3.05
= South Korea	3.05

* In those countries/latest year for which data available

Source: United Nations

The demographics of divorce are more complex than the Top 10 suggests, varying according to age at marriage (highest among those who marry in their early twenties), higher for second, and higher still for third marriages.

Death

The writing on the wall
Worldwide, AIDS has claimed over 25 million lives in 25 years, making it one of the most devastating epidemics of all time.

THE 10 **MOST COMMON CAUSES OF DEATH BY INFECTIOUS AND PARASITIC DISEASES**

	CAUSE	APPROXIMATE DEATHS (2002)
1	Lower-respiratory infections	3,884,000
2	HIV/AIDS	2,777,000
3	Diarrhoeal diseases	1,798,000
4	Tuberculosis	1,566,000
5	Malaria	1,272,000
6	Measles	611,000
7	Whooping cough (pertussis)	294,000
8	Neonatal tetanus	214,000
9	Meningitis	173,000
10	Syphilis	157,000

Source: World Health Organization, *World Health Report 2004*

In 2002, infectious and parasitic diseases accounted for some 10,904,000 of the 57,029,000 deaths worldwide. After declining, certain childhood diseases—including measles and whooping cough—showed an increase in this year.

THE 10 **MOST COMMON CAUSES OF DEATH IN THE USA**

CAUSE / DEATHS (2004)

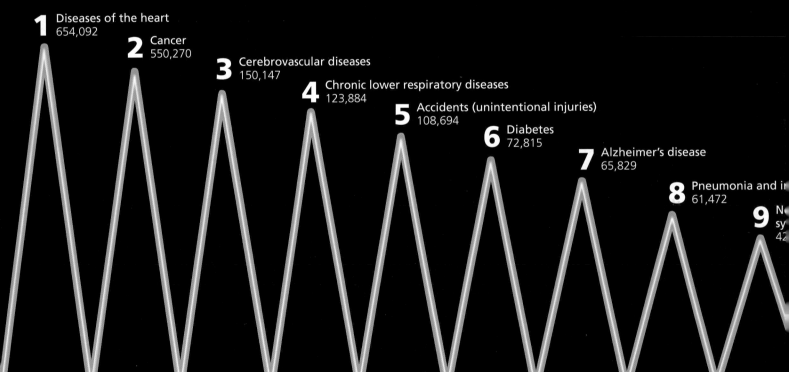

1 Diseases of the heart
654,092

2 Cancer
550,270

3 Cerebrovascular diseases
150,147

4 Chronic lower respiratory diseases
123,884

5 Accidents (unintentional injuries)
108,694

6 Diabetes
72,815

7 Alzheimer's disease
65,829

8 Pneumonia and i
61,472

9 N
sy
42

The Chinese way of death
China has almost 20 percent of the global population and accounts for some 17 percent of annual deaths worldwide.

TOP 10 **COUNTRIES WITH THE MOST DEATHS**

COUNTRY / ESTIMATED DEATHS (2008)

1 China 9,350,214
2 India 7,347,174
3 USA 2,512,630
4 Nigeria 2,269,228
5 Russia 2,259,676
6 Indonesia 1,482,077
7 Pakistan 1,355,937
8 Bangladesh 1,228,375
9 Japan 1,222,013
10 Brazil 1,193,671
World 55,771,877

enza

itis, nephrotic
ome, and nephrosis
2

10 Septicaemia
34,464

Total (all causes)
2,398,365

THE 10 **COUNTRIES WITH THE LOWEST DEATH RATES**

COUNTRY	ESTIMATED DEATH RATE (DEATHS PER 1,000, 2008)
1 Kuwait	2.37
2 Saudi Arabia	2.52
3 Jordan	2.72
4 Libya	3.46
5 Brunei	3.54
6 Oman	3.74
7 Solomon Islands	3.82
8 Ecuador	4.21
9 Bahrain	4.29
10 Nicaragua	4.39

Source: US Census Bureau, International Data Base

The crude death rate is derived by dividing the total number of deaths in a given year by the total population and multiplying by 1,000. Age-standardized death rates take account of the age structure of the population to produce a more accurate assessment.

THE 10 **MOST SUICIDAL COUNTRIES**

	SUICIDES PER 100,000 PER ANNUM*		
COUNTRY	MALE	FEMALE	TOTAL
1 Lithuania	74.3	13.9	42.1
2 Russia	69.3	11.9	38.7
3 Belarus	63.3	10.3	35.1
4 Kazakhstan	50.2	8.8	28.8
5 Slovenia	45.0	12.0	28.1
6 Hungary	44.9	12.0	27.7
7 Estonia	47.7	9.8	27.3
8 Ukraine	46.7	8.4	26.1
9 Latvia	45.0	9.7	26.0
10 Japan	35.2	12.8	23.8
USA	*17.6*	*4.1*	*10.7*

* In those countries/latest year for which data available

Source: World Health Organization

Suicide rates in certain countries appear low, partly because of extended family support networks and because of the cultural taboos attached to suicide.

World Religions

TOP 10 **RELIGIOUS BELIEFS**

	RELIGION	FOLLOWERS
1	Christianity	2,135,784,198
2	Islam	1,313,983,654
3	Hinduism	870,047,346
4	Chinese folk religions	404,922,244
5	Buddhism	378,809,103
6	Ethnic religions	256,340,652
7	New religions	108,131,713
8	Sikhism	25,373,879
9	Judaism	15,145,702
10	Spiritists	13,030,538

Source: World Christian Database

While some mainstream religious groups have experienced a decline in formal attendance, certain fringe religions have grown. Today, about one-third of the world's population are nominally (self-declared), if not practicing, Christians, and one-fifth are followers of Islam. At least 15 percent of the world's population profess no religious beliefs of any kind.

TOP 10 **LARGEST MUSLIM POPULATIONS**

	COUNTRY	MUSLIMS
1	Pakistan	154,563,023
2	India	134,149,817
3	Bangladesh	132,868,312
4	Indonesia	121,606,358*
5	Turkey	71,322,513
6	Iran	67,724,004
7	Egypt	63,503,397
8	Nigeria	54,665,801
9	Algeria	31,858,555
10	Morocco	31,000,895
	USA	*4,657,005*
	World	*1,313,983,654*

* An additional 46 million people are considered Muslims by the Indonesian government but are more properly categorized as New Religionists (Islamisized syncretistic religions)

Source: World Christian Database

TOP 10 **LARGEST ROMAN CATHOLIC POPULATIONS**

	COUNTRY	ROMAN CATHOLICS
1	Brazil	155,929,000
2	Mexico	99,200,000
3	Philippines	68,252,000
4	USA	65,900,000
5	Italy	55,300,000
6	France	46,274,000
7	Colombia	42,200,000
8	Spain	38,473,000
9	Poland	35,300,000
10	Argentina	35,000,000
	World	*1,118,991,707*

Source: World Christian Database

Below: High church
The statue of Christ towers over Rio de Janeiro. Brazil is home to one in seven of the world's Roman Catholics.

TOP 10 **LARGEST JEWISH POPULATIONS**

	COUNTRY	JEWS
1	USA	5,764,208
2	Israel	4,772,138
3	France	607,111
4	Argentina	520,130
5	Palestine	451,001
6	Canada	414,452
7	Brazil	383,837
8	UK	312,173
9	Russia	244,719
10	Germany	222,689
	World	*15,145,702*

Source: World Christian Database

The Diaspora, or scattering, of Jewish people has established Jewish communities in almost every country in the world. In 1939 the estimated total Jewish population was 17 million. Some six million fell victim to Nazi persecution, reducing the figure to about 11 million, since when it has grown to over 15 million.

TOP 10 **LARGEST HINDU POPULATIONS**

	COUNTRY	HINDUS
1	India	810,387,411
2	Nepal	19,020,312
3	Bangladesh	17,029,336
4	Indonesia	7,632,941
5	Sri Lanka	2,173,114
6	Pakistan	2,100,342
7	Malaysia	1,855,194
8	USA	1,143,864
9	South Africa	1,078,667
10	Myanmar	1,006,804
	World	*870,047,346*

Source: World Christian Database

Hindus constitute some 74 percent of the population of India and 72 percent of that of Nepal, but only 11 percent of Bangladesh's population and as little as three percent of Indonesia's.

TOP 10 **LARGEST BUDDHIST POPULATIONS**

	COUNTRY	BUDDHISTS
1	China	111,358,666
2	Japan	70,722,505
3	Thailand	53,294,170
4	Vietnam	40,780,825
5	Myanmar	37,151,956
6	Sri Lanka	13,234,600
7	Cambodia	12,697,958
8	India	7,596,701
9	South Korea	7,281,110
10	Taiwan	4,823,361
	USA	*2,721,335*
	World	*378,809,103*

Source: World Christian Database

Although India now features in 8th place among countries with high Buddhist populations, the religion originated there in the 6th century BC. Its espousal of peace and tolerant coexistence ensured its appeal and encouraged the spread of Buddhism throughout Asia and beyond.

Spiritual leader
Tenzin Gyatso was declared as the 14th Dalai Lama at the age of five, and enthroned when he was 15.

THE 10 **LATEST DALAI LAMAS**

NAME / BORN/DIED

1 Tenzin Gyatso (1935–)
2 Thubten Gyatso (1876–1933)
3 Trinley Gyatso (1856–75)
4 Khendrup Gyatso (1838–56)
5 Tsultrim Gyatso (1816–37)
6 Lungtok Gyatso (1806–15)
7 Jamphel Gyatso (1758–1804)
8 Kelzang Gyatso (1708–57)
9 Tsangyang Gyatso (1683–1706)
10 Lobsang Gyatso (1617–82)

The current Dalai Lama is the 14th in line since the first, Gedun Truppa (1391–1475). Each is believed to be the reincarnation of his predecessor and proclaimed as a child soon after the previous incumbent's death—although they do not take office until they are older.

Rulers & Leaders

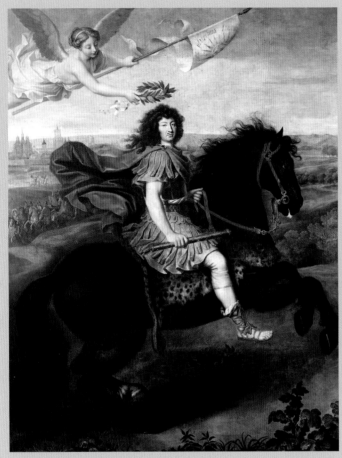

72 years in the saddle
Discounting the doubtful 95 years claimed for King Mihti of Arakan (Myanmar), 94 for Egyptian pharaoh Phiops (Pepi) II, and long reigns of other early monarchs, that of French "Sun King" Louis XIV establishes him as the world's longest-serving ruler.

TOP 10 **LONGEST-REIGNING MONARCHS***

MONARCH / COUNTRY / REIGN	AGE AT ACCESSION	REIGN		
		YEARS	MONTHS	DAYS
1 King Louis XIV, France May 14, 1643–Sep 1, 1715	5	72	3	18
2 King John II, Liechtenstein Nov 12, 1858–Feb 11, 1929	18	70	2	30
3 Emperor Franz-Josef, Austria-Hungary Dec 2, 1848–Nov 21, 1916	18	67	11	19
4 Queen Victoria, UK Jun 20, 1837–Jan 22, 1901	18	63	7	2
5 James I, Aragon Sep 12, 1213–Jul 27, 1276	5	62	10	15
6 Emperor Hirohito, Japan Dec 25, 1926–Jan 7, 1989	25	62	0	13
7 Emperor K'ang Hsi, China Feb 5, 1661–Dec 20, 1722	7	61	10	15
8 King Sobhuza II#, Swaziland Dec 22, 1921–Aug 21, 1982	22	60	7	30
9 Emperor Ch'ien Lung, China Oct 18, 1735–Feb 9, 1796	25	60	3	22
10 King Christian IV, Denmark Apr 4, 1588–Feb 21, 1648	11	59	10	17

* During past 1,000 years, excluding earlier rulers of dubious authenticity
# Paramount chief until 1967, when Great Britain recognized him as king with the granting of internal self-government

TOP 10 **LONGEST-REIGNING QUEENS**

QUEEN*	COUNTRY	REIGN	YEARS
1 Victoria	UK	1837–1901	63
2 Wilhelmina	Netherlands	1890–1948	58
3 Elizabeth II	UK	1952–	55#
4 Wu Chao	China	AD 655–705	50
5 Salote Tubou	Tonga	1918–65	47
6 Elizabeth I	England	1558–1603	44
7 Maria Theresa	Hungary	1740–80	40
8 Maria I	Portugal	1777–1816	39
9 Joanna I	Italy	1343–81	38
10 Suiko Tenno	Japan	AD 592–628	36

* Queens and empresses who ruled in their own right, not as consorts of kings or emperors
# As at February 6, 2007

THE 10 **YOUNGEST BRITISH MONARCHS**

MONARCH	REIGN	AGE AT ACCESSION		
		YEARS	MONTHS	DAYS
1 Henry VI	1422–61	0	8	25
2 Henry III	1216–72	9	0	18
3 Edward VI	1547–53	9	3	16
4 Richard II	1377–99	10	5	16
5 Edward V	1483	12	5	14
6 Edward III	1327–77	14	2	12
7 Jane	1553	15	8	23*
8 Henry VIII	1509–47	17	9	25
9 Victoria	1837–1901	18	0	27
10 Charles II	1649–85#	18	8	1

* Circa—precise birthdate unknown
# Succeeded on death of father, but did not reign until 1660

Henry VI was born on December 6, 1421 and became king of England on September 1, 1422 after the death of his father, Henry V. At the age of 10 months 15 days, following the death of his grandfather, Charles VI, he also became king of France. Before the Norman Conquest, Edward the Martyr became king in AD 975 aged about 12 and Ethelred II ("the Unready") in AD 978 at the age of about 10.

Desert reign
Colonel Gaddafi towers over his rivals as one of Africa's most durable leaders.

TOP 10 **LONGEST-SERVING PRESIDENTS TODAY**

PRESIDENT / COUNTRY	TOOK OFFICE
1 El Hadj Omar Bongo, Gabon	Dec 2, 1967
2 Colonel Mu'ammar Gaddafi, Libya	Sep 1, 1969*
3 Fidel Castro, Cuba	Nov 2, 1976
4 Ali Abdullah Saleh, Yemen	Jul 17, 1978
5 Maumoon Abdul Gayoom, Maldives	Nov 11, 1978
6 Teodoro Obiang Nguema Mbasogo, Equatorial Guinea	Aug 3, 1979
7 José Eduardo dos Santos, Angola	Sep 21, 1979
8 Hosni Mubarak, Egypt	Oct 6, 1981
9 Paul Biya, Cameroon	Nov 7, 1982
10 Lansana Conté, Guinea	Apr 3, 1984

* Since a reorganization in 1979, Colonel Gaddafi has held no formal position, but continues to rule under the ceremonial title of "Leader of the Revolution"

All the presidents in this list have been in power for more than 20 years. Fidel Castro became prime minister of Cuba in February 1959. He was chief of the army and as there was no opposition party, he effectively ruled as dictator from then, but was not technically president until the Cuban constitution was revised in 1976.

THE 10 **FIRST FEMALE PRIME MINISTERS AND PRESIDENTS**

PRIME MINISTER/PRESIDENT / COUNTRY	FIRST PERIOD IN OFFICE
1 Sirimavo Bandaranaike (PM), Sri Lanka	Jul 21, 1960–Mar 27, 1965
2 Indira Gandhi (PM), India	Jan 19, 1966–Mar 24, 1977
3 Golda Meir (PM), Israel	Mar 17, 1969–Jun 3, 1974
4 Maria Estela Perón (President), Argentina	Jul 1, 1974–Mar 24, 1976
5 Elisabeth Domitien (PM), Central African Republic	Jan 3, 1975–Apr 7, 1976
6 Margaret Thatcher (PM), UK	May 4, 1979–Nov 28, 1990
7 Dr. Maria Lurdes Pintasilgo (PM), Portugal	Aug 1, 1979–Jan 3, 1980
8 Mary Eugenia Charles (PM), Dominica	Jul 21, 1980–Jun 14, 1995
9 Vigdís Finnbogadóttir (President), Iceland	Aug 1, 1980–Aug 1, 1996
10 Gro Harlem Brundtland (PM), Norway	Feb 4–Oct 14, 1981

Following the assassination of her husband Solomon West Ridgeway Dias Bandaranaike, Sirimavo Ratwatte Dias Bandaranaike (1916–2000) took over as leader of the Ceylon (later Sri Lanka) Freedom Party, won the election, and thereby became the world's first female prime minister, serving three terms.

All the Presidents

THE 10 US PRESIDENTS WITH THE MOST CHILDREN

	PRESIDENT / YEARS IN OFFICE / WIFE	CHILDREN
1	**John Tyler** (1841–45) 1st Letitia Christian (7*) 2nd Julia Gardiner (7)	14
2	**William H. Harrison** (1841) Anna Tuthill Symmes	10
3	**Rutherford B. Hayes** (1877–81) Lucy Ware Webb	8
4	**James Garfield** (1881) Lucretia Rudolph	7
5	**= George H. W. Bush** (1989–93) Barbara Pierce	6
	= Thomas Jefferson (1801–09) Martha Wayles Skelton	6
	= Franklin D. Roosevelt (1933–45) Anna Eleanor Roosevelt#	6*
	= Theodore Roosevelt (1901–09) 1st Alice Hathaway Lee (1) 2nd Edith Kermit Carow (5)	6
	= Zachary Taylor (1849–50) Margaret Smith	6
10	**= John Adams** (1797–1801) Abigail Smith	5
	= Grover Cleveland (1893–97) Frances Folsom	5
	= Andrew Johnson (1865–69) Eliza McCardle	5

* Including one child deceased
# Niece of Theodore Roosevelt

Ronald Reagan had five children, but one was adopted. George Washington, James Buchanan (the only unmarried president), Andrew Jackson, James Polk, and James Madison did not have any.

Millard Fillmore's Bathtub

In the *New York Evening Mail* of December 28, 1917, American journalist H. L. Mencken described as "A Neglected Anniversary" the installation of the first bathtub in the USA, in Cincinnati in 1842, followed by the first in the White House, by President Millard Fillmore in 1851. Mencken's tale of a tub was, of course, entirely invented—baths had been common long before these dates—and he admitted as much in print, but for 90 years the story has appeared as an authentic historical account in numerous articles, reputable reference books, and on websites.

THE 10 SHORTEST-SERVING US PRESIDENTS

	PRESIDENT / YEARS IN OFFICE	PERIOD IN OFFICE YEARS	MONTHS	DAYS
1	William H. Harrison (1841)*	–	–	30
2	James Garfield (1881)*	–	6	15
3	Zachary Taylor (1849–50)*	1	4	5
4	Warren Harding (1921–23)*	2	4	29
5	Gerald Ford (1974–77)	2	5	11
6	Millard Fillmore (1850–53)	2	5	25
7	John F. Kennedy (1961–63)*	2	10	2
8	Chester A. Arthur (1881–85)	3	5	13
9	Andrew Johnson (1865–69)	3	10	17
10	John Tyler (1841–45)	3	11	0

* Died in office

TOP 10 FATTEST US PRESIDENTS

	PRESIDENT / YEARS IN OFFICE	BMI
1	William H. Taft (1909–13)	45.4
2	Grover Cleveland (1885–89)	34.6
3	William McKinley (1897–1901)	31.1
4	= Theodore Roosevelt (1901–09)	30.2
	= Zachary Taylor (1849–50)	30.2
6	Chester A. Arthur (1881–85)	28.7
7	Bill Clinton (1993–2001)	28.3
8	Herbert Hoover (1929–33)	27.7
9	James Buchanan (1857–61)	26.9
10	George W. Bush (2001–)	26.8

BMI stands for "Body-Mass Index." A person's weight in kilograms is divided by the square of their height in meters. A person with a BMI of over 25 is considered overweight, and more than 30 is regarded as clinically obese. Taft was 5 ft 11 in (1.8 m) tall and weighed 325 lb (147 kg) when he took office. He had to have a giant bath constructed in the White House to accommodate him.

Left: Senior citizen
40th US President Ronald Reagan was both the oldest-elected (69) and oldest-serving (77) of all time.

Below: Young Teddy
Theodore Roosevelt was 42 when he took office and 45 at the time of his re-election in 1904.

THE 10 **YOUNGEST US PRESIDENTS**

PRESIDENT	TOOK OFFICE	AGE ON TAKING OFFICE		
		YEARS	MONTHS	DAYS
1 Theodore Roosevelt	Sep 14, 1901	42	10	18
2 John F. Kennedy	Jan 20, 1961	43	7	22
3 Bill Clinton	Jan 20, 1993	46	5	1
4 Ulysses S. Grant	Mar 4, 1869	46	10	5
5 Grover Cleveland	Mar 4, 1893	47	11	14
6 Franklin Pierce	Mar 4, 1804	48	3	9
7 James Garfield	Mar 4, 1881	49	3	13
8 James Polk	Mar 4, 1845	49	4	2
9 Millard Fillmore	Jul 10, 1850	50	6	3
10 John Tyler	Apr 6, 1841	51	0	8

TOP 10 **OLDEST US PRESIDENTS**

PRESIDENT	LEFT OFFICE	AGE ON LEAVING OFFICE		
		YEARS	MONTHS	DAYS
1 Ronald Reagan	Jan 20, 1989	77	11	14
2 Dwight D. Eisenhower	Jan 20, 1961	70	3	6
3 Andrew Jackson	Mar 3, 1837	69	11	16
4 James Buchanan	Mar 3, 1841	69	10	8
5 Harry S. Truman	Jan 20, 1953	68	8	10
6 George H. W. Bush	Jan 20, 1993	68	7	8
7 William H. Harrison	Apr 4, 1841*	68	1	26
8 Zachary Taylor	Jul 9, 1850*	65	7	15
9 John Adams	Mar 3, 1801	65	4	3
10 Gerald Ford	Jan 20, 1977	63	6	6

* Died in office

Born on February 6, 1911, Ronald Reagan took the record when he completed his second term on January 20, 1989.

The US Constitution requires that a president must be at least 35 years old on taking office. Vice-president Theodore Roosevelt assumed the presidency following the assassination of William McKinley. John F. Kennedy was the youngest president to be elected. Polk holds the record for the shortest lifespan after leaving office, ending his four-year term on March 3, 1849 and dying 103 days later at the age of 53 years 6 months 17 days. George W. Bush was aged 54 years 6 months 14 days when he became president.

Organizations

TOP 10 CHARITIES IN THE USA

	CHARITY	INCOME (2004) TOTAL ($)
1	YMCAs in the United States	4,831,582,000
2	Catholic Charities USA	3,179,622,682
3	Salvation Army	3,104,086,000
4	American Red Cross	3,065,541,356
5	United Jewish Communities	2,864,000,000
6	Goodwill Industries International	2,389,719,000
7	Boys & Girls Club of America	1,186,300,097
8	Feed the Children	958,778,536
9	Habitat for Humanity International	902,424,175
10	Shriners Hospitals for Children	894,723,000

Source: *NonProfit Times*

TOP 10 OLDEST GOLF CLUBS IN THE USA

	CLUB	FOUNDED
1	South Carolina Golf Club, Charleston, South Carolina (now the Country Club of Charleston)	1786
2	Savannah Golf Club, Savannah, Georgia	1794
3	Philadelphia Cricket Club, Philadelphia, Pennsylvania	1854
4	Germania Town and Country Club, Saginaw, Michigan	1856
5	Vesper Country Club, Tyngsboro, Massachusetts	1875
6	Rockaway Hunting Club, Cedarhurst, New York	1878
7	Olympic Club, San Francisco, California	1879
8	Edgewood Club of Tivoli, Tivoli, New York	1880
9	Meadow Brook Club, Jericho, New York	1881
10 =	Pittsburgh Field Club, Pittsburgh, Pennsylvania	1882
=	The Country Club, Brookline, Massachusetts	1882

Most of these clubs included golf as one of several activities, and most were later disbanded. St. Andrew's Golf Club, Yonkers, New York, founded in 1888, is the oldest continuously operating golf club in the USA.

TOP 10 OLDEST YACHT CLUBS IN THE WORLD

	CLUB	FOUNDED
1	Royal Cork Yacht Club (founded as Water Club of the Harbour of Cork; dormant 1763–1803), Cork, Ireland	1720
2	Lough Ree Yacht Club, Athlone, Ireland	1770
3	Starcross Yacht Club, Exeter, Devon, UK	1772
4	Cumberland Sailing Society (Royal Thames Yacht Club since 1830), London, UK	1775
5	Royal Yacht Squadron, Cowes, Isle of Wight, UK	1815
6	Royal Northern Yacht Club, Glasgow, UK	1824
7	Republic of Singapore Yacht Club, Singapore	1826
8	Port of Plymouth Royal Clarence Regatta Club (Royal Western Yacht Club of England since 1842), Plymouth, UK	1827
9	Royal Gibraltar Yacht Club (Royal since 1933), Gibraltar	1829
10	Kungliga Svenska Segel Sällskapet (Royal Swedish Yacht Club), Stockholm, Sweden	1830

Sail of the centuries
A regatta of the Royal Northern. Yacht clubs are among the world's longest-established membership organizations.

TOP 10 COUNTRIES WITH THE HIGHEST GIRL-GUIDE AND GIRL-SCOUT MEMBERSHIP

	COUNTRY	GUIDING FOUNDED	MEMBERSHIP*
1	USA	1912	3,854,202
2	India	1911	1,170,262
3	Philippines	1919	671,267
4	UK	1909	555,420
5	Canada	1910	149,387
6	Kenya	1920	120,805
7	Nigeria	1919	100,198
8	Egypt	1913	92,000
9	Poland	1910	86,591
10	Italy	1912	83,601

* Latest year for which data available

Source: World Association of Girl Guides and Girl Scouts

100 YEARS AGO: BOY SCOUTS FOUNDED

Robert Baden-Powell (1857–1941), the hero of the Siege of Mafeking during the Boer War (1899), organized an experimental camp attended by 20 boys, held from July 29 to August 9, 1907 on Brownsea Island, Poole, Dorset, England. His book, *Scouting for Boys*, outlining the principles of scouting, much of it based on Baden-Powell's army career in Africa, was published in six two-weekly parts from January 15, 1908. The first edition of the magazine *The Scout* appeared on April 14, 1908, and the first official camp was held at Humshaugh, Northumberland later that year. By 1909 the scouting movement had gained such momentum that a rally held at Crystal Palace, London, attracted 11,000 scouts. The Boy Scouts of America, Sea Scouts, and Girl Guides were all established the following year, by which time there were over 100,000 scouts worldwide. The current figure exceeds 38 million.

Stamp of success
A 1960 postage stamp celebrates 50 years of scouting in the USA.

TOP 10 COUNTRIES WITH THE HIGHEST SCOUT MEMBERSHIP

COUNTRY / FOUNDED / MEMBERSHIP AS AT SEPTEMBER 2005

1 Indonesia 1912
8,909,435

2 USA 1910
6,239,435

3 India 1909
2,138,015

4 Philippines 1923
1,956,131

5 Thailand 1911
1,305,027

6 Bangladesh 1972
908,435

7 Pakistan 1947
526,403

8 UK 1907
498,888

9 South Korea 1922
252,157

10 Japan 1913
220,223

Endeavor & Achievement

THE 10 **FIRST WOMEN TO WIN A NOBEL PRIZE**

WINNER	COUNTRY	PRIZE	YEAR
1 Marie Curie* (1867–1934)	Poland	Physics	1903
2 Bertha von Suttner (1843–1914)	Austria	Peace	1905
3 Selma Lagerlöf (1858–1940)	Sweden	Literature	1909
4 Marie Curie (1867–1934)	Poland	Chemistry	1911
5 Grazia Deledda (1875–1936)	Italy	Literature	1926#
6 Sigrid Undset (1882–1949)	Norway	Literature	1928
7 Jane Addams† (1860–1935)	USA	Peace	1931
8 Irène Joliot-Curie§ (1897–1956)	France	Chemistry	1935
9 Pearl Buck (1892–1973)	USA	Literature	1938
10 Gabriela Mistral (1899–1957)	Chile	Literature	1945

* Shared half with husband Pierre Curie; other half to Henri Becquerel
\# Awarded 1927
† Shared with Nicholas Murray Butler
§ Shared with husband Frédéric Joliot-Curie

THE 10 **YOUNGEST NOBEL PRIZE WINNERS**

WINNER / COUNTRY / BORN	AWARD	AGE
1 William Lawrence Bragg, UK Mar 31, 1890	Physics 1915	25
2 Paul Adrien Maurice Dirac, UK Aug 8, 1902	Physics 1933	31
3 Carl David Anderson, USA Sep 3, 1905	Physics 1936	31
4 Werner Karl Heisenberg, Germany Dec 5, 1901	Physics 1932	31
5 Tsung-Dao Lee, China Nov 24, 1926	Physics 1957	31
6 Rudolf Ludwig Mössbauer, West Germany, Jan 31, 1929	Physics 1961	32
7 Frederick Grant Banting, Canada Nov 14, 1891	Medicine 1923	32
8 Brian David Josephson, UK Jan 4, 1940	Physics 1973	33
9 Joshua Lederberg, USA May 23, 1925	Medicine 1958	33
10 James Dewey Watson, USA Apr 6, 1928	Medicine 1962	34

Nobel first
The first of Marie Curie's two Nobel Prizes, for Physics in 1903, is one of only two by women in this field. Maria Goeppert-Mayer (Germany/USA) won the other in 1963.

THE 10 **FIRST MOUNTAINEERS TO CLIMB EVEREST**

MOUNTAINEER / COUNTRY	DATE
1 Edmund Hillary, New Zealand	May 29, 1953
2 Tenzing Norgay, Nepal	May 29, 1953
3 Jürg Marmet, Switzerland	May 23, 1956
4 Ernst Schmied, Switzerland	May 23, 1956
5 Hans-Rudolf von Gunten, Switzerland	May 24, 1956
6 Adolf Reist, Switzerland	May 24, 1956
7 Wang Fu-chou, China	May 25, 1960
8 Chu Ying-hua, China	May 25, 1960
9 Konbu, Tibet	May 25, 1960
10 = Nawang Gombu, India	May 1, 1963
= James Whittaker, USA	May 1, 1963

Some 15 reconnaissance expeditions and attempts on Everest—several resulting in the deaths of the mountaineers—preceded the first successful conquest of the world's tallest peak. Nawang Gombu and James Whittaker are 10th equal because, neither wishing to deny the other the privilege of being first, they ascended the last steps to the summit side by side.

Above: Pole position
Jean-Louis Etienne trekked for 63 days solo 750 miles (1,200 km) overland, hauling a sled, to reach the North Pole.

Below: Over a barrel
After becoming the first man to survive Niagara Falls, Bobby Leach (1858–1925) died after tripping on an orange peel.

THE 10 **FIRST EXPEDITIONS TO REACH THE NORTH POLE OVERLAND***

NAME# / COUNTRY	DATE
1 Ralph S. Plaisted, USA	Apr 19, 1968
2 Wally W. Herbert, UK	Apr 5, 1969
3 Naomi Uemura, Japan	May 1, 1978
4 Dmitri Shparo, USSR	May 31, 1979
5 Sir Ranulph Fiennes/ Charles Burton, UK	Apr 11, 1982
6 Will Steger/ Paul Schurke, USA	May 1, 1986
7 Jean-Louis Etienne, France	May 11, 1986
8 Fukashi Kazami, Japan	Apr 20, 1987
9 Helen Thayer, USA†	Apr 20, 1988
10 Robert Swan, UK	May 14, 1989

* Confirmed only
\# Expedition leader or co-leader
† New Zealand-born

THE 10 **FIRST PEOPLE TO GO OVER NIAGARA FALLS AND SURVIVE**

	NAME / COUNTRY	METHOD	DATE
1	Annie Edson Taylor, USA	Wooden barrel	Oct 24, 1901
2	Bobby Leach, UK	Steel barrel	Jul 25, 1911
3	Jean Lussier, Canada	Steel and rubber ball fitted with oxygen cylinders	Jul 4, 1928
4	Nathan Boya (aka William Fitzgerald), USA	Steel and rubber ball fitted with oxygen cylinders	Jul 15, 1961
5	Karel Soucek, Canada	Wood and plastic barrel	Jul 3, 1984
6	Steven Trotter, USA	Metal barrel with inner tubes	Aug 18, 1985
7	Dave Mundy, Canada	Steel container	Oct 5, 1985
8	=Peter deBernardi, Canada	Steel container	Sep 28, 1989
	=Jeffrey Petkovich, Canada	Steel container	Sep 28, 1989
10	Dave Mundy	Steel diving bell	Sep 26, 1993

Source: Niagara Falls Museum

Criminal Records

TOP 10 **MOST COMMON CRIMES IN THE USA**

CRIME / NO. RECORDED (2005)

1 Property crime 9,277,285

2 Larceny-theft 6,143,800

3 Burglary 1,966,159

4 Violent crime 1,273,754

5 Motor-vehicle theft 1,167,326

6 Aggravated assault 777,461

7 Robbery 397,356

8 Forcible rape 83,312

9 Arson 64,062

10 Murder and non-negligent manslaughter 15,625

Source: Crime in the United States 2005

TOP 10 **COUNTRIES WITH THE HIGHEST REPORTED CAR-THEFT RATES**

COUNTRY / RATE PER 100,000 (2000*)

1 Switzerland 962.80

2 New Zealand 818.01

3 England and Wales 752.95

4 Sweden 738.47

5 Australia 726.19

6 Denmark 604.18

7 Scotland 555.33

8 Italy 537.00

9 Canada 521.20

10 Norway 518.25

USA 414.17

* Or latest year for which data available

Source: Interpol

TOP 10 **MOST STOLEN MAKES OF CAR**

MAKE / NO. STOLEN*

1 TOYOTA 404,217

2 VOLKSWAGEN 307,680

3 FORD 264,017

4 FIAT 215,225

5 NISSAN 185,292

6 RENAULT 148,767

7 LADA 148,239

8 MITSUBISHI 137,627

9 PEUGEOT 126,157

10 HONDA 125,766

* On Interpol's database as at May 2006

Source: Interpol

TOP 10 COUNTRIES WITH THE HIGHEST REPORTED CRIME RATES

COUNTRY / REPORTED CRIMES PER 100,000 POPULATION

1 Dominica 11,382

2 New Zealand 10,588

3 Finland 10,153

4 Denmark 9,283

5 Chile 8,823

6 UK 8,555

7 Montserrat 8,040

8 USA 8,007

9 Netherlands 7,958

10 South Africa 7,719

Source: United Nations

An appearance in this list does not confirm these as the most crime-ridden countries, since the rate of reporting relates closely to such factors as confidence in local law-enforcement authorities. In certain countries crime is so common and law enforcement so inefficient or corrupt that countless incidents go unreported, while for propaganda purposes, many countries do not publish accurate figures. However, a rate of approximately 1,000 per 100,000 may be considered average, so those in the Top 10 are well above it.

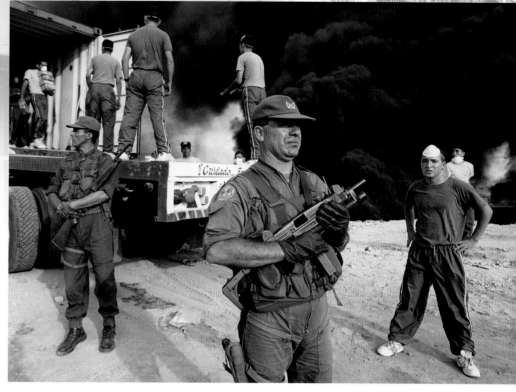

Powder burns
Armed drug-enforcement authorities in Chile destroy a quantity of cocaine seized in raids.

TOP 10 COUNTRIES WITH THE HIGHEST PRISON POPULATIONS

COUNTRY	PRISONERS PER 100,000 POPULATION	TOTAL PRISONERS*
1 USA	737	2,193,798
2 China	118	1,548,498
3 Russia	613	871,693
4 Brazil	203	385,317
5 India	30	332,112
6 Mexico	197	214,452
7 Thailand	256	164,443
8 Ukraine	350	162,602
9 South Africa	336	160,198
10 Iran	214	147,926

* As at date of most recent data

Source: International Centre for Prison Studies

TOP 10 US PRISONS WITH THE HIGHEST OCCUPANCY

INSTITUTION / LOCATION	CURRENT OCCUPANCY*
1 Fort Dix Federal Correctional Institution, New Jersey	4,326
2 Big Spring CI#, Texas	2,845
3 California City CI#, California	2,594
4 Brooklyn Metropolitan Detention Center, New York	2,483
5 Reeves CI#, Texas	2,189
6 Coleman FCI (low security), Florida	2,122
7 Atlanta US Penitentiary, Georgia	2,045
8 Beaumont FCI (low security), Texas	1,888
9 Seagonville FCI, Texas	1,863
10 Elkton FCI, Ohio	1,829
Total federal inmates	*192,266*

* As at October 12, 2006
\# Privately managed prison

Source: Bureau of Federal Prisons

Murder File

TOP 10 COUNTRIES WITH THE HIGHEST MURDER RATES

COUNTRY / MURDERS PER 100,000 POPULATION

1 Colombia 61.8
2 South Africa 49.6
3 Jamaica 32.4
4 Venezuela 31.6
5 Russia 20.2
6 Mexico 13.0
7 Estonia 10.7
8 Latvia 10.4
9 Lithuania 10.3
10 Belarus 9.8

Source: United Nations

THE 10 WORST YEARS FOR MURDER IN THE USA

	YEAR	MURDER RATE PER MILLION POPULATION	TOTAL*
1	1991	9.8	24,703
2	1993	9.5	24,526
3	1992	9.3	23,760
4	1990	9.4	23,438
5	1994	9.0	23,326
6	1980	10.2	23,040
7	1981	9.8	22,520
8	1989	8.7	21,500
9	1979	9.7	21,460
10	1982	9.1	21,010

* Includes non-negligent manslaughter victims; victims of September 11, 2001 terrorist attacks are excluded

Source: Bureau of Justice Statistics

Murders in the USA first exceeded 2,000 in 1910 and increased rapidly as a result of gang warfare during the Prohibition era, topping 10,000 in 1930. The total rose to over 20,000 for the first time in 1974.

TOP 10 MURDER CIRCUMSTANCES IN THE USA

REASON / MURDERS (2005)

1 Argument (unspecified) 3,692
2 Robbery 921
3 Juvenile gang killing 754
4 Contravention of narcotic drug laws 589
5 Argument over money or property 211
6 Brawl due to influence of alcohol 120
7 Romantic triangle 117
8 Brawl due to influence of narcotics 97
9 Gangland killings 96
10 Burglary 88

Source: FBI Uniform Crime Reports

THE 10 MOST COMMON MURDER WEAPONS AND METHODS IN THE USA

WEAPON/METHOD	VICTIMS (2005)
1 Firearms	10,100
2 Knives or cutting instruments	1,914
3 "Personal weapons" (hands, feet, fists, etc.)	888
4 Blunt objects (hammers, clubs, etc.)	597
5 Fire	123
6 Strangulation	120
7 Asphyxiation	96
8 Narcotics	44
9 Drowning	20
10 Poison	9
Other/weapons not stated	943
Total	14,860

Source: FBI Uniform Crime Reports

In 2005 "other weapons or weapons not stated" were used in 943 murders, and unspecified firearms in 1,598 cases. Relatively less common methods included drowning (20) and explosives (2).

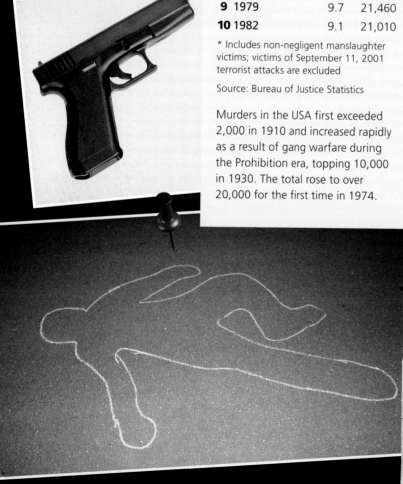

THE 10 MOST PROLIFIC SERIAL KILLERS*

MURDERER / COUNTRY / VICTIMS

1 **Behram** (India) 931
Behram (or Buhram) was the leader of the Thugee cult in India, which it is reckoned was responsible for the deaths of up to two million people. At his trial Behram was found guilty of personally committing 931 murders between 1790 and 1830.

2 **Countess Erszébet Báthory** (Hungary) up to 650
In the period up to 1610 in Hungary, Báthory, known as "Countess Dracula," was alleged to have murdered between 300 and 650 girls in the belief that drinking their blood would prevent her from ageing.

3 **Pedro Alonso López** (Colombia) 300
Captured in 1980, López, nicknamed the "Monster of the Andes," led police to 53 graves, but probably murdered at least 300 in Colombia, Ecuador, and Peru.

4 **Dr Harold Shipman** (UK) 215
In January 2000, Dr. Shipman was found guilty of the murder of 15 women patients; the official inquiry into his crimes put the figure at 215, with 45 possible further cases.

Doctor Death
Harold Shipman (1946–2004) of Hyde, Manchester, is Britain's worst serial killer.

5 **Henry Lee Lucas** (USA) 200
Lucas (1936–2001) admitted in 1983 to 360 murders, many committed with his partner-in-crime Ottis Toole. He died while on Death Row in Huntsville Prison, Texas.

6 **Gilles de Rais** (France) up to 200
A fabulously wealthy French aristocrat, Gilles de Laval, Baron de Rais (1404–40) committed murders as sacrifices during black-magic rituals. He was accused of having kidnapped and killed between 60 and 200 children.

7 **Hu Wanlin** (China) 196
Posing as a doctor specializing in ancient Chinese medicine, Hu Wanlin was sentenced on October 1, 2000 to 15 years imprisonment for three deaths, but authorities believe he was responsible for considerably more.

8 **Luis Alfredo Garavito** (Colombia) 189
Garavito confessed in 1999 to a spate of murders. On May 28, 2000 he was sentenced to a total of 835 years imprisonment.

9 **Hermann Webster Mudgett** (USA) up to 150
Mudgett (1860–96), was believed to have lured over 150 women to his Chicago "castle," which he operated as a hotel. It was fully equipped for torturing, murdering, and dissecting his victims and disposing of their bodies in furnaces or an acid bath.

10 **Dr Jack Kevorkian** (USA) 130
In 1999 Kevorkian, who admitted to assisting in 130 suicides since 1990, was convicted of second-degree murder.

* Includes only individual murderers; excludes murders by bandits, those carried out by terrorist groups, political and military atrocities, and gangland slayings

The World at War

	COUNTRY	PERSONNEL*
1	Russia	12,000,000
2	Germany	11,000,000
3	British Empire	8,904,467
4	France	8,410,000
5	Austria-Hungary	7,800,000
6	Italy	5,615,000
7	USA	4,355,000
8	Turkey	2,850,000
9	Bulgaria	1,200,000
10	Japan	800,000

* Total at peak strength

Russia's armed forces were relatively small in relation to the country's population—some six percent, compared with 17 percent in Germany. Several other European nations had forces that were similarly substantial in relation to their populations: Serbia's army comprised some 14 percent of its population. In total, more than 65 million combatants were involved.

Historic ship
Commissioned in 1944, the USS Missouri *was the ship on which the Japanese signed their surrender document on September 2, 1945. It is now an exhibit at Pearl Harbor, Hawaii.*

TOP 10 **LARGEST BATTLESHIPS OF WORLD WAR II**

	NAME	COUNTRY	STATUS	LENGTH FT	M	TONNAGE
1 =	Musashi	Japan	Sunk Oct 25, 1944	862	263	80,258
=	Yamato	Japan	Sunk Apr 7, 1945	862	263	80,258
3 =	Iowa	USA	Decommissioned Oct 26, 1990	887	270	61,410
=	Missouri	USA	Decommissioned Mar 31, 1992	887	270	61,410
=	New Jersey	USA	Decommissioned Feb 8, 1991	887	270	61,410
=	Wisconsin	USA	Decommissioned Sep 30, 1991	887	270	61,410
7 =	Bismarck	Germany	Sunk May 27, 1941	823	251	55,284
=	Tirpitz	Germany	Sunk Nov 12, 1944	823	251	55,284
9 =	Jean Bart	France	Survived WWII, later scrapped	812	247	52,360
=	Richelieu	France	Survived WWII, later scrapped	812	247	52,360

THE 10 **HIGHEST PROPORTIONS OF MILITARY VICTIMS IN WORLD WAR I**

	COUNTRY	DEAD*
1	Romania	44.76
2	France	16.36
3	Germany	16.12
4	Austria-Hungary	15.38
5	Russia	14.17
6	Italy	11.58
7	Turkey	11.40
8	Great Britain	10.20
9	Bulgaria	7.29
10	Portugal	7.22

* As percentage of troops mobilized

THE 10 COUNTRIES SUFFERING THE GREATEST AIRCRAFT LOSSES IN WORLD WAR II

	COUNTRY	AIRCRAFT LOST
1	Germany	116,584
2	USSR	106,652
3	USA	59,296
4	Japan	49,485
5	UK	33,090
6	Australia	7,160
7	Italy	5,272
8	Canada	2,389
9	France	2,100
10	New Zealand	684

Reports of aircraft losses vary considerably from country to country, some including aircraft damaged, lost as a result of accidents, or scrapped, as well as those destroyed during combat.

Bomb damage
Frankfurt am Main, one of the German cities devastated by Allied bombing during World War II.

THE 10 AREAS OF EUROPE MOST BOMBED BY ALLIED AIRCRAFT*, 1939–45

AREA / BOMBS DROPPED (TONS)   * British and US

1 Germany 1,488,474

2 France 642,998

3 Italy 404,024

4 Austria, Hungary, and the Balkans 199,329

5 Belgium and Netherlands 97,819

6 Southern Europe and Mediterranean 84,332

7 Czechoslovakia and Poland 23,610

8 Norway and Denmark 5,819

9 Sea targets 622

10 British Channel Islands 103

Modern Military

TOP 10 LARGEST ARMED FORCES

COUNTRY	ARMY	ESTIMATED ACTIVE FORCES NAVY	AIR	TOTAL
1 China	1,600,000	255,000	400,000	2,255,000
2 USA	595,946	376,750	347,400	1,506,757*
3 India	1,100,000	46,000	161,000	1,316,000
4 North Korea	950,000	46,000	110,000	1,106,000
5 Russia	395,000	142,000	160,000	1,027,000#
6 South Korea	560,000	63,000	64,000	687,000
7 Pakistan	550,000	24,000	45,000	619,000
8 Iran	350,000	18,000	52,000	545,000†
9 Turkey	402,000	52,750	60,100	514,850
10 Egypt	340,000	18,500	30,000	468,500§

* Includes 186,661 Marine Corps, 40,500 Coast Guard
# Includes 80,000 Strategic Deterrent Forces, 250,000 Command and Support
† Includes 125,000 Revolutionary Guard Corps
§ Includes 70,000 Air Defense Command

Source: The International Institute for Strategic Studies, *The Military Balance 2005–2006*

Several countries also have substantial reserves on standby: South Korea's has been estimated at some 4.5 million plus 3.5 Paramilitary, Vietnam's at 5 million and China's 800,000. North Korea has the highest number of troops in relation to it population—47.85 per 1,000.

TOP 10 ARMOR COUNTRIES*

COUNTRY	UNITS
1 Russia	48,270
2 USA	29,920
3 Israel	14,200
4 China	13,200
5 Syria	9,650
6 Egypt	9,357
7 Germany	8,384
8 Iraq	7,430
9 Turkey	7,165
10 France	6,875

* Tracked and wheeled MBTs (Main Battle Tanks) and APCs (Armored Personnel Carriers)

Source: GlobalFirePower.com

TOP 10 MILITARY EXPENDITURE COUNTRIES

COUNTRY	$ (2005)
1 USA	518,100,000,000
2 China	81,480,000,000
3 France	45,000,000,000
4 Japan	44,310,000,000
5 UK	42,836,500,000
6 Germany	35,063,000,000
7 Italy	28,182,800,000
8 South Korea	21,060,000,000
9 India	19,040,000,000
10 Saudi Arabia	18,000,000,000

Source: GlobalFirePower.com

TOP 10 WORLD MILITARY RANKING*

1 USA
2 Russia
3 China
4 India
5 Germany
6 France
7 Japan
8 Turkey
9 Brazil
10 UK

* Based on GlobalFirePower's collective averages across a range of military criteria

Source: GlobalFirePower.com

Air power
The USA operates over 500 F-15 fighters in an armory of more than 18,000 military aircraft—almost double that of China, its closest rival.

TOP 10 MILITARY AIRCRAFT COUNTRIES

	COUNTRY	MILITARY AIRCRAFT IN SERVICE
1	USA	18,169
2	China	9,218
3	Russia	7,331
4	India	3,382
5	Ukraine	2,451
6	France	2,175
7	Turkey	1,964
8	Japan	1,957
9	UK	1,891
10	Germany	1,641

Source: GlobalFirePower.com

TOP 10 MISSILE DEFENSE SYSTEMS COUNTRIES*

	COUNTRY	SYSTEMS
1	USA	35,324
2	Russia	19,250
3	China	18,500
4	North Korea	16,075
5	Syria	11,233
6	India	7,125
7	South Korea	7,032
8	Iraq	5,210
9	Egypt	3,334
10	Israel	3,153

* Including Heavy Antitank and SAM Missile Systems

Source: GlobalFirePower.com

TOP 10 NAVAL SHIPS COUNTRIES*

	COUNTRY	NAVAL VESSELS IN SERVICE
1	USA	1,866
2	North Korea	708
3	Russia	701
4	China	284
5	Turkey	182
6	Japan	172
7	UK	164
8	India	145
9	France	140
10	Germany	129

* Includes all military, logistical, survey, and research craft under military control

Source: GlobalFirePower.com

4
TOWN & COUNTRY

Countries—Size

State within a state
Vatican City is the world's smallest and least populated state, and the country with the shortest (virtual) border.

THE 10 **SMALLEST COUNTRIES**

COUNTRY	AREA SQ MILES	SQ KM
1 Vatican City	0.17	0.44
2 Monaco	0.75	1.95
3 Nauru	8.18	21.20
4 Tuvalu	9.89	25.63
5 San Marino	23.63	61.20
6 Liechtenstein	61.77	160.00
7 Marshall Islands	70.05	181.43
8 Saint Kitts and Nevis	104.01	269.40
9 Maldives	115.05	298.00
10 Malta	121.66	315.10

TOP 10 **LARGEST COUNTRIES**

COUNTRY	AREA SQ MILES	SQ KM	% OF WORLD TOTAL
1 Russia	6,592,772	17,075,200	11.5
2 Canada	3,855,103	9,984,670	6.7
3 USA	3,718,712	9,631,420	6.5
4 China	3,705,407	9,596,960	6.4
5 Brazil	3,286,488	8,511,965	5.7
6 Australia	2,967,910	7,686,850	5.2
7 India	1,269,346	3,287,590	2.2
8 Argentina	1,068,302	2,766,890	2.1
9 Kazakhstan	1,049,156	2,717,300	1.9
10 Sudan	967,499	2,505,810	1.7
World total	*57,506,062*	*148,940,000*	*100.0*

Source: CIA, *The World Factbook 2007*

This list is based on the area of a country within its borders, including offshore islands and inland water, and may thus differ from versions in which these are excluded. The countries in the Top 10 collectively comprise 50 percent of the total Earth's land surface.

TOP 10 COUNTRIES WITH THE MOST NEIGHBORS

COUNTRY / NEIGHBORS	NO. OF NEIGHBORS
1 = China Afghanistan, Bhutan, India, Kazakhstan, Kyrgyzstan, Laos, Mongolia, Myanmar, Nepal, North Korea, Pakistan, Russia, Tajikistan, Vietnam	14
= Russia Azerbaijan, Belarus, China, Estonia, Finland, Georgia, Kazakhstan, Latvia, Lithuania, Mongolia, North Korea, Norway, Poland, Ukraine	14
3 Brazil Argentina, Bolivia, Colombia, French Guiana, Guyana, Paraguay, Peru, Suriname, Uruguay, Venezuela	10
4 = Dem. Rep. of Congo Angola, Burundi, Central African Republic, Congo, Rwanda, Sudan, Tanzania, Uganda, Zambia	9
= Germany Austria, Belgium, Czech Republic, Denmark, France, Luxembourg, Netherlands, Poland, Switzerland	9
= Sudan Central African Republic, Chad, Dem. Rep. of Congo, Egypt, Eritrea, Ethiopia, Kenya, Libya, Uganda	9
7 = Austria Czech Republic, Germany, Hungary, Italy, Liechtenstein, Slovakia, Slovenia, Switzerland	8
= France Andorra, Belgium, Germany, Italy, Luxembourg, Monaco, Spain, Switzerland	8
= Serbia Albania, Bosnia-Herzegovina, Bulgaria, Croatia, Hungary, Republic of Macedonia, Montenegro, Romania	8
= Tanzania Burundi, Dem. Rep. of Congo, Kenya, Malawi, Mozambique, Rwanda, Uganda, Zambia	8
= Turkey Armenia, Azerbaijan, Bulgaria, Georgia, Greece, Iran, Iraq, Syria	8

TOP 10 LONGEST BORDERS

COUNTRY	TOTAL BORDERS MILES	KM
1 China	13,642	22,117
2 Russia	12,437	20,017
3 Brazil	9,128	14,691
4 India	8,763	14,103
5 USA	7,477	12,034
6 Kazakhstan	7,463	12,012
7 Dem. Rep. of Congo	6,667	10,730
8 Argentina	6,005	9,665
9 Canada	5,525	8,893
10 Mongolia	5,107	8,220

Source: CIA, *The World Factbook 2007*

The total length of the world's land boundaries is approximately 155,636 miles (250,472 km), with shared boundaries counted once.

THE 10 SHORTEST BORDERS

COUNTRIES	LAND BORDERS MILES	KM
1 Vatican/Italy	2.0	3.2
2 Monaco/France	2.7	4.4
3 Azerbaijan/Turkey	5.6	9.0
4 North Korea/Russia	11.8	19.0
5 Cuba/USA (Guantánamo Bay)	18.0	29.0
6 Liechtenstein/Austria	21.7	34.9
7 Armenia/Iran	21.7	35.0
8 San Marino/Italy	24.2	39.0
9 Liechtenstein/Switzerland	25.5	41.1
10 Andorra/France	35.2	56.6

Source: CIA, *The World Factbook 2007*

Line of defense
The Great Wall of China once marked China's border with Mongolia.

Countries—Population

TOP 10 **MOST DENSELY POPULATED COUNTRIES**

	COUNTRY	AREA (SQ KM)	POPULATION (2008 EST.)	POPULATION PER SQ KM
1	Macau	25	460,823	18,432.9
2	Monaco	1.95	32,796	16,818.5
3	Singapore	693	4,608,167	6,649.6
4	Hong Kong	1,092	7,018,636	6,427.3
5	Vatican City	0.44	932*	2,118.2
6	Malta	315.10	403,532	1,280.6
7	Maldives	298.00	379,174	1,272.4
8	Bangladesh	133,911	153,546,901	1,146.6
9	Bahrain	665	718,306	1,080.2
10	Nauru	21	13,770	655.7
	USA	*9,631,418*	*303,824,646*	*31.5*
	World	*148,940,000*	*6,682,477,937*	*44.9*

* July 2006 estimate

Source: US Census Bureau, International Data Base

Both Macau and Hong Kong are special administrative regions within China, but are still considered countries for the purposes of statistical comparison. Other territories with high population densities include the Gaza Strip with its population of 1,537,269 occupying a land area of 360 sq km (4,270.2 people per sq km), Gibraltar with a population of 28,002 occupying 7 sq km (4,000.3 people per sq km), and Bermuda with 66,536 people occupying 53 sq km (1,255.4 people per sq km).

THE 10 **LEAST DENSELY POPULATED COUNTRIES**

	COUNTRY	AREA (SQ KM)	POPULATION (2008 EST.)	POPULATION PER SQ KM
1	Mongolia	1,564,116	2,916,865	1.86
2	Namibia	825,418	2,063,927	2.50
3	Australia	7,686,850	20,600,856	2.68
4	Suriname	163,270	475,996	2.69
5	Botswana	600,370	1,638,393	2.72
6	Iceland	103,000	304,367	2.95
7	Mauritania	1,030,700	3,364,940	3.26
8	Canada	9,984,670	33,679,263	3.37
9	Libya	1,759,540	6,173,579	3.50
10	Guyana	214,970	770,794	3.58

Source: US Census Bureau, International Data Base

Greenland is not an independent country, but if included it would be in first place with an area of 2,166,086 sq km and a population of 56,326—a density of just 0.03 people per sq km.

Above: Population explosion
India currently has more than 16 percent of the world's population on 2.4 percent of the land area. It is predicted that by 2035 its population will exceed 1.46 billion, overtaking China's—which by then will be declining.

Background: Namib Desert
Although Namibia is larger than Pakistan, its harsh terrain—one-sixth is desert—is occupied by a population one-eighty-fourth the size of Pakistan's, making it, after Mongolia, the least densely populated country on the planet.

TOP 10 **MOST POPULATED COUNTRIES**

	COUNTRY	POPULATION (2008 EST.)
1	China	1,330,044,605
2	India	1,147,995,898
3	USA	303,824,646
4	Indonesia	237,512,355
5	Brazil	191,908,598
6	Pakistan	172,730,891
7	Bangladesh	153,546,901
8	Russia	140,702,094
9	Nigeria	138,283,240
10	Japan	127,425,722
	World	*6,682,477,937*

Source: US Census Bureau, International Data Base

The population of the USA—which had reached 100 million in 1915 and 200 million in 1967—passed 300 million on October 17, 2006. On average, one American is born every seven seconds and one dies every 13 seconds. Taking account of immigration and emigration, its population increases by one every 10 seconds.

THE 10 **LEAST POPULATED COUNTRIES**

	COUNTRY	POPULATION (2008 EST.)
1	Vatican City	932*
2	Tuvalu	12,181
3	Nauru	13,770
4	Palau	21,093
5	San Marino	29,973
6	Monaco	32,796
7	Liechtenstein	34,498
8	Saint Kitts and Nevis	39,619
9	Marshall Islands	63,139
10	Dominica	69,080

* July 2006 estimate

Source: US Census Bureau, International Data Base/CIA, *The World Factbook 2007*

TOP 10 **COUNTRIES IN WHICH WOMEN MOST OUTNUMBER MEN**

	COUNTRY	ESTIMATED WOMEN PER 100 MEN (2008)
1	Estonia	118.9
2	Ukraine	116.8
3	Russia	116.7
4	Latvia	116.0
5	Belarus	114.7
6	Lithuania	112.6
7	Armenia	112.0
8	Hungary	110.1
9	Georgia	109.8
10 =	Moldova	109.6
=	Monaco	109.6
	USA	*103.4*

Source: US Census Bureau, International Data Base

The male/female ratio of the world is balanced virtually 50:50—in Mongolia, the Philippines, and Senegal precisely so—although in many Western countries male births slightly outnumber female by a very small percentage. There are certain countries, however, where one sex dominates more markedly for reasons that may include imprecise recording or the nonenumeration of women in countries where their status is considered inferior, or the presence of large numbers of immigrant male workers.

TOP 10 **COUNTRIES IN WHICH MEN MOST OUTNUMBER WOMEN**

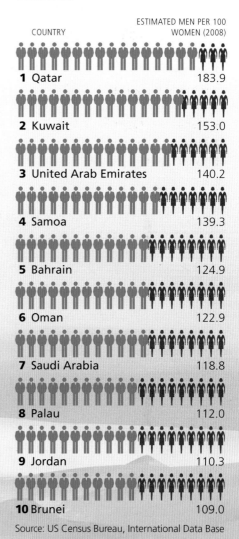

	COUNTRY	ESTIMATED MEN PER 100 WOMEN (2008)
1	Qatar	183.9
2	Kuwait	153.0
3	United Arab Emirates	140.2
4	Samoa	139.3
5	Bahrain	124.9
6	Oman	122.9
7	Saudi Arabia	118.8
8	Palau	112.0
9	Jordan	110.3
10	Brunei	109.0

Source: US Census Bureau, International Data Base

The United States

THE 10 **FIRST US STATES**

STATE	ENTERED UNION
1 Delaware	Friday, Dec 7, 1787
2 Pennsylvania	Wednesday, Dec 12, 1787
3 New Jersey	Tuesday, Dec 18, 1787
4 Georgia	Wednesday, Jan 2, 1788
5 Connecticut	Wednesday, Jan 9, 1788
6 Massachusetts	Wednesday, Feb 6 1788
7 Maryland	Monday, Apr 28, 1788
8 South Carolina	Friday, May 23, 1788
9 New Hampshire	Saturday, Jun 21, 1788
10 Virginia	Wednesday, Jun 25, 1788

The names of two of the first 10 American states commemorate early colonists. Delaware Bay (and hence the river, and later the state) was named after Thomas West, Lord De La Warr, a governor of Virginia. Pennsylvania was called "Pensilvania,", or "Penn's woodland," in its original charter, issued in 1681 to the Quaker leader William Penn. He had acquired the territory as part settlement of a debt owed to his father, Admiral William Penn, by King Charles II.

Two states were named after places with which their founders had associations: New Jersey was the subject of a deed issued in 1644 by the Duke of York to John Berkeley and Sir George Carteret, who came from Jersey in the Channel Islands, and New Hampshire was called after the English county by settler Captain John Mason.

Two names are of native American origin: Connecticut after the Algonquin Indian name "kuenihtekot," meaning "long river at" (the extra syllable "c" was probably added by a writer with "connect" in mind); and Massachusetts, which is believed to be native American for "high hill, little plain," the name of a place and of a tribe.

The remaining four states' names have royal connections: Virginia after Queen Elizabeth I, the "Virgin Queen," and Georgia, so-called by English soldier and politician James Oglethorpe in honor of King George II, who in 1732 issued a charter allowing him to colonize the area. Maryland, named after Queen Henrietta Maria, wife of Charles I, was planned by George Calvert, Baron Baltimore, but he died two months before the charter was signed and it was his son Cecilius who established it. Carolina was originally a French settlement called La Caroline after the French king Charles IX, but the tract of land was issued in 1629 to Sir Robert Heath, who named it Carolina after the English king Charles I.

New Jersey flies the flag
Several US states have names that reflect the British origins of their settlers. New Jersey, the third state to join the union, took its name from the British Channel island Jersey.

TOP 10 **LARGEST US STATES**

	STATE	LAND AREA*	
		SQ MILES	SQ KM
1	Alaska	571,951	1,481,347
2	Texas	261,797	678,051
3	California	155,959	403,933
4	Montana	145,552	376,979
5	New Mexico	121,356	314,309
6	Arizona	113,635	294,312
7	Nevada	109,826	284,448
8	Colorado	103,718	268,627
9	Wyoming	97,100	251,489
10	Oregon	95,997	248,631
	Total (all states)	*3,537,438*	*9,161,923*

* Excluding water

The total land area of the United States has grown progressively: in 1800 it was 867,980 sq miles (2,248,058 sq km), and by 1900 it had grown to 2,974,159 sq miles (7,703,036 sq km). The admission of Alaska to the Union on January 3 and Hawaii on August 20, 1959 increased the total by almost 20 percent, bringing the total area to its present extent.

TOP 10 **MOST DENSELY POPULATED US STATES**

	STATE	POPULATION DENSITY (2005)	
		SQ MILES	SQ KM
1	New Jersey	1,175.3	453.79
2	Rhode Island	1,029.9	396.74
3	Massachusetts	816.2	315.13
4	Connecticut	724.5	279.73
5	Maryland	573.0	221.23
6	Delaware	431.8	166.71
7	New York	407.8	157.45
8	Florida	329.9	127.37
9	Ohio	280.0	108.10
10	Pennsylvania	277.3	107.06
	US average	*83.8*	*32.35*
	District of Columbia	*8,966.1*	*3,461.83*

Source: US Census Bureau

THE 10 **SMALLEST US STATES**

	STATE	LAND AREA*	
		SQ MILES	SQ KM
1	Rhode Island	1,045	2,706
2	Delaware	1,955	5,063
3	Connecticut	4,845	12,548
4	Hawaii	6,423	16,635
5	New Jersey	7,419	19,215
6	Massachusetts	7,838	20,300
7	New Hampshire	8,969	23,229
8	Vermont	9,249	23,955
9	Maryland	9,775	25,317
10	West Virginia	24,087	62,385

* Excluding water

Smallest state Rhode Island has the longest official name, "State of Rhode Island and Providence Plantations." A total of 546 Rhode Islands—which also includes some 500 sq miles (1,295 sq km) of inland water—could be fitted into the land area of largest state Alaska. The District of Columbia has a total area of 61 sq miles (159 sq km).

THE 10 **LEAST DENSELY POPULATED US STATES**

	STATE	POPULATION DENSITY (2005)	
		SQ MILES	SQ KM
1	Alaska	1.2	0.46
2	Wyoming	5.2	2.00
3	Montana	6.4	2.47
4	North Dakota	9.2	3.55
5	South Dakota	10.2	3.93
6	New Mexico	15.9	6.13
7	Idaho	17.3	6.67
8	Nevada	22.0	8.49
9	Nebraska	22.9	8.84
10	Utah	30.1	11.62

Source: US Census Bureau

China

TOP 10 EXPORTS FROM CHINA

COMMODITY / VALUE ($) (2005)

1 Electrical goods 322,008,000,000

2 Textiles and products 107,661,000,000

3 Metals 57,086,000,000

4 Chemicals 31,853,000,000

5 Vehicles and transport 28,410,000,000

6 Scientific, etc. instruments 28,398,000,000

7 Plastics 23,286,000,000

8 Footwear and accessories 22,773,000,000

9 Minerals 20,920,000,000

10 Leather products 15,601,000,000

Total 761,953,000,000

Source: *China Statistical Yearbook 2006*

TOP 10 PATENT CATEGORIES IN CHINA

CATEGORY	PATENT APPLICATIONS	PATENTS GRANTED (2005)
1 Electrical	18,911	10,251
2 Medical and veterinary science and hygiene	24,875	10,179
3 Telecommunications	21,578	7,013
4 Measuring and testing	11,507	5,421
5 Furniture, domestic items	10,865	5,313
6 Computing, calculating, counting	12,441	4,316
7 Packing/conveying flammable materials	7,143	4,175
8 Engineering, general	9,047	3,988
9 Stoves, ranges, and ventilation	6,491	3,400
10 Organic chemistry	6,507	3,248
Total	*287,162*	*132,654*

Source: *China Statistical Yearbook 2006*

TOP 10 TYPES OF BOOK PUBLISHED IN CHINA

CATEGORY	TITLES PUBLISHED	COPIES PRINTED (2005)
1 Culture, science, education, sports	85,668	4,896,590,000
2 History and geography	8,525	294,020,000
3 Industrial technology	29,511	196,980,000
4 Arts	10,622	179,760,000
5 Languages	11,659	169,860,000
6 Economics	18,389	142,990,000
7 Literature	13,428	139,740,000
8 Politics and law	10,104	119,340,000
9 Medicine and healthcare	9,565	65,150,000
10 Mathematics and chemistry	4,669	42,810,000
Total	*222,473*	*6,465,970,000*

Source: *China Statistical Yearbook 2006*

Little Emperors

In the 1980s, as the population of China passed the one billion mark, fears of overpopulation led to an official policy of one-child families. Without it the current population would be as much as 400 million greater. One consequence, as social commentators have observed, has been the emergence of "little emperors"—a generation of overindulged only children.

TOP 10 ETHNIC GROUPS IN CHINA

	GROUP	POPULATION
1	Han	1,136,703,824
2	Zhuang	15,555,800
3	Manchu	8,846,800
4	Hui	8,612,000
5	Miao	7,383,600
6	Uygur	7,207,000
7	Yi	6,578,500
8	Tujia	5,725,000
9	Mongolian	4,802,400
10	Tibetan	4,593,100

Miao women
Members of one of the 55 minority ethnic groups officially recognized in China, distinctively dressed Miao women prepare for a festival in Guizhou, the southern province that is home to about half the Miao population of China.

TOP 10 SUNNIEST MAJOR CITIES IN CHINA

	CITY	AVERAGE ANNUAL SUNSHINE HOURS
1	Lhasa	3,100.0
2	Hohhot	2,816.8
3	Yinchuang	2,813.4
4	Dalian	2,749.7
5	Taiyuan	2,620.9
6	Beijing	2,576.1
7	Urumqi	2,528.7
8	Xining	2,477.5
9	Lanzhou	2,469.9
10	Jinan	2,369.5

Source: *China Statistical Yearbook 2006*

Lhasa, the former capital of Tibet, is popularly known as the "sunlit city." It benefits from being one of the highest in the world, at 11,975 ft (3,650 m) and has an equable climate, without extreme temperatures or daytime cloud cover.

TOP 10 TALLEST BUILDINGS IN CHINA

BUILDING / LOCATION	YEAR COMPLETED	STORIES	HEIGHT FT	HEIGHT M
1 Shanghai World Financial Center, Shanghai	2007*	101	1,613	492
2 International Commerce Centre, Hong Kong	2007*	108	1,587	484
3 Oriental Pearl Tower, Shanghai Guangzhou TV & Sightseeing	1994	14	1,535	468
4 Tower, Guangzhou	2009*	37	1,490	454
5 Guangzhou Twin Towers, Guangzhou	2009*	103	1,417	432
6 Jin Mao Tower, Shanghai	1998	88	1,381	421
7 Dailian International Trade Center, Dalian	2007*	78	1,377	420
8 Two International Finance Centre, Hong Kong	2003	88	1,362	415
9 CITIC Plaza, Guangzhou	1997	80	1,283	391
10 Shun Hing Square, Shenzhen	1996	69	1,260	384

* Under construction—scheduled completion date

India

TOP 10 LARGEST STATES IN INDIA

	STATE	AREA	
		SQ MILES	SQ KM
1	Rajasthan	132,138	342,236
2	Madhya Pradesh	118,975	308,144
3	Maharashtra	118,809	307,713
4	Andhra Pradesh	106,204	275,068
5	Uttar Pradesh	92,111	238,566
6	Jammu and Kashmir	85,806	222,236
7	Gujarat	75,685	196,024
8	Karnataka	74,051	191,791
9	Orissa	60,119	155,707
10	Chhattisgarh	52,199	135,194
	India total	*1,269,346*	*3,287,590*

TOP 10 MOST POPULATED STATES IN INDIA

	STATE	POPULATION*
1	Uttar Pradesh	166,197,921
2	Maharashtra	96,878,627
3	Bihar	82,998,509
4	West Bengal	80,176,197
5	Andhra Pradesh	76,210,007
6	Tamil Nadu	62,405,679
7	Madhya Pradesh	60,348,023
8	Rajasthan	56,507,188
9	Karnataka	52,850,562
10	Gujarat	50,671,017

* As at 2001 census

TOP 10 LANGUAGES IN INDIA

	LANGUAGE	SPEAKERS
1	Hindi	363,839,000
2	Bengali	70,561,000
3	Telugu	69,634,000
4	Marathi	68,030,000
5	Tamil	61,527,000
6	Urdu	48,062,000
7	Gujarati	45,479,000
8	Malayalam	35,351,000
9	Kannada	35,346,000
10	Oriya	31,666,000

Source: Central Institute of Indian Languages

Ancient and modern
21st-century India has a technologically skilled labor force, but faces the challenges of a huge population and disparity between the very rich and very poor.

TOP 10 **RICHEST INDIANS**

	NAME	COMPANY / INDUSTRY	NET WORTH ($)
1	Lakshmi Mittal	Mittal Steel/metals	32,000,000,000
2	Mukesh Ambani	Reliance/diversified	20,100,000,000
3	Anil Ambani	ADAG/diversified	18,200,000,000
4	Azim Premji	Wipro/ITeS, Software	17,100,000,000
5	Kushal Pal Singh	DLF/property	10,000,000,000
6	Sunil Mittal	Airtel (Bharti Televentures)/telecoms	9,500,000,000
7	Kumar Birla	Aditya Birla Group/diversified	8,000,000,000
8	Ramesh Chandra	Unitech/property	6,400,000,000
9	Pallonji Mistry	Shapoorji Pallonji Group/textiles, construction	5,600,000,000
10	Adi Godrej	Godrej/manufacturing	4,100,000,000

Source: *Forbes* magazine, *The World's Richest People 2006*

TOP 10 **TALLEST HABITABLE BUILDINGS IN INDIA***

	BUILDING	YEAR COMPLETED	STORIES	HEIGHT FT	M
1	MVRDC World Trade Centre	2008#	35	511	156
2	Shreepati Arcade	2002	45	500	153
3	Belvedere Court	2000	40	490	149
4	Kalpataru Heights	2000	39	472	144
5	Heritage (Hiranandani Gardens)	2005	36	452	138
6	Verona (Hiranandani Gardens)	2004	30	422	129
7	Avalon (Hiranandani Gardens)	2004	30	419	128
8	ITC Grand Central Sheraton & Towers	2005	30	417	127
9	Phiroze Jeejeebhoy Towers	1980	28	387	118
10	Hilton Towers	1973	35	383	117

* All Mumbai (Bombay)
# Under construction—scheduled completion date

While skyscrapers have become commonplace elsewhere in Asia, tall buildings are rare in India. All those in the Top 10 are in Mumbai, where land is at a premium and population density high.

Megacities

TOP 10 **CITIES WITH THE HIGHEST PROPORTION OF A COUNTRY'S POPULATION**

CITY / COUNTRY / % OF TOTAL COUNTRY POPULATION

1 Singapore
100.0

2 San Juan, Puerto Rico
60.1

3 Beirut, Lebanon
49.1

4 Kuwait City, Kuwait
48.5

5 Tel Aviv, Israel
45.3

6 Montevideo, Uruguay
39.3

7 Tripoli, Libya
36.1

8 Yerevan, Armenia
35.3

9 Santiago, Chile
34.7

10 Buenos Aires, Argentina
34.0

New York,

USA 6.2

Source: United Nations Population Division

THE 10 **FIRST CITIES WITH POPULATIONS OF MORE THAN ONE MILLION**

CITY / COUNTRY

1 Rome, Italy

2 Alexandria, Egypt

3 Angkor, Cambodia

4 Hangchow (Hangzhou), China

5 London, UK

6 Paris, France

7 Peking (Beijing), China

8 Canton (Guangzhou), China

9 Berlin, Prussia

10 New York, USA

Rome's population was reckoned to have exceeded one million some time in the second century BC, and Alexandria soon after. Angkor reached this figure by about AD 900, but was abandoned in the 15th century, and Hangchow in c.1200. London passed the million mark early in the 19th century, followed by others between about 1850 and the late 1870s.

TOP 10 **COUNTRIES WITH THE MOST MILLION-PLUS CITIES**

COUNTRY	CITIES WITH POPULATIONS OF OVER ONE MILLION
1 = China	52
= USA	52
3 India	45
4 Brazil	20
5 Russia	15
6 Japan	13
7 Germany	11
8 Mexico	10
9 = Pakistan	8
= UK	8

Some 437 cities in the world have populations of more than one million. Although such megacities are found in 100 different countries, many of them contain only one with a population of one million-plus—usually its capital.

Seoul mate
The population of Seoul, South Korea is second only to that of Tokyo, with over 23 million people in the metropolitan area.

TOP 10 **LARGEST CITIES**

CITY / COUNTRY	ESTIMATED POPULATION, 2006
1 Tokyo, Japan	33,400,000
2 Seoul, South Korea	23,100,000
3 Mexico City, Mexico	22,000,000
4 New York, USA	21,800,000
5 Mumbai (Bombay), India	21,100,000
6 Delhi, India	20,800,000
7 São Paulo, Brazil	20,300,000
8 Shanghai, China	18,600,000
9 Los Angeles, USA	17,900,000
10 Jakarta, Indonesia	16,900,000

Source: Th. Brinkhoff: The Principal Agglomerations of the World, http://www.citypopulation.de, 2006-11-22

This is based on "urban agglomerations" as defined by the United Nations, which disregards administrative boundaries in favor of often very extensive built-up areas stretching across densely populated suburbs.

TOP 10 **LARGEST CAPITAL CITIES**

CITY / COUNTRY	ESTIMATED POPULATION, 2006
1 Tokyo (including Yokohama and Kawasaki), Japan	34,400,000
2 Seoul (including Bucheon, Goyang, Incheon, Seongnam and Suweon), South Korea	23,100,000
3 Mexico City (including Nezahualcóyotl, Ecatepec and Naucalpan), Mexico	22,000,000
4 Delhi (including Faridabad and Ghaziabad), India	20,800,000
5 Jakarta (including Bekasi, Bogor, Depok and Tangerang), Indonesia	16,900,000
6 Cairo (including Al-Jizah and Shubra al-Khaymah), Egypt	15,800,000
7 Manila (including Kalookan and Quezon City), Philippines	15,200,000
8 Dhaka, Bangladesh	13,600,000
9 Buenos Aires (including San Justo and La Plata), Argentina	13,500,000
10 Moscow, Russia	13,400,000

Source: Th. Brinkhoff: The Principal Agglomerations of the World, http://www.citypopulation.de, 2006-11-22

Tall Buildings & Structures

TOP 10 **HIGHEST DAMS**

	DAM / RIVER / LOCATION	YEAR COMPLETED	HEIGHT FT	HEIGHT M
1	**Rogun**, Vakhsh, Tajikistan	1985	1,099	335
2	**Nurek**, Vakhsh, Tajikistan	1980	984	300
3	**Xiaowan**, Lancangjiang, China	2012*	958	292
4	**Grande Dixence**, Dixence, Switzerland	1962	935	285
5	**Inguri**, Inguri, Georgia	1984	892	272
6	**Vaiont**, Vaiont, Italy	1961	860	262
7 =	**Manuel M. Torres**, Chicoasén,Grijalva, Mexico	1981	856	261
=	**Tehri**, Bhagirathi, India	2006	856	261
9	**Alvaro Obregón**, Mextiquic, Mexico	1946	853	260
10	**Mauvoisin**, Drance de Bagnes, Switzerland	1957	820	250

* Under construction—scheduled completion date

Source: International Commission on Large Dams (ICOLD), *World Register of Dams*

THE 10 **LAST BUILDINGS AND STRUCTURES TO HOLD THE TITLE OF "WORLD'S TALLEST"**

	STRUCTURE	YEAR	HEIGHT FT	HEIGHT M
1	**Warszawa Radio Mast**, Konstantynow, Poland Operational July 30, 1974, collapsed August 8, 1991 during renovation, killing 3 and injuring 12	1974	2,118	645
2	**KVLY (formerly-KTHI) TV Mast**, Blanchard, North Dakota, USA Since the destruction of the Warszawa Radio Mast, it is again the world's tallest structure	1963	2,063	628
3	**Nexstar Broadcasting Tower Vivian**, Vivian, Louisiana, USA	1961	1,752	534
4	**KFVS TV Mast**, Egypt Mills, Missouri, USA	1960	1,677	511
5	**KOBR-TV Tower (KSWS-TV Transmitter)** Caprock, New Mexico, USA	1960	1,608	490
6	**KWTV Mast**, Oklahoma City, Oklahoma, USA	1954	1,572	479
7	**Empire State Building**, New York, USA	1930	1,250	381
8	**Chrysler Building**, New York, USA	1930	1,046	319
9	**Eiffel Tower**, Paris, France	1889	984	300
10	**Washington Monument**, Washington D.C., USA	1884	555	169

The Great Pyramid, Giza, Egypt (c. 2580 BC), originally 479 ft (146 m), held the record as the world's tallest structure until 1311, when Lincoln Cathedral (524 ft/159.7 m) overtook it. A succession of cathedrals held the title until the completion of the Washington Monument. All the "world's tallests" for over 50 years have been guyed masts.

SINGER CENTENARY

Although the Eiffel Tower was taller, at its completion in 1908 the 612-ft (186.5-m) Singer Building, Manhattan, New York, built for the Singer sewing-machine company, became the tallest habitable building in the world—but only briefly, as the 700-ft (213-m) Metropolitan Life Insurance Company Tower overtook it the following year. It was demolished in 1968 and the 743-ft (226-m) One Liberty Plaza (1973) built on the site. The Singer Building was the tallest ever destroyed prior to the collapse of the twin towers of the World Trade Center in the 9/11 attacks of 2001.

TOP 10 **CITIES WITH MOST SKYSCRAPERS***

CITY / LOCATION	SKYSCRAPERS
1 Hong Kong, China	195
2 New York City, USA	186
3 Chicago, USA	87
4 Shanghai, China	72
5 Tokyo, Japan	65
6 Singapore City, Singapore	38
7 Houston, USA	29
8 Seoul, South Korea	27
9 Sydney, Australia	25
10 Kuala Lumpur, Malaysia	24

* Completed habitable buildings of more than 500 ft (152 m)

TOP 10 **TALLEST TWIN TOWERS**

	BUILDING / LOCATION / YEAR COMPLETED	STORIES	HEIGHT FT	M
1	Petronas Towers, Kuala Lumpur, Malaysia, 1997	96	1,482	452
	roof height		1,244	379
2	Guangzhou Twin Towers, Guangzhou, China, 2009*	104	1,417	432
3	Emirates Park Tower, Dubai, UAE, 2009*	77	1,296	395
4	The Imperial, Mumbai, India, 2007*	60	815	249
5	Al Fattan Towers, Dubai, UAE, 2006	60	802	245
6	Dalian Futures Square, Dalian, China, 2007*	62	755	230
7	Grand Gateway, Shanghai, China, 2005	52	738	225
8	Atlantic Richfield, Tower, Los Angeles, USA, 1972	52	699	213
9	Huaxia Financial Square, Shanghai, China, 2003/2005	42	670	202
10	Parque Central Offinicas, Caracas, Venezuela, 1986	56	656	200

* Under construction—scheduled completion date

TOP 10 **TALLEST CHURCHES**

	CHURCH / LOCATION	YEAR COMPLETED	HEIGHT* FT	M
1	Sagrada Família, Barcelona, Spain	2020#	558	170
2	Ulm Cathedral, Ulm, Germany	1890	530	162
3	Notre-Dame Cathedral, Rouen, France	1876	518	158
4	Cologne Cathedral, Cologne, Germany	1880	516	157
5	Our Lady of Peace Basilica, Yamoussoukro, Côte d'Ivoire	1990	489	149
6	St. Nicholas, Hamburg, Germany	1847	482	147
7	Notre Dame Cathedral, Strasbourg, France	1439	472	144
8	St. Peter's, Rome, Italy	1626	452	138
9	St. Stephen's Cathedral, Vienna, Austria	1570	448	137
10	Neuer Dom, Linz, Austria	1924	439	134

* To tip of spire
# Under construction—scheduled completion date

The Chicago Methodist Temple, Chicago, USA is 568 ft (173 m) high, but is sited atop a 25-storey, 328-ft (100-m) building. Salisbury Cathedral at 404 ft (123 m) is the UK's tallest religious building. St. Paul's Cathedral and Liverpool Anglican Cathedral are the only others over 328 ft (100 m) tall.

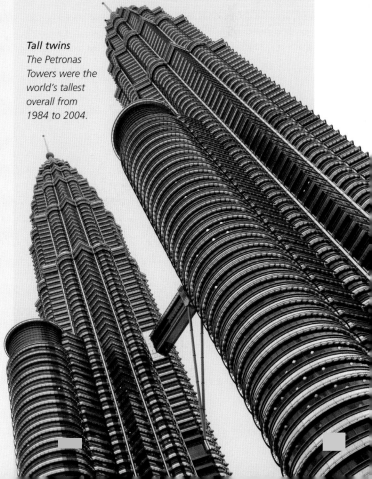

Tall twins
The Petronas Towers were the world's tallest overall from 1984 to 2004.

Bridges & Tunnels

The Akashi-Kaikyo, currently the world's longest bridge.

TOP 10 **LONGEST SUSPENSION BRIDGES**

BRIDGE / LOCATION	YEAR COMPLETED*	LENGTH OF MAIN SPAN FT	M
1 = Kitan Straight, Japan	u/c	8,202	2,500
= Qiongzhou Haixia, China	u/c	8,202	2,500
3 Akashi-Kaikyo, Kobe-Naruto, Japan	1998	6,532	1,991
4 Izmit Bay, Turkey	2002	5,472	1,668
5 Donmgfang, China	u/c	5,413	1,650
6 Great Belt, Denmark	1997	5,328	1,624
7 Ryungyang, China	2005	4,888	1,490
8 Ging Lon Da Qiao, China	2007#	4,652	1,418
9 Humber Estuary, UK	1980	4,625	1,410
10 Jiangyin, China	1998	4,543	1,385

* u/c—under construction
\# Scheduled completion date

The design of a suspension bridge, in which the weight of the deck is borne by cables, enables single spans to be longer than any other type of bridge. The proposed Messina Strait Bridge between Sicily and Calabria, Italy, would have broken all records with a center span of 10,827 ft (3,300 m), but the project was canceled.

TOP 10 **LONGEST CABLE-STAYED BRIDGES**

BRIDGE / LOCATION	YEAR COMPLETED*	LENGTH OF MAIN SPAN FT	M
1 Suzhou-Nantong, China	u/c	3,569	1,088
2 Stonecutters, Hong Kong	2008#	3,339	1,018
3 = Dongfang, China	u/c	2,952	900
= Linding, China	u/c	2,952	900
5 Tatara, Onomichi-Imabari, Japan	1999	2,920	890
6 Pont de Normandie, Le Havre, France	1994	2,808	856
7 Zhenyang, China	u/c	2,788	850
8 Gaopu, China	u/c	2,296	700
9 Nancha (Second Nanjing), China	2001	2,060	628
10 Wuhan Baishazhou, China	2000	2,027	618

* u/c—under construction
\# Scheduled completion date

The towers of a cable-stayed bridge bear the weight of the deck, to which they are connected by cables. Multiple towers enable them to be very long—the Hanzhou Bay Bridge, China (2008), will measure 22 miles (36 km) overall.

TOP 10 **LONGEST BRIDGES IN THE USA**

BRIDGE / LOCATION	YEAR COMPLETED	LENGTH OF MAIN SPAN FT	M
1 Verrazano Narrows, New York	1964	4,260	1,298
2 Golden Gate, San Francisco, California	1937	4,200	1,280
3 Mackinac Straits, Michigan	1957	3,800	1,158
4 George Washington, New York	1931/62*	3,500	1,067
5 Tacoma Narrows II, Washington	1950	2,800	853
6 Transbay, San Francisco, California#	1936	2,310	704
7 Bronx-Whitestone, New York	1939	2,300	701
8 Delaware Memorial, Wilmington, Delaware#	1951/68	2,150	655
9 Walt Whitman, Philadelphia, Pennsylvania	1957	2,000	610
10 Ambassador, Detroit, Michigan/Windsor, Ontario, Canada	1929	1,850	564

* Lower deck added
\# Twin spans

All 10 are suspension bridges. The USA also has the two longest steel arch bridges in the world, the New River Gorge Bridge, Fayetteville, West Virginia (1977: 1,700 ft/518 m), and the Kill van Kull at Bayonne, New Jersey (1931: 1,652 ft/504 m).

Bridge-Building Tragedies
Few of America's best-known bridges have been built without loss of life. Some 27 died during the construction of the Brooklyn Bridge (1883), but the Golden Gate Bridge, which is three time longer, used a safety net that saved the lives of at least 19 until, on February 17, 1937, just before it was opened, 10 workers died when a section of scaffolding collapsed.

TOP 10 **LONGEST RAIL TUNNELS**

TUNNEL / LOCATION / YEAR COMPLETED	LENGTH FT	M
1 AlpTransit Gotthard, Switzerland, 2015*	187,244	57,072
2 Seikan, Japan, 1988	176,673	53,850
3 Channel Tunnel, France/England, 1994	165,518	50,450
4 Moscow Metro (Serpukhovsko-Timiryazevskaya line), Russia, 1983	127,625	38,900
5 Guadarrama, Spain, 2007*	97,100	28,377
6 London Underground (East Finchley/Morden, Northern Line), UK, 1939	91,339	27,840
7 Hakkouda, Japan, 2013*	86,795	26,455
8 Iwate, Japan, 2013*	84,678	25,810
9 Lainzer/Wienerwald, Austria, 2015*	78,228	23,844
10 Iiyama, Japan, 2013*	72,917	22,225

* Under construction—scheduled completion date

The world's longest rail tunnel, the AlpTransit Gotthard, Switzerland, was proposed as early as 1947 and given the go-ahead in 1998 after a referendum of the Swiss electorate. When completed, trains will travel through it at 155 mph (250 km/h).

TOP 10 **LONGEST ROAD TUNNELS**

TUNNEL / LOCATION / YEAR COMPLETED	LENGTH FT	M
1 Laerdal, Norway, 2000	80,413	24,510
2 Zhongnanshan, China, 2007*	59,186	18,040
3 St. Gotthard, Switzerland, 1980	55,505	16,918
4 Arlberg, Austria, 1978	45,850	13,972
5 Hsuehshan, Taiwan, 2006	42,323	12,900
6 Fréjus, France/Italy, 1980	42,306	12,895
7 Mont-Blanc, France/Italy, 1965	38,094	11,611
8 Gudvangen, Norway, 1991	37,493	11,428
9 Folgefonn, Norway, 2001	36,417	11,100
10 Kan-Etsu II (southbound), Japan, 1991	36,122	11,010

* Under construction—scheduled completion date

Nos. 1, 3, 4, and 7 have all held the record as "world's longest road tunnel." Previous record-holders include the 19,206-ft (5,854-m) Grand San Bernardo (Italy–Switzerland, 1964); the 16,841-ft (5,133-m) Alfonos XIII or Viella (Spain, 1948); the 10,620-ft (3,237-m) Queensway (Mersey) Tunnel (connecting Liverpool and Birkenhead, UK, 1934); and the 10,453-ft (3,186-m) Col de Tende (France–Italy, 1882), originally built as a rail tunnel and converted for road use in 1928.

5

CULTURE

World Culture

THE 10 **FIRST EUROPEAN CAPITALS OF CULTURE**

	CITY / COUNTRY	YEAR
1	Athens, Greece	1985
2	Florence, Italy	1986
3	Amsterdam, Netherlands	1987
4	West Berlin, West Germany	1988
5	Paris, France	1989
6	Glasgow, UK	1990
7	Dublin, Ireland	1991
8	Madrid, Spain	1992
9	Antwerp, Belgium	1993
10	Lisbon, Portugal	1994

Each year since 1985, a European city has been designated European Capital (originally "City") of Culture, providing it with an opportunity to draw attention to its cultural attractions for the year. Each country in the European Union has an opportunity to participate in turn, with two capitals being selected from 2008.

Left: Cultural icon
Michelangelo's statue of David is one of the world's most widely recognized works of art. Completed in 1504, the 17-ft (5.17-m) sculpture is housed in the Gallereria dell'Accademia, Florence, Italy.

THE 10 **LATEST ARAB CULTURAL CAPITALS**

YEAR	CITY / COUNTRY
2007	Algiers, Algeria
2006	Muscat, Oman
2005	Khartoum, Sudan
2004	Sana'a, Yemen
2003	Rabat, Morocco
2002	Amman, Jordan
2001	Kuwait City, Kuwait
2000	Riyadh, Saudi Arabia
1999	Beirut, Lebanon
1998	Sharjah, United Arab Emirates

Source: UNESCO

Initiated by the Cultural Capitals Programme of the United Nations Educational, Scientific and Cultural Organization (UNESCO) to promote Arab culture and foster cooperation throughout the Arab world, Cairo, Egypt, was declared the first Arab Cultural Capital in 1996.

Below: Cultural capital
Athens, Greece, was the pioneering European City (now Capital) of Culture, since when, up to 2007, over 30 cities have been designated.

THE 10 **FIRST NATIONAL HISTORIC SITES IN THE USA**

NATIONAL HISTORIC SITE	DESIGNATED*
1 Ford's Theatre, Washington, D.C.	Apr 7, 1866
2 Abraham Lincoln Birthplace, Kentucky	Jul 17, 1916
3 Andrew Johnson, Tennessee	Aug 29, 1935
4 Jefferson National Expansion Memorial, Missouri	Dec 20, 1935
5 Whitman Mission, Washington	Jun 29, 1936
6 Salem Maritime, Massachusetts	Mar 17, 1938
7 Fort Laramie, Wyoming	Jul 16, 1938
8 Hopewell Furnace, Pennsylvania	Aug 3, 1938
9 Vanderbilt Mansion, New York	Dec 18, 1940
10 Fort Raleigh, North Carolina	Apr 5, 1941

* Dates include those for locations originally assigned other designations but later authorized as Historic Sites

THE 10 **LATEST WORLD HERITAGE SITES IN THE USA**

SITE / LOCATION	YEAR
1 = Carlsbad Caverns National Park, New Mexico	1995
= Waterton Glacier International Peace Park, Montana (and Alberta, Canada)	1995
3 Pueblo de Taos, New Mexico	1992
4 Chaco Culture, New Mexico	1987
5 = Hawaii Volcanoes National Park, Hawaii	1987
= Monticello and the University of Virginia in Charlottesville, Virginia	1987
7 = Statue of Liberty, New York	1984
= Yosemite National Park, California	1984
9 = Great Smoky Mountains National Park, Tennessee/North Carolina	1983
= La Fortaleza and San Juan National Historic Site, Puerto Rico	1983

TOP 10 **OLDEST MUSEUMS AND ART GALLERIES IN THE USA**

MUSEUM/ART GALLERY / FOUNDED

1 Charleston Museum, Charleston, South Carolina 1773

2 Peabody Essex Museum, Salem, Massachusetts 1799

3 Pennsylvania Academy of Fine Arts, Philadelphia, Pennsylvania 1805

4 Peale Museum, Baltimore, Maryland 1814

5 Yale (originally Trumbull) Art Gallery, New Haven, Connecticut 1832

6 Wadsworth Athenaeum, Hartford, Connecticut 1842

7 West Point Museum, West Point, New York 1854

8 American Museum of Natural History, New York City 1869

9 Metropolitan Museum of Art, New York City 1872

10 Corcoran Gallery of Art, Washington, D.C. 1874

Words & Language

TOP 10 **LANGUAGES SPOKEN IN THE USA**

	LANGUAGE	SPEAKERS
1	English	215,423,557
2	Spanish	28,101,052
3	Chinese	2,022,143
4	French	1,643,838
5	German	1,382,613
6	Tagalog	1,224,241
7	Vietnamese	1,009,627
8	Italian	1,008,370
9	Korean	894,063
10	Russian	706,242

Source: US Census Bureau, Census 2000

Studying the Qu'ran
Widely spoken in North Africa and the Middle East, Arabic is the first language of upward of 200 million people.

TOP 10 **LANGUAGES OFFICIALLY SPOKEN IN THE MOST COUNTRIES**

	LANGUAGE	COUNTRIES
1	English	51
2	French	31
3	Arabic	26
4	Spanish	22
5	Portuguese	10
6	German	7
7	Italian	6
8	=Dutch	5
	=Russian	5
10	=Croatian	4
	=Turkish	4

There are many countries in the world with more than one official language—both English and French are recognized officially in Canada, for example. English is used in numerous countries as the *lingua franca*, the common language that enables people who speak mutually unintelligible languages to communicate with each other.

TOP 10 **LANGUAGES THAT WILL BE SPOKEN BY THE YOUTH OF 2050**

	LANGUAGE	ESTIMATED NO. OF 15–24-YEAR-OLD SPEAKERS, 2050
1	Chinese	166,000,000
2	Hindu/Urdu	73,700,000
3	Arabic	72,200,000
4	English	65,000,000
5	Spanish	62,800,000
6	Portuguese	32,500,000
7	Bengali	31,600,000
8	Russian	22,500,000
9	Japanese	18,200,000
10	Malay	10,500,000

Source: David Graddol, *The Future of English?*, British Council

TOP 10 **MOST COMMON WORDS IN ENGLISH**

WRITTEN		SPOKEN
the	**1**	be
of	**2**	the
and	**3**	I
a	**4**	you
in	**5**	and
to	**6**	it
is	**7**	have
was	**8**	a
it	**9**	not
for	**10**	do

Source: British National Corpus

A survey of a wide range of texts containing a total of almost 90 million words indicated that, in written English, one word in every 16 is "the."

100 Years Ago

Also known as *Dji'ts Bud dnaca*, or "Flying Bird", Fidelia Hoscott Fielding (1827–1908) was the last known speaker of Mohegan Pequot, a native American language of Connecticut. When she died the language became extinct, but the diaries she kept have enabled some elements of it to be preserved.

TOP 10 **COUNTRIES WITH THE MOST SPANISH-LANGUAGE SPEAKERS**

	COUNTRY	APPROXIMATE NO. OF NATIVE SPEAKERS
1	Mexico	106,255,000
2	Colombia	45,600,000
3	Spain	44,400,000
4	Argentina	41,248,000
5	USA	31,000,000
6	Venezuela	26,021,000
7	Peru	23,191,000
8	Chile	15,795,000
9	Cuba	11,285,000
10	Ecuador	10,946,000

TOP 10 **ONLINE LANGUAGES**

	LANGUAGE	% OF ALL INTERNET USERS	INTERNET USERS*
1	English	29.5	328,666,386
2	Chinese	14.3	159,001,513
3	Spanish	8.0	89,077,232
4	Japanese	7.7	86,300,000
5	German	5.3	58,711,687
6	French	5.0	55,521,294
7	Portuguese	3.6	40,216,760
8	Korean	3.1	34,120,000
9	Italian	2.8	30,763,940
10	Arabic	2.6	28,540,700
	Top 10 languages	*81.8*	*910,919,512*
	Rest of world languages	*18.2*	*203,354,914*
	World total	*100.0*	*1,114,274,426*

* As at March 2007

Source: Internet World Stats
http://www.internetworldstats.com/

Education

TOP 10 COUNTRIES WITH THE MOST PRIMARY SCHOOL PUPILS

	COUNTRY	PRIMARY SCHOOL PUPILS
1	India	125,568,597
2	China	120,998,605
3	Indonesia	29,050,834
4	USA	24,848,518
5	Nigeria	21,110,707
6	Brazil	19,380,387
7	Bangladesh	17,953,300
8	Pakistan	16,207,286
9	Mexico	14,857,191
10	Philippines	12,970,635
	World total	682,646,764

Source: UNESCO, *Global Education Digest 2006*

TOP 10 COUNTRIES WITH THE MOST SECONDARY SCHOOL PUPILS

	COUNTRY	% FEMALE	SECONDARY SCHOOL PUPILS
1	China	47	98,762,802
2	India	43	81,050,129
3	Brazil	52	26,789,210
4	USA	49	23,854,458
5	Indonesia	49	15,872,535
6	Russia	49	14,521,818
7	Bangladesh	51	11,051,234
8	Iran	47	10,312,561
9	Mexico	51	10,188,185
10	Vietnam	48	9,588,698

Source: UNESCO, *Global Education Digest 2006*

TOP 10 OLDEST SECONDARY SCHOOLS IN THE USA

	SCHOOL	FOUNDED
1	Roxbury Latin School, West Roxbury, Massachusetts	1645
2	Hopkins School New Haven, Connecticut	1660
3	= Friends Select School, Philadelphia, Pennsylvania	1689
	= William Penn Charter School, Philadelphia, Pennsylvania	1689
5	Abington Friends School, Jenkintown, Pennsylvania	1697
6	Trinity School, New York, New York	1709
7	Moravian Academy, Bethlehem, Pennsylvania	1742
8	Linden Hall School for Girls, Lititz, Pennsylvania	1746
9	Governor Dummer Academy, Byfield, Massachusetts	1763
10	Columbia Grammar and Preparatory School, New York, New York	1764

TOP 10 **LARGEST UNIVERSITIES**

UNIVERSITY / COUNTRY / STUDENTS

1 Kameshwar Singh Darbhanga Sanskrit, India 515,000

2 Calicut, India 300,000

3 Paris, France 279,978

4 Mexico, Mexico 269,000

5 Mumbai, India 262,350

6 Chhatrapati Shahuji Maharaj University, India 220,000

7 Utkal, India 200,000

8 Rome, Italy 189,000

9 Buenos Aires, Argentina 183,397

10 Guadalajara, Mexico 180,776

Some distance-learning establishments, such as the Indira Gandhi National Open University, India, with 1.43 million students, are considerably larger than these.

Paris University
Founded in the mid-12th century, the University of Paris was reorganized in 1970 and today comprises 13 separate bodies located across the city, each of which offers a range of specialized subjects.

TOP 10 **LARGEST UNIVERSITIES IN THE USA**

UNIVERSITY / LOCATION / ENROLLMENT (2006)

1 Ohio State University, Columbus, Ohio 51,818

2 Arizona State University, Tempe, Arizona 51,234

3 University of Florida, Gainesville, Florida 50,785

4 University of Minnesota Twin Cities, Minneapolis, Minnesota 50,402

5 University of Texas at Austin, Austin, Texas 49,738

6 University of Central Florida, Orlando, Florida 46,719

7 Texas A&M University-College Station, College Station, Texas 45,487

8 Michigan State University, East Lansing, Michigan 45,166

9 University of South Florida, Tampa, Florida 44,038

10 Pennsylvania State University, University Park, Pennsylvania 42,914

TOP 10 **OLDEST UNIVERSITIES** *

UNIVERSITY	COUNTRY	FOUNDED
1 Parma	Italy	1064
2 Bologna	Italy	1088
3 Paris	France	1150
4 Oxford	England	1167
5 Modena	Italy	1175
6 Cambridge	England	1209
7 Salamanca	Spain	1218
8 Padua	Italy	1222
9 Naples	Italy	1224
10 Toulouse	France	1229

* Only those in continuous operation since founding

Books & Libraries

TOP 10 BESTSELLING NON-FICTION BOOKS

BOOK / FIRST PUBLISHED	MINIMUM ESTIMATED SALES*
1 The Bible	6,000,000,000
2 Quotations from the Works of Mao Tse-tung, 1966	900,000,000
3 Xinhua Zidian (Chinese dictionary), 1953	400,000,000
4 Qur'an (Koran)	200,000,000
5 Noah Webster, The American Spelling Book, 1783	100,000,000
6 William Holmes McGuffey, The McGuffey Readers, 1836	60,000,000
7 Benjamin Spock, The Common Sense Book of Baby and Child Care, 1946	50,000,000
8 Elbert Hubbard, A Message to Garcia, 1899	45,000,000
9 = Rev Charles Monroe Sheldon, In His Steps: 'What Would Jesus Do?', 1896	30,000,000
= Napoleon Hill, Think and Grow Rich, 1918	30,000,000
= A. S. Hornby, et al, Oxford Advanced Learner's Dictionary, 1948	30,000,000

* Including translations; excluding annual publications and series

TOP 10 BESTSELLING NOVELS

BOOK / FIRST PUBLISHED	MINIMUM ESTIMATED SALES*
1 J. R. R. Tolkien, The Lord of the Rings, 1954–55	100,000,000
2 J. K. Rowling, Harry Potter and the Sorcerer's Stone, 1997	87,000,000
3 = Dan Brown, The Da Vinci Code, 2003	65,000,000
= J. K. Rowling, Harry Potter and the Half-Blood Prince, 2005	65,000,000
5 = J. D. Salinger, The Catcher in the Rye, 1951	60,000,000
= J. K. Rowling, Harry Potter and the Chamber of Secrets, 1998	60,000,000
7 = J. K. Rowling, Harry Potter and the Prisoner of Azkaban, 1999	55,000,000
= J. K. Rowling, Harry Potter and the Goblet of Fire, 2000	55,000,000
= J. K. Rowling, Harry Potter and the Order of the Phoenix, 2003	55,000,000
10 = Johanna Spyri, Heidi, 1880	50,000,000
= Antoine de Saint-Exupéry, Le Petit Prince (The Little Prince), 1943	50,000,000

* Including translations

Pottermania
The launch of each new Harry Potter title has generated a frenzy of publicity and multimillion sales in over 60 languages.

TOP 10 MOST EXPENSIVE BOOKS AND MANUSCRIPTS

BOOK / MANUSCRIPT / SALE*	PRICE ($)#
1 The Codex Hammer (formerly Codex Leicester), 1506–10 Christie's New York, Nov 11, 1994 This is one of Leonardo da Vinci's notebooks, which includes many scientific drawings and diagrams. It was purchased by Bill Gates, the billionaire founder of Microsoft.	30,802,500
2 The Rothschild Prayerbook, c. 1503 Christie's London, Jul 8, 1999 This holds the world-record price for an illuminated manuscript.	13,387,140
3 The Gospels of Henry the Lion, c. 1173–75 Sotheby's London, Dec 6, 1983 At the time of its sale, it became the most expensive manuscript, book, or work of art other than a painting ever sold.	10,656,000
4 John James Audubon's The Birds of America, 1827–38 Christie's New York, Mar 10, 2000 The record for any printed book. Further copies of the same book, a collection of more than 400 large, hand-colored engravings, have also fetched high prices. A facsimile reprint of *The Birds of America* published in 1985 by Abbeville Press, New York, was listed at $30,000, making it the most expensive book ever published.	8,802,500
5 The Canterbury Tales, Geoffrey Chaucer, c. 1476–77 Christie's London, Jul 8, 1998 Printed by William Caxton and purchased by Sir Paul Getty, it set the record for a work of English literature.	7,579,260
6 Comedies, Histories, and Tragedies, The First Folio of William Shakespeare, 1623 Christie's New York, 8 Oct 8, 2001 This sale marks the world auction record for a 17th-century book. Another was sold privately in 2003 (by Oriel College Oxford to Sir Paul Getty) for a rumored £3,500,000, and one owned by Dr Williams's Library at Sotheby's, London, on July 13, 2006 for £2,800,000.	6,166,000
7 The Gutenberg Bible, 1455 Christie's New York, USA, Oct 22, 1987 One of the first books ever printed, by Johann Gutenberg and Johann Fust.	5,390,000
8 The Northumberland Bestiary, c. 1250–60 Sotheby's, London, Nov 29, 1990	5,319,000
9 The Burdett Psalter and Hours, c. 1282–86 Sotheby's London, Jun 23, 1998	4,100,000
10 The Cornaro Missal, c. 1503 Christie's London, Jul 8, 1999 This manuscript, formerly owned by the Barons Nathaniel and Albert von Rothschild, achieved a world-record price for an Italian manuscript.	4,056,000

* Excludes collections
# Includes buyer's premium

THE 10 LATEST WINNERS OF THE PULITZER PRIZE FOR FICTION

YEAR	AUTHOR / TITLE
2006	Geraldine Brooks, March
2005	Marilynne Robinson, Gilead
2004	Edward P. Jones, The Known World
2003	Jeffrey Eugenides, Middlesex
2002	Richard Russo, Empire Falls
2001	Michael Chabon, The Amazing Adventures of Kavalier & Clay
2000	Jhumpa Lhiri, Interpreter of Maladies
1999	Michael Cunningham, The Hours
1998	Philip Roth, American Pastoral
1997	Steven Millhauser, Martin Dressler: The Tale of an American Dreamer

THE 10 FIRST PUBLIC LIBRARIES IN THE USA

LIBRARY / FOUNDED

1 Peterboro Public Library, Peterboro, NH 1833

2 Buffalo and Erie County Public Library, NY 1836

3 New Orleans Public Library, New Orleans, LA 1843

4 Boston Public Library, Boston, MA 1848

5 Public Library of Cincinnati and Hamilton County, Cincinnati, OH 1853

6 Springfield City Library, Springfield, MA 1857

7 Worcester Public Library, Worcester, MA 1859

8 Multnomah County Library, Portland, OR 1864

9 Detroit Public Library, Detroit, MI 1865

10 Atlanta-Fulton Public Library, Atlanta, GA 1867

The Press

TOP 10 **OLDEST NEWSPAPERS IN THE WORLD**

NEWSPAPER	COUNTRY	FOUNDED
1 Haarlems Dagblad	Netherlands	1656
2 Gazzetta di Mantova	Italy	1664
3 The London Gazette	UK	1665
4 Wiener Zeitung	Austria	1703
5 Hildesheimer Allgemeine Zeitung	Germany	1705
6 Berrow's Worcester Journal	UK	1709
7 Newcastle Journal	UK	1711
8 Stamford Mercury	UK	1712
9 Northampton Mercury	UK	1720
10 Hanauer Anzeiger	Germany	1725

This list includes only newspapers that have been published continuously since their founding. The former No. 1 on this list, the *Swedish Post-och Inrikes Tidningar*, founded in 1645, ceased publication on paper on January 1, 2007 and is now available only online.

The word on the street
Despite the wide choice of alternative media, from TV to the Internet, traditional newspapers have maintained their importance, with some 50 worldwide selling more than a million copies a day.

TOP 10 **LONGEST-RUNNING MAGAZINES IN THE USA**

MAGAZINE	FIRST PUBLISHED
1 Scientific American	1845
2 Town & Country*	1846
3 Harper's#	1850
4 The Moravian	1856
5 The Atlantic Monthly	1857
6 Armed Forces Journal†	1863
7 The Nation	1865
8 American Naturalist	1867
9 Harper's Bazaar§	1867
10 Animals¶	1868

* Originally *The National Press*, then *The Home Journal*
\# Originally *Harper's New Monthly Magazine*
† Originally *Army and Navy Journal*
§ Originally spelled *Bazar*
¶ Originally *Our Dumb Animals*

America's longest continuously published magazine, *Scientific American*, was published on August 28, 1845, the brainchild of Rufus Porter. Originally a four-page newspaper, it included features on both science and technology, and nonscientific topics such as religion and poetry. Soon afterward, Porter sold it for $800 to 22-year-old Orson Desaix Munn and a schoolfriend, 19-year-old Alfred Ely Beach, whose father published the New York *Sun*. They revised the format, focussing on science and establishing the magazine as the world's most popular scientific journal.

TOP 10 **DAILY NEWSPAPERS IN THE USA**

NEWSPAPER	AVERAGE US CIRCULATION*
1 USA Today	2,528,437
2 The Wall Street Journal	2,058,342
3 The New York Times	1,683,855
4 Los Angeles Times	1,231,318
5 The Washington Post	960,684
6 Chicago Tribune	957,212
7 New York Daily News	795,153
8 The Philadelphia Inquirer	705,965
9 Denver Post/ Rocky Mountain News	704,806
10 Houston Chronicle	692,557

* Average for six months to March 31, 2006

Source: Audit Bureau of Circulations

TOP 10 **MAGAZINES IN THE USA**

MAGAZINE	AVERAGE CIRCULATION (2005)
1 AARP The Magazine	22,675,655
2 AARP Bulletin	22,075,011
3 Reader's Digest	10,111,773
4 TV Guide	8,211,581
5 Better Homes and Gardens	7,620,932
6 National Geographic	5,403,934
7 Good Housekeeping	4,634,763
8 Family Circle	4,296,370
9 Ladies' Home Journal	4,122,460
10 Woman's Day	4,048,799

Source: Audit Bureau of Circulations/Magazine Publishers of America

TOP 10 **DAILY NEWSPAPERS IN THE WORLD**

NEWSPAPER	COUNTRY	AVERAGE DAILY CIRCULATION, 2006
1 Yomiuri Shimbun	Japan	14,246,000
2 Asahi Shimbun	Japan	12,326,000
3 Mainichi Shimbun	Japan	5,635,000
4 Nihon Keizai Shimbun	Japan	4,737,000
5 Chunichi Shimbun	Japan	4,571,000
6 Bild	Germany	4,220,000
7 The Sun	UK	3,461,000
8 Sankei Shimbun	Japan	2,665,000
9 USA Today	USA	2,603,000
8 Canako Xiaoxi (Beijing)	China	2,530,000

Source: World Association of Newspapers

Yomiuri Shimbun was founded in Japan 1874. In 1998 it became the country's and the world's bestselling daily newspaper, achieving a record average sale of 14,532,694 copies a day.

TOP 10 **MAGAZINES IN THE WORLD**

MAGAZINE	COUNTRY	AVERAGE CIRCULATION
1 Reader's Digest	USA	12,078,000
2 Better Homes and Gardens	USA	7,605,000
3 Family Circle	USA	4,634,000
4 Women's Day	USA	4,205,000
5 Time	USA	4,112,000
6 Ladies' Home Journal	USA	4,101,000
7 Kampioen	Netherlands	3,756,000
8 People	USA	3,625,000
9 Playboy	USA	3,215,000
10 Newsweek	UK	3,183,000

Source: International Federation of Audit Bureaux of Circulations

Art on Show

TOP 10 **BEST-ATTENDED ART EXHIBITIONS, 2006**

	EXHIBITION	VENUE / CITY / DATES	ATTENDANCE* DAILY	ATTENDANCE* TOTAL
1	Tutankhamun and the Golden Age of the Pharaohs	Museum of Art, Fort Lauderdale, Florida, USA, Dec 15, 2005–Apr 23, 2006	5,443	707,534
2	Russia!	Guggenheim Museum, Bilbao, Spain, Mar 29–10 Sep 10	4,392	621,188
3	Klimt, Schiele, Moser, Kokoschka	Grand Palais, Paris, France, Oct 5, 2005–Jan 23, 2006	6,297	600,000
4	Gauguin/Van Gogh: The Adventure of Colour	Museo Santa Giulia, Breshia, Italy, Oct 22, 2005–Mar 26, 2006	3,517	541,547
5 =	Egypt's Sunken Treasures	Martin-Gropius-Bau Museum, Berlin, Germany, May 13–Sep 4	4,559	450,000
=	The Phillips Collection in Paris	Musée du Luxembourg, Paris, France, Nov 20, 2005–Mar 26, 2006	3,543	450,000
7	The King's Jewels	Green Vault, Residenzschloss, Dresden, Germany, Dec 3, 2005–Jul 24, 2006	2,165	434,506
8	Edvard Munch: The Modern Life of the Soul	Museum of Modern Art, New York, USA, Feb 19–May 8	6,184	419,653
9	Cézanne and Pissarro, 1865–85	Musée d'Orsay, Paris, France, Feb 28–May 28	5,242	405,165
10	Picasso: Tradition and Avant-garde	Reina Sofia, Madrid, Spain, Jun 6–Sep 25	4,211	404,879

* Includes exhibitions spanning 2005–2006

Source: *The Art Newspaper*

TOP 10 **BEST-ATTENDED ART EXHIBITIONS IN THE USA, 2006**

	EXHIBITION	VENUE / CITY / DATES	ATTENDANCE* DAILY	ATTENDANCE* TOTAL
1	Tutankhamun and the Golden Age of the Pharaohs	Museum of Art, Fort Lauderdale, Florida, Dec 15, 2005–Apr 23, 2006	5,443	707,534
2	Edvard Munch: The Modern Life of the Soul	Museum of Modern Art, New York, Feb 19–May 8	6,184	419,653
3	Russia!	Guggenheim Museum, New York, Sep 16, 2005–Jan 11, 2006	4,006	405,780
4	Dada	Museum of Modern Art, New York, Jun 18–Sep 11	5,107	377,205
5	AngloMania	Metropolitan Museum of Art, New York, May 2–Sep 4	4,488	377,201
6	Zaha Hadid	Guggenheim Museum, New York, Jun 3–Oct 25	2,884	358,830
7	Directions: Jim Lambie	Hirshhorn Museum, Washington, D.C., May 13–Oct 4	2,452	355,457
8	Cézanne in Provence	National Gallery of Art, Washington, D.C, Jan 29–May 7	3,385	335,164
9	Black Box: Francis Alÿs	Hirshhorn Museum, Washington, D.C., Apr 17–Aug 13	2,741	326,202
10	Audubon's Dreams Realized	National Gallery of Art, Washington, D.C. Sep 25, 2005–Mar 26, 2006	1,733	317,096

* Approximate totals provided by museums Source: *The Art Newspaper*

THE 10 **MOST-VISITED ART GALLERIES AND MUSEUMS IN THE USA**

ATTRACTION / LOCATION / ANNUAL VISITORS

1 The Smithsonian Institution, DC 20,100,000

2 United States Capitol Historical Society, DC 8,000,000

3 National Museum of American History, DC 5,900,000

4 National Museum of Natural History, DC 5,542,000

5 Metropolitan Museum of Art, NY 5,400,000

6 National Gallery of Art, DC 4,000,000

7 American Museum of Natural History, NY 4,000,000

8 Statue of Liberty National Monument and Ellis Island Immigration Museum, NY 3,408,560

9 Museum of Modern Art, NY 1,585,000

10 Museum of Science, MA 1,429,685

Source: *The Official Museum Directory*

Russian art
Yuri Pimenov's New Moscow (1935), one of more than 250 works of art shown at the Guggenheim's major Russia! exhibition.

TOP 10 **BEST-ATTENDED EXHIBITIONS AT THE METROPOLITAN MUSEUM OF ART, NEW YORK**

	EXHIBITION	YEAR	ATTENDANCE
1	The Treasures of Tutankhamun	1978–79	1,226,467
2	Mona Lisa	1963	1,007,521
3	The Vatican Collection: The Papacy and Art	1983	896,743
4	Glory Of Russian Costume	1976–77	835,862
5	Origins of Impressionism	1994–95	794,108
6	Romantic and Glamorous Hollywood	1974–75	788,665
7	The Horses of San Marco	1980	742,221
8	Man and the Horse	1984–85	726,523
9	Masterpieces of Fifty Centuries	1979–81	690,471
10	Seurat	1991–92	642,408

TOP 10 **TALLEST EGYPTIAN OBELISKS**

	OBELISK / LOCATION	FT	HEIGHT IN	M
1	Lateran, Piazza San Giovanni in Laterano, Rome, Italy	105	7	32.18
2	Hatsheput, Karnak, Egypt	97	0	29.56
3	Tuthmosis III*, Istanbul, Turkey	95	0	28.95
4	St Peter's, Rome, Italy	83	3	25.37
5	Rameses II, Luxor, Egypt	82	0	25.00
6	Piazza del Popolo, Rome, Italy	76	1	23.20
7	Rameses II, Place de la Concorde, Paris, France	74	0	22.55
8	Piazza di Montecitorio, Rome, Italy	71	62	1.79
9	Tuthmosis III, Central Park, New York, USA	69	7	21.21
10	Tuthmosis III ('Cleopatra's Needle'), Thames Embankment, London, UK	68	6	20.88

* Broken, total height estimated (actual surviving fragment 65 ft/19.8 m)

There are some 27 surviving ancient Egyptian obelisks—tall columns built at the entrance to temples—only eight of which remain in Egypt. The rest have been plundered by or donated to other countries at various stages of Egypt's history, including 11 in Italy and those from Heliopolis set up in Paris (1833), New York (1881), and London (1878), popularly known as "Cleopatra's Needles"—despite having no connection with Queen Cleopatra.

Royal treasure
The mask of Tutankhamun was the star attraction of a series of record-breaking exhibitions.

Art on Sale

TOP 10 **MOST EXPENSIVE PAINTINGS BY GUSTAV KLIMT**

WORK / YEAR / SALE	PRICE ($)
1 Portrait of Adele Bloch-Bauer II, 1912 Christie's New York, Nov 8, 2006	87,936,000
2 Birch Forest, 1903, Christie's New York, Nov 8, 2006	40,336,000
3 Apple Tree I, 1912, Christie's New York, Nov 8, 2006	33,056,000
4 Houses at Unterach on the Attersee, 1916, Christie's New York, Nov 8, 2006	31,376,000
5 Landhaus am Attersee, 1914, Sotheby's New York, Nov 5, 2003	29,128,000
6 Schloss Kammer am Attersee II, 1909 Christie's London, Oct 9, 1997	23,490,000
7 Litzlbergerkeller am Attersee, 1915–16 Sotheby's New York, May 13, 1997	14,742,500
8 Dame mit Facher, 1917–18, Sotheby's New York, May 11, 1994	11,662,500
9 Bauergarten, 1905–07, Christie's London, Nov 28, 1994	5,844,270
10 Obstbäume am Attersee (Fruit trees by Lake Attersee), 1901, Sotheby's London, Dec 8, 1997	5,548,740

TOP 10 **MOST EXPENSIVE PAINTINGS SOLD PRIVATELY**

ARTIST / PAINTING / YEAR / TRANSACTION LOCATION / YEAR	ESTIMATED PRICE ($)
1 Jackson Pollock, No. 5, 1948, New York, 2006	140,000,000
2 Willem De Kooning, Woman III, 1952/53, New York, 2006	137,500,000
3 Gustav Klimt, Portrait of Adele Bloch-Bauer I, 1907, New York, 2006	135,000,000
4 Jasper Johns, False Start, 1959, New York, 2006	80,000,000
5 Willem De Kooning, Police Gazette, 1955, New York, 2006	63,500,000
6 Vincent Van Gogh, Champ de blé avec cyprès, 1889, New York, 1993	57,000,000
7 Vincent Van Gogh, Peasant Woman Against a Background of Wheat, 1890, New York, 1997	47,500,000*
8 Vassily Kandinsky, Composition V, 1911, unknown, 1998	40,000,000
9 = Paul Cézanne, Nature morte avec pot de gingembre, sucrier et pommes, 1888–90, London, 1996	35,000,000
= Paul Gauguin, Famille Tahitienne (Promenade au bord de la mer), 1902, London, 1996	35,000,000

* Resold in 2005 with Gauguin's *The Bathers* for total of $100 million

The precise details of private (as contrasted with public auction) sales of works of art range from those that are totally secret to others where the vendor or purchaser deliberately publishes—and perhaps exaggerates—them in order to derive the maximum publicity. This Top 10 is therefore based on those for which reliable evidence is available, and may exclude certain similarly or even higher-priced but unknown transactions. In 2006 Pablo Picasso's *Le rêve*, the 6th most expensive by the artist ever sold, hit the headlines when its new owner, Las Vegas casino magnate Steve Wynn, agreed to sell it in a private transaction for $139 million, which would have made it the world's most expensive work of art. The sale was abandoned when Mr. Wynn accidentally damaged it by poking his elbow through the canvas.

Portrait of Adele Bloch-Bauer II
This work, painted in 1912, and the earlier Portrait of Adele Bloch-Bauer I *(1907), along with other works by Gustav Klimt, were looted by the Nazis during World War II. After a protracted legal battle, they were restored to their owner Maria Altmann, a niece of the sitter. Both paintings were sold for record sums in 2006, this at auction, the other privately.*

TOP 10 **MOST EXPENSIVE PAINTINGS**

	PAINTING / ARTIST	SALE	PRICE* ($)
1	Garçon à la pipe, Pablo Picasso (Spanish, 1881–1973)	Sotheby's New York, May 5, 2004	104,168,000
2	Dora Maar au chat, Pablo Picasso	Sotheby's New York, May 3, 2006	95,216,000
3	Portrait of Adele Bloch-Bauer II, Gustav Klimt (Austrian, 1862–1918)	Christie's New York, Nov 8, 2006	87,936,000
4	Portrait du Dr Gachet, Vincent van Gogh (Dutch, 1853–90)	Christie's New York, May 15, 1990	82,500,000
5	Bal au Moulin de la Galette, Montmartre Pierre-Auguste Renoir (French, 1841–1919)	Sotheby's New York, May 17, 1990	78,100,000
6	Massacre of the Innocents, Sir Peter Paul Rubens (Flemish, 1577–1640)	Sotheby's London, Jul 10, 2002	75,930,440
7	Portrait de l'Artiste Sans Barbe, Vincent van Gogh	Christie's New York, Nov 19, 1998	71,502,496
8	Rideau, Cruchon et Compôtier, Paul Cézanne (French, 1839–1906)	Sotheby's New York, May 10, 1999	60,502,500
9	Femme aux Bras Croises, Pablo Picasso	Christie's New York, Nov 8, 2000	55,006,000
10	Irises, Vincent van Gogh	Sotheby's New York, Nov 11, 1987	53,900,000

* Including buyer's premium

TOP 10 **MOST EXPENSIVE PAINTINGS BY PABLO PICASSO***

	PAINTING / YEAR / SALE	PRICE ($)
1	Garçon à la pipe, 1905, Sotheby's New York, May 5, 2004	104,168,000
2	Dora Maar au chat, 1941, Sotheby's New York, May 3, 2006	95,216,000
3	Femme aux bras croisés, 1901–02, Christie's New York, Nov 8, 2000	55,006,000
4	Les Noces de Pierrette, Binoche et Godeau, Paris, Nov 30, 1989	51,796,432
5	Femme assise dans un jardin, 1938, Sotheby's New York, Nov 10, 1999	49,502,500
6	Le rêve, 1932, Christie's New York, Nov 10, 1997	48,402,500
7	Self-portrait: Yo Picasso, 1901, Sotheby's New York, May 9, 1989	47,850,000
8	Nu au fauteuil noir, 1932, Christie's New York, Nov 9, 1999	45,102,500
9	Au Lapin Agile, 1905, Sotheby's New York, Nov 15, 1989	40,700,000
10	Acrobate et jeune Arlequin, 1905, Christie's London, Nov 28, 1988	38,138,700

* Sold at auction up to January 1, 2007, including buyer's premium

TOP 10 **MOST EXPENSIVE WORKS BY ANDY WARHOL**

	WORK / YEAR / SALE	PRICE ($)
1	Mao, 1972, Christie's New York, Nov 15, 2006	17,376,000
2	Orange Marilyn, 1964, Sotheby's New York, May 14, 1998	17,327,500
3	Orange Marilyn, 1962, Christie's New York, Nov 15, 2006	16,256,000
4	Sixteen Jackies, 1964, Christie's New York, Nov 15, 2006	15,696,000
5	Mustard Race Riot (2 panels), 1963, Christie's New York, Nov 10, 2004	15,127,500
6	Liz, 1963, Sotheby's New York, May 10, 2005	12,616,000
7	Small Torn Campbell's Soup Can (Pepper pot), 1962, Christie's New York, May 9, 2006	11,776,000
8	Brigitte Bardot, 1974, Christie's London, Feb 8, 2007	10,633,047
8	Jackie Frieze (13 parts), 1964, Sotheby's New York, Nov 9, 2005	9,200,000
10	Three Women, 1963, Christie's London, Feb 8, 2007	8,748,031

American icon
Now considered classics of pop art, Andy Warhol's pictures have commanded ever-higher prices. The first to sell for over $1 million did so within months of his death in 1987.

6

MUSIC

Singles

TOP 10 SINGLES OF ALL TIME IN THE USA

TITLE / ARTIST / YEAR OF ENTRY	ESTIMATED US SALES
1 "Candle in the Wind (1997)"/"Something About the Way You Look Tonight," Elton John, 1997	11,000,000
2 "White Christmas," Bing Crosby, 1942	8,000,000
3 = "Hey Jude," The Beatles, 1968	4,000,000
= "Hound Dog"/"Don't Be Cruel," Elvis Presley, 1956	4,000,000
= "I Will Always Love You," Whitney Houston, 1992	4,000,000
= "We Are the World," USA for Africa, 1985	4,000,000
= "Whoomp! (There it Is)," Tag Team, 1993	4,000,000
8 = "(Every Thing I Do) I Do It For You," Bryan Adams, 1991	3,000,000
= "How Do I Live," LeAnn Rimes, 1997	3,000,000
= "I'll Be Missing You," Puff Daddy and Faith Evans (featuring 112), 1997	3,000,000
= "Love Me Tender"/"Any Way You Want Me," Elvis Presley, 1956	3,000,000
= "Macarena," Los Del Rio, 1995	3,000,000

Source: RIAA

THE 10 FIRST SINGLES BY FOREIGN* ARTISTS TO TOP THE US CHART

TITLE / ARTIST / NATIONALITY	DATE
1 "Cherry Pink and Apple Blossom White," Perez "Prez Prado" (Cuban)	Apr 30, 1955
2 "Diana," Paul Anka (Canadian)	Sep 14, 1957
3 "Patricia," Perez "Prez Prado" (Cuban)	Aug 2, 1958
4 "Nel Blu Dipinto Di Blue (Volare)," Domenico Modugno (Italian)	Aug 23, 1958
5 "Lonely Boy," Paul Anka (Canadian)	Jul 18, 1959
6 "The Theme from 'A Summer Place'," Percy Faith (Canadian)	Feb 27, 1960
7 "Wonderland by Night," Bert Kaempfert (German)	Jan 14, 1961
8 "Sukiyaki," Kyu Sakamoto (Japanese)	Jun 15, 1963
9 "Dominique," The Singing Nun (Belgian)	Dec 7, 1963
10 "Ringo," Lorne Greene (Canadian)	Dec 5, 1964

* Excluding UK

Source: Music Information Database

TOP 10 SINGLES OF THE PAST 10 YEARS IN THE USA

YEAR	TITLE	ARTIST
2006	"Bad Day"	Daniel Powter
2005	"Hollaback Girl"	Gwen Stefani
2004	"I Believe"	Fantasia
2003	"Bridge Over Troubled Water"	Clay Aiken
2002	"Before Your Love"/ "A Moment Like This"	Kelly Clarkson
2001	"Loverboy"	Mariah Carey
2000	"Maria Maria"	Santana featuring the Product G&B
1999	"Believe"	Cher
1998	"The Boy is Mine"	Brandy and Monica
1997	"Candle in the Wind (1997)"/ "Something About the Way You Look Tonight"	Elton John

Source: Music Information Database

The bestselling singles of 2002, 2003, and 2004 were all by the participants of the TV show *American Idol*.

King of the singles
Through numerous posthumous re-releases, Elvis Presley's death in 1977 at the age of 42 failed to end his run of hits, with more No. 1s and more chart entries overall than any other artist.

TOP 10 **ARTISTS WITH THE MOST NO. 1 SINGLES IN THE USA**

ARTIST (TOTAL CHART HITS) / NO. 1 SINGLES

1 Elvis Presley (131) 22

2 The Beatles (72) 20

3 Mariah Carey (34) 18

4 Michael Jackson (46) 13

5 = Madonna (52) 12

5 = The Supremes (45) 12

7 Whitney Houston (38) 11

8 Janet Jackson (36) 10

9 = The Bee Gees (43) 9

9 = Paul McCartney/Wings (45) 9

9 = Stevie Wonder (61) 9

Source: Music Information Database

Pop princes
Although the Beatles' career spanned just 10 years, compared with Elvis Presley's 23, they scored only two fewer No. 1 singles in the USA.

TOP 10 **SINGLES THAT STAYED LONGEST IN THE US CHARTS**

	TITLE / ARTIST	FIRST CHART ENTRY	WEEKS IN CHART
1	"How Do I Live," LeAnn Rimes	1997	69
2	"Foolish Games"/"You Were Meant For Me," Jewel	1996	65
3	"Macarena (Bayside Boys Mix)," Los Del Rio	1996	60
4	"Smooth," Santana featuring Rob Thomas	1999	58
5	"Higher," Creed	1999	57
6	= "I Don't Want to Wait," Paula Cole	1997	56
	= "The Way You Love Me," Faith Hill	2000	56
8	= "Barely Breathing," Duncan Sheik	1996	55
	= "Missing," Everything But The Girl	1996	55
	= "Amazed," Lonestar	1999	55

Source: Music Information Database

Jewel's "You Were Meant For Me" charted for 41 weeks, but then became a double-A side for the remainder of its chart run. Otherwise, all the Top 10 were achieved with consecutive runs.

Albums

TOP 10 ALBUMS IN THE USA

	TITLE / ARTIST / YEAR OF ENTRY	EST. SALES
1	Their Greatest Hits, 1971–1975, The Eagles, 1976	29,000,000
2	Thriller, Michael Jackson, 1982	27,000,000
3	Led Zeppelin IV, Led Zeppelin, 1971	23,000,000
4	Back in Black, AC/DC, 1980	21,000,000
5	Come On Over, Shania Twain, 1997	20,000,000
6	Rumours, Fleetwood Mac, 1977	19,000,000
7 =	The Bodyguard, Soundtrack, 1992	17,000,000
=	Boston, Boston, 1976	17,000,000
9 =	Greatest Hits, Elton John, 1974	16,000,000
=	Physical Graffiti, Led Zeppelin, 1975	16,000,000
=	Hotel California, The Eagles, 1976	16,000,000
=	No Fences, Garth Brooks, 1990	16,000,000
=	Cracked Rear View, Hootie and the Blowfish, 1994	16,000,000
=	Jagged Little Pill, Alanis Morissette, 1995	16,000,000

Source: RIAA

The Eagles' *Their Greatest Hits, 1971–1975* was the first album ever to be certified platinum (for sales of over one million copies) and long vied with Jackson's *Thriller* as the USA's all-time No. 1.

Still rolling
Mick Jagger and the Rolling Stones have been performing and recording for over 45 years, during which their album releases have put them hard on the heels of Elvis and list-topping Beatles.

THE 10 FIRST FOREIGN* ARTISTS TO TOP THE US ALBUM CHART

	TITLE / ARTIST / NATIONALITY	DATE
1	Crazy Otto, Crazy Otto (German)	May 28, 1955
2	Film Encores, Mantovani and His Orchestra (Italian)	Jul 18, 1959
3	Wonderland By Night, Bert Kaempfert (German)	Jan 21, 1961
4	The Singing Nun, The Singing Nun (Belgian)	Dec 7, 1963
5	Blooming Hits, Paul Mauriat and His Orchestra (French)	Mar 2, 1968
6	Harvest, Neil Young (Canadian)	Mar 11, 1972
7	Sundown, Gordon Lightfoot (Canadian)	Jun 22, 1974
8	Not Fragile, Bachman-Turner Overdrive (Canadian)	Oct 19, 1974
9	Chariots of Fire, Vangelis (Greek)	Apr 17, 1982
10	Business As Usual, Men At Work (Australian)	Nov 13, 1982*

* Excluding UK

Source: Music Information Database

TOP 10 ALBUMS IN THE USA IN THE PAST 10 YEARS

YEAR / TITLE / ARTIST

2006
High School Musical, Soundtrack

2005
The Emancipation of Mimi, Mariah Carey

2004
Confessions, Usher

2003
Get Rich Or Die Tryin', 50 Cent

2002
The Eminem Show, Eminem

2001
Hybrid Theory, Linkin Park

2000
No Strings Attached, *NSync

1999
Millennium, Backstreet Boys

1998
Titanic, Soundtrack

1997
Spice, The Spice Girls

Source: Music Information Database

TOP 10 ALBUMS THAT STAYED LONGEST IN THE US CHARTS

	TITLE / ARTIST	FIRST CHART ENTRY	WEEKS IN CHART
1	The Dark Side of the Moon, Pink Floyd (593)	1973	741
2	Johnny's Greatest Hits, Johnny Mathis (208)	1958	490
3	My Fair Lady, Original Cast (192)	1956	480
4	Highlights from the Phantom of the Opera, Original Cast (331)	1990	331
5	Oklahoma!, Soundtrack (95)	1955	305
6	Tapestry, Carole King (302)	1971	302
7	Heavenly, Johnny Mathis (155)	1959	295
8	MCMXC A.D., Enigma (252)	1991	282
9	Metallica, Metallica (281)	1991	281
10	The King and I, Soundtrack (96)	1956	277

Source: Music Information Database

Numbers in parentheses denote the longest consecutive run on the charts. Three of the albums listed (*Phantom of the Opera*, *Tapestry*, and *Metallica*) all notched up their runs in a single chart stay.

In the pink
Pink Floyd in concert: their iconic The Dark Side of the Moon *made US No. 1 and holds the record for the longest-ever US chart residence—a total of 741 weeks.*

TOP 10 ARTISTS WITH THE MOST NO. 1 ALBUMS IN THE USA

	ARTIST	NO. 1 ALBUMS
1	The Beatles (46)	19
2	Elvis Presley (105)	10
3	The Rolling Stones (45)	9
4	= Barbra Streisand (46)	8
	= Garth Brooks (15)	8
6	= Elton John (39)	7
	= Paul McCartney/Wings (33)	7
	= Bruce Springsteen (21)	7
	= Led Zeppelin (18)	7
10	= Madonna (16)	6
	= U2 (17)	6

Source: Music Information Database

Figures in parentheses denote total chart albums. The comparable list for the UK features the same three artists at Nos. 1, 2, and 3.

Male Singers

TOP 10 **MALE SOLO ARTISTS WITH THE MOST NO. 1 ALBUMS IN THE USA**

	ARTIST (TOTAL CHART HITS)	NO. 1 ALBUMS
1	Elvis Presley (109)	10
2	Garth Brooks (14)	8
3	= Elton John (40)	7
	= Bruce Springsteen (23)	7
5	Jay-Z (11)	6
6	Michael Jackson (18)	5
7	= Frank Sinatra (69)	4
	= 2Pac (12)	4
	= Kenny Chesney (10)	4
	= Eminem (5)	4
	= Billy Joel (20)	4
	= R. Kelly (11)	4
	= Rod Stewart (34)	4

Source: Music Information Database

Left: Career achievement
As he approaches his 50th birthday in 2008,
Michael Jackson's success appears unassailable.

Right: Made in the USA
Bruce Springsteen shares third place in the most
successful artist list with Brit Elton John.

THE 10 **LAST RECORDS BY A FOREIGN MALE ARTIST TO TOP THE US SINGLES CHART** *

	TITLE / ARTIST / NATIONALITY	DATE
1	"Get Busy," Sean Paul (Jamaican)	Mar 10, 2003
2	"Angel," Shaggy feat. Rayvon (Jamaican)	Mar 31, 2001
3	"It Wasn't Me," Shaggy feat. Ricardo "Rikrok" Ducent (Jamaican)	Feb 3, 2001
4	"Be With You," Enrique Iglesias (Spanish)	Jun 24, 2000
5	"Livin' La Vida Loca," Ricky Martin (Puerto Rican)	May 8, 1999
6	"Bailamos," Enrique Iglesias	Sep 4, 1999
7	"Have You Ever Really Loved A Woman?," Bryan Adams (Canadian)	Jun 3, 1995
8	"Here Comes The Hotstepper," Ini Kamoze (Jamaican)	Dec 16, 1994
9	"(Everything I Do) I Do It For You," Bryan Adams	Jul 27, 1991
10	"Get Outta My Dreams, Get Into My Car," Billy Ocean (Trinidadian)	Apr 9, 1988

* Excluding UK acts

Source: Music Information Database

TOP 10 **BESTSELLING ALBUMS BY A MALE ARTIST IN THE USA**

	TITLE / ARTIST / YEAR	SALES
1	Thriller, Michael Jackson, 1982	26,000,000
2	= Greatest Hits, Elton John, 1974	16,000,000
	= No Fences, Garth Brooks, 1990	16,000,000
4	Born in the USA, Bruce Springsteen, 1984	15,000,000
5	= Bat Out of Hell, Meat Loaf, 1977	14,000,000
	= Ropin' the Wind, Garth Brooks, 1991	14,000,000
7	= Breathless, Kenny G, 1992	12,000,000
	= Greatest Hits, Kenny Rogers, 1980	12,000,000
	= No Jacket Required, Phil Collins, 1985	12,000,000
10	= Devil Without a Cause, Kid Rock, 1999	11,000,000
	= James Taylor's Greatest Hits, James Taylor, 1976	11,000,000

Source: RIAA

Within two years of its release, Michael Jackson's *Thriller* album had sold a record total of 20 million copies, but it continued to sell into its second and third decades, being certified for record sales of 26 million copies in 2000. To these US sales must be added those in other countries, bringing the world total to more than 50 million.

TOP 10 **SINGLES BY MALE SOLO SINGERS IN THE USA**

	TITLE / ARTIST	YEAR
1	"Candle in the Wind (1997)"/"Something About the Way You Look Tonight," Elton John	1997
2	"White Christmas," Bing Crosby	1942
3	"Hound Dog"/"Don't Be Cruel," Elvis Presley	1956
4	"Gangsta's Paradise," Coolio featuring L.V.	1995
5	"(Everything I Do) I Do It For You," Bryan Adams	1991
6	"Love Me Tender"/"Any Way You Want Me," Elvis Presley	1956
7	"All Shook Up," Elvis Presley	1957
8	"Jailhouse Rock," Elvis Presley	1957
9	"Heartbreak Hotel"/"I Was the One," Elvis Presley	1956
10	"Baby Got Back," Sir Mix-A-Lot	1992

Source: Music Information Database

THE 10 **FIRST RECORDS BY A UK MALE ARTIST TO TOP THE US SINGLES CHART**

	TITLE / ARTIST	DATE
1	"He's Got the Whole World (In His Hands)," Laurie London	Apr 19, 1958
2	"Stranger on the Shore," Mr. Acker Bilk	May 26, 1962
3	"The Stripper," David Rose	Jul 7, 1963
4	"A World Without Love," Peter & Gordon	Jun 27, 1964
5	"You Make Me Feel Like Dancing," Leo Sayer	Jan 15, 1977
6	"Pop Muzik," M	Nov 3, 1979
7	"(Just Like) Starting Over," John Lennon	Dec 27, 1980
8	"One More Night," Phil Collins	Mar 30, 1985
9	"Sussudio," Phil Collins	Jul 6, 1985
10	"Everytime You Go Away," Paul Young	Jul 27, 1985

Source: Music Information Database

Female Singers

THE 10 LAST RECORDS BY A FOREIGN FEMALE ARTIST TO TOP THE US SINGLES CHART*

	TITLE / NATIONALITY	DATE
1	"My Heart Will Go On," Celine Dion (Canadian)	Feb 28, 1998
2	"Because You Loved Me," Celine Dion	Mar 23, 1996
3	"The Power of Love," Celine Dion	Feb 12, 1994
4	"Coming Out of the Dark," Gloria Estefan (Cuban)	Mar 30, 1991
5	"Nothing Compares 2 U," Sinead O'Connor (Irish)	Apr 21, 1990
6	"Black Velvet," Alannah Myles (Canadian)	Mar 14, 1990
7	"Don't Wanna Lose You," Gloria Estefan	Sep 16, 1989
8	"You Needed Me," Anne Murray (Canadian)	Nov 11, 1978
9	"Angie Baby," Helen Reddy (Australian)	Dec 28, 1974
10	"Delta Dawn," Helen Reddy	Sep 15, 1973

* Excluding UK acts

Source: Music Information Database

Twain makes her mark
Although it combines rock, pop, and country genres, Canadian-born Shania Twain's 1998 album Come On Over *ranks as the all-time bestselling country album in UK, topping the album chart for 11 weeks and selling over 4.8 million copies.*

TOP 10 SINGLES BY FEMALE SOLO SINGERS IN THE USA

	TITLE / ARTIST	YEAR
1	"I Will Always Love You," Whitney Houston	1992
2	"How Do I Live," LeAnn Rimes	1998
3	"Un-break My Heart," Toni Braxton	1996
4	"You're Still the One," Shania Twain	1998
5	"Fantasy," Mariah Carey	1996
6	"Vogue," Madonna	1990
7	"The First Night," Monica	1998
8	"You're Makin'Me High"/"Let It Flow," Toni Braxton	1996
9	"Exhale (Shoop Shoop)," Whitney Houston	1995
10	"You Were Meant For Me," Jewel	1997

TOP 10 ALBUMS BY A FEMALE ARTIST IN THE USA

	TITLE / ARTIST	YEAR
1	Come On Over, Shania Twain	1997
2	Jagged Little Pill, Alanis Morissette	1995
3	...Baby One More Time, Britney Spears	1999
4	Whitney Houston, Whitney Houston	1986
5	Pieces of You, Jewel	1996
6	The Woman in Me, Shania Twain	1995
7	Falling Into You, Celine Dion	1996
8	Up!, Shania Twain	2002
9	Tapestry, Carole King	1971
10	Music Box, Mariah Carey	1993

Source: Music Information Database

TOP 10 **FEMALE ARTISTS WITH THE MOST NO. 1 SINGLES IN THE USA**

	ARTIST (TOTAL CHART HITS)*	NO. 1 SINGLES
1	Mariah Carey (24)	14
2	= Madonna (51)	12
	= Supremes (40)	12
4	Whitney Houston (31)	11
5	Janet Jackson (28)	10
6	= Paula Abdul (13)	5
	= Diana Ross (34)	5
8	= Britney Spears (13)	4
	= Cher (32)	4
	= Destiny's Child (12)	4
	= Olivia Newton-John (32)	4
	= TLC (15)	4

* Duets and "featuring" are not included

Source: Music Information Database

Golden girl
Following the success of her 1.2 million-selling debut single "...Baby One More Time," Britney Spears enjoyed spectacular success in the US chart.

TOP 10 **ALBUMS BY FEMALE SOLO ARTISTS IN THE USA IN THE PAST 10 YEARS**

YEAR	TITLE / ARTIST
2006	Some Hearts, Carrie Underwood
2005	The Emancipation of Mimi, Mariah Carey
2004	Feels Like Home, Norah Jones
2003	Come Away With Me, Norah Jones
2002	Let Go, Avril Lavigne
2001	A Day Without Rain, Enya
2000	Oops! ... I Did it Again, Britney Spears
1999	...Baby One More Time, Britney Spears
1998	Let's Talk About Love, Celine Dion
1997	Pieces of You, Jewel

Source: Music Information Database

Grammy Awards

THE 10 LATEST GRAMMY POP VOCALISTS OF THE YEAR (MALE)

YEAR* VOCALIST / SONG

2007 John Mayer
"Waiting on the World to Change"

2006 Stevie Wonder
"From the Bottom of My Heart"

2005 John Mayer "Daughters"

2004 Justin Timberlake "Cry Me a River"

2003 John Mayer
"Your Body is a Wonderland"

2002 James Taylor
"Don't Let Me Be Lonely Tonight"

2001 Sting "She Walks this Earth
(Soberana Rosa)"

2000 Sting "Brand New Day"

1999 Eric Clapton "My Father's Eyes"

1998 Elton John
"Candle in the Wind 1997"

* Awards are for singles released during the previous year

THE 10 LATEST GRAMMY AWARDS FOR BEST RAP PERFORMANCE*

YEAR DUO/GROUP

2007 Chamillionaire feat. Krayzie Bone

2006 Black Eyed Peas

2005 Black Eyed Peas

2004 P. Diddy, Murphy Lee and Nelly

2003 OutKast and Killer Mike

2002 OutKast

2001 Dr. Dre and Eminem

2000 The Roots and Erykah Badu

1999 Beastie Boys

1998 Puff Daddy, Faith Evans and 112

* By a duo or group

THE 10 LATEST GRAMMY NEW ARTISTS OF THE YEAR

YEAR* ARTIST

2007 Carrie Underwood

2006 John Legend

2005 Maroon 5

2004 Evanescence

2003 Norah Jones

2002 Alicia Keys

2001 Shelby Lynne

2000 Christina Aguilera

1999 Lauryn Hill

1998 Paula Cole

* Awards are for achievements during the previous year

THE 10 LATEST GRAMMY AWARDS FOR BEST ROCK PERFORMANCE*

YEAR DUO/GROUP

2007 Red Hot Chili Peppers

2006 U2

2005 U2

2004 Bruce Springsteen
& Warren Zevon

2003 Coldplay

2002 U2

2001 U2

2000 Everlast and Santana

1999 Aerosmith

1998 The Wallflowers

* By a duo or group with vocal

THE 10 LATEST WINNERS OF BEST FEMALE POP VOCAL PERFORMANCE GRAMMYS

YEAR* VOCALIST / SONG

2007 Christina Aguilera
"Ain't No Other Man"

2006 Kelly Clarkson
"Since U Been Gone"

2005 Norah Jones
"Sunrise"

2004 Christina Aguilera
"Beautiful"

2003 Norah Jones
"Don't Know Why"

2002 Nelly Furtado
"I'm Like a Bird"

2001 Macy Gray
"I Try"

2000 Sarah McLachlan
"I Will Remember You"

1999 Celine Dion
"My Heart Will Go On"

1998 Sarah McLachlan
"Building a Mystery"

* Awards are for singles released during the previous year

Back on track
Taken from her No. 1 US and UK Back to Basics album, Christina Aguilera's "Ain't No Other Man" single clocked up over one million downloads in the US and won her the Best Female Pop Vocal Performance Grammy.

THE 10 **LATEST GRAMMY RECORDS OF THE YEAR**

YEAR*	SINGLE	PERFORMING ARTIST(S)
2007	"Not Ready to Make Nice"	Dixie Chicks
2006	"Boulevard of Broken Dreams"	Green Day
2005	"Here We Go Again"	Ray Charles & Norah Jones
2004	"Clocks"	Coldplay
2003	"Don't Know Why"	Norah Jones
2002	"Walk On"	U2
2001	"Beautiful Day"	U2
2000	"Smooth"	Rob Thomas & Santana
1999	"My Heart Will Go On"	Celine Dion
1998	"Sunny Came Home"	Shawn Colvin

* Awards are for singles released during the previous year

THE 10 **LATEST GRAMMY ALBUMS OF THE YEAR**

YEAR*	ALBUM	PERFORMING ARTIST(S)
2007	Taking the Long Way	Dixie Chicks
2006	How to Dismantle an Atomic Bomb	U2
2005	Genius Loves Company	Ray Charles and various artists
2004	Speakerboxxx/The Love Below	OutKast
2003	Come Away with Me	Norah Jones
2002	O Brother, Where Art Thou? (Soundtrack)	Various artists
2001	Two Against Nature	Steely Dan
2000	Supernatural	Santana
1999	The Miseducation of Lauryn Hill	Lauryn Hill
1998	Time Out of Mind	Bob Dylan

* Awards are for albums released during the previous year

Classical Music

TOP 10 CLASSICAL ALBUMS IN THE USA

	TITLE	PERFORMER/ORCHESTRA	YEAR
1	The Three Tenors In Concert	José Carreras, Placido Domingo, Luciano Pavarotti	1990
2	Romanza	Andrea Bocelli	1997
3	Sogno	Andrea Bocelli	1999
4	Voice of an Angel	Charlotte Church	1999
5	Chant	Benedictine Monks of Santo Domingo De Silos	1994
6	The Three Tenors— In Concert 1994	José Carreras, Placido Domingo, Luciano Pavarotti	1994
7	Sacred Arias	Andrea Bocelli	1999
8	Tchaikovsky: Piano Concerto No. 1	Van Cliburn	1958
9	Fantasia (50th Anniversary Edition)	Soundtrack (Philadelphia Orchestra)	1990
10	Perhaps Love	Placido Domingo	1981

Source: Music Information Database

TOP 10 CLASSICAL ALBUMS IN THE USA, 2006

	ALBUM	ARTIST
1	Songs from the Labyrinth	Sting
2	No Boundaries	5 Browns
3	The Flying Dutchman	André Rieu
4	Voice of the Violin	Joshua Bell
5	Sacred Songs	Renée Fleming
6	Tuscany	André Rieu
7	New Year's in Vienna	André Rieu
8	Opera Proibita	Cecilia Bartoli
9	Yo-Yo Ma Plays Ennio Morricone	Yo-Yo Ma with the Roma Sinfonietta Orchestra
10	Silk Road Journeys: Beyond the Horizon	Yo-Yo Ma with the Roma Sinfonietta Orchestra

Source: Billboard

Church music
Charlotte Church's debut album Voice of an Angel *is America's bestselling by a female singer.*

THE 10 LATEST GRAMMY AWARDS FOR BEST CLASSICAL CONTEMPORARY COMPOSITION

YEAR	COMPOSER	WORK
2007	Osvaldo Golijov	Ainadamar: Fountain of Tears
2006	William Bolcom	Songs of Innocence and of Experience
2005	John Adams	On the Transmigration of Souls
2004	Dominick Argento	Casa Guidi
2003	John Tavener	Lamentations and Praises
2002	Christopher Rouse	Concert de Gaudí for Guitar and Orchestra
2001	George Crumb	Star Child
2000	Pierre Boulez	Répons
1999	Krzysztof Penderecki	Violin Concerto No. 2: Metamorphosen
1998	John Adams	El Dorado

TOP 10 OPERAS MOST FREQUENTLY PERFORMED AT THE METROPOLITAN OPERA HOUSE, NEW YORK

	OPERA	COMPOSER	FIRST PERFORMANCE	TOTAL*
1	La Bohème	Giacomo Puccini	Dec 26, 1900	1,183
2	Aïda	Giuseppi Verdi	Nov 12, 1886	1,093
3	Carmen	Georges Bizet	Jan 9, 1884	936
4	La Traviata	Giuseppi Verdi	Nov 5, 1883	919
5	Tosca	Giacomo Puccini	Feb 4, 1901	891
6	Madama Butterfly	Giacomo Puccini	Feb 11, 1907	812
7	Rigoletto	Giuseppi Verdi	Nov 16, 1883	810
8	Faust	Charles Gounod	Oct 22, 1883	727
9	Pagliacci	Ruggero Leoncavallo	Dec 11, 1893	700
10	Cavalleria Rusticana	Pietro Mascagni	Dec 30, 1891	660

* As at January 1, 2007, including performances by company at other venues

Source: Metropolitan Opera

The most popular operas at the Met closely mirror those of the Royal Opera House, London, where *La Bohème*, *Aïda*, and *Carmen* similarly occupy the top three places. The only notable difference is the presence of Vincenzo Bellini's *Norma* in 10th position in London, in place of the Met's *Cavalleria Rusticana*.

THE 10 LATEST WINNERS OF THE BEST CLASSICAL ALBUM GRAMMY AWARD

YEAR*	COMPOSER / TITLE	CONDUCTOR / SOLOIST / ORCHESTRA
2007	Gustav Mahler, Symphony No. 7	Michael Tilson Thomas, San Francisco Symphony Orchestra
2006	William Bolcom, Songs of Innocence and of Experience	Leonard Slatkin, University of Michigan School of Music Symphony Orchestra
2005	John Adams, On the Transmigration of Souls	Lorin Maazel, Brooklyn Youth Chorus and New Choral Artists, New York Philharmonic
2004	Gustav Mahler, Symphony No. 3; Kindertotenlieder	Michael Tilson Thomas, Michelle DeYoung, San Francisco Symphony Orchestra
2003	Vaughan Williams, A Sea Symphony (Symphony No. 1)	Robert Spano, Norman Mackenzie, Brett Polegato, Christine Goerke, Atlanta Symphony Orchestra
2002	Hector Berlioz, Les Troyens	Sir Colin Davis, Ben Heppner, Kenneth Tarver, Michelle De Young, Peter Mattei, Petra Lang, Sara Mingardo, Stephen Milling, London Symphony Orchestra
2001	Dmitri Shostakovich, The String Quartets	Emerson String Quartet
2000	Igor Stravinsky, Firebird; The Right of Spring; Perséphone	Michael Tilson Thomas, Stuart Neill, San Francisco Symphony Orchestra
1999	Samuel Barber, Prayers of Kierkegaard/ Ralph Vaughan Williams, Dona Nobis Pacem/Béla Bartók, Cantata Profana	Robert Shaw, Richard Clement, Nathan Gunn, Atlanta Symphony Orchestra and Chorus
1998	Richard Danielpour, Leon Kirchner, Christopher Rouse, Premieres – Cello Concertos	Yo-Yo Ma, David Zinman, Philadelphia Orchestra

* Awards are for albums released during the previous year

Source: NARAS

TOP 10 LARGEST OPERA HOUSES

	THEATER / LOCATION	CAPACITY*
1	Arena di Verona# Verona, Italy	15,000
2	Metropolitan Opera House New York, USA	3,800
3	NHK Hall Tokyo, Japan	3,677
4	Civic Opera House Chicago, USA	3,563
5	Music Hall Cincinnati, USA	3,516
6	Music Hall Dallas, USA	3,420
7	War Memorial Opera House San Francisco, USA	3,176
8	The Hummingbird Centre Toronto, Canada	3,167
9	Dorothy Chandler Pavilion Los Angeles, USA	3,098
10	Civic Theatre San Diego, USA	2,992

* Seating capacity only, excluding standing
# Open-air venue

Although there are many more venues in the world where opera is also performed, such as the 13,000-seat Municipal Opera Theatre ("Muny") open-air auditorium, St. Louis, this list is limited to those where the principal performances are opera.

Movie Music

TOP 10 **MOVIE MUSICALS ADAPTED FROM STAGE VERSIONS**

	MUSICAL	THEATER OPENING	MOVIE RELEASE
1	Grease	1972	1978
2	Chicago	1975	2002
3	The Sound of Music	1959	1965
4	The Phantom of the Opera	1986	2004
5	Evita	1978	1996
6	The Rocky Horror (Picture) Show	1973	1975
7	Dreamgirls	1981	2006
8	Fiddler on the Roof	1964	1971
9	My Fair Lady	1956	1964
10	The Best Little Whorehouse in Texas	1978	1982

The adapting of stage musicals as films has a long history, with these the most successful cinematic versions of, in most instances, long-running theatrical productions. Some followed even longer routes from stage to screen, having been nonmusical theatrical productions before being adapted as stage musicals, among them the recent success *Chicago*, which started life in 1926 as a play by Maurine Dallas Watkins and was made into two films, *Chicago* (1927) and *Roxie Hart* (1942), before Bob Fosse wrote the 1975 musical.

Still alive
Over 40 years after its release, The Sound of Music *maintains its place among the most successful stage-to-film adaptations.*

TOP 10 **POP STAR MOVIE DEBUTS**

	MOVIE	STAR	YEAR
1	The Bodyguard	Whitney Houston	1992
2	Austin Powers in Goldmember	Beyonce Knowles	2002
3	8 Mile	Eminem	2002
4	Rocky Horror Picture Show	Meat Loaf	1975
5	The Dukes of Hazzard	Jessica Simpson	2005
6	Nine to Five	Dolly Parton	1980
7	Crash	Ludacris	2005
8	Spice World	Spice Girls	1998
9	Money Train	Jennifer Lopez	1995
10	Romeo Must Die	Aaliyah	2000

Since Al Jolson's debut role in the pioneering talkie *The Jazz Singer* (1927), many popular vocalists have made the transition to movies, with those listed ranked as the most successful (although some had minor parts, often uncredited, in movies before starring in these), the first six of them earning more than $100 million each worldwide. Since the 1930s this catalog has included artists of the caliber of Bing Crosby, Marlene Dietrich, Elvis Presley, The Beatles, David Bowie, Sting, Madonna, and Björk.

TOP 10 MGM MUSICALS

	MOVIE	YEAR
1	Victor/Victoria	1982
2	That's Entertainment!	1974
3	The Wizard of Oz	1939
4	De-Lovely	2004
5	Gigi	1958
6	Seven Brides For Seven Brothers	1954
7	I'll Cry Tomorrow	1955
8	High Society	1956
9	The Unsinkable Molly Brown	1964
10	Meet Me in St. Louis	1944

From the earliest years of talking pictures, MGM established itself as the pre-eminent studio for musicals, making some 200 and winning the first Best Picture Oscar for *The Broadway Melody* (1929) and subsequently for *The Great Ziegfeld* (1936), *An American in Paris* (1951), and *Gigi* (1958). MGM's *That's Entertainment*, like its two sequels (1976 and 1994), was a compilation of clips rather than a single narrative film, while *De-Lovely* is a musical biopic based on the life and songs of Cole Porter.

TOP 10 MUSICIAN FILM BIOPICS

	MOVIE	SUBJECT	YEAR
1	Walk the Line	Johnny Cash	2005
2	The Sound of Music	von Trapp family	1965
3	Ray	Ray Charles	2004
4	Shine	David Helfgott	1996
5	Coal Miner's Daughter	Loretta Lynn	1980
6	La Bamba	Ritchie Valens	1987
7	Amadeus	Wolfgang Amadeus Mozart	1984
8	What's Love Got to Do with It	Tina Turner	1993
9	Selena	Selena Quintanilla	1997
10	The Doors	The Doors	1991

Biopics on the lives of famous musicians have been a Hollywood staple for over 50 years. Those within and outside the Top 10 have encompassed both classical and popular musicians, including such artists as Hank Williams (*Your Cheatin' Heart*, 1964), Peter Tchaikovsky (*The Music Lovers*, 1970), Billie Holiday (*Lady Sings the Blues*, 1972), Buddy Holly (*The Buddy Holly Story*, 1978), John Lennon (*Imagine: John Lennon*, 1988), and Jacqueline du Pré (*Hilary and Jackie*, 1998).

TOP 10 SOUNDTRACK ALBUMS IN THE USA

	TITLE	YEAR
1	The Bodyguard	1992
2	Purple Rain	1984
3	Forrest Gump	1994
4	= Dirty Dancing	1987
	= Titanic	1997
6	The Lion King	1994
7	= Footloose	1984
	= Top Gun	1986
9	Grease	1978
10	Saturday Night Fever	1977

Source: RIAA

Over 17 million copies of *The Bodyguard* soundtrack have been sold in North America and a total of 37 million worldwide. It held US No.1 for 20 weeks and won the Album of the Year Grammy Award in 1994.

Profitable line
With world earnings approaching $200 million, Walk the Line has overtaken The Sound of Music as the most successful musical biopic ever.

7

STAGE & SCREEN

Stage

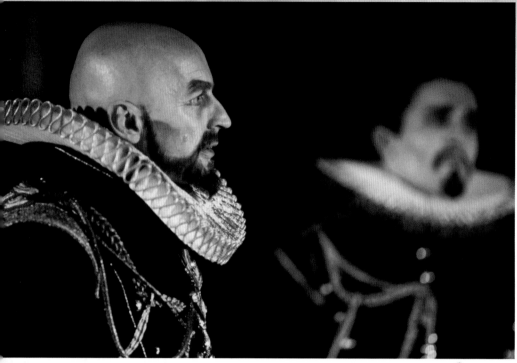

We like it
Although possibly unperformed in his lifetime, Shakespeare's comedy As You Like It *has become the most popular of all his plays in the modern era.*

TOP 10 MOST-PRODUCED PLAYS BY SHAKESPEARE, 1878–2006

	PLAY	PRODUCTIONS
1	As You Like It	80
2	Hamlet	78
3	= The Taming of the Shrew	77
	= Twelfth Night	77
5	A Midsummer Night's Dream	74
6	Much Ado About Nothing	72
7	The Merchant of Venice	70
8	Macbeth	66
9	The Merry Wives of Windsor	62
10	Romeo and Juliet	60

Source: Shakespeare Centre

This list is based on an analysis of Shakespearean productions (rather than individual performances) from December 31, 1878 to December 31, 2006 at Stratford upon Avon and by the Royal Shakespeare Company at home and on tour.

TOP 10 LONGEST-RUNNING MYSTERIES AND THRILLERS ON BROADWAY

	SHOW	RUN	PERFORMANCES
1	Deathtrap	Feb 26, 1978–Jul 13, 1982	1,793
2	Arsenic and Old Lace	Jan 10, 1941–Jun 17, 1944	1,444
3	Angel Street	Dec 5, 1941–Dec 30, 1944	1,295
4	Sleuth	Nov 12, 1970–Oct 13, 1973	1,222
5	The Bat	Aug 23, 1920–Sep 1922	867
6	Dracula	Oct 20, 1977–Jan 6, 1980	925
7	Witness for the Prosecution	Dec 16, 1954–Jun 30, 1956	645
8	Dial "M" for Murder	Oct 29, 1952–Feb 27, 1954	552
9	Sherlock Holmes	Nov 12, 1974–Jan 4, 1976	471
10	An Inspector Calls	Apr 27, 1994–May 28, 1995	454

Deathtrap by Ira Levin opened at the Music Box Theatre. Though nominated for four Tony Awards, it failed to win any, but went on to achieve a record four-year run, transferring for the last six months to the Biltmore Theatre. Marian Seldes appeared in almost every one of its 1,793 performances. The film version of *Deathtrap*, released the year the play closed, starred Michael Caine—who also appeared in *Sleuth*, another Broadway thriller noted for its longevity.

TOP 10 OLDEST BROADWAY THEATERS

	THEATER / OPENING SHOW	OPENED
1	New Victory Theatre (originally Theatre Republic), Sag Harbor	Sep 27, 1900
2	= Lyceum Theatre, The Proud Prince	Nov 2, 1903
	= New Amsterdam Theatre, A Midsummer Night's Dream	Nov 2, 1903
4	Belasco Theatre (originally Stuyvesant), A Grand Army Man	Oct 16, 1907
5	Lunt-Fontanne Theatre, (originally Globe Theatre), The Old Town	Jan 10, 1910
6	Winter Garden Theatre, La Belle Paree	Mar 20, 1911
7	Helen Hayes Theatre, (originally Little Theatre), The Pigeon	Mar 12, 1912
8	Cort Theatre, Peg o' My Heart	Dec 20, 1912
9	Palace Theatre, Vaudeville show	Mar 24, 1913
10	Longacre Theatre, Are You a Crook?	May 1, 1913

Unlike their London counterparts, several of which date back to the 17th century, no Broadway theater can claim an ancestry earlier than 1900. The oldest, the New Victory Theatre, was built by Oscar Hammerstein (1846–1919), the grandfather of the lyricist Oscar Hammerstein II, and underwent a radical makeover in 1995. Outside New York, the Walnut Street Theatre in Philadelphia, Pennsylvania, has operated continuously since it opened in 1809 and is claimed as America's oldest.

Grand Opera
With a run of over 20 years in London and approaching that on Broadway, and numerous productions including a Las Vegas spectacular, The Phantom of the Opera *has become a global phenomenon.*

TOP 10 **LONGEST-RUNNING MUSICALS ON BROADWAY**

SHOW	PERFORMANCES
1 The Phantom of the Opera (Jan 26, 1988–)	8,000*
2 Cats (Sep 23, 1982–Sep 10, 2000)	7,485
3 Les Misérables (Mar 12, 1987–May 18, 2003)	6,680
4 A Chorus Line (Jul 25, 1975–Apr 28, 1990)	6,137
5 Beauty and the Beast (Mar 9, 1994–)	5,328*
6 Rent (Apr 29, 1996–)	4,548*
7 Chicago (Nov 14, 1996–)	4,325*
8 Miss Saigon (Apr 11, 1991–Jan 28, 2001)	4,092
9 The Lion King (Nov 13, 1997–)	3,910*
10 42nd Street (Aug 18, 1980–Jan 8, 89)	3,486

* Still running, total as at April 4, 2007

All the longest-running musicals date from the past 40 years. Prior to these record-breakers, the longest runner of the 1940s was *Oklahoma!*, which debuted in 1943 and ran for 2,212 performances up to 1948, and from the 1950s *My Fair Lady*, which opened in 1956 and closed in 1962 after 2,717 performances. With 3,388 performances, *Grease* (1972–80) just fails to enter the Top 10.

TOP 10 **LONGEST-RUNNING COMEDIES ON BROADWAY**

SHOW	PERFORMANCES
1 Life with Father (Nov 8, 1939–Jul 12, 1947)	3,224
2 Abie's Irish Rose (May 23, 1922–Oct 1, 1927)	2,327
3 Gemini (May 21, 1977–Sep 6, 1981)	1,819
4 Harvey (Nov 1, 1944–Jan 15, 1949)	1,775
5 Born Yesterday (Feb 4, 1946–Dec 31, 1949)	1,642
6 Mary, Mary (Mar 8, 1961–Dec 12, 1964)	1,572
7 The Voice of the Turtle (Dec 8, 1943–Jan 3, 1948)	1,557
8 Barefoot in the Park (Oct 23, 1963–Jun 25, 1967)	1,530
9 Same Time, Next Year (Mar 14, 1975–Sep 3, 1978)	1,453
10 Brighton Beach Memoirs (Mar 27, 1983–May 11, 1986)	1,299

Shown at the Empire Theatre, Howard Lindsay and Russel Crouse's *Life with Father*, adapted from stories in *New Yorker*, owed its success in part to the show's nostalgic view of bygone America that appeared under threat as it opened on the eve of World War II.

Theater Awards

THE 10 **LATEST TONY AWARDS FOR A PLAY**

YEAR	PLAY / PLAYWRIGHT
2007	The History Boys, Alan Bennett
2006	Doubt, John Patrick Shanley
2005	I Am My Own Wife, Doug Wright
2004	Take Me Out, Richard Greenberg
2003	The Goat or Who is Sylvia, Edward Albee
2002	Proof, David Auburn
2001	Copenhagen, Michael Frayn
2000	Side Man, Warren Leight
1999	Art, Yasmina Reza
1998	The Last Night of Ballyhoo, Alfred Uhry

The Tony Awards, established in 1947 by the American Theater Wing, honor outstanding Broadway plays and musicals, actors and actresses, music, costume, and other contributions. They are named for the actress and director Antoinette Perry (1888–1946), who headed the American Theater Wing during World War II.

THE 10 **LATEST TONY AWARDS FOR AN ACTOR**

YEAR	ACTOR / PLAY
2007	Richard Griffiths, The History Boys
2006	Bill Irwin, Who's Afraid of Virginia Woolf?
2005	Jefferson Mays, I Am My Own Wife
2004	Brian Dennehy, Long Day's Journey into Night
2003	Alan Bates, Fortune's Fool
2002	Richard Easton, The Invention of Love
2001	Stephen Dillane, The Real Thing
2000	Brian Dennehy, Death of a Salesman
1999	Anthony LaPaglia, A View From the Bridge
1998	Christopher Plummer, Barrymore

THE 10 **LATEST DRAMA DESK AWARDS FOR AN ACTRESS IN A PLAY**

YEAR	ACTRESS / PLAY
2006	Lois Smith, The Trip to Bountiful
2005	Cherry Jones, Doubt
2004	Viola Davis, Intimate Apparel and Phylicia Rashad, A Raisin in the Sun (tie)
2003	Vanessa Redgrave, Long Day's Journey Into Night
2002	Lindsay Duncan, Private Lives
2001	Mary-Louise Parker, Proof
2000	Eileen Heckart, The Waverly Gallery
1999	Kathleen Chalfant, Wit
1998	Cherry Jones, Pride's Crossing
1997	Janet McTeer, A Doll's House

THE 10 **LATEST DRAMA DESK AWARDS FOR AN ACTOR IN A PLAY**

YEAR	ACTOR / PLAY
2006	Richard Griffiths, The History Boys
2005	Brian F. O'Byrne, Doubt
2004	Kevin Kline, Henry IV
2003	Eddie Izzard, A Day in the Death of Joe Egg
2002	Alan Bates, Fortune's Fool
2001	Richard Easton, The Invention of Love
2000	Stephen Dillane, The Real Thing
1999	Brian Dennehy, Death of a Salesman
1998	Anthony LaPaglia, A View From the Bridge
1997	David Morse, How I Learned to Drive and Christopher Plummer, Barrymore (tie)

Production number
The stage musical version of Mel Brooks' 1968 film The Producers *won a Drama Desk Award for Best Musical.*
The musical of the film about a musical in turn became a musical film (2005).

THE 10 **LATEST DRAMA DESK AWARDS FOR A PLAY**

YEAR	PLAY / PLAYWRIGHT
2006	The History Boys, Alan Bennett
2005	Doubt, John Patrick Shanley
2004	I Am My Own Wife, Doug Wright
2003	Take Me Out, Richard Greenbergn
2002	The Goat or Who is Sylvia, Edward Albee and **Metamorphoses**, Mary Zimmerman (tie)
2001	Proof, David Auburn
2000	Copenhagen, Michael Frayn
1999	Wit, Margaret Edson
1998	The Beauty Queen of Leenane, Martin McDonough
1997	How I Learned to Drive, Paula Vogel

THE 10 **LATEST TONY AWARDS FOR AN ACTRESS**

YEAR	ACTRESS / PLAY
2006	Cynthia Nixon, Rabbit Hole
2005	Cherry Jones, Doubt
2004	Phylicia Rashad, A Raisin in the Sun
2003	Vanesa Redgrave, Long Day's Journey into Night
2002	Lindsay Duncan, Private Lives
2001	Mary-Louise Parker, Proof
2000	Jennifer Ehle, The Real Thing
1999	Judi Dench, Amy's View
1998	Marie Mullen, The Beauty Queen of Leenane
1997	Janet McTeer, A Doll's House

THE 10 **LATEST DRAMA DESK AWARDS FOR A MUSICAL**

YEAR	MUSICAL
2006	The Drowsy Chaperone
2005	Spamalot
2004	Wicked
2003	Hairspray
2002	Thoroughly Modern Millie
2001	The Producers
2000	Contact
1999	Parade
1998	Ragtime
1997	The Life

Film Industry

TOP 10 **COUNTRIES WITH THE MOST CINEMA SCREENS**

COUNTRY / SCREENS (2005)

 China 39,425

 USA 38,852

 India 10,500

 France 5,366

 Germany 4,889

 Spain 4,398

 Italy 3,865

 Mexico 3,544

 UK 3,486

 Canada 2,933

Source: *Screen Digest*

TOP 10 **MOVIE BUDGETS**

	MOVIE	YEAR	ESTIMATED BUDGET ($)
1	Spider-Man 3	2007	300,000,000
2	Superman Returns	2006	270,000,000
3	Pirates of the Caribbean: Dead Man's Chest	2006	225,000,000
4	X-Men: The Last Stand	2006	210,000,000
5	King Kong	2005	207,000,000
6	= Titanic	1997	200,000,000
	= Terminator 3: Rise of the Machines	2003	200,000,000
	= Spider-Man 2	2004	200,000,000
	= Pirates of the Caribbean: At World's End	2007	200,000,000
	= Avatar	2008 *	200,000,000
	= The Curious Case of Benjamin Button	2008 *	200,000,000
	= Battle Angel	2009 *	200,000,000

* Scheduled

Budget burden
Industry sources claim the production budget of Superman Returns *to have been $270 million.*

Bollywood spectacle
Hrishitaa Bhatt in Kisna: The Warrior Poet,
one of more than 1,000 films produced by
the Indian movie industry in 2005.

TOP 10 **YEARS FOR CINEMA ADMISSIONS IN THE USA***

	YEAR	ADMISSIONS
1	1946	4,067,300,000
2	1947	3,664,400,000
3	1948	3,422,700,000
4	1949	3,168,500,000
5	1950	3,017,500,000
6	1951	2,840,100,000
7	1952	2,777,700,000
8	1953	2,630,600,000
9	1954	2,270,400,000
10	1955	2,072,300,000

* 1946–present

Source: Motion Picture Association of America

The year 1955 was the last year on record that US movie attendance was greater than two billion. From 1956, admissions continued to decline (until 1963, when there was a slight increase), in 1971 reaching a low of 820,300,000. Since 1991, admissions have increased each year, in 2002 hitting 1,639,300,000 (a figure last exceeded in 1957), although in 2005 it slipped back to 1,402,700,000.

TOP 10 **MOVIE-PRODUCING COUNTRIES**

	COUNTRY	FEATURE FILMS PRODUCED (2005)
1	India	1,041
2	USA	699
3	Japan	356
4	China	260
5	France	240
6	Russia	160
7	Spain	142
8	UK	124
9	Germany	103
10	Bangladesh	102

Source: *Screen Digest*

Hollywood's "golden age" was the 1920s and 1930s, with 854 films made in 1921, and its nadir 1978 with just 354. In 2005 the USA made 600 movies at a cost of $13,945,000,000, an average of $19,950,000 per movie. Total world feature film production reached 4,603, an increase of 7.8 percent on the previous year, led by growth among European and South American producers. The total cost was $22,598,000,000, an average of less than $5 million per movie.

TOP 10 **COUNTRIES BY BOX-OFFICE REVENUE**

	COUNTRY	ESTIMATED TOTAL BOX-OFFICE GROSS, 2006 ($)
1	USA	9,420,000,000
2	Japan	1,839,600,000
3	UK	1,397,000,000
4	France	1,387,600,000
5	Germany	1,018,300,000
6	Spain	788,300,000
7	Canada	685,900,000
8	Italy	680,200,000
9	Australia	661,000,000
10	Mexico	557,900,000

Source: *Screen Digest*

Blockbuster Movies

TOP 10 **MOVIES OF ALL TIME**

	MOVIE	YEAR	USA	GROSS INCOME ($) OVERSEAS	WORLD TOTAL
1	Titanic*	1997	600,788,188	1,244,246,000	1,845,034,188
2	The Lord of the Rings: The Return of the King	2003	377,027,325	752,191,927	1,129,219,252
3	Pirates of the Caribbean: Dead Man's Chest	2006	423,315,812	642,344,000	1,065,659,812
4	Harry Potter and the Sorcerer's Stone	2001	317,575,550	668,242,109	985,817,659
5	The Lord of the Rings: The Two Towers	2002	341,786,758	584,500,642	926,287,400
6	Star Wars: Episode I— The Phantom Menace	1999	431,088,301	493,229,257	924,317,558
7	Shrek 2#	2004	441,226,247	479,439,411	920,665,658
8	Jurassic Park	1993	357,067,947	562,632,053	919,700,000
9	Harry Potter and the Goblet of Fire	2005	290,013,036	602,200,000	892,213,036
10	Harry Potter and the Chamber of Secrets	2002	261,988,482	614,700,000	876,688,482

* Won Best Picture Oscar
# Animated

Prior to the release of *Star Wars* in 1977, no movie had ever made more than $500 million worldwide. Since then, some 47 films have done so, 15 of them earning over $800 million each. *Titanic* remains the only movie to have made more than this amount in the USA alone, and just 13 films have exceeded this total outside the USA.

Hot pursuit
Pirates of the Caribbean: Dead Man's Chest *became only the third film ever to earn more than $1 billion globally, with the 2007 release of* Pirates of the Caribbean: At World's End, *set to consolidate the success of the series.*

TOP 10 **MOVIES IN THE USA, 2006**

	MOVIE	US GROSS ($)
1	Pirates of the Caribbean: Dead Man's Chest	421,284,468
2	Cars*	244,082,982
3	X-Men: The Last Stand	234,362,462
4	The Da Vinci Code	217,536,138
5	Superman Returns	200,028,903
6	Ice Age: The Meltdown*	195,330,621
7	Over the Hedge*	155,019,340
8	Talladega Nights: The Ballad of Ricky Bobby	148,213,377
9	Click	137,340,146
10	Mission: Impossible III	133,501,348

* Animated

Winning the war
The Star Wars *series has (just) outearned the* Bond *franchise.*

TOP 10 **MOVIES WORLDWIDE, 2006**

MOVIE / WORLDWIDE GROSS, 2006 ($)

  Pirates of the Caribbean: Dead Man's Chest
1,059,696,468

 The Da Vinci Code
756,220,423

 Ice Age: The Meltdown*
646,593,702

 X-Men: The Last Stand
458,602,385

 Cars*
456,005,982

 Mission: Impossible III
395,695,255

 Superman Returns
391,028,903

 Over the Hedge*
319,942,172

 The Devil Wears Prada
233,210,662

Click
224,319,234

* Animated

TOP 10 **MOVIE FRANCHISES OF ALL TIME**

	FRANCHISE	NO. OF MOVIES	YEARS	TOTAL WORLD GROSS ($)*
1	Star Wars	6	1977–2005	4,421,000,000
2	James Bond	21#	1963–2006	4,325,000,000
3	Harry Potter	4	2001–06	3,545,000,000
4	The Lord of the Rings	3	2001–03	2,927,000,000
5	Jurassic Park	3	1993–2001	1,902,000,000
6	Pirates of the Caribbean	2	2003–06	1,720,000,000
7	Batman	5	1989–2005	1,643,000,000
8	The Matrix	3	1999–2003	1,624,000,000
9	Spider-Man	2	2002–04	1,606,000,000
10	Shrek	2	2001–04	1,405,000,000

* Cumulative global earnings of the original film and all its sequels to March 20, 2007
# Excluding "unofficial" *Casino Royale* and *Never Say Never Again*

TOP 10 **OPENING WEEKENDS IN THE USA**

	MOVIE	RELEASE DATE	OPENING WEEKEND GROSS ($)
1	Pirates of the Caribbean: Dead Man's Chest	Jul 7, 2006	135,634,554
2	Spider-Man	May 3, 2002	114,844,116
3	Star Wars: Episode III—Revenge of the Sith	May 19, 2005	108,435,841
4	Shrek 2*	May 19, 2004	108,037,878
5	X-Men: The Last Stand	May 26, 2006	102,750,665
6	Harry Potter and the Goblet of Fire	Nov 18, 2005	102,335,066
7	Harry Potter and the Prisoner of Azkaban	Jun 4, 2004	93,687,367
8	The Matrix Reloaded	May 15, 2003	91,774,413
9	Harry Potter and the Sorcerer's Stone	Nov 16, 2001	90,294,621
10	Harry Potter and the Chamber of Secrets	Nov 15, 2002	88,357,488

* Animated

A high-earning opening weekend (generally three days, Friday to Sunday, but sometimes a four-day holiday weekend) in the USA is usually a pointer to the ongoing success of a movie, but does not guarantee it. Conversely, a movie may start its run relatively quietly and then gather momentum.

Movies Through the Decades

Monster hit
Despite being released during the Depression, King Kong (1933) was one of the most commercially successful movies of the decade and through numerous rereleases.

TOP 10 MOVIES OF THE 1930s

	MOVIE	YEAR	WORLD BOX OFFICE ($)
1	Gone with the Wind*	1939	400,176,459
2	Snow White and the Seven Dwarfs#	1937	187,670,866
3	King Kong	1933	62,815,000
4	The Hurricane	1937	17,300,000
5	The Wizard of Oz	1939	14,800,000
6	Frankenstein	1931	12,000,000
7	Ingagi	1931	4,000,000
8	Top Hat	1935	3,000,000
9	=42nd Street	1933	2,300,000
	=Ninotchka	1939	2,300,000

* Won Best Picture Oscar
# Animated

TOP 10 MOVIES OF THE 1940s

	MOVIE	YEAR	WORLD BOX OFFICE ($)
1	Bambi*	1942	267,997,150
2	Pinocchio*	1940	84,254,167
3	Fantasia*	1940	76,408,097
4	Song of the South#	1946	65,000,000
5	Samson and Delilah	1949	28,800,000
6	The Best Years of Our Lives†	1946	23,650,000
7	The Bells of St Mary's	1945	21,333,333
8	Duel in the Sun	1946	20,408,163
9	This is the Army	1943	19,500,000
10	The Jolson Story	1946	19,000,000

* Animated
# Part animated, part live action
† Won Best Picture Oscar

TOP 10 MOVIES OF THE 1950s

	MOVIE	YEAR	WORLD BOX OFFICE ($)
1	Lady and The Tramp*	1955	93,602,326
2	Peter Pan*	1953	87,404,651
3	The Ten Commandments	1956	80,000,000
4	Ben-Hur#	1959	74,000,000
5	Sleeping Beauty*	1959	51,600,000
6	Around the World in 80 Days#	1956	42,000,000
7	This is Cinerama	1952	41,600,000
8	South Pacific	1958	36,800,000
9	Rear Window	1954	36,764,313
10	=The Greatest Show on Earth#	1952	36,000,000
	=The Robe	1953	36,000,000

* Animated
# Won Best Picture Oscar

TOP 10 MOVIES OF THE 1960s

	MOVIE	YEAR	WORLD BOX OFFICE ($)
1	One Hundred and One Dalmatians	1961	224,000,000
2	The Jungle Book*	1967	205,843,612
3	2001: A Space Odyssey	1968	190,700,000
4	The Sound of Music#	1965	163,214,286
5	Thunderball	1965	141,195,658
6	Goldfinger	1964	124,881,062
7	Doctor Zhivago	1965	112,950,721
8	You Only Live Twice	1967	111,584,787
9	The Graduate	1967	104,397,102
10	Butch Cassidy and the Sundance Kid	1969	102,308,889

* Animated
# Won Best Picture Oscar

Over the moon
E.T. *was the 1980s' biggest earner, and the 16th of all time.*

TOP 10 **MOVIES OF THE** 1970s

MOVIE	YEAR	WORLD BOX OFFICE ($)
1 Star Wars: Episode IV— A New Hope	1977	775,398,007
2 Jaws	1975	470,653,000
3 The Exorcist	1973	441,071,011
4 Grease	1978	394,589,888
5 Close Encounters of the Third Kind	1977	303,788,635
6 Superman	1978	300,218,018
7 Saturday Night Fever	1977	285,400,000
8 The Godfather*	1972	245,044,459
9 Jaws 2	1978	209,040,376
10 Moonraker	1979	202,708,099

* Won Best Picture Oscar

TOP 10 **MOVIES OF THE** 1980s

MOVIE	YEAR	WORLD BOX OFFICE ($)
1 E.T. the Extra-Terrestrial	1982	792,910,554
2 Star Wars: Episode VI— Return of the Jedi	1983	573,006,177
3 Star Wars: Episode V— The Empire Strikes Back	1980	538,375,067
4 Indiana Jones and the Last Crusade	1989	494,771,806
5 Rain Man*	1988	416,011,462
6 Batman	1989	413,388,924
7 Raiders of the Lost Ark	1981	384,140,454
8 Back to the Future	1985	381,109,762
9 Top Gun	1986	353,816,701
10 Indiana Jones and the Temple of Doom	1984	333,107,271

* Won Best Picture Oscar

TOP 10 **MOVIES OF THE** 1990s

MOVIE	YEAR	WORLD BOX OFFICE ($)
1 Titanic*	1997	1,845,034,188
2 Star Wars: Episode I— The Phantom Menace	1999	924,317,554
3 Jurassic Park	1993	919,700,000
4 Independence Day	1996	816,969,255
5 The Lion King#	1994	783,841,776
6 Forrest Gump*	1994	677,386,686
7 The Sixth Sense	1999	672,804,617
8 Jurassic Park: The Lost World	1997	618,638,999
9 Men in Black	1997	589,390,539
10 Armageddon	1998	553,709,788

* Won Best Picture Oscar
# Animated

TOP 10 **MOVIES OF THE** 2000s*

MOVIE	YEAR	WORLD BOX OFFICE ($)
1 The Lord of the Rings: The Return of the King#	2003	1,129,219,252
2 Pirates of the Caribbean: Dead Man's Chest	2006	1,065,659,812
3 Harry Potter and the Sorcerer's Stone	2001	985,817,659
4 The Lord of the Rings: The Two Towers	2002	926,287,400
5 Shrek 2†	2004	920,665,658
6 Harry Potter and the Goblet of Fire	2005	892,213,036
7 Harry Potter and the Chamber of Secrets	2002	876,688,482
8 The Lord of the Rings: The Fellowship of the Ring	2001	871,368,364
9 Finding Nemo†	2003	864,625,978
10 Star Wars: Episode III – Revenge of the Sith	2005	848,797,674

* To end of 2006
# Won Best Picture Oscar
† Animated

Movie Genres

Crossing America
Borat's tour of the USA crosses the road-trip and mockumentary genres, topping both in world earnings of $250 million.

TOP 10 **DISASTER MOVIES**

MOVIE / YEAR

1 Titanic
1997

2 Armageddon
1998

3 The Day After Tomorrow
2004

4 Twister
1996

5 Die Hard: With a Vengeance
1995

6 Apollo 13
1995

7 Deep Impact
1998

8 The Perfect Storm
2000

9 Die Hard 2: Die Harder
1990

10 Outbreak
1995

Excluding science-fiction subjects (alien attacks, rampaging dinosaurs, and other fantasy themes), disasters involving blazing buildings, natural disasters such as volcanoes, earthquakes, tidal waves, train and air crashes, sinking ships, and terrorist attacks, have long been a staple of Hollywood movies, while latterly asteroid impacts, tornadoes, exploding space capsules, and killer viruses have been added to the genre.

TOP 10 **COMEDY ROAD-TRIP MOVIES**

MOVIE	YEAR
1 Borat: Cultural Learnings of America for Make Benefit Glorious Nation of Kazakhstan	2006
2 Dumb and Dumber	1994
3 Road Trip	2000
4 The Blues Brothers	1980
5 Sideways	2004
6 Are We There Yet?	2005
7 Little Miss Sunshine	2006
8 Forces of Nature	1999
9 RV	2006
10 Rat Race	2001

TOP 10 **MOVIES ADAPTED FROM COMICS**

MOVIE*	COMIC FIRST PUBLISHED	MOVIE RELEASED
1 Spider-Man	1962	2002
2 Men in Black	1990	1997
3 X-Men: The Last Stand	1963	2006
4 Batman	1939	1989
5 Superman Returns	1938	2006
6 The Mask	1991	1994
7 Fantastic Four	1961	2005
8 Superman	1938	1978
9 Casper#	1949	1995
10 Hulk	1962	2003

* If series, highest-earning only
\# Original movie made 1946

The transition from cartoons and comic strips to film has been commonplace since the 1920s, and there are many popular predecessors to those appearing in the Top 10, each of which earned over $245 million at the global box office. Disney's animated *Tarzan* (1999) has been excluded since although Tarzan became a comic strip in 1929, the film derived from Edgar Rice Burroughs' 1914 *Tarzan of the Apes* novel and its sequels.

TOP 10 **MOCKUMENTARIES**

MOVIE	YEAR
1 Borat: Cultural Learnings of America for Make Benefit Glorious Nation of Kazakhstan	2006
2 Best in Show	2000
3 A Mighty Wind	2003
4 Drop Dead Gorgeous	1999
5 Zelig	1983
6 Sweet and Lowdown	1999
7 Take the Money and Run	1969
8 For Your Consideration	2006
9 Bob Roberts	1992
10 This is Spinal Tap	1984

Spoof comedy documentaries by Christopher Guest (2, 3, and 8) and Woody Allen (5, 6, and 7) feature prominently in this list.

TOP 10 **TREASURE-HUNT MOVIES**

MOVIE	YEAR
1 Pirates of the Caribbean: Dead Man's Chest	2006
2 Pirates of the Caribbean: The Curse of the Black Pearl	2003
3 Indiana Jones and the Last Crusade	1989
4 Raiders of the Lost Ark	1981
5 National Treasure	2004
6 Lara Croft: Tomb Raider	2001
7 Lara Croft Tomb Raider: The Cradle of Life	2003
8 Sahara	2005
9 Romancing the Stone	1984
10 Treasure Planet	2002

TOP 10 **CHRISTMAS MOVIES**

MOVIE	YEAR
1 Dr. Seuss's How the Grinch Stole Christmas	2000
2 The Santa Clause	1994
3 The Santa Clause 2: The Mrs Clause	2002
4 Jingle All the Way	1996
5 The Santa Clause 3: The Escape Clause	2006
6 Christmas with the Kranks	2004
7 Bad Santa	2003
8 The Nightmare Before Christmas	1993
9 National Lampoon's Christmas Vacation	1989
10 Scrooged	1988

These are movies in which Christmas and/or Santa Claus provide the principal theme, rather than films containing Christmas or holiday scenes—which would be led by movies such as *Home Alone*. The top five in the list earned over $100 million each worldwide, with the No. 1 scooping a festive $345 million.

TOP 10 **JAMES BOND MOVIES**

MOVIE	BOND ACTOR	YEAR
1 Casino Royale	Daniel Craig	2006
2 Die Another Day	Pierce Brosnan	2002
3 The World is Not Enough	Pierce Brosnan	1999
4 GoldenEye	Pierce Brosnan	1995
5 Tomorrow Never Dies	Pierce Brosnan	1997
6 Moonraker	Roger Moore	1979
7 For Your Eyes Only	Roger Moore	1981
8 The Living Daylights	Timothy Dalton	1987
9 The Spy Who Loved Me	Roger Moore	1977
10 Octopussy	Roger Moore	1983

Ian Fleming wrote 12 James Bond novels, only two of which—*Moonraker* (1955) and *The Spy Who Loved Me* (1962)—figure in this Top 10. After his death in 1964, *For Your Eyes Only*, *Octopussy*, *The Living Daylights* and *GoldenEye* were developed by other writers from his short stories, while subsequent releases were written without reference to Fleming's writings. The original *Casino Royale* (book 1953, movie 1967), featuring 56-year-old David Niven as the retired spy Sir James Bond, is an oddity in that it was presented as a comedy. This and *Never Say Never Again* (1983), effectively a remake of *Thunderball*, are not considered "official" Bond movies, making the 2006 *Casino Royale* the 21st in the canonical series.

High-yield Bond
Casino Royale, *Daniel Craig's debut as James Bond, is the highest-earning Bond film to date. Craig is also to star in the 22nd in the series, scheduled for release in 2008.*

Animated Movies

Ice breaker
Ice Age: The Meltdown *was made with a budget of $80 million, but has earned more than eight times as much worldwide.*

TOP 10 **ANIMATED MOVIES**

	MOVIE	YEAR	WORLDWIDE TOTAL GROSS ($)
1	Shrek 2*	2004	920,665,658
2	Finding Nemo#	2003	864,625,978
3	The Lion King#	1994	783,841,776
4	Ice Age: The Meltdown†	2006	651,552,216
5	The Incredibles#	2004	631,436,092
6	Monsters, Inc.#	2001	529,061,238
7	Madagascar*	2005	528,898,225
8	Aladdin#	1992	504,050,219
9	Toy Story 2#	1999	485,015,179
10	Shrek*	2001	484,409,218

* DreamWorks
\# Disney
† 20th Century Fox Animation

TOP 10 **ANIMATED MOVIE BUDGETS**

	MOVIE	YEAR	BUDGET ($)
1	The Polar Express	2004	170,000,000
2	Tarzan	1999	145,000,000
3	Flushed Away	2006	143,000,000
4	Treasure Planet	2002	140,000,000
5	Final Fantasy: The Spirits Within	2001	137,000,000
6	Dinosaur	2000	127,500,000
7	Cars	2006	120,000,000
8	Monsters, Inc.	2001	115,000,000
9	Home on the Range	2004	110,000,000
10	The Emperor's New Groove	2000	100,000,000

Snow White and the Seven Dwarfs (1937) set a record animated movie budget of $1.49 million. Subsequent milestones include *Pinocchio* (1940) at $2.28 million, *Sleeping Beauty* (1959) $6 million, *Robin Hood* (1973) $15 million, and *The Lion King* (1994) $79.3 million.

TOP 10 **ANIMATED MOVIE OPENING WEEKENDS IN THE USA**

	MOVIE	YEAR	OPENING WEEKEND GROSS ($)
1	Shrek 2	2004	108,037,878
2	The Incredibles	2004	70,467,623
3	Finding Nemo	2003	70,251,710
4	Ice Age: The Meltdown	2006	68,033,544
5	Monsters, Inc.	2001	62,577,067
6	Cars	2006	60,119,509
7	Toy Story 2*	1999	57,388,839
8	Shark Tale	2004	47,604,606
9	Madagascar	2005	47,224,594
10	Ice Age	2002	46,312,454

* Second weekend; opening weekend release in limited number of theaters only

TOP 10 **ANIMATED MOVIES IN THE USA**

	MOVIE	YEAR	US TOTAL GROSS ($)
1	Shrek 2*	2004	441,226,247
2	Finding Nemo#	2003	339,714,978
3	The Lion King#	1994	328,541,776
4	Shrek*	2001	267,665,011
5	The Incredibles#	2004	261,441,092
6	Monsters, Inc.#	2001	255,873,250
7	Toy Story 2#	1999	245,852,179
8	Cars#	2006	244,082,982
9	Aladdin*	1992	217,350,219
10	Ice Age: The Meltdown†	2006	195,330,621

* DreamWorks # Disney † 20th Century Fox Animation

THE 10 **LATEST WINNERS OF ANNIE AWARDS FOR BEST ANIMATED FEATURE**

YEAR*	MOVIE
2006	Cars
2005	Wallace & Gromit: The Curse of the Were-Rabbit
2004	The Incredibles
2003	Finding Nemo
2002	Spirited Away
2001	Shrek
2000	Toy Story 2
1999	The Iron Giant
1998	Mulan
1997	Cats Don't Dance

* Of movie—awards are made the following year

The Annie Awards have been presented by the International Animated Film Society (ASIFA-Hollywood) since 1972. In addition to the individual and specialist category awards presented from then, it has been honoring Best Animated Features (originally Outstanding Achievement in an Animated Theatrical Feature) since 1992, when it was won by *Beauty and the Beast*. The Academy Award (Oscar) for Best Animated Feature was first presented in 2001.

Figures of fun
First presented in 1992, the International Animated Film Society's Annie Award went to British feature Wallace & Gromit *in 2005.*

Actors

TOP 10 **JOHNNY DEPP MOVIES**

MOVIE	YEAR
1 Pirates of the Caribbean: Dead Man's Chest	2006
2 Pirates of the Caribbean: The Curse of the Black Pearl	2003
3 Charlie and the Chocolate Factory	2004
4 Sleepy Hollow	1999
5 Platoon	1986
6 Chocolat	2000
7 Donnie Brasco	1997
8 Finding Neverland	2004
9 Desperado II: Once Upon a Time in Mexico	2003
10 Secret Window	2004

The first eight of Johnny Depp's Top 10 movies have earned more than $100 million each, his run of successes led—by a considerable margin—by the first two *Pirates of the Caribbean* films.

TOP 10 **TOM HANKS MOVIES**

MOVIE	YEAR
1 The Da Vinci Code	2006
2 Forrest Gump*	1994
3 Saving Private Ryan	1998
4 Cast Away	2000
5 Apollo 13	1995
6 Catch Me if You Can	2002
7 The Green Mile	1999
8 You've Got M@il	1998
9 Sleepless in Seattle	1993
10 The Terminal	2004

* Won Best Actor Oscar

Tom Hanks also appeared in a voice-only part as Woody in *Toy Story* (1995), *Toy Story 2* (1999), *The Polar Express* (2004), and *Cars* (2006). If included, these would be part of his personal Top 10, every one of which has earned more than $200 million worldwide.

TOP 10 **HARRISON FORD MOVIES**

MOVIE	YEAR
1 Star Wars: Episode IV— A New Hope	1977
2 Star Wars: Episode VI— Return of the Jedi	1983
3 Star Wars: Episode V— The Empire Strikes Back	1980
4 Indiana Jones and the Last Crusade	1989
5 Raiders of the Lost Ark	1981
6 The Fugitive	1993
7 Indiana Jones and the Temple of Doom	1984
8 Air Force One	1997
9 What Lies Beneath	2000
10 Presumed Innocent	1990

Billion-dollar Bloom
British actor Orlando Bloom has starred in two of only three movies ever to earn more than $1 billion worldwide.

TOP 10 **ORLANDO BLOOM MOVIES**

MOVIE	YEAR
1 The Lord of the Rings: The Return of the King	2003
2 Pirates of the Caribbean: Dead Man's Chest	2006
3 The Lord of the Rings: The Two Towers	2002
4 The Lord of the Rings: The Fellowship of the Ring	2001
5 Pirates of the Caribbean: The Curse of the Black Pearl	2003
6 Troy	2004
7 Kingdom of Heaven	2005
8 Black Hawk Down	2001
9 Elizabethtown	2005
10 Ned Kelly	2004

Orlando Bloom's role in *Black Hawk Down* was minor; if discounted, the 10th entry in his Top 10 would be his first movie, *Wilde* (1998)—in which his role was also small—or his most recent, *Haven* (2006).

TOP 10 **DANIEL CRAIG MOVIES**

MOVIE	YEAR
1 Casino Royale	2006
2 Lara Croft: Tomb Raider	2001
3 Road to Perdition	2002
4 Munich	2005
5 Elizabeth	1998
6 The Jacket	2005
7 I Dreamed of Africa	2000
8 A Kid in King Arthur's Court	1995
9 Layer Cake	2004
10 The Power of One	1992

Daniel Wroughton Craig (born 1968) made his film debut in *The Power of One*, but also appeared in numerous TV dramas, including *Our Friends in the North* (1996). His roles in *Lara Croft: Tomb Raider* and *Road to Perdition* secured his fame and led to his casting as the new James Bond in *Casino Royale*. He appears as Lord Asriel in *His Dark Materials: The Golden Compass*, released in 2007.

On the right track
Based on a children's book by Milan Trenc, Night at the Museum, *starring Ben Stiller, received a negative critical response, but has made over $500 million worldwide, placing it among the highest-earning comedies of all time.*

TOP 10 **BEN STILLER MOVIES**

	MOVIE	YEAR
1	Night at the Museum	2006
2	Meet the Fockers	2004
3	There's Something About Mary	1998
4	Meet the Parents	2000
5	Along Came Polly	2004
6	Starsky and Hutch	2004
7	DodgeBall: A True Underdog Story	2004
8	The Cable Guy	1996
9	The Royal Tenenbaums	2001
10	Zoolander	2001

TOP 10 **NICOLAS CAGE MOVIES**

	MOVIE	YEAR
1	National Treasure	2004
2	The Rock	1996
3	Face/Off	1997
4	Gone in 60 Seconds	2000
5	Con Air	1997
6	City of Angels	1998
7	Ghost Rider	2006
8	The Family Man	2000
9	Snake Eyes	1998
10	8MM	1999

TOP 10 **DENZEL WASHINGTON MOVIES**

	MOVIE	YEAR
1	Philadelphia	1993
2	The Pelican Brief	1993
3	Inside Man	2006
4	Déjà Vu	2006
5	Crimson Tide	1995
6	The Bone Collector	1999
7	Remember the Titans	2000
8	Man on Fire	2004
9	The Siege	1998
10	Training Day*	2001

* Won Best Actor Oscar

Actresses

TOP 10 CAMERON DIAZ MOVIES

MOVIE	YEAR
1 There's Something About Mary	1998
2 The Mask	1994
3 My Best Friend's Wedding	1997
4 Charlie's Angels	2000
5 Charlie's Angels: Full Throttle	2003
6 Vanilla Sky	2001
7 Gangs of New York	2002
8 The Holiday	2006
9 Any Given Sunday	1999
10 In Her Shoes	2005

Cameron Diaz's Top 10 movies include some of the highest-earning of recent years, the top nine here having earned between $100 million and $370 million worldwide. She also provided the voice of Princess Fiona in *Shrek* (2001) and *Shrek 2* (2004)—which have outearned them all.

Song and dance
Renée Zellweger stars as Roxie Hart in the film musical Chicago. *Her first singing and dancing role and her most successful film to date, grossing over $300 million globally,* Chicago *was based on a 1975 stage musical, in turn derived from a 1926 play.*

TOP 10 RACHEL WEISZ MOVIES

MOVIE	YEAR
1 The Mummy Returns	2001
2 The Mummy	1999
3 Constantine	2005
4 About a Boy	2002
5 Enemy at the Gates	2001
6 The Constant Gardener	2005
7 Runaway Jury	2003
8 Chain Reaction	1996
9 Confidence	2003
10 Envy	2004

TOP 10 SCARLETT JOHANSSON MOVIES

MOVIE	YEAR
1 The Horse Whisperer	1998
2 The Island	2005
3 Lost in Translation	2003
4 The Prestige	2006
5 Home Alone 3	1997
6 Match Point	2005
7 Just Cause	1995
8 In Good Company	2004
9 The Black Dahlia	2006
10 Eight Legged Freaks	2002

Scarlett Johansson (born 1984) began her career as a child actress in *North* (1994), making *The Horse Whisperer*, her 7th and to date highest-earning movie, by the age of 13. She won the BAFTA Best Actress award for her role in *Lost in Translation*.

TOP 10 RENÉE ZELLWEGER MOVIES

MOVIE	YEAR
1 Chicago*	2002
2 Bridget Jones's Diary	2001
3 Jerry Maguire	1996
4 Bridget Jones: The Edge of Reason	2004
5 Cold Mountain	2003
6 Me, Myself & Irene	2000
7 Cinderella Man	2005
8 Down with Love	2003
9 Nurse Betty	2000
10 The Bachelor	1999

* Won Best Picture Oscar

Renée Zellweger gained consecutive Best Actress Oscar nominations for *Bridget Jones's Diary* (2001) and *Chicago* (2002), and won as Best Actress in a Supporting Role for *Cold Mountain* (2003).

TOP 10 REESE WITHERSPOON MOVIES

MOVIE	YEAR
1 Sweet Home Alabama	2002
2 Walk the Line*	2005
3 Legally Blonde	2001
4 Legally Blonde 2: Red, White and Blonde	2003
5 Just Like Heaven	2005
6 Cruel Intentions	1999
7 Little Nicky	2000
8 Pleasantville	1998
9 American Psycho	2000
10 Fear	1996

* Won Best Actress Oscar

Reese Witherspoon's role in *Little Nicky* was only a cameo; if discounted, her starring part in *Vanity Fair* (2004) occupies 10th place among her highest-earning movies.

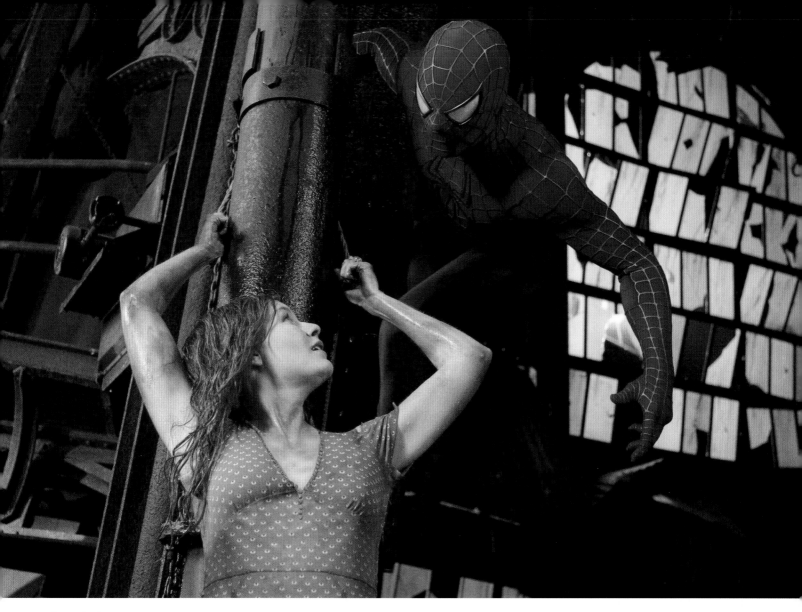

Second spin
Kirsten Dunst in Spider-Man 2. *The first two movies in the franchise earned a total of $1.6 billion at the world box office.*

TOP 10 **KIRSTEN DUNST** MOVIES

	MOVIE	YEAR
1	Spider-Man	2002
2	Spider-Man 2	2004
3	Jumanji	1995
4	Interview with the Vampire: The Vampire Chronicles	1994
5	Mona Lisa Smile	2003
6	Bring It On	2000
7	Small Soldiers	1998
8	Eternal Sunshine of the Spotless Mind	2004
9	Wag the Dog	1997
10	Marie Antoinette	2006

TOP 10 **KEIRA KNIGHTLEY** MOVIES

	MOVIE	YEAR
1	Pirates of the Caribbean: Dead Man's Chest	2006
2	Star Wars: Episode I— The Phantom Menace	1999
3	Pirates of the Caribbean: The Curse of the Black Pearl	2003
4	Love Actually	2003
5	King Arthur	2004
6	Pride and Prejudice	2005
7	Bend it Like Beckham	2003
8	Domino	2005
9	The Jacket	2005
10	Pure	2005

TOP 10 **KATE WINSLET** MOVIES

	MOVIE	YEAR
1	Titanic*	1997
2	The Holiday	2006
3	Sense and Sensibility	1995
4	Finding Neverland	2004
5	Eternal Sunshine of the Spotless Mind	2004
6	The Life of David Gale	2003
7	Quills	2000
8	Iris	2001
9	Enigma	2001
10	A Kid in King Arthur's Court	1995

* Won Best Picture Oscar

Best Picture Oscars

THE 10 FIRST COLOR MOVIES TO WIN BEST PICTURE OSCARS*

MOVIE	YEAR
1 Gone With the Wind	1939
2 An American in Paris	1951
3 The Greatest Show on Earth	1952
4 Around the World in 80 Days	1956
5 The Bridge on the River Kwai	1957
6 Gigi	1958
7 Ben-Hur	1959
8 West Side Story	1961
9 Lawrence of Arabia	1962
10 Tom Jones	1963

* Oscar® is a Registered Trade Mark

THE 10 LAST BLACK-AND-WHITE MOVIES TO WIN BEST PICTURE OSCARS

MOVIE	YEAR
1 Schindler's List*	1993
2 The Apartment	1960
3 Marty	1955
4 On the Waterfront	1954
5 From Here to Eternity	1953
6 All About Eve	1950
7 All the King's Men	1949
8 Hamlet	1948
9 Gentleman's Agreement	1947
10 The Best Years of Our Lives	1946

* With color sequences

THE 10 LATEST BEST PICTURE OSCAR-WINNERS ADAPTED FROM A NOVEL

MOVIE	YEAR
1 The Lord of the Rings: The Return of the King	2003
2 A Beautiful Mind	2001
3 The English Patient	1996
4 Forrest Gump	1994
5 Schindler's List	1993
6 The Silence of the Lambs	1991
7 Dances with Wolves	1990
8 Out of Africa	1985
9 Terms of Endearment	1983
10 Ordinary People	1980

The third-ever Oscar-winner, *All Quiet on the Western Front* (1930), based on a novel by Erich Maria Remarque, was the first adapted work of fiction.

Above: List topper
Schindler's List *is the only black-and-white film to win a Best Picture Oscar since 1960.*

Left: Scarlett in color
Gone with the Wind *won 10 Oscars, including Best Picture—the first color film to do so.*

The Departed *arrives*
As well as winning Oscars for Best Picture, Adapted Screenplay, and Editing, The Departed gained its director Martin Scorsese his first Academy Award after eight nominations since 1980.

TOP 10 **LONGEST BEST PICTURE OSCAR MOVIES**

	MOVIE / YEAR	LENGTH (MINS)
1	Gone with the Wind 1939	238
2	Lawrence of Arabia 1962	216
3	Ben-Hur 1959	212
4	The Lord of the Rings: The Return of the King 2003	201
5	The Godfather: Part II 1974	200
6	Schindler's List 1993	197
7	Titanic 1997	194
8	Gandhi 1982	188
9	=Dances with Wolves 1990	183
	=The Deer Hunter 1978	183

THE 10 **SHORTEST BEST PICTURE OSCAR MOVIES**

	MOVIE / YEAR	LENGTH (MINS)
1	Marty 1955	91
2	Annie Hall 1977	93
3	Driving Miss Daisy 1989	99
4	The Lost Weekend 1945	101
5	Casablanca 1942	102
6	The French Connection 1971	104
7	=It Happened One Night 1934	105
	=Kramer vs. Kramer 1979	105
9	On the Waterfront 1954	108
10	=In the Heat of the Night 1967	109
	=All the King's Men 1949	109

THE 10 **LATEST BEST PICTURE OSCAR-WINNERS**

YEAR	MOVIE / DIRECTOR
2006	The Departed Martin Scorsese
2005	Crash Paul Haggis*
2004	Million Dollar Baby Clint Eastwood
2003	The Lord of the Rings: The Return of the King Peter Jackson
2002	Chicago Rob Marshall*
2001	A Beautiful Mind Ron Howard
2000	Gladiator Ridley Scott*
1999	American Beauty Sam Mendes
1998	Shakespeare in Love John Madden*
1997	Titanic James Cameron

* Did not also win Best Director Oscar

Oscar-Winning Actors

TOP 10 **ACTORS WITH THE MOST NOMINATIONS***

	ACTOR	WINS SUPPORTING	WINS BEST	NOMINATIONS
1	Jack Nicholson	1	2	12
2	Laurence Olivier	0	1	10
3	= Paul Newman	0	1	9
	= Spencer Tracy	0	2	9
5	= Marlon Brando	0	2	8
	= Jack Lemmon	1	1	8
	= Al Pacino	0	1	8
	= Peter O'Toole	0	0	8
9	= Richard Burton	0	0	7
	= Dustin Hoffman	0	2	7

* In all acting categories

Left: Here's Jack!
Out of his dozen nominations, Jack Nicholson won Oscars for One Flew Over the Cuckoo's Nest *(1975),* Terms of Endearment *(1983), and* As Good as It Gets *(1997).*

TOP 10 **ACTORS WITH THE MOST NOMINATIONS WITHOUT A WIN***

	ACTOR	NOMINATIONS
1	Peter O'Toole	8
2	Richard Burton	7
3	= Albert Finney	5
	= Arthur Kennedy	5
5	= Warren Beatty	4
	= Charles Boyer	4
	= Jeff Bridges	4
	= Montgomery Clift	4
	= Ed Harris	4
	= Claude Rains	4
	= Mickey Rooney	4

* In any acting categories

THE 10 **LATEST ACTORS TO WIN A BEST ACTOR OSCAR WITH THEIR ONE AND ONLY NOMINATION**

	ACTOR	MOVIE	YEAR
1	Forest Whitaker	The Last King of Scotland	2006
2	Philip Seymour Hoffman	Capote	2005
3	Jamie Foxx	Ray	2004
4	Adrien Brody	The Pianist	2002
5	Roberto Benigni	La Vita è Bela/ Life is Beautiful	1998
6	Jeremy Irons	Reversal of Fortune	1990
7	Michael Douglas	Wall Street	1987
8	F. Murray Abraham	Amadeus	1984
9	Art Carney	Harry and Tonto	1974
10	Cliff Robertson	Charly	1968

In the first year of the Oscars, Emil Jannings won for two films, but since single-film nominations have been the norm, all these actors won the Oscar after being nominated in this category once and never again.

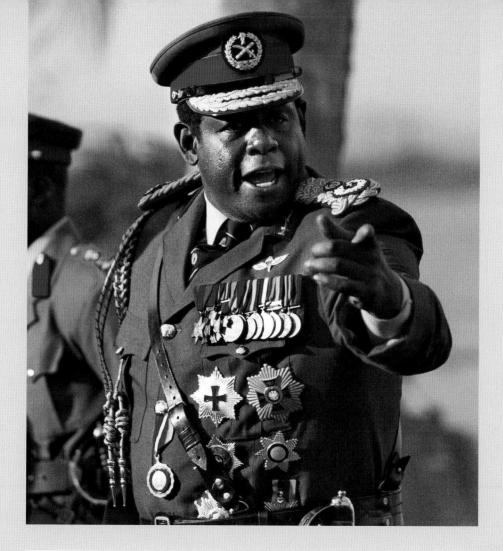

Last first
Best Actor Oscar-winner Forest Whitaker as Idi Amin in The Last King of Scotland.

THE 10 **LATEST BEST ACTOR OSCAR-WINNERS**

YEAR	ACTOR / MOVIE
2006	**Forest Whitaker** The Last King of Scotland
2005	**Philip Seymour Hoffman** Capote
2004	**Jamie Foxx** Ray
2003	**Sean Penn** Mystic River
2002	**Adrien Brody** The Pianist
2001	**Denzel Washington** Training Day
2000	**Russell Crowe** Gladiator*
1999	**Kevin Spacey** American Beauty*
1998	**Roberto Benigni** Life is Beautiful
1997	**Jack Nicholson** As Good as It Gets

* Won Best Picture Oscar

TOP 10 **OLDEST OSCAR-WINNING ACTORS**

	ACTOR	MOVIE	YEAR	YEARS	AGE* MONTHS	DAYS
1	George Burns	The Sunshine Boys	1975	80	2	9
2	Melvyn Douglas	Being There	1979	79	0	9
3	John Gielgud	Arthur	1981	77	11	15
4	Don Ameche	Cocoon	1985	77	9	24
5	Henry Fonda	On Golden Pond	1981	76	10	13
6	Edmund Gwenn	Miracle on 34th Street	1947	72	5	24
7	Jack Palance	City Slickers	1991	72	0	1
8	John Houseman	The Paper Chase	1973	71	6	0
9	Morgan Freeman	Million Dollar Baby#	2004	67	8	27
10	Charles Coburn	The More the Merrier	1943	66	8	13

* At the time of the Award ceremony
# Won Best Picture Oscar

All the Academy Awards listed are for Best Supporting Actor, apart from Henry Fonda's award for Best Actor in *On Golden Pond*. The oldest person to win the Best Actor award prior to Henry Fonda was John Wayne, who was 62 when he received his 1969 award for *True Grit*.

Oscar-Winning Actresses

THE 10 YOUNGEST OSCAR-WINNING ACTRESSES

	ACTRESS	AWARD / MOVIE (WHERE SPECIFIED)	YEAR	AGE* YRS	MTHS	DAYS
1	Shirley Temple	Special Award: Outstanding Contribution during 1934	1934	6	10	4
2	Margaret O'Brien	Special Award: Outstanding Child Actress of 1944 (Meet Me in St. Louis)	1944	8	2	0
3	Tatum O'Neal	Best Supporting Actress (Paper Moon)	1973	10	4	28
4	Anna Paquin	Best Supporting Actress (The Piano)	1993	11	7	25
5	Hayley Mills	Special Award: Outstanding Juvenile Performance of 1960 (Pollyanna)	1960	13	11	30
6	Peggy Ann Garner	Special Award: Outstanding Child Performer of 1945 (A Tree Grows in Brooklyn)	1945	14	4	18
7	Patty Duke	Best Supporting Actress (The Miracle Worker)	1962	16	3	25
8	Deanna Durbin	Special Award: Juvenile Players Setting a High Standard of Ability and Achievement#	1938	17	2	19
9	Judy Garland	Special Award (Wizard of Oz)	1939	17	8	19
10	Marlee Matlin	Best Actress (Children of a Lesser God)	1986	21	7	6

* At the time of the Award ceremony
\# Shared with fellow teen star Mickey Rooney

British actress Hayley Mills, the 12th and last winner of the Special Award miniature Oscar, won her award precisely one day before her 14th birthday. Subsequent winners have had to compete on the same basis as adult actors and actresses for the major acting awards. Tatum O'Neal is thus the youngest winner of—as well as the youngest ever nominee for—an "adult" Oscar. The youngest Best Actress nominee is Keisha Castle-Hughes (Australia), who was 13 in 2004 when she was nominated for her role in *Whale Rider*. The Academy Awards ceremony usually takes place at the end of February in the year following that in which the movie was released, so the winners are generally at least a year older when they receive their Oscars than when they acted in their award-winning movies.

Child star
Shirley Temple made her first film at the age of three and won a special Oscar at six.

TOP 10 ACTRESSES WITH THE MOST OSCAR NOMINATIONS*

	ACTRESS	WINS SUPPORTING	BEST	NOMS
1	Meryl Streep	1	1	14
2	Katharine Hepburn	0	4	12
3	Bette Davis	0	2	10
4	Geraldine Page	0	1	8
5 =	Ingrid Bergman	1	2	7
=	Jane Fonda	0	2	7
=	Greer Garson	0	1	7
8 =	Ellen Burstyn	0	1	6
=	Judi Dench	1	0	6
=	Deborah Kerr	0	0	6
=	Jessica Lange	1	1	6
=	Vanessa Redgrave	1	0	6
=	Thelma Ritter	0	0	6
=	Norma Shearer	0	0	6
=	Maggie Smith	1	1	6
=	Sissy Spacek	0	1	6

* In all acting categories

THE 10 LATEST BEST SUPPORTING ACTRESS OSCAR-WINNERS

YEAR	ACTRESS / MOVIE
2006	Jennifer Hudson — Dreamgirls
2005	Rachel Weisz — The Constant Gardener
2004	Cate Blanchett — The Aviator
2003	Renée Zellweger — Cold Mountain
2002	Catherine Zeta Jones — Chicago*
2001	Jennifer Connelly — A Beautiful Mind*
2000	Marcia Gay Harden — Pollock
1999	Angelina Jolie — Girl, Interrupted
1998	Judi Dench — Shakespeare in Love*
1997	Kim Basinger — L.A. Confidential

* Won Best Picture Oscar

One has won
Helen Mirren's title role in The Queen *earned her the Best Actress Oscar.*

THE 10 **LATEST ACTRESSES TO WIN A BEST ACTRESS OSCAR WITH THEIR ONE AND ONLY NOMINATION**

	ACTRESS	MOVIE	YEAR
1	Reese Witherspoon	Walk the Line	2005
2	Halle Berry	Monster's Ball	2001
3	Gwyneth Paltrow	Shakespeare in Love	1998
4	Helen Hunt	As Good As It Gets	1997
5	Marlee Matlin	Children of a Lesser God	1986
6	Louise Fletcher	One Flew Over the Cuckoo's Nest	1975
7	Grace Kelly	The Country Girl	1954
8	Shirley Booth	Come Back, Little Sheba	1952
9	Judy Holliday	Born Yesterday	1950
10	Ginger Rogers	Kitty Foyle	1940

The first actress to win a Best Actress Oscar with her unique nomination was Mary Pickford for *Coquette* (1929), although in 1976, at the age of 84, she was presented with an honorary award. In the first ceremony in 1929, Janet Gaynor was nominated for and won a Best Actress Oscar for three films.

THE 10 **LATEST BEST ACTRESS OSCAR-WINNERS**

YEAR	ACTRESS / MOVIE
2006	Helen Mirren, The Queen
2005	Reese Witherspoon, Walk the Line
2004	Hilary Swank, Million Dollar Baby*
2003	Charlize Theron, Monster
2002	Nicole Kidman, The Hours
2001	Halle Berry, Monster's Ball
2000	Julia Roberts, Erin Brockovich
1999	Hilary Swank, Boys Don't Cry
1998	Gwyneth Paltrow, Shakespeare in Love*
1997	Helen Hunt, As Good as It Gets

* Won Best Picture Oscar

Other Film Awards

The Wind That Shakes The Barley
Ken Loach's film is the first British Palm d'Or winner since Mike Leigh's Secrets and Lies *in 1996.*

THE **AMERICAN FILM INSTUTUTE'S 10 GREATEST ACTORS**

ACTOR

1 Humphrey Bogart
2 Cary Grant
3 James Stewart
4 Marlon Brando
5 Fred Astaire
6 Henry Fonda
7 Clark Gable
8 James Cagney
9 Spencer Tracy
10 Charlie Chaplin

Source: American Film Institute

THE **AMERICAN FILM INSTUTUTE'S 10 GREATEST FILMS**

FILM

1 Citizen Kane (1941)
2 Casablanca (1942)
3 The Godfather (1972)
4 Gone with the Wind (1939)
5 Lawrence of Arabia (1962)
6 The Wizard of Oz (1939)
7 The Graduate (1967)
8 On the Waterfront (1954)
9 Schindler's List (1993)
10 Singin' in the Rain (1952)

Source: American Film Institute

These are the Top 10 of a long list identified by members of the American movie community for a poll conducted by the American Film Institute.

THE 10 **LATEST PALM D'OR WINNERS AT THE CANNES FILM FESTIVAL**

YEAR*   FILM

2006 The Wind That Shakes the Barley
2005 The Child
2004 Fahrenheit 9/11
2003 Elephant
2002 The Pianist
2001 The Son's Room
2000 Dancer in the Dark
1999 Rosetta
1998 Eternity and a Day
1997 A Taste of Cherry

* Of award

Animal magic Animated movies such as Madagascar *appear high in the annual lists of bestselling DVDs.*

TOP 10 **VIDEO PIRACY COUNTRIES**

	COUNTRY	ESTIMATED LOSSES ($) 2005*
1	Mexico	483,000,000
2	Russia	266,000,000
3	China	244,000,000
4	Italy	161,000,000
5	Thailand	149,000,000
6	Brazil	120,000,000
7	Canada	118,000,000
8	= Hungary	102,000,000
	= Poland	102,000,000
10	Taiwan	98,000,000

* Or latest year for which data available, including illicit broadcasts

Source: International Intellectual Property Alliance (IIPA)

The IIPA calculates that losses affecting the motion picture business—primarily through illicit DVDs, each of them robbing the industry of a legitimate sale—totaled almost $2 billion in 2005.

TOP 10 **DVD RENTALS IN THE USA, 2006**

1 Flightplan
2 Wedding Crashers
3 Walk the Line
4 Failure to Launch
5 Fun With Dick and Jane
6 Click
7 Inside Man
8 King Kong
9 RV
10 Lord of War

Source: Video Business

The total US video rental market (DVD and VHS) in 2006 was worth $7.67 billion. DVD now dominates the market: of the total revenue, VHS accounted for just $281 million (3.7 percent), down from 14.1 percent the previous year.

TOP 10 **VIDEO COUNTRIES**

	COUNTRY	SPENDING ($)*
1	USA	24,915,000,000
2	Japan	6,408,000,000
3	UK	4,973,000,000
4	Canada	2,483,000,000
5	France	2,465,000,000
6	Germany	2,099,000,000
7	Australia	1,347,000,000
8	Spain	917,000,000
9	Italy	880,000,000
10	Netherlands	623,000,000

* 2005, DVD and VHS

Source: *Screen Digest*

TV & Radio

THE 10 FIRST COUNTRIES TO HAVE TELEVISION*

	COUNTRY	DATE
1	UK	Nov 2, 1936
2	USSR	Dec 31, 1938
3	USA	Apr 30, 1939
4	France	Jun 29, 1949
5	Mexico	Aug 31, 1950
6	Brazil	Sep 18, 1950
7	Cuba	Oct 24, 1950
8	=Denmark	Oct 2, 1951
	=Netherlands	Oct 2, 1951
10	Argentina	Oct 17, 1951

* High-definition regular public broadcasting service

TOP 10 COUNTRIES WITH THE MOST TV STATIONS

	COUNTRY	TELEVISION STATIONS
1	Russia	7,306
2	China	3,240
3	USA	2,218
4	Turkey	635
5	France	584
6	India	562
7	South Africa	556
8	Germany	373
9	Norway	360
10	Italy	358

Source: CIA, *The World Factbook 2007*

TOP 10 LONGEST-RUNNING TV SERIES IN THE USA*

	PROGRAM	EPISODES
1	Gunsmoke	633
2	Lassie	588
3	Death Valley Days	452
4	Ozzie and Harriett	435
5	Bonanza	430
6	The Simpsons	1387
7	Law and Order	381
8	My Three Sons	369
9	Alfred Hitchcock Presents	361
10	Dallas	357

* To December 6, 2006

TOP 10 **TV AUDIENCES IN THE USA**

	PROGRAM	DATE	VIEWERS
1	M*A*S*H Special	Feb 28, 1983	50,150,000
2	Dallas	Nov 21, 1980	41,470,000
3	Roots Part 8	Jan 30, 1977	36,380,000
4	Super Bowl XVI	Jan 24, 1982	40,020,000
5	Super Bowl XVII	Jan 30, 1983	40,480,000
6	XVII Winter Olympics	Feb 23, 1994	45,690,000
7	Super Bowl XX	Jan 26, 1986	41,490,000
8	Gone With the Wind Pt.1	Nov 7, 1976	33,960,000
9	Gone With the Wind Pt.2	Nov 8, 1976	33,750,000
10	Super Bowl XII	Jan 15, 1978	34,410,000

Source: Nielsen Media Research

The 2½-hour feature-length "Goodbye, Farewell, and Amen" episode of *M*A*S*H* was the last in a series that had run for more than 10 years. An estimated 50.15 million households, or almost 106 million individual viewers, tuned in, making it the most-watched broadcast of all time. The screening of Dallas gained its audience and hence its position in the list because it was the episode that revealed who had shot J. R. Ewing exactly eight months earlier.

In 2006 there were an estimated 110.2 million television households in the USA, so a single ratings point would represent 1 percent, or 1,102,000 households, and so on. Historically, as more households acquired television sets, audiences generally increased, but the rise in channel choice and use of recording has checked this trend, and it is unlikely that such high viewing figures will ever again be attained.

TOP 10 **TV COUNTRIES***

1 China 186,679,720

2 USA 112,884,190

3 India 83,512,900

4 Japan 48,842,920

5 Brazil 48,390,910

6 Russia 40,822,010

7 Germany 38,715,850

8 Indonesia 34,334,330

9 UK 25,269,160

10 France 24,369,170

World total 1,176,019,000

* Households with color TVs, 2007 forecast Source: Euromonitor

THE 10 **LAST EMMY COMEDY AWARD-WINNNG SERIES***

YEAR	SHOW / NETWORK
2006	The Office, NBC
2005	Everybody Loves Raymond, CBS
2004	Arrested Development, Fox
2003	Everybody Loves Raymond, CBS
2002	Friends, NBC
2001	Sex and the City, HBO
2000	Will & Grace, NBC
1999	Ally McBeal, FOX
1998	Frasier, NBC
1997	Frasier, NBC

* Primetime Emmy Award for Outstanding Comedy Series

TOP 10 **COUNTRIES WITH THE MOST RADIO STATIONS***

	COUNTRY	RADIO STATIONS AM	FM	TOTAL
1	USA	4,789	8,961	13,750
2	France	41	3,500	3,541
3	Russia	323	1,500	1,823
4	Brazil	1,365	296	1,661
5	Mexico	850	545	1,395
6	Philippines	369	583	952
7	Spain	208	715	923
8	Germany	51	787	838
9	Canada	245	582	827
10	Poland	14	777	781

* 2006 or latest year for which data available

Source: CIA, *The World Factbook 2007*

Tiny TV
Hailed as the "world's smallest TV," the Seiko TV Watch was launched in 1982 and used by Roger Moore as James Bond in *Octopussy*. Unfortunately, its poor-quality black and white screen, the bulky receiver to which it was connected, and its $495 price tag made it a commercial failure.

8

THE COMMERCIAL WORLD

Trade

TOP 10 **GLOBAL RETAILERS**

COMPANY / BASE	RETAIL SALES, 2005* ($)
1 Wal-Mart Stores, Inc., USA	312,427,000,000
2 Carrefour, France	92,778,000,000
3 Home Depot, Inc., USA	81,511,000,000
4 METRO AG, Germany	69,134,000,000
5 Tesco plc, UK	68,866,000,000
6 Kroger Co., USA	60,553,000,000
7 Target Corp., USA	52,620,000,000
8 Costco Wholesale Corp., USA	51,862,000,000
9 Sears Holdings, USA	49,124,000,000
10 Schwarz Unternehmens Treuhand KG, Germany	45,891,000,000

* Financial year

Source: *Stores* magazine, 2007 Global Powers of Retailing

TOP 10 **COMPANIES SPENDING THE MOST ON ADVERTISING**

COMPANY / COUNTRY	WORLD ADVERTISING* SPENDING, 2005 ($)
1 Procter & Gamble Company, USA	8,190,000,000
2 Unilever, UK/Netherlands	4,272,000,000
3 General Motors Corporation, USA	4,173,000,000
4 Toyota Motor Corporation, Japan	2,800,000,000
5 L'Oréal, France	2,773,000,000
6 Ford Motor Company, USA	2,645,000,000
7 Time Warner, USA	2,479,000,000
8 DaimlerChrysler, Germany/USA	2,104,000,000
9 Nestlé, Switzerland	2,033,000,000
10 Johnson & Johnson, USA	1,968,000,000

* Includes newspapers, magazines, billboards, television, radio, Internet, and Yellow Pages

Source: *Advertising Age Global Marketing Report 2006*

TOP 10 **IMPORTERS**

COUNTRY	GOODS AND SERVICES IMPORTS, 2004 ($)
1 USA	1,769,031,000,000
2 Germany	912,587,000,000
3 China	606,543,000,000
4 UK	604,562,000,000
5 Japan	542,380,000,000
6 France	526,635,000,000
7 Italy	423,241,000,000
8 Netherlands	341,622,000,000
9 Canada	336,733,000,000
10 Spain	307,365,000,000
World total	*11,096,960,000,000*

Source: The World Bank, *World Development Indicators 2006*

TOP 10 **EXPORTERS**

COUNTRY	GOODS AND SERVICES EXPORTS, 2004 ($)
1 USA	1,151,448,000,000
2 Germany	1,051,303,000,000
3 China	655,827,000,000
4 Japan	636,610,000,000
5 UK	533,167,000,000
6 France	531,488,000,000
7 Italy	435,871,000,000
8 Netherlands	388,899,000,000
9 Canada	377,646,000,000
10 South Korea	299,174,000,000
World total	*11,238,500,000,000*

Source: The World Bank, *World Development Indicators 2006*

The real thing
Launched in 1886, Coca-Cola is recognized internationally and considered the world's most valued brand.

TOP 10 **MOST VALUABLE GLOBAL BRANDS**

	BRAND NAME*	INDUSTRY	BRAND VALUE 2006 ($)
1	Coca-Cola	Beverages	67,000,000,000
2	Microsoft	Technology	56,962,000,000
3	IBM	Technology	56,201,000,000
4	General Electric	Diversified	48,907,000,000
5	Intel	Technology	32,319,000,000
6	Nokia, Finland	Technology	30,131,000,000
7	Toyota, Japan	Automotive	27,941,000,000
8	Disney	Leisure	27,848,000,000
9	McDonald's	Food retail	27,501,000,000
10	Mercedes	Automotive	21,795,000,000

* All US-owned unless otherwise stated

Source: Interbrand/BusinessWeek

Brand consultants Interbrand use a method of estimating value that takes account of the profitability of individual brands within a business (rather than the companies that own them), as well as such factors as their potential for growth.

TOP 10 **MOST-ADVERTISED PRODUCTS***

	CATEGORY	WORLD ADVERTISING SPENDING, 2005 ($)
1	Automotive	22,761,000,000
2	Personal care	19,491,000,000
3	Entertainment and media	11,029,000,000
4	Food	8,129,000,000
5	Pharmaceuticals	7,470,000,000
6	Soft drinks	3,971,000,000
7	Restaurants	3,349,000,000
8	Computers	3,106,000,000
9	Telephone	3,104,000,000
10	Financial	3,000,000,000
	World total	*98,273,000,000*

* Based on total worldwide spend by Top 100 companies

Source: *Advertising Age Global Marketing Report 2006*

Rich Lists

TOP 10 **RICHEST WOMEN** *

	NAME / COUNTRY	SOURCE	NET WORTH ($)
1	Liliane Bettencourt, France	L'Oreal	20,700,000,000
2	Alice L. Walton, USA	Wal-Mart	16,600,000,000
3	Helen R. Walton, USA	Wal-Mart	16,400,000,000
4	Abigail Johnson, USA	Finance	13,000,000,000
5 =	Anne Cox Chambers, USA	Media/entertainment	12,600,000,000
=	Barbara Cox Anthony, USA	Media/entertainment	12,600,000,000
7	Jacqueline Mars, USA	Candy	10,500,000,000
8	Susanne Klatten, Germany	Pharmaceuticals	9,600,000,000
9	Charlene de Carvalho-Heineken, Netherlands	Beverages	7,200,000,000
10	Johanna Quandt, Germany	BMW cars	6,700,000,000

* Excluding rulers and family fortunes

Source: *Forbes* magazine, *The World's Billionaires, 2007*

TOP 10 **COUNTRIES WITH THE MOST DOLLAR BILLIONAIRES**

	COUNTRY*	$ BILLIONAIRES
1	USA	369
2	Germany	45
3	UK	33
4	Russia	32
5	Japan	27
6	Hong Kong	22
7 =	Switzerland	21
=	Turkey	21
9 =	Canada	19
=	India	19
	World total	*746*

* Of residence, irrespective of citizenship

Source: *Forbes* magazine, *The World's Billionaires, 2007*

TOP 10 **HIGHEST-EARNING CELEBRITIES**

	CELEBRITY*	PROFESSION	EARNINGS# ($)
1	Steven Spielberg	Film producer/director	332,000,000
2	Howard Stern	Radio shock jock	302,000,000
3	George Lucas	Film producer/director	235,000,000
4	Oprah Winfrey	Talk-show host/producer	225,000,000
5	Jerry Seinfeld	Actor/producer	100,000,000
6	Tiger Woods	Golfer	90,000,000
7	Dan Brown	Author	88,000,000
8	Jerry Bruckheimer	Movie and TV producer	84,000,000
9	J. K. Rowling (UK)	Author	75,000,000
10	Dick Wolf	Director/producer	70,000,000

* Individuals, excluding groups; US unless otherwise stated
# 2005–2006

Source: *Forbes* magazine, *The Celebrity 100, 2006*

Director rules
The sale of part of DreamWorks and box-office revenue combine to make Steven Spielberg the highest-earning celebrity.

TOP 10 **HIGHEST-EARNING DEAD CELEBRITIES**

	CELEBRITY	PROFESSION	DEATH	EARNINGS 2005 ($)
1	Kurt Cobain	Rock star	Apr 5, 1994	50,000,000
2	Elvis Presley	Rock star	Aug 16, 1977	42,000,000
3	Charles Schultz	"Peanuts" cartoonist	Feb 12, 2000	35,000,000
4	John Lennon	Rock star	Dec 8, 1980	24,000,000
5	Albert Einstein	Scientist	Apr 18, 1955	20,000,000
6	Andy Warhol	Artist	Feb 22, 1987	19,000,000
7	=Theodor "Dr Seuss" Geisel	Author	Sep 24, 1991	10,000,000
	=Ray Charles	Musician	Jun 10, 2004	10,000,000
9	=Marilyn Monroe	Actress	Aug 5, 1962	8,000,000
	=Johnny Cash	Musician	Sep 12, 2003	8,000,000

Source: *Forbes* magazine, *Top-Earning Dead Celebrities, 2006*

Dead rich
Income from the sale of part of his band
Nirvana's song catalogue places Kurt Cobain
at the head of the dead rich list.

TOP 10 **RICHEST MEN***

	NAME / COUNTRY (CITIZEN/ RESIDENCE, IF DIFFERENT)	SOURCE	NET WORTH ($)
1	William H. Gates III, USA	Microsoft (software)	56,000,000,000
2	Warren Edward Buffett, USA	Berkshire Hathaway (investments)	52,000,000,000
3	Carlos Slim Helu, Mexico	Communications	49,000,000,000
4	Ingvar Kamprad, Sweden/Switzerland	Ikea (home furnishings)	33,000,000,000
5	Lakshmi Mittal, India/UK	Mittal Steel	32,000,000,000
6	Sheldon Adelson, USA	Casinos and hotels	26,500,000,000
7	Bernard Arnault, France	Louis Vuitton, etc. (luxury goods)	26,000,000,000
8	Amancio Ortega, Spain	Zara, etc. (clothing)	24,000,000,000
9	Li Ka-shing, China	Diverse investments	23,000,000,000
10	David Thomson, Canada	Media, entertainment	22,000,000,000

* Excluding rulers and family fortunes

Source: *Forbes* magazine, *The World's Billionaires, 2007*

Richest 50 Years Ago

In 1957, *Fortune* magazine published a list of America's 76 richest people. It was headed by oil magnate J. Paul Getty (1892–1976), whose fortune was estimated at between $700 million and $1 billion—worth some six times as much in today's values, yet still little more than one-tenth of the wealth of today's richest man, Bill Gates.

Resources

TOP 10 **STEEL PRODUCERS**

COUNTRY	PRODUCTION 2006 (TONS)
1 China	461,647,972
2 Japan	128,088,573
3 USA	108,577,663
4 Russia	77,823,178
5 South Korea	53,351,867
6 Germany	52,029,093
7 India	48,501,697
8 Ukraine	44,974,301
9 Italy	34,833,037
10 Brazil	34,061,419
World total	*1,366,314,856*

Source: International Iron & Steel Institute

The world's largest steel producer, Mittal Steel, produced 69.4 million tons of steel in 2005. In 2006, it merged with second largest Arcelor (51.5 million tons). Its Indian owner Lakshmi Mittal is the fifth-richest man in the world ($32 billion).

TOP 10 **URANIUM PRODUCERS**

COUNTRY	PRODUCTION 2005 (TONS)
1 Canada	12,818
2 Australia	10,493
3 Kazakhstan	4,803
4 Russia*	3,782
5 Namibia	3,469
6 Niger	3,409
7 Uzbekistan	2,535
8 USA	1,145
9 Ukraine*	882
10 China*	827
World total	*45,851*

* Estimated

Source: World Nuclear Association

Forging ahead
As its economy has expanded, China's steel output has grown—the country now makes more than one-third of the world's steel.

TOP 10 **PLATINUM PRODUCERS**

COUNTRY	PRODUCTION 2005 LB	KG
1 South Africa	372,027	168,749
2 Russia*	66,138	30,000
3 Canada	14,109	6,400
4 Zimbabwe	10,657	4,834
5 USA	8,642	3,920
6 Colombia	2,385	1,082
7 Finland	1,763	800
8 Japan	1,609	730
9 Botswana*	661	300
10 Australia*	529	240
World total	*217,000*	*478,402*

* Estimated

Source: US Geological Survey, *Minerals Yearbook*

TOP 10 **SILVER PRODUCERS**

COUNTRY	% OF WORLD TOTAL	PRODUCTION 2005 (TONS)
1 Peru	16.0	3,517
2 Mexico	14.4	3,165
3 Australia	12.1	2,635
4 China	10.1	2,218
5 Chile	6.9	1,519
6 Russia	6.6	1,447
7 Poland	6.3	1,389
8 USA	6.1	1,344
9 Canada	5.3	1,170
10 Kazakhstan	4.0	885
World total	*100.0*	*21,998*

Source: The Silver Institute, *World Silver Survey 2006*

Total world silver production hit a new record in 2005, up from 16,710 tons in the 10 years since 1995, with leading producer Peru's output growing by 67 percent.

TOP 10 **GOLD PRODUCERS**

COUNTRY	% OF WORLD TOTAL	PRODUCTION 2006 (TONS)
1 South Africa	11.8	321.7
2 USA	10.2	277.6
3 China	10.0	272.5
4 Australia	10.4	269.5
5 Peru	9.9	224.1
6 Russia	7.0	190.5
7 Indonesia	6.6	125.8
8 Canada	4.6	114.6
9 Uzbekistan	3.2	86.5
10 Ghana	2.8	77.4
World total	*100.0*	*2,723.9*

Source: Gold Fields Mineral Services Ltd, *Gold Survey 2007*

Although still below its all-time production high of 682.9 tons, South Africa continues to dominate world production. That of Australia peaked at 345.2 tons in 1997, and in 2005 just overtook the USA for the first time.

THE CULLINAN DIAMOND

The largest diamond ever found, the 3,106.75-carat (621.35-g) Cullinan, was discovered in South Africa in 1905. It was presented to King Edward VII on his 66th birthday on November 9, 1907. For security, a fake was carried to London under armed guard, while the real gem was secretly sent by parcel post. Cut into 105 separate gems by Dutch expert Joseph Asscher, it produced the Great Star of Africa (530.20 carats), which is mounted in the Queen's Sceptre, the Second Star of Africa (317.40 carats), set in the Imperial State Crown, and the Third Star of Africa (94.40 carats) and Fourth Star of Africa (63.60 carats), both once set in Queen Mary's Crown, but now set in a brooch which, with other gems cut from the Cullinan, is worn by Queen Elizabeth II.

TOP 10 **DIAMOND PRODUCERS (BY VOLUME)**

COUNTRY	VALUE (2004) ($)	VOLUME (2004) (CARATS)
1 Russia	1,989,000,000	35,000,000
2 Botswana	2,940,000,000	31,125,000
3 Dem. Rep. of Congo	790,000,000	29,000,000
4 Australia	343,000,000	20,673,000
5 South Africa	1,458,000,000	14,233,000
6 Canada	1,646,000,000	12,618,000
7 Angola	1,300,000,000	7,500,000
8 Namibia	698,000,000	2,011,000
9 Ghana	26,000,000	900,000
10 Brazil	35,000,000	700,000

Source: Northwest Territories, *Diamond Facts 2005*

Diamond anniversary Fredrick Wells, an official at the Premier Diamond Mine, discovered the world's largest diamond on June 25, 1905. It was purchased from him and named the Cullinan Diamond after Sir Thomas Cullinan, the mine's owner, and cut in 1907, producing a superb collection of gems that are among the British Crown Jewels.

Food

TOP 10 **EGG CONSUMERS**

COUNTRY / CONSUMPTION PER CAPITA PER DAY (2004)/OZ/G

	Denmark	Netherlands	Japan	China	Hungary	Brunei	France	USA	Paraguay	Belgium
	2.15 / 61.19	1.85 / 52.58	1.84 / 52.25	1.70 / 48.29	1.68 / 47.83	1.67 / 47.61	1.64 / 46.69	1.64 / 46.62	1.55 / 44.09	1.51 / 42.85

Source: Food and Agriculture Organization of the United Nations

You Say "Potato"

English adventurer Sir John Hawkins first took potatoes from Florida to Ireland in about 1565, in the same year introducing the word in English when he wrote, "These potatoes be the most delicate rootes that may be eaten, and doe far exceede our passeneps or carets."

TOP 10 **POTATO CONSUMERS**

COUNTRY	CONSUMPTION (OZ PER CAPITA PER DAY, 2004)
1 Belarus	17.24
2 Kyrgyzstan	13.60
3 Rwanda	13.46
4 Lithuania	13.18
5 Poland	13.17
6 Ukraine	13.08
7 Latvia	13.07
8 Russia	12.67
9 Portugal	12.39
10 Ireland	12.28
USA	5.87

Source: Food and Agricultural Organization of the United Nations

TOP 10 **FOOD, DRINK, AND RESTAURANT BRANDS**

BRAND*	BRAND VALUE (2006)
1 Coca-Cola	67,000,000,000
2 McDonald's	27,501,000,000
3 Pepsi	12,690,000,000
4 Nescafé, Switzerland	12,507,000,000
5 Budweiser	11,662,000,000
6 Kellogg's	8,776,000,000
7 Heinz	6,223,000,000
8 Wrigley's	5,449,000,000
9 KFC	5,350,000,000
10 Nestlé, Switzerland	4,932,000,000

* US unless otherwise stated

Source: *Interbrand's Best Global Brands 2006*

A number of these multibillion dollar global brands have a long history, Nestlé dating back to 1866 and Heinz to 1869.

TOP 10 FAST FOOD OUTLETS IN THE USA

	TYPE*	SALES ($)
1	Burgers	85,130,200,000
2	Bakery products	29,715,700,000
3	Chicken	14,400,600,000
4	Latin American	10,881,500,000
5	Convenience stores	6,764,300,000
6	Asian	3,795,700,000
7	Pizza	2,593,300,000
8	Ice cream	2,525,500,000
9	Fish	2,129,300,000
10	Middle Eastern	214,800,000

* Excluding nonspecific categories

Source: Euromonitor, Consumer Foodservice in the US, 2005

Now the dominant fast food item in the US diet, the word "hamburger" first appeared in print on January 5, 1889, in the *Walla Walla Union*, a Washington newspaper, hidden within the bizarre phrase, "You are asked if you will have porkchopbeefsteakhamandegghamburgersteak orliverandbacon."

TOP 10 FOODS CONSUMED IN THE USA*

	ITEM	ANNUAL PER CAPITA CONSUMPTION (2003)		
		LB	OZ	KG
1	Milk and cream	205	4	93.1
2	Meat (red meat 111 lb 14 oz/50.7 kg)	199	6	90.4
3	= Fresh vegetables (excl. potatoes)	148	3	67.2
	= Processed fruit	148	3	67.2
5	Sweeteners (sugar 61 lb 1 oz/27.7 kg#)	141	11	64.2
6	Potatoes (fresh and processed)	138	8	62.8
7	Wheat flour and flour products	137	14	62.5
8	Processed vegetables (excl. potatoes)	129	1	58.5
9	Fresh fruit	126	11	57.4
10	Fats	87	14	39.8

* By weight
# Excludes sugar imported in blends and mixtures

Source: US Department of Agriculture, Economic Research Service

TOP 10 FISH CONSUMERS*

	COUNTRY	CONSUMPTION PER CAPITA PER DAY (2004)	
		OZ	G
1	Maldives	12.82	363.51
2	Samoa	4.68	132.72
3	Kiribati	3.29	93.27
4	Malta	2.79	79.15
5	Grenada	2.51	71.23
6	Barbados	2.41	68.44
7	Saint Lucia	2.01	56.99
8	South Korea	2.00	56.85
9	Dominica	1.88	53.41
10	Ghana	1.85	52.46
	USA	*0.21*	*6.04*

* Pelagic (marine) only, excluding crustaceans, molluscs, etc.

Source: Food and Agriculture Organization of the United Nations

Drink

TOP 10 COFFEE DRINKERS

COUNTRY / CONSUMPTION PER HEAD (2005) (LB/OZ / KG / CUPS*)

3 Sweden 18/4/8.3/1,245

2 Denmark 19/2/8.7/1,305

1 Finland 21/6/9.7/1,455

7 Austria 12/12/5.8/870

6 Switzerland 15/10/7.1/1,065

5 Netherlands 16/1/7.3/1,095

4 Norway 18/1/8.2/1,230

10 Brazil 8/9/3.9/585

8 Germany 12/2/5.5/825

9 Belgium 11/14/5.4/810

USA   6/2 / 2.8 / 420

World average   1/9 / 0.7 / 105

* Based on 150 cups per 2 lb 3 oz (1 kg) Source: Euromonitor

TOP 10 SOFT-DRINK BRANDS IN THE USA

BRAND	SALES 2005 (GALLONS)
1 Coca-Cola Classic	4,848,200,000
2 Pepsi	3,124,900,000
4 Mountain Dew	1,301,300,000
6 Dr. Pepper	1,168,200,000
5 Sprite	993,700,000
6 Gatorade	958,000,000
7 Minute Maid	672,000,000
8 Tropicana	632,000,000
9 Aquafina	506,100,000
10 Dasani	448,000,000

Source: Beverage Marketing Corporation

A total of 28,882,500,000 gallons of soft drinks were sold in the USA in 2005.

TOP 10 BREWERS

BREWERY / COUNTRY	% OF WORLD TOTAL	PRODUCTION (2005) PINTS	LITERS
1 InBev, Belgium	12.6	35,564,000,000	20,210,000,000
2 SABMiller, UK	11.0	30,971,000,000	17,600,000,000
3 Anheuser-Busch, USA	10.9	30,531,000,000	17,350,000,000
4 Heineken, Netherlands	7.4	20,870,000,000	11,860,000,000
5 = Carlsberg, Denmark	3.0	8,499,000,000	4,830,000,000
= Molson Coors, USA/Canada	3.0	8,499,000,000	4,830,000,000
7 Modelo, Mexico	2.9	8,006,000,000	4,550,000,000
8 Baltik Beverage, Russia	2.6	7,302,000,000	4,150,000,000
9 Tsingtao, China	2.6	7,197,000,000	4,090,000,000
10 Yan Jing, China	2.0	5,490,000,000	3,120,000,000
World total	*100.0*	*281,224,000,000*	*159,808,800,000*

Source: The Barth Report 2005/2006

TOP 10 **CHAMPAGNE CONSUMERS**

COUNTRY / CONSUMPTION (2005) (GALLONS/BOTTLES)

Source: Euromonitor

1 France 34,712,000 / 175,200,000
2 UK 5,944,000 / 30,000,000
3 USA 3,487,000 / 17,600,000
4 Germany 1,955,000 / 9,866,000
5 Belgium 1,506,000 / 7,600,000
6 Italy 1,321,000 / 6,666,000
7 Japan 1,189,000 / 6,000,000
8 Switzerland 1,136,000 / 5,733,000
9 Netherlands 528,000 / 2,666,000
10 Spain 502,000 / 2,533,000

World total 57,325,000 / 289,333,000

TOP 10 **MILK CONSUMERS**

COUNTRY	CONSUMPTION PER CAPITA PER DAY (2005)	
	OZ	G
1 France	31.33	888.05
2 Albania	30.86	874.76
3 Switzerland	30.26	857.80
4 Iceland	30.10	853.33
5 Ireland	29.99	850.04
6 Sweden	29.41	833.74
7 Finland	29.21	828.20
8 Australia	26.91	762.95
9 Kazakhstan	26.90	762.82
10 Romania	26.58	753.39
USA	*24.94*	*707.10*

Source: Food and Agriculture Organization of the United Nations

While these countries are the principal consumers of milk, the USA is the world's leading producer, with more than 80 million tons a year. France produces over 26 million tons a year and maintains its place as the leading consumer. The UK formerly appeared in both the Top 10 of consumers and (at almost 15 million tons per annum) producers, but health concerns have seen its per capita consumption reduce.

TOP 10 **COLA-DRINK CONSUMERS**

COUNTRY	CONSUMPTION PER HEAD (2005)	
	PINTS	LITERS
1 USA	204.3	116.1
2 Mexico	171.0	97.2
3 Australia	130.0	73.9
4 Canada	125.1	71.1
5 Chile	124.6	70.8
6 Belgium	123.0	69.9
7 Norway	121.8	69.2
8 Spain	103.6	58.9
9 New Zealand	101.0	57.4
10 Argentina	99.3	56.4
World average	*29.91*	*17.0*

Source: Euromonitor

In marked contrast to the countries in the Top 10, India and Vietnam (2.3 pints/ 1.3 liters per capita) and Indonesia (1.4 pints/0.8 liters), and many African nations, fall well below the average in a world market that in 2005 drank 191.3 billion pints (108.7 billion liters) of cola drinks.

Energy

TOP 10 **COUNTRIES WITH THE GREATEST NATURAL-GAS RESERVES**

	COUNTRY	RESERVES 2005 TRILLION FT³	TRILLION M³
1	Russia	1,688.0	47.82
2	Iran	943.9	26.74
3	Qatar	910.1	25.78
4	Saudi Arabia	243.6	6.90
5	United Arab Emirates	213.0	6.04
6	USA	192.5	5.45
7	Nigeria	184.6	5.23
8	Algeria	161.7	4.58
9	Venezuela	152.3	4.32
10	Iraq	111.9	3.17
	World total	*6,348.10*	*179.83*

Source: *BP Statistical Review of World Energy 2006*

Cold comfort
A natural gas plant in Siberia, Russia. The country has the world's greatest proved reserves.

TOP 10 **COUNTRIES WITH THE GREATEST COAL RESERVES**

	COUNTRY	RESERVES AT END OF 2005 (TONS)
1	USA	271,877,365,966
2	Russia	173,073,897,213
3	China	126,214,643,850
4	India	101,903,168,129
5	Australia	86,531,437,050
6	South Africa	53,737,675,875
7	Ukraine	37,647,237,829
8	Kazakhstan	34,479,195,153
9	Poland	15,432,358,200
10	Brazil	11,147,674,177
	World total	*1,002,071,519,623*

Source: *BP Statistical Review of World Energy 2006*

Coal reserves are quantities of coal that can be economically recovered from known deposits using current engineering techniques.

TOP 10 **COAL-CONSUMING COUNTRIES**

	COUNTRY	CONSUMPTION 2005 (TONS OF OIL EQUIVALENT)
1	China	1,192,590,595
2	USA	634,269, 922
3	India	234,682,076
4	Japan	133,710,361
5	Russia	123,017,941
6	South Africa	101,302,408
7	Germany	90,499,758
8	Poland	62,501,051
9	South Korea	60,406,659
10	Australia	57,540,650
	World total	*3,229,551,647*

Source: *BP Statistical Review of World Energy 2006*

TOP 10 **COAL-PRODUCING COUNTRIES**

	COUNTRY	PRODUCTION 2005 (TONS OF OIL EQUIVALENT)
1	China	1,221,030,227
2	USA	635,151,771
3	Australia	223,107,807
4	India	220,021,335
5	South Africa	153,111,050
6	Russia	151,016,648
7	Indonesia	91,712,300
8	Poland	75,728,786
9	Germany	58,642,961
10	Kazakhstan	48,501,697
	World total	*3,182,593,185*

Source: *BP Statistical Review of World Energy 2006*

TOP 10 NATURAL GAS-CONSUMING COUNTRIES

COUNTRY	CONSUMPTION 2005 (TONS OF OIL EQUIVALENT)
1 USA	628,427,672
2 Russia	401,902,700
3 UK	93,806,692
4 Canada	90,720,220
5 Iran	87,743,979
6 Germany	85,208,663
7 Japan	80,468,725
8 Italy	78,374,333
9 Ukraine	72,311,621
10 Saudi Arabia	69,004,687
World total	*2,727,889,774*

Source: *BP Statistical Review of World Energy 2006*

TOP 10 COUNTRIES WITH THE GREATEST OIL RESERVES

COUNTRY	2005 RESERVES (TONS)
1 Saudi Arabia	40,013,900,190
2 Iran	20,833,683,570
3 Iraq	17,085,825,150
4 Kuwait	15,432,358,200
5 United Arab Emirates	14,330,046,900
6 Venezuela	12,676,579,950
7 Russia	11,243,575,260
8 Kazakhstan	5,952,481,020
9 Libya	5,621,787,630
10 Nigeria	5,291,094,240
World total	*180,338,128,680*

Source: *BP Statistical Review of World Energy 2006*

TOP 10 OIL-CONSUMING COUNTRIES

COUNTRY	CONSUMPTION 2005 (TONS)
1 USA	1,041,243,254
2 China	360,786,488
3 Japan	269,184,419
4 Russia	143,300,469
5 Germany	133,930,823
6 India	127,537,417
7 South Korea	116,293,842
8 Canada	110,341,361
9 France	102,625,182
10 Saudi Arabia	96,121,545
World total	*4,152,516,898*

Source: *BP Statistical Review of World Energy 2006*

TOP 10 OIL-PRODUCING COUNTRIES

COUNTRY / PRODUCTION 2005 (TONS)

1 Saudi Arabia 580,036,206
2 Russia 518,086,311
3 USA 341,936,965
4 Iran 220,903,183
5 Mexico 206,242,444
6 China 199,297,883
7 Venezuela 170,527,558
8 Norway 165,236,464
9 Canada 152,339,422
10 Kuwait 143,410,700

World total 4,293,502,514

Source: *BP Statistical Review of World Energy 2005*

Environmental Issues

TOP 10 **CARBON DIOXIDE-EMITTING COUNTRIES**

	COUNTRY	CO_2 EMISSIONS PER CAPITA, 2004 (TONS OF CO_2)
1	United Arab Emirates	61.64
2	Qatar	50.98
3	Bahrain	36.95
4	Kuwait	34.04
5	Trinidad and Tobago	33.10
6	Singapore	32.77
7	Luxembourg	29.34
8	USA	22.24
9	Australia	21.37
10	Canada	19.94
	World average	*4.67*

Source: Energy Information Administration

The concentration of atmospheric carbon dioxide varies, but averages 0.0383 percent by volume or 0.0582 percent by weight. Any increase is significant as CO_2 is a major contributor to the greenhouse effect and global warming. CO_2 emissions derive from three principal sources—fossil-fuel burning, cement manufacturing, and gas flaring—as well as various industrial processes. In the past 60 years, increasing industrialization in many countries has resulted in huge increases in carbon output, a trend that most countries are now actively attempting to reverse, with some degree of success among the former leaders in this Top 10, although the USA remains the worst offender in total, with over 6.6 billion tons released in 2004. Around the world there are a number of island territories with small populations but a high CO_2 output resulting from such industries as the production of liquid fuels. Among them, Gibraltar (165.06 tons per head) and the US Virgin Islands (161.89 tons per head), have greater per capita emissions than those countries in the Top 10.

THE 10 **WORST AIR-QUALITY COUNTRIES**

	COUNTRY	SCORE*
1	Bangladesh	6.9
2	Pakistan	8.2
3	Albania	14.4
4	Egypt	14.8
5	Mali	21.2
6	China	22.3
7	Niger	22.9
8	Chad	24.4
9	Sudan	24.9
10	Indonesia	25.1

* Out of 100

Source: *Pilot 2006 Environmental Performance Index*

TOP 10 **ENVIRONMENTAL PERFORMANCE INDEX COUNTRIES**

	COUNTRY	EPI SCORE*
1	New Zealand	88.0
2	Sweden	87.8
3	Finland	87.0
4	Czech Republic	86.0
5	UK	85.6
6	Austria	85.2
7	Denmark	84.2
8	Canada	84.0
9 =	Ireland	83.3
=	Malaysia	83.3
	USA	*78.5*

* Out of 100

Source: *Pilot 2006 Environmental Performance Index*

The Environmental Performance Index is a measure of environmental health and ecosystem vitality based on an assessment of 16 indicators in each country. These include air quality, water resources, biodiversity and habitat, productive natural resources, and sustainable energy.

TOP 10 **AIR-QUALITY COUNTRIES**

	COUNTRY	SCORE*
1	Uganda	98.0
2	Gabon	96.1
3	Rwanda	91.1
4	Burundi	90.9
5	Ghana	87.3
6	Kenya	87.0
7	Liberia	86.5
8	Tanzania	86.2
9	New Zealand	83.7
10 =	Dem. Rep. of Congo	82.3
=	Togo	82.3
	USA	*44.7*

* Out of 100

Source: *Pilot 2006 Environmental Performance Index*

Air pollution is a major factor in environmental health. It is caused by power generation, industrial production, motor vehicles, and residential heating and cooking, especially through the consumption of fossil fuels. Atmospheric pollutants such as sulfur dioxide cause acid rain, which affect fish stocks and agricultural production. Countries with low-level vehicle use and industrialization score the highest on the Environmental Performance Index.

THE 10 WORST ENVIRONMENTAL PERFORMANCE INDEX COUNTRIES

	COUNTRY	EPI SCORE*
1	Niger	25.7
2	Chad	30.5
3	Mauritania	32.0
4	Mali	33.9
5	Ethiopia	36.7
6	Angola	39.3
7	Pakistan	41.1
8	Burkina Faso	43.2
9	Bangladesh	43.5
10	Sudan	44.0

* Out of 100

Source: *Pilot 2006 Environmental Performance Index*

TOP 10 COUNTRIES WITH THE LOWEST OZONE CONCENTRATION

	COUNTRY	OZONE (PARTS PER BILLION)*
1	São Tomé and Principe	11.7
2	Gabon	12.3
3	= Congo	12.6
	= Equatorial Guinea	12.6
5	Rwanda	14.1
6	Uganda	14.2
7	Burundi	14.7
8	Kenya	15.8
9	Liberia	17.1
10	Dem. Rep. of Congo	17.7

* In the atmosphere at ground level

Source: *Pilot 2006 Environmental Performance Index*

TOP 10 GARBAGE PRODUCERS

	COUNTRY*	DOMESTIC WASTE PER CAPITA 2003# LB	KG
1	Ireland	1,676	760
2	USA	1,631	740
3	Iceland	1,609	730
4	Norway	1,543	700
5	Australia	1,521	690
6	Denmark	1,477	670
7	Switzerland	1,455	660
8	= Luxembourg	1,433	650
	= Spain	1,433	650
10	Germany	1,411	640

* In those countries for which data available
# Or latest year for which data available

TOP 10 COUNTRIES WITH THE HIGHEST OZONE CONCENTRATION

	COUNTRY	OZONE (PARTS PER BILLION)*
1	Belize	64.5
2	Guatemala	64.4
3	Mexico	64.2
4	China	63.4
5	East Timor	62.7
6	Mongolia	60.9
7	Australia	60.6
8	Bhutan	58.9
9	Nepal	58.6
10	USA	57.5

* In the atmosphere at ground level

Source: *Pilot 2006 Environmental Performance Index*

While the ozone layer in the stratosphere protects us from ultraviolet light from the Sun, and its breakdown is therefore a cause for concern, at lower levels of the atmosphere ozone is a pollutant and affects the health of those who breathe it.

Industrial Disasters

THE 10 **WORST INDUSTRIAL-SITE DISASTERS***

LOCATION / DATE / INCIDENT	NO. KILLED
1 Bhopal, India, Dec 3, 1984 Methylisocyante gas escape at Union Carbide plant	3,849
2 Jesse, Nigeria, Oct 17, 1998 Oil-pipeline explosion	>700
3 Oppau, Germany, Sep 21, 1921 Bradishe Aniline chemical-plant explosion	561
4 San Juanico, Mexico, Nov 19, 1984 Explosion at a PEMEX liquefied petroleum gas plant	540
5 Cubatão, Brazil, Feb 25, 1984 Oil-pipeline explosion	508
6 Durunkah, Egypt, Nov 2, 1994 Fuel storage depot fire	>500
7 Mexico City, Mexico, Nov 19, 1984 Butane-storage explosion	>400
8 Adeje, Nigeria, Jul 10, 2000 Oil-pipeline explosion	>250
9 Guadalajara, Mexico, Apr 22, 1992 Explosions caused by gas leak into sewers	230
10 Oakdale, Pennsylvania, May 18, 1918 TNT explosion at Aetna Chemical Company	210

* Including industrial sites, factories, fuel depots, and pipelines; excluding military, munitions, bombs, mining, marine, and other transport disasters, dam failures and mass poisonings

Officially, the meltdown of the nuclear reactor at Chernobyl, Ukraine, on April 26, 1986 caused the immediate death of 31 people, but it has been suggested that by 1992 some 6,000 to 8,000 people had died as a result of radioactive contamination, a toll that will continue for many years. Extending the parameters of "industrial" to include construction work, as many as 25,000 workers may have died during the building of the Panama Canal in the period 1881–1914, largely as a result of diseases such as yellow fever, malaria, and cholera, while the building of the Madeira-Mamore railways in Brazil (1870–1912) resulted in over 6,000 deaths from disease, poison-arrow attacks, and snakebite. The boring of the Gauley Bridge Water Tunnel, West Virginia, killed some 476 workers in 1935 as a result of inhalation of silica dust, with perhaps 1,500 becoming disabled.

THE 10 **WORST EXPLOSIONS***

LOCATION / DATE / INCIDENT	ESTIMATED NO. KILLED
1 Rhodes, Greece, Apr 3, 1856 Lightning strike of gunpowder store	4,000
2 Breschia, Italy, Aug 18, 1769 Church of San Nazaire caught fire after being struck by lightning, gunpowder store exploded	>3,000
3 Salang Tunnel, Afghanistan, Nov 3, 1982 Gas-tanker collision	>2,000
4 Lanchow, China, Oct 26, 1935 Arsenal	2,000
5 Halifax, Nova Scotia, Dec 6, 1917 Ammunition ship *Mont Blanc*	1,963
6 Hamont Station, Belgium, Aug 3, 1918 Ammunition trains	1,750
7 Memphis, USA, Apr 27, 1865 Sultana paddle-steamer boiler explosion	1,547
8 = Archangel, Russia, Feb 20, 1917 Munitions ship	1,500
= Smederovo, Yugoslavia, Jun 9, 1941 Ammunition dump	1,500
10 Bombay, India, Apr 14, 1944 Ammunition ship *Fort Stikine*	1,376

* Excluding mining disasters, terrorist, and military bombs, and natural explosions, such as volcanoes

All these "best-estimate" figures should be treated with caution, since, as with fires and shipwrecks, body counts following explosions are notoriously unreliable.

THE 10 **WORST SINGLE-BUILDING FIRES**

LOCATION / DATE / BUILDING	NO. KILLED
1 London Bridge, UK, Jul 11, 1212	3,000*
2 Santiago, Chile, Dec 8, 1863, Church of La Compañía	2,500#
3 Canton, China, May 25, 1845, theater	1,670
4 Shanghai, China, Jun 1871, theater	900
5 Vienna, Austria, 8 Dec 1881, Ring Theatre	640–850
6 St Petersburg, Russia, Feb 14, 1836, Lehmann Circus	800
7 Antoung, China, Feb 13, 1937, Cinema	658
8 Chicago, USA, Dec 30, 1903, Iroquois Theatre	602
9 Mandi Dabwali, India, Dec 23, 1995, school tent	>500
10 Boston, USA, Nov 28, 1942, Cocoanut Grove Night Club	491

* Burned, crushed, and drowned in ensuing panic; some chroniclers give the year as 1213
# Precise figure uncertain

Sampoong disaster
The sudden and catastrophic collapse of the crowded five-year-old Seoul
department store left 501 staff and customers dead and 937 injured.

THE 10 **WORST MINING DISASTERS**

	LOCATION / DATE	NO. KILLED
1	Honkeiko, China, Apr 26, 1942	1,549
2	Courrières, France, Mar 10, 1906	1,060
3	Omuta, Japan, Nov 9, 1963	447
4	Senghenydd, Wales, UK, Oct 14, 1913	439
5	=Coalbrook, South Africa, Jan 21, 1960	437
	=Hokkaido, Japan, Dec 1, 1914	437
7	Wankie, Rhodesia, Jun 6, 1972	427
8	Tsinan, China, May 13, 1935	400
9	Dhanbad, India, May 28, 1965	375
10	Chasnala, India, Dec 27, 1975	372

A mine disaster at the Fushun mines, Manchuria, on February 12, 1931 may have resulted in up to 3,000 deaths, but information was suppressed by the Chinese government. Soviet security was also responsible for obscuring details of an explosion at the East German Johanngeorgendstadt uranium mine on November 29, 1949, when as many as 3,700 may have died.

THE 10 **WORST SHOP AND OFFICE DISASTERS**

	LOCATION / DATE / INCIDENT	NO. KILLED
1	Seoul, Korea, Jun 29, 1995 Collapse of Sampoong department store	501
2	Asuncíon, Paraguay, Aug 1, 2004 Fire from gas leak in a supermarket	>400
3	Brussels, Belgium, May 22, 1967 L'Innovation department-store fire	322
4	Luoyang, China, Dec 25, 2000 Fire in shopping mall disco	>309
5	Lima, Peru, Dec 29, 2001 Fire in the Mesa Redonda shopping area began in an illegal firework shop, rapidly spreading to other buildings	>290
6	São Paulo, Brazil, Feb 1, 1974 Fire in Joelma bank and office building	188
7	Paris, France, May 4, 1897 Fire in Grand Bazar de Charité	129
8	Osaka, Japan, May 13, 1972 Fire in night club in Sennichi department store	119
9	Kumamoto, Japan, Nov 29, 1973 Taiyo department-store fire	101
10	Bogota, Colombia, Dec 16, 1958 Fire at El Almacen Vida department store	84

Research & Development

TOP 10 COUNTRIES FOR HIGH-TECHNOLOGY EXPORTS

COUNTRY	HIGH-TECHNOLOGY EXPORTS, 2004 ($)
1 China (includes Hong Kong, $80,109,000,000)	241,712,000,000
2 USA	216,016,000,000
3 Germany	131,838,000,000
4 Japan	124,045,000,000
5 Singapore	87,742,000,000
6 South Korea	75,742,000,000
7 France	64,871,000,000
8 UK	64,295,000,000
9 Netherlands	55,211,000,000
10 Malaysia	52,868,000,000

Source: The World Bank, *World Development Indicators 2006*

TOP 10 COUNTRIES REGISTERING THE MOST PATENTS

COUNTRY	PATENTS GRANTED (2004)*
1 USA	164,291
2 Japan	124,192
3 China	49,360
4 South Korea	49,068
5 Germany	29,586
6 Russia	23,191
7 Canada	13,060
8 Australia	12,739
9 France	11,841
10 UK	10,541

* Resident and nonresident applications

Source: World Intellectual Property Organization

TOP 10 COUNTRIES WITH THE MOST INDUSTRIAL ROBOTS

COUNTRY	NO. OF OPERATIONAL INDUSTRIAL ROBOTS (2005)
1 Japan	373,481
2 North America (USA, Canada, Mexico)	139,553
3 Germany	126,725
4 South Korea	61,576
5 Italy	56,198
6 France	30,434
7 Spain	24,081
8 Taiwan	15,464
9 UK	14,948
10 China	11,557
World total	*922,875*

Source: International Federation of Robotics

TOP 10 INTERNATIONAL COMPANIES FOR RESEARCH AND DEVELOPMENT

	COMPANY / COUNTRY	INDUSTRY	R&D SPENDING 2005–06 ($)
1	Ford Motor, USA	Automobiles and parts	9,262,815,000
2	Pfizer, USA	Pharmaceuticals	8,618,817,000
3	General Motors, USA	Automobiles and parts	7,759,482,000
4	DaimlerChrysler, Germany	Automobiles and parts	7,716,461,000
5	Microsoft, USA	Software and IT services	7,624,274,000
6	Toyota, Japan	Automobiles and parts	7,409,028,000
7	Johnson & Johnson, USA	Pharmaceuticals	7,309,307,000
8	Siemens, Germany	Electronic and electrical	7,040,362,000
9	Samsung, South Korea	Electronic and electrical	6,299,590,000
10	GlaxoSmithKline, UK	Pharmaceuticals	6,232,669,000

Source: Department of Trade and Industry, *The R&D Scorecard 2006*

A survey of the leading 1,250 global companies indicated that in the year 2005–06 they invested a total of $495 billion in research and development—an increase of seven percent over the previous year. R&D is concentrated in firms from five countries (82 percent in the USA, Japan, Germany, France, and the UK), in five sectors (70 percent in technology hardware, pharmaceuticals, automotive, electronics, and software) and in the top 100 companies (61 percent of the total).

I, robot
More than 125,000 new robots are installed worldwide every year.

TOP 10 MOST VALUABLE TECHNOLOGY BRANDS*

	BRAND NAME	BRAND VALU 2006 ($
1	Microsoft, USA	67,000,000,000
2	IBM, USA	56,201,000,000
3	Intel, USA	32,319,000,000
4	Nokia, Finland	30,131,000,000
5	Hewlett-Packard, USA	20,458,000,000
6	Cisco, USA	17,532,000,000
7	Samsung, South Korea	16,169,000,000
8	Dell, USA	12,256,000,000
9	Sony, Japan	11,695,000,000
10	Oracle, USA	11,459,000,000

* Includes computer, telecommunications, and consumer electronics brands

Source: Interbrand/*BusinessWeek*

Brand consultants Interbrand estimate value by taking account of the profitabilit of individual brands within a business and such factors as their potential for growth.

TOP 10 MOST-CITED SCIENTIFIC JOURNALS

	JOURNAL	PAPERS 1996–2006	CITATIONS
1	Journal of Biological Chemistry	59,061	1,761,650
2	Proceedings of the National Academy of Science, USA	29,703	1,382,162
3	Nature	10,947	1,217,027
4	Science	10,296	1,181,938
5	Physical Review Letters	32,732	843,70
6	Journal of the American Chemical Society	27,362	717,785
7	Physical Review B	52,173	601,422
8	Cell	3,780	573,285
9	Journal of Immunology	17,904	520,93
10	New England Journal of Medicine	3,864	511,08.

* Most-cited of over 7 million scientific-journal articles

Source: *Essential Science Indicators*

Essential Science Indicators considers more than seven million papers published in over 11,500 journals over the previous decade, in 22 main fields of science and the social sciences, to arrive at this ranking.

Wired World

TOP 10 COUNTRIES WITH THE MOST TELEPHONES

COUNTRY	TELEPHONE LINES PER 100	TOTAL (2004)
1 China	23.98	311,756,000
2 USA	60.60	177,947,000
3 Japan	46.00	58,788,000
4 Germany	66.15	54,574,000
5 India	4.07	43,960,000
6 Brazil	23.46	42,382,000
7 Russia	27.47	39,616,000
8 France	56.04	33,870,200
9 UK	56.35	33,700,000
10 South Korea	55.31	26,595,100
World	*18.89*	*1,206,247,200*

Source: International Telecommunications Union, *World Telecommunication/ICT Development Report 2006*

Of the world's telephone lines, 538,981,500 are in Asia, 327,580,000 in Europe, 295,306,500 in North and South America, 25,925,000 in Africa, and 13,773,000 in Oceania. In many developing countries, mobile phones have replaced often-defunct, inefficient, or nonexistent fixed lines, enabling their telephone systems rapidly to adopt 21st-century technology.

TOP 10 COMPUTER COUNTRIES

COUNTRY	% OF WORLD TOTAL	COMPUTERS (2005)
1 USA	25.49	230,400,000
2 Japan	8.15	73,660,000
3 China	7.03	63,520,000
4 Germany	5.58	50,420,000
5 UK	4.27	38,620,000
6 France	3.58	32,400,000
7 South Korea	3.14	28,380,000
8 Italy	2.87	25,960,000
9 Canada	2.63	23,770,000
10 Russia	2.52	22,760,000
World total	*100.00*	*903,900,000*

Source: Computer Industry Almanac Inc.

TOP 10 CELLPHONE COUNTRIES

COUNTRY / CELLPHONE SUBSCRIBERS

China
398,000,000

USA
202,000,000

Russia
115,000,000

Japan
95,000,000

Brazil
86,000,000

India
79,000,000

Germany
73,000,000

Italy
59,000,000

UK
58,000,000

France
47,000,000

World total   *2,065,000,000*

Source: Computer Industry Almanac Inc.

TOP 10 **INTERNET COUNTRIES**

COUNTRY	% OF WORLD TOTAL	INTERNET USERS (2007)
1 USA	18.9	211,108,086
2 China	12.3	137,000,000
3 Japan	7.7	86,300,000
4 Germany	4.5	50,471,212
5 India	3.6	40,000,000
6 UK	3.4	37,600,000
7 South Korea	3.1	34,120,000
8 Brazil	2.9	32,130,000
9 France	2.8	30,837,592
10 Italy	2.8	30,763,848
World total	*100.0*	*1,114,274,426*

Source: Internet World Stats

TOP 10 **BROADBAND COUNTRIES**

COUNTRY	BROADBAND SUBSCRIBERS (2006)
1 USA	54,558,000
2 China	48,576,000
3 Japan	25,843,000
4 South Korea	13,898,000
5 Germany	12,744,000
6 France	12,643,000
7 UK	12,317,000
8 Italy	8,377,000
9 Canada	7,615,000
10 Spain	6,091,000
World total	*263,801,000*

Source: Point Topic, *World Broadband Statistics*, December 2006

While these represent the leading users of broadband in terms of subscriber numbers, the percentage of the population connecting to the Internet via broadband varies greatly around the world, from more than 25 percent in Scandinavian countries to about 20 percent in the UK and USA, down to under four percent in China, and less than one percent in India.

9 TRANSPORT & TOURISM

Cars & Road Transport

The car in front...
...is a Toyota—the Corolla is the bestselling ever.

TOP 10 MOTOR VEHICLE-OWNING COUNTRIES

COUNTRY	CARS	COMMERCIAL VEHICLES	TOTAL (2004)
1 USA	132,822,614	98,575,667	231,398,281
2 Japan	55,994,005	17,011,782	73,005,787
3 Germany	45,375,526	3,539,658	48,915,184
4 Italy	33,973,147	4,250,896	38,224,043
5 France	29,990,000	6,139,000	36,039,000
6 UK	29,378,190	3,396,446	33,074,636
7 Russia	24,208,000	5,536,200	29,744,200
8 China	7,900,000	19,800,000	27,700,000
9 Spain	19,541,900	4,660,400	24,202,300
10 Brazil	17,600,000	4,400,000	22,000,000
World total	*603,433,437*	*233,536,876*	*836,970,313*

Source: Ward's Motor Vehicle Facts & Figures 2006

TOP 10 BESTSELLING CARS OF ALL TIME

MANUFACTURER / MODEL	YEARS IN PRODUCTION	APPROXIMATE SALES*
1 Toyota Corolla	1966–	31,600,000
2 Volkswagen Golf	1974–	24,000,000
3 Volkswagen Beetle	1937–2003#	21,529,464
4 Ford Escort/Orion	1968–2003	20,000,000
5 Ford Model T	1908–27	16,536,075
6 Honda Civic	1972–	16,500,000
7 Nissan Sunny/Sentra/Pulsar	1966–	15,900,100
8 Volkswagen Passat	1973–	14,000,000
9 Lada Riva	1980–	13,500,000
10 Chevrolet Impala/Caprice	1958–	13,000,000

* To 2006, except where otherwise indicated
# Produced in Mexico 1978–2003

TOP 10 CAR MANUFACTURERS

COMPANY / COUNTRY	PASSENGER-CAR PRODUCTION 2005
1 Toyota (Japan)	6,157,038
2 General Motors (USA)	5,657,225
3 Volkswagen group (Germany)	4,979,487
4 Ford (USA)	3,514,496
5 Honda (Japan)	3,324,282
6 PSA Peugeot Citroën (France)	2,982,690
7 Hyundai-Kia (South Korea)	2,726,600
8 Nissan (Japan)	2,697,362
9 Renault-Dacia-Samsung (France)	2,195,162
10 DaimlerChrysler (Germany)	1,965,410
World total (including manufacturers outside Top 10)	*45,855,503*

Source: OICA Statistics Committee

TOP 10 CAR-PRODUCING COUNTRIES

COUNTRY / CAR PRODUCTION 2005

Japan	Germany	USA	South Korea	France	China	Spain	Brazil	UK	Canada
9,016,375	5,350,187	4,321,272	3,357,094	3,112,961	3,078,153	2,098,168	2,009,494	1,596,296	1,356,198

Source: The International Organization of Motor Vehicle Manufacturers

TOP 10 COUNTRIES WITH THE LONGEST ROAD NETWORKS

COUNTRY / TOTAL ROAD NETWORK MILES/KM

 1 USA
3,995,643 / 6,430,366

 2 India
2,102,312 / 3,383,344

 3 China
1,162,374 / 1,870,661

 4 Brazil
1,088,560 / 1,751,868

 5 Japan
735,982 / 1,183,000

 6 Canada
647,655 / 1,042,300

 7 France
594,219 / 956,303

 8 Russia
541,214 / 871,000

 9 Australia
503,708 / 810,641

10 Spain
414,014 / 666,292

World total 20,098,350 / 32,345,165

Source: CIA, *The World Factbook 2007*

The CIA's assessment of road lengths includes both paved (mostly tarmac-surfaced) and unpaved highways (gravel and earth-surfaced). In many developing countries the proportion of unpaved is greater than paved. The world total is equivalent to over 800 times the circumference of the Earth at the Equator.

THE CENTENARY OF THE MODEL T FORD

The Model T Ford was long the world's most popular car.

Considered the most influential car of the 20th century, the first Model T Ford left the company's Detroit, Michigan, factory on September 27, 1908. The application of revolutionary production-line methods enabled the Model T, popularly known as the "Tin Lizzie," to be assembled quickly and hence made it affordable: its original price was $850.50, but fell to under $300 by 1925. The well-known slogan that it was available in "any color so long as it's black" was not always true—it was available in various colors in the early and late years of its long life, but restricted to black in the middle period. Model T Fords were also assembled in Canada and the UK.

In 1911, Henry Alexander drove one to the top of Ben Nevis, Britain's highest mountain. So popular did it become that in 1921 642,750, or 50.4 percent of the world total car production of 1,275,324 vehicles were Model Ts. The last Model T was made on May 26, 1927.

Fastest on Land

THE 10 **FIRST HOLDERS OF THE LAND SPEED RECORD**

DRIVER / CAR	LOCATION	DATE	SPEED MPH	SPEED KM/H
1 Gaston de Chasseloup-Laubat, Jeantaud	Achères, France	Dec 18, 1898	39.24	62.78
2 Camille Jenatzy, Jenatzy	Achères, France	Jan 17, 1899	41.42	66.27
3 Gaston de Chasseloup-Laubat, Jeantaud	Achères, France	Jan 17, 1899	43.69	69.90
4 Camille Jenatzy, Jenatzy	Achères, France	Jan 27, 1899	49.92	79.37
5 Gaston de Chasseloup-Laubat, Jeantaud	Achères, France	Mar 4, 1899	57.60	92.16
6 Camille Jenatzy, Jenatzy	Achères, France	Apr 29, 1899	65.79	105.26
7 Leon Serpollet, Serpollet	Nice, France	Apr 13, 1902	75.06	120.09
8 William Vanderbilt, Mors	Albis, France	Aug 5, 1902	76.08	121.72
9 Henri Fournier, Mors	Dourdan, France	Nov 5, 1902	76.60	122.56
10 M. Augières, Mors	Dourdan, France	Nov 17, 1902	77.13	123.40

The official land speed record was set and broken five times within a year. The first six holders were rival racers Comte Gaston de Chasseloup-Laubat (France) and Camille Jenatzy (Belgium).

THE 10 **LATEST HOLDERS OF THE LAND SPEED RECORD**

DRIVER / CAR	DATE	SPEED MPH	SPEED KM/H
1 Andy Green (UK), ThrustSSC*	Oct 15, 1997	763.04	1,227.99
2 Richard Noble (UK), Thrust2*	Oct 4, 1983	633.47	1,013.47
3 Gary Gabelich (USA), The Blue Flame	Oct 23, 1970	622.41	995.85
4 Craig Breedlove (USA), Spirit of America – Sonic 1	Nov 15, 1965	600.60	960.96
5 Art Arfons (USA), Green Monster	Nov 7, 1965	576.55	922.48
6 Craig Breedlove (USA), Spirit of America – Sonic 1	Nov 2, 1965	555.48	888.76
7 Art Arfons (USA), Green Monster	Oct 27, 1964	536.71	858.73
8 Craig Breedlove (USA), Spirit of America	Oct 15, 1964	526.28	842.04
9 Craig Breedlove (USA), Spirit of America	Oct 13, 1964	468.72	749.95
10 Art Arfons (USA), Green Monster	Oct 5, 1964	434.02	694.43

* Location: Black Rock Desert, Nevada, USA; all other speeds were achieved at Bonneville Salt Flats, Utah, USA

Second pioneer
Camille Jenatzy (1868–1913) held successive land speed records and was the first person to exceed the symbolic 100 km/h barrier, in an electric-powered vehicle, La Jamais Contente ("Never Satisfied"). He went on to win major races, but died tragically in a hunting accident.

World's fastest car
Designed by previous record-holder Richard Noble and driven by RAF pilot Andy Green, the ThrustSSC (SuperSonic Car), powered by two Rolls Royce jet engines from Phantom fighter aircraft, became the first car to break the sound barrier as it set a new land speed record.

THE 10 **LATEST HOLDERS OF THE MOTORCYCLE SPEED RECORD**

	RIDER*	MOTORCYCLE	DATE	SPEED MPH	SPEED KM/H
1	Chris Carr	BUB Number Seven	Sep 5, 2006	350.88	564.68
2	Rocky Robinson	Ack Attack, dual-Suzuki-Hayabusa	Sep 3, 2006	342.80	551.68
3	Dave Campos	Twin 91 cu in/1,491 cc Ruxton Harley-Davidson Easyriders	Jul 14, 1990	322.15	518.45
4	Donald A. Vesco	Twin 1,016 cc Kawasaki Lightning Bolt	Aug 25, 1978	318.60	512.73
5	Donald A. Vesco	Twin 1,016 cc Kawasaki Lightning Bolt	Aug 23, 1978	315.44	507.65
6	Donald A. Vesco	1,496 cc Yamaha Silver Bird	Sep 28, 1975	302.93	487.51
7	Donald A. Vesco	Yamaha	Oct 1, 1974	281.71	453.36
8	Calvin Rayborn	1,480 cc Harley-Davidson	Oct 16, 1970	265.49	427.26
9	Calvin Rayborn	1,480 cc Harley-Davidson	Oct 15, 1970	255.38	410.99
10	Donald A. Vesco	700 cc Yamaha	Sep 17, 1970	251.92	405.42

* All USA

All the records listed here were achieved at the Bonneville Salt Flats. To break a Fédération Internationale Motorcycliste record, the motorcycle has to cover a measured distance, making two runs within one hour, and taking the average of the two. American Motorcycling Association records require a turnround within two hours.

TOP 10 **FASTEST RAIL JOURNEYS**

	JOURNEY*	TRAIN	DISTANCE MILES	DISTANCE KM	SPEED MPH	SPEED KM/H
1	Lyon-St Exupéry to Aix-en-Provence, France	TGV 6171	179.9	289.6	163.6	263.3
2	Hiroshima to Kokura, Japan	15 Nozomi	119.3	192.0	162.7	261.8
3	Frankfurt Flughafen to Siegburg/Bonn, Germany	17 ICE trains	89.5	144.0	145.1	233.5
4	Brussels Midi to Marseilles-St Charles, Belgium/France	ThalysSoleil	654.9	1,054.0	145.0	233.4
5	Madrid Atocha to Cuidad Atocha, Spain	6 AVE trains	160.1	170.7	127.3	204.8
6	Falköping to Katrineholm, Sweden	X2000 438	130.3	209.7	118.4	190.6
7	Seoul to Taejeon, South Korea	5 KTX trains	96.3	155.0	117.9	189.8
8	Stevenage to Grantham, UK	1 IC255	77.9	125.3	112.5	181.1
9	Roma (Rome) Termini to Firenze (Florence) SMN, Italy	Eurostar 9458	162.2	261.0	103.5	166.6
10	Wilmington to Baltimore, USA	13 Acela Expresses	68.4	110.1	102.6	165.1

* Fastest journey for each country; all those in the Top 10 have other equally or similarly fast services

Source: *Railway Gazette International*, 2005 World Speed Survey

Fastest Man—On a Sled
On December 10, 1954, Lt. Col. John P. Stapp (1910–99) became the fastest man in the world on a rocket-propelled sled, Sonic Wind No. 1, at the Holloman Air Force Base, New Mexico, which attained a speed of 632 mph (1,017 km/h). The fastest speed on land in an unmanned vehicle was achieved on April 30, 2003 by a rocket-powered sled that reached 6,416 mph (10,326 km/h) or Mach 8.5.

French revolution
In service since 1981, the French TGV (Train à Grande Vitesse—high-speed train) has consistently offered some of the world's fastest scheduled services. On April 3, 2007, a TGV set a new world rail-speed record of 357.2 mph (574.8 km/h).

On the Water

Queen rules
The Queen Mary *twice held the Blue Riband for the fastest Atlantic crossing in both directions, seizing the coveted title from the French* Normandie. *She maintained the record until 1952 and retired from service in 1967.*

TOP 10 **LONGEST CRUISE SHIPS**

SHIP / YEAR BUILT / COUNTRY	LENGTH FT	M
1 Genesis of the Seas 2009*, Finland	1,181	360
2 Queen Mary 2 2004, France	1,132	345
3 = Freedom of the Seas 2006, Finland	1,112	339
= Liberty of the Seas 2007, Finland	1,112	339
5 = Fantasia 2008*, France	1,092	333
= Serenata 2009*, France	1,092	333
7 = Voyager of the Seas 1999, Finland	1,021	311
= Explorer of the Seas 2000, Finland	1,021	311
9 = Adventure of the Seas 2001, Finland	1,020	311
= Navigator of the Seas 2003, Finland	1,020	311
= Mariner of the Seas 2004, Finland	1,020	311

* Scheduled launch

For comparison, the *Great Eastern* (launched 1858) measured 692 ft (211 m), while the *Titanic* was 882 ft (269 m) long, and until the influx of new vessels in 1998, would have ranked 8th in this Top 10. Former entrant in this list the *Queen Mary* (1,020 ft/311 m) is now a floating museum at Long Beach, California, while the 1,031-ft (314-m) *Queen Elizabeth* was taken out of service in 1972. One-time record longest ship, the 1,035-m (316-m) *Norway* (former *France*), ceased sailing in 2003, but plans to scrap her have been halted following protests from environmentalists.

THE 10 **LATEST BLUE RIBAND WINNERS** *

SHIP / COMPANY	DATE	DAYS	DURATION HRS	MINS	AVERAGE SPEED (KNOTS)
1 Cat-Link V, Scandlines	Jul 20, 1998	2	20	9	41.28
2 Catalonia, Buquebus	Jun 10, 1998	3	9	55	38.85
3 Hoverspeed Great Britain, Hoverspeed	Jun 24, 1990	3	7	54	36.97
4 United States, US Line	Jul 7, 1952	3	10	40	35.59
5 Queen Mary, Cunard White Star	Aug 14, 1938	3	20	42	31.69
6 Normandie, French Line	Aug 8, 1937	3	22	7	31.20
7 Normandie, French Line	Mar 22, 1937	4	0	6	30.99
8 Queen Mary, Cunard White Star	Aug 30, 1936	3	23	57	30.63
9 Normandie, French Line	Jun 11, 1935	4	3	25	30.31
10 Bremen, Norddeutscher Lloyd	Jun 15, 1933	4	16	15	28.51

* Eastbound crossings

Steamships began carrying passengers across the Atlantic between Europe and the USA from 1838 onward. In the early years, it could take 18 days or longer to make the journey, a distance—depending on the route—of about 3,000 miles (4,828 km). Shipping companies competed with each other, with the fastest ship carrying a blue flag, or "Blue Riband." There were separate Blue Ribands for westbound and eastbound crossings, and after 1934 the Hales Trophy was presented to the ship with the fastest average speed.

THE 10 **LATEST HOLDERS OF THE WATER SPEED RECORD—JET-POWERED**

DRIVER / BOAT / LOCATION / DATE	SPEED MPH	SPEED KM/H
1 Ken Warby (Australia), Spirit of Australia, Blowering Dam, Australia Oct 8, 1978	511.13	317.60
2 Ken Warby, Spirit of Australia, Blowering Dam, Nov 20, 1977	463.78	288.18
3 Lee Taylor (USA), Hustler, Lake Guntersville, Alabama, USA Jun 30, 1967	459.02	285.22
4 Donald Campbell (UK), Bluebird K7, Lake Dumbleyung, Australia Dec 31, 1964	444.71	276.33
5 Donald Campbell, Bluebird K7, Coniston Water, UK, May 14, 1959	418.99	260.35
6 Donald Campbell, Bluebird K7, Coniston Water, Nov 10, 1958	400.12	248.62
7 Donald Campbell, Bluebird K7, Coniston Water, Nov 7, 1957	384.75	239.07
8 Donald Campbell, Bluebird K7, Coniston Water, Sep 19, 1956	363.12	225.63
9 Donald Campbell, Bluebird K7, Lake Mead, Nevada, USA, Nov 16, 1955	347.94	216.20
10 Donald Campbell, Bluebird K7, Ullswater, Jul 23, 1955	325.60	202.32

Jet-powered craft have long held the World Unlimited water speed record, with Ken Warby's self-built *Spirit of Australia* unbeaten for 30 years.

THE 10 **LATEST HOLDERS OF THE WATER SPEED RECORD—PROPELLER-DRIVEN**

DRIVER / BOAT / LOCATION / DATE	SPEED MPH	SPEED KM/H
1 Dave Villwock, Miss Budweiser, Lake Oroville, California, USA Mar 13, 2004	220.493	354.849
2 Russ Wicks, Miss Freei, Lake Washington, Washington, USA Jun 15, 2000	205.494	330.711
3 Roy Duby, Miss US1, Lake Guntersville, Alabama, USA Apr 17, 1962	200.419	322.543
4 Bill Muncey, Miss Thriftaway, Lake Washington, Feb 16, 1960	192.001	308.996
5 Jack Regas, Hawaii Kai III, Lake Washington, Nov 10, 1957	187.627	301.956
6 Art Asbury (Canada), Miss Supertest II, Lake Ontario, Canada, Nov 1, 1957	184.540	296.988
7 Stanley Sayres, Slo-Mo-Shun IV, Lake Washington, Jul 7, 1952	178.497	287.263
8 Stanley Sayres, Slo-Mo-Shun IV, Lake Washington, Jun 26, 1950	160.323	258.015
9 Malcolm Campbell (UK), Bluebird K4, Coniston Water, UK, Aug 19, 1939	141.740	228.108
10 Malcolm Campbell, Bluebird K3, Hallwiler See, Switzerland, Aug 17, 1938	130.910	210.679

* USA unless otherwise stated

All these record-holders were propeller-driven craft, taking the average of two runs over a measured mile or kilometer course.

Fastest hydroplane
Miss Budweiser *set a new record for propeller-driven craft, hitting 229 mph (369 km/h) on the return leg of its two runs.*

In the Air

Transatlantic cruiser
One of three Douglas World Cruisers that embarked on a round-the-world journey in 1924, two of them successfully crossing the Atlantic.

THE 10 **FIRST TRANSATLANTIC FLIGHTS**

FLIGHT DETAILS / AIRCRAFT   DATE*

1 Trepassy Harbor, Newfoundland, to Lisbon, Portugal
US Navy Curtiss flying boat *NC-4*   May 16–27, 1919
Lt.-Cdr. Albert Cushing Read and a crew of five crossed the Atlantic in a series of hops, refueling at sea.

2 St. John's, Newfoundland, to Galway, Ireland
Twin Rolls-Royce-engined
converted Vickers Vimy bomber   Jun 14–15, 1919
British pilot Capt. John Alcock and navigator Lt. Arthur Whitten Brown achieved the first nonstop flight, ditching in Derrygimla bog after their epic 16 hr 28 min journey.

3 East Fortune, Scotland to Roosevelt Field, New York
British *R-34* airship   Jul 2–6,1919
Major George Herbert Scott and a crew of 30 made the first east–west crossing, the first airship to do so.

4 Lisbon, Portugal to Recife, Brazil
Fairey IIID seaplane *Santa Cruz*   Mar 30–Jun 5, 1922
Portuguese pilots Admiral Gago Coutinho and Commander Sacadura Cabral were the first to fly the South Atlantic in stages.

5 Orkneys, Scotland to Labrador, Canada
Two Douglas seaplanes, *Chicago*
and *New Orleans*   Aug 2–31, 1924
Lt. Lowell H. Smith and Leslie P. Arnold in one biplane and Erik Nelson and John Harding in another set out and crossed the North Atlantic in a series of hops via Iceland and Greenland.

6 Friedrichshafen, Germany to Lakehurst, New Jersey
Los Angeles, a renamed German-built
ZR 3 airship   Oct 12–15, 1924
Piloted by Dr. Hugo Eckener, with 31 passengers and crew.

7 Huelva, Spain to Recife, Brazil
Plus Ultra, a Dornier Wal
twin-engined flying boat   Jan 22–Feb 10, 1926
A crew of three Spaniards including General Franco's brother Ramón plus a photographer crossed the South Atlantic in stages.

8 Cagliari, Sardinia to Recife, Brazil   Feb 8–24, 1927
Santa Maria, a Savoia-Marchetti S.55 flying boat
Francesco Marquis de Pinedo, Capt. Carlo del Prete, and Lt. Vitale Zacchetti crossed in stages as part of a goodwill trip.

9 Lisbon, Portugal to Natal, Brazil
Dornier Wal flying boat   Mar 16–17, 1927
Portuguese flyers Sarmento de Beires and Jorge de Castilho took the route via Casablanca.

10 Genoa, Italy to Natal, Brazil
Savoia-Marchetti flying boat   Apr 28–May 14, 1927
A Brazilian crew set out on October 17, 1926, flying in stages via the Canaries and Cape Verde Islands.

* All dates refer to the Atlantic legs of the journeys; some started earlier and ended beyond their first transatlantic landfalls

TOP 10 **LONGEST AIRCRAFT**

		LENGTH	
AIRCRAFT	FT	IN	M
1 Ekranoplan KM Caspian Sea Monster	348	0	106.1
2 Antonov An-225 Cossack	275	7	84.0
3 Lockheed C-5 Galaxy	247	10	75.5
4 Airbus A340-600	246	11	75.3
5 Boeing 777	242	4	73.9
6 Lun Ekranoplan	240	0	73.2
7 Airbus A380-800	239	6	73.0
8 Boeing 747	231	10	70.7
9 Antonov An-124 Condor	226	9	69.1
10 H-4 Hercules ("Spruce Goose")	218	6	66.6

THE 10 **FIRST ROCKET AND JET AIRCRAFT**

AIRCRAFT	COUNTRY	FIRST FLIGHT
1 Heinkel He 176*	Germany	Jun 20, 1939
2 Heinkel He 178	Germany	Aug 27, 1939
3 DFS 194*	Germany	Aug 1940#
4 Caproni-Campini N-1	Italy	Aug 28, 1940
5 Heinkel He 280V-1	Germany	Apr 2, 1941
6 Gloster E.28/39	UK	May 15, 1941
7 Messerschmitt Me 163 Komet*	Germany	Aug 13, 1941
8 Messerschmitt Me 262V-3	Germany	Jul 18, 1942
9 Bell XP-59A Airacomet	USA	Oct 2, 1942
10 Gloster Meteor F Mk 1	UK	Mar 5, 1943

* Rocket-powered
# Precise date unknown

Fastest jet
In 1976 the Lockheed SR-71A "Blackbird" set a jet record of Mach 3.3 that still stands over 30 years later.

THE 10 **LATEST AIR SPEED RECORDS HELD BY JETS***

PILOT	COUNTRY	LOCATION	AIRCRAFT	SPEED MPH	SPEED KM/H	DATE
1 Eldon W. Joersz/ George T. Morgan Jr	USA	Beale AFB, California, USA	Lockheed SR-71A	2,193.167	3,529.560	Jul 28, 1976
2 Adolphus Bledsoe/ John T. Fuller	USA	Beale AFB, USA	Lockheed SR-71A	2,092.294	3,367.221	Jul 27, 1976
3 Robert L. Stephens/ Daniel Andre	USA	Edwards AFB, California, USA	Lockheed YF-12A	2,070.102	3,331.507	May 1, 1965
4 Georgi Mossolov	USSR	Podmoskownoe, USSR	Mikoyan E-166	1,665.896	2,681.000	Jul 7, 1962
5 Robert B. Robinson	USA	Edwards AFB, USA	McDonnell F4H-1F Phantom II	1,606.509	2,585.425	Nov 22, 1961
6 Joseph W. Rogers	USA	Edwards AFB, USA	Convair F-106A Delta Dart	1,525.924	2,455.736	Dec 15, 1959
7 Georgi Mossolov	USSR	Jukowski- Petrowskol, USSR	Mikoyan E-66	1,483.834	2,388.000	Oct 31, 1959
8 Walter W. Irwin	USA	Edwards AFB, USA	Lockheed YF-104A Starfighter	1,404.012	2,259.538	May 16, 1958
9 Adrian E. Drew	USA	Edwards AFB, USA	McDonnell F-101A Voodoo	1,207.635	1,943.500	Dec 12, 1957
10 Peter Twiss	UK	Chichester, UK	Fairey Delta Two	1,132.138	1,822.000	Mar 10, 1956

* Ground-launched only, hence excluding X-15 records

The speed of 822.268 mph (1,323.312 km/h) achieved on August 20, 1955 by Horace A. Hanes (USA) at Palmdale, USA, in a North American F-100C Super Sabre, was the first official supersonic record-holder. The next holder, that of Peter Twiss, was the greatest-ever incremental increase in the air speed record—309.870 mph (498.688 km/h). It should be noted that although air records are customarily expressed to three decimal places, few flights have ever been recorded to such a level of accuracy.

Transport Disasters

THE 10 **WORST MARINE DISASTERS**

LOCATION / DATE / INCIDENT — NO. KILLED

1 Off Gdansk, Poland, Jan 30, 1945 — up to 7,800
The German liner *Wilhelm Gustloff*, laden with refugees, was torpedoed by a Soviet submarine, S-13. The precise death toll remains uncertain, but recent research suggests a total of 10,582 on board.

2 Off Cape Rixhöft (Rozeewie), Poland, Apr 16, 1945 — 6,800
German ship *Goya*, carrying evacuees from Gdansk, was torpedoed in the Baltic.

3 Off Yingkow, China, Dec 3, 1948 — >6,000
The boilers of an unidentified Chinese troopship carrying soldiers from Manchuria exploded, detonating ammunition.

4 Off Sumatra, Sep 18, 1944 — 5,620
The Japanese ship *Junyo Maru*, carrying Dutch, British, American, and Australian prisoners of war and Javanese slave laborers, was torpedoed by British submarine HMS *Tradewind*.

5 En route for Okinawa, Jun 29, 1944 — 5,400
Japanese troop transport *Toyama Maru* was torpedoed by American submarine USS *Sturgeon*.

6 Lübeck, Germany, May 3, 1945 — 5,000
The German ship *Cap Arcona*, carrying concentration-camp survivors, was bombed and sunk by British fighter-bombers.

7 Off British coast, Aug to Oct 1588 — 4,000
Military conflict and storms combined to destroy the Spanish Armada.

8 Off Stolpmünde (Ustka), Poland, Feb 10, 1945 — 3,500
German war-wounded and refugees were lost when the *General Steuben* was torpedoed by the same Russian submarine that had sunk the *Wilhelm Gustloff* 10 days earlier.

9 Off St Nazaire, France, Jun 17, 1940 — >3,000
The British ship *Lancastria*, carrying troops and French refugees, sank after a dive-bombing attack by Luftwaffe aircraft.

10 Tabias Strait, Philippines, Dec 21, 1987 — up to 3,000
The ferry *Doña Paz* was struck by oiltanker *MV Vector*. The *Doña Paz* was so overcrowded that a death toll of 4,341 claimed by some sources may be possible.

Recent reassessments of the death tolls in some of the World War II marine disasters means that the most famous marine disaster of all, the *Titanic*, which sank on April 15, 1912 with the loss of 1,517 lives, no longer ranks in the Top 10. However, the *Titanic* tragedy remains one of the worst peacetime disasters, along with such incidents as the *General Slocum*, a steamboat that caught fire off New York on June 15, 1904 with the loss of 1,021.

THE 10 **WORST RAIL DISASTERS**

LOCATION / DATE / INCIDENT — NO. KILLED

1 Telwatta, Sri Lanka, Dec 26, 2004 — up to 2,000
The *Queen of the Sea* train was struck by the Indian Ocean tsunami. It was impossible to determine the precise number of casualties in the devastation.

2 Bagmati River, India, Jun 6, 1981 — c. 800
The carriages of a train plunged off a bridge over the river Bagmati near Mansi when the driver braked, apparently to avoid hitting a sacred cow.

3 Chelyabinsk, Russia, Jun 3, 1989 — up to 800
Two passenger trains, laden with holidaymakers, were destroyed when liquid gas from a nearby pipeline exploded.

4 Guadalajara, Mexico, Jan 18, 1915 — >600
A train derailed on a steep incline, but political strife in the country meant that full details of the disaster were suppressed.

5 Modane, France, Dec 12, 1917 — 573
A troop-carrying train ran out of control, and it has been claimed that it was overloaded and that as many as 1,000 may have died.

6 Balvano, Italy, Mar 2, 1944 — 521
A heavily laden train stalled in the Armi Tunnel, and many passengers were asphyxiated.

7 Torre, Spain, Jan 3, 1944 — >500
A double collision and fire in a tunnel resulted in many deaths.

8 Awash, Ethiopia, Jan 13, 1985 — 428
A derailment hurled a train into a ravine.

9 Cireau, Romania, Jan 7, 1917 — 374
An overcrowded passenger train crashed into a military train and was derailed.

10 Reqa al-Gharbiya, Egypt, Feb 20, 2002 — 373
A fire on the Cairo-Luxor train engulfed the carriages. Passengers were burned or leaped from the train to their deaths.

THE 10 **WORST AIR DISASTERS**

LOCATION / DATE / INCIDENT   NO. KILLED

1 **New York**, USA, Sep 11, 2001   c. 1,622
Following a hijacking by terrorists, an American Airlines Boeing 767 was deliberately flown into the North Tower of the World Trade Center, killing all 81 passengers (including five hijackers), 11 crew on board, and an estimated 1,530 on the ground, both as a direct result of the crash and the subsequent fire and collapse of the building, which also killed 479 rescue workers.

2 **New York**, USA, Sep 11, 2001   c. 677
As part of the coordinated attack, hijackers commandeered a second Boeing 747 and crashed it into the South Tower of the World Trade Center, killing all 56 passengers and 9 crew on board, and approximately 612 on the ground.

3 **Tenerife**, Canary Islands, Mar 27, 1977   583
Two Boeing 747s (PanAm and KLM, carrying 380 passengers and 16 crew, and 234 passengers and 14 crew respectively) collided and caught fire on the runway of Los Rodeos airport after the pilots received incorrect control-tower instructions. A total of 61 escaped.

4 **Mt. Ogura**, Japan, Aug 12, 1985   520
A JAL Boeing 747 on an internal flight from Tokyo to Osaka crashed, killing all but four of the 509 passengers and all 15 crew on board.

5 **Charkhi Dadri**, India, Nov 12, 1996   349
Soon after taking off from New Delhi's Indira Gandhi International Airport, a Saudi Arabian Airlines Boeing 747 collided with a Kazakh Airlines Ilyushin IL76 cargo aircraft on its descent and exploded, killing all 312 (289 passengers and 23 crew) on the Boeing and all 37 (27 passengers and 10 crew) on the Ilyushin in the world's worst midair crash.

LOCATION / DATE / INCIDENT   NO. KILLED

6 **Paris**, France, Mar 3, 1974   346
Immediately after takeoff for London, a Turkish Airlines DC-10 suffered an explosive decompression when a door burst open, and crashed at Ermenonville, north of Paris, killing all 335 passengers, including many England rugby supporters, and its crew of 11.

7 **Off the Irish coast**, Jun 23, 1985   329
An Air India Boeing 747 on a flight from Vancouver to Delhi exploded in midair, probably as a result of a terrorist bomb, killing all 307 passengers and 22 crew.

8 **Riyadh**, Saudi Arabia, Aug 19, 1980   301
Following an emergency landing a Saudia (Saudi Arabian) Airlines Lockheed TriStar caught fire. The crew were unable to open the doors and all 287 passengers and 14 crew died from smoke inhalation.

9 **Off the Iranian coast**, Jul 3, 1988   290
An Iran Air A300 airbus was shot down in error by a missile fired by the USS *Vincennes*, which mistook the airliner for an Iranian fighter aircraft, resulting in the deaths of all 274 passengers and 16 crew. In 1996 the USA paid $61.8 million in compensation to the families of the victims.

10 **Sirach Mountain**, Iran, Feb 19, 2003   275
An Ilyushin 76 on a flight from Zahedan to Kerman crashed into the mountain in poor weather. It was carrying 257 Revolutionary Guards and a crew of 18, none of whom survived.

No survivors
The aftermath of the Charkhi Dadri disaster, the world's worst involving a midair collision.

World Tourism

TOP 10 **TOURIST DESTINATIONS**

COUNTRY	INTERNATIONAL VISITORS (2005)
1 France	76,000,000
2 Spain	55,600,000
3 USA	49,400,000
4 China	46,800,000
5 Italy	36,500,000
6 UK	30,000,000
7 Mexico	21,900,000
8 Germany	21,500,000
9 Turkey	20,300,000
10 Austria	20,000,000
World total	*806,000,000*

Source: World Tourism Organization

TOP 10 **DESTINATIONS FOR US TOURISTS**

COUNTRY	VISITORS (2005)
1 Mexico	20,325,000
2 Canada	14,390,000
3 UK	3,829,000
4 France	2,217,000
5 Italy	2,044,000
6 Germany	1,670,000
7 Japan	1,497,000
8 Dominican Republic	1,439,000
9 Jamaica	1,353,000
10 China	1,295,000

Source: US Department of Commerce, International Trade Administration, Office of Travel and Tourism Industries

TOP 10 **COUNTRIES WITH THE BIGGEST INCREASE IN TOURISM**

COUNTRY	VISITORS INCREASE 2004–05 (%)
1 Swaziland	82.8
2 Laos	65.1
3 Venezuela	45.2
4 Cambodia	34.7
5 Honduras	25.9
6 Turkey	20.5
7 El Salvador	19.5
8 Vietnam	18.4
9 Colombia	18.0
10 Algeria	16.9
USA	*7.2*

Source: World Tourism Organization

French leave
The tranquility of rural France combines with its urban attractions and culinary delights to make it the world's foremost tourist destination.

Fall and rise
The appeal of such features as Venezuela's Angel Falls have prompted a substantial rise in its tourist numbers.

TOP 10 **TOURIST EARNING COUNTRIES**

COUNTRY	INTERNATIONAL TOURISM RECEIPTS, 2005 ($)
1 USA	81,680,000,000
2 Spain	47,891,000,000
3 France	42,276,000,000
4 Italy	35,398,000,000
5 UK	30,669,000,000
6 China	29,296,000,000
7 Germany	29,204,000,000
8 Turkey	18,152,000,000
9 Austria	15,467,000,000
10 Australia	14,952,000,000
World total	*680,000,000,000*

Source: World Tourism Organization

TOP 10 **TOURISM SPENDING COUNTRIES**

COUNTRY	INTERNATIONAL TOURISM EXPENDITURE, 2005 ($)
1 Germany	71,000,000,000
2 USA	69,200,000,000
3 UK	59,600,000,000
4 Japan	37,500,000,000
5 France	31,200,000,000
6 Italy	22,400,000,000
7 China	21,800,000,000
8 Canada	18,400,000,000
9 Russia	17,800,000,000
10 Netherlands	16,200,000,000
World total	*680,000,000,000*

Source: World Tourism Organization

La Serenissima
A magnet for tourists since the days of the Grand Tour, Venice remains of one of Italy's most popular cities.

Gambling capital
Almost 40 million people a year visit Las Vegas, placing it among the USA's principal tourist venues.

Tourist Attractions

TOP 10 **AMUSEMENT PARKS IN THE USA**

PARK / LOCATION	VISITORS (2006)
1 Magic Kingdom, Walt Disney World, Orlando, FL	16,640,000
2 Disneyland, Anaheim, CA	14,730,000
3 Epcot, Walt Disney World, Orlando, FL	10,460,000
4 Disney-MGM Studios, Walt Disney World, Orlando, FL	9,100,000
5 Disney's Animal Kingdom, Walt Disney World, Orlando, FL	8,910,000
6 Universal Studios, Orlando, FL	6,000,000
7 Disney's California Adventure, Anaheim, CA	5,950,000
8 SeaWorld, Orlando, FL	5,740,000
9 Universal's Islands of Adventure, Orlando, FL	5,300,000
10 Universal Studios, Hollywood, CA	4,700,000

Source: TEA/ERA Theme Park Attendance Report 2006

TOP 10 **OLDEST OPERATING ROLLERCOASTERS IN THE USA***

ROLLERCOASTER / LOCATION	OPENED
1 Leap-the-Dips, Lakemont Park, Altoona, PA	1902
2 Jack Rabbit, Sea Breeze Park, Rochester, NY	1920
3 =Jack Rabbit, Kennywood, West Mifflin, PA	1921
=Roller Coaster, Lagoon, Farmington, UT	1921
5 Giant Dipper, Santa Cruz Beach Boardwalk, Santa Cruz, CA	1924
6 =Big Dipper, Geauga Lake, Aurora, OH	1925
=Giant Dipper, Belmont Park, San Diego, CA	1925
8 =Wildcat, Lake Compounce, Bristol, CT	1927
=Giant Coaster, Arnolds Park, Arnolds Park, IA	1927
=Cyclone, Astroland—Coney Island, Brooklyn, NY	1927
=Racer, Kennywood, West Mifflin, PA	1927

* In operation at same location

TOP 10 COUNTRIES OF ORIGIN OF OVERSEAS VISITORS TO THE USA

	COUNTRY	OVERSEAS VISITORS (2005)
1	Canada	14,865,000
2	Mexico	12,858,000
3	UK	4,344,957
4	Japan	3,883,906
5	Germany	1,415,530
6	France	878,648
7	South Korea	705,093
8	Australia	581,773
9	Italy	545,546
10	Brazil	485,373
	Total all countries	49,401,528

Source: US Department of Commerce, International Trade Administration, Office of Travel and Tourism Industries

TOP 10 MOST-VISITED US CITIES

	STATE	MARKET SHARE %	OVERSEAS VISITORS, 2005
1	New York City	26.8	5,810,000
2	Los Angeles	11.9	2,580,000
3	San Francisco	9.8	2,124,000
4	Miami	9.6	2,081,000
5	Orlando	9.3	2,016,000
6	Oahu/Honolulu	8.4	1,821,000
7	Las Vegas	8.2	1,778,000
8	Washington, D.C.	5.1	1,106,000
9	Chicago	5.0	1,084,000
10	Boston	3.7	802,000

Source: Tourism Industries/International Trade Administration, Department of Commerce

TOP 10 MOST-VISITED US STATES AND TERRITORIES

	STATE	MARKET SHARE %	OVERSEAS VISITORS, 2005
1	New York	28.1	6,092,000
2	California	22.1	4,791,000
3	Florida	20.2	4,379,000
4	Hawaii	10.4	2,255,000
5	Nevada	8.4	1,821,000
6	Illinois	5.3	1,149,000
7	Guam	5.2	1,127,000
8	New Jersey	4.6	997,000
9	Texas	4.4	954,000
10	Massachusetts	4.0	867,000

Source: Tourism Industries/International Trade Administration, Department of Commerce

10

SPORT & LEISURE

Winter Sports

TOP 10 **MEDAL-WINNING COUNTRIES AT THE WINTER OLYMPICS***

	COUNTRY	G	S	B	TOTAL
1	USSR/Unified Team/Russia	121	87	86	294
2	Norway	98	100	85	280
3	USA	78	81	59	218
4	Germany/West Germany	71	73	52	196
5	Austria	51	64	70	185
6	Finland	42	58	52	152
7	Sweden	46	33	45	124
8	Canada	39	38	43	120
9	Switzerland	38	37	43	118
10	East Germany	40	38	37	115

* Up to and including the 2006 Turin Games, and also includes medals won at figure skating and ice hockey included in the Summer games prior to the launch of the Winter Olympics in 1924

G—Gold; S—Silver; B—Bronze

Speed skater
American speed skater Shani Davis took gold in the 1,000 metres and silver in the 1,500 metres at Turin 2006.

TOP 10 **LONGEST BOBSLEIGH AND TOBOGGAN TRACKS***

	LOCATION / COUNTRY	CURVES	LENGTH FT	LENGTH M
1	Nagano, Japan	13	5,780	1,762
2	St. Moritz, Switzerland	13	5,649	1,722
3	La Plagne, France	19	4,944	1,507
4	Calgary, Canada	14	4,839	1,475
5	Lake Placid, USA	20	4,773	1,455
6	Cesana, Italy	19	4,708	1,435
7	Altenberg, Germany	17	4,635	1,413
8	Lillehammer, Norway	16	4,478	1,365
9	Cortina d'Ampezzo, Italy	11	4,429	1,350
10	Salt Lake City, USA	15	4,396	1,340

The most famous of all bobsleigh and toboggan tracks is the Cresta Run at St. Moritz. Toboggan racing has taken place there since the first Grand National in 1885, which attracted 20 entrants.

* Top-level competition tracks

TOP 10 **MOST SKIING WORLD CUP RACE WINS IN A CAREER (MEN)***

	NAME / COUNTRY	FIRST SEASON	LAST SEASON	WINS
1	Ingemar Stenmark, Sweden	1974–75	1988–89	86
2	Hermann Maier, Austria	1996–97	2005–06	53
3	Alberto Tomba, Italy	1987–88	1997–98	50
4	Marc Girardelli, Luxembourg	1982–83	1995–96	46
5	Pirmin Zurbriggen, Switzerland	1981–82	1989–90	40
6	= Stephan Eberharter, Austria	1997–98	2003–04	29
	= Benjamin Raich, Austria	1998–99	2006–07	29
8	Phil Mahre, USA	1976–77	1982–83	27
9	Franz Klammer, Austria	1973–74	1983–84	26
10	Bode Miller, USA	2000–01	2006–07	25

* Up to and including the 2006–07 season

TOP 10 **MOST WORLD FIGURE SKATING TITLES***

	NAME / COUNTRY	MEN	WOMEN	PAIRS	DANCE	TOTAL
1	= Sonja Henie, Norway	0	10	0	0	10
	= Irina Rodnina, USSR	0	0	10	0	10
	= Ulrich Salchow, Sweden	10	0	0	0	10
4	= Herma Planck (*née* Szabo), Austria	0	5	2	0	7
	= Karl Schafer, Austria	7	0	0	0	7
6	= Aleksandr Gorshkov, USSR	0	0	6	0	6
	= Lyudmila Pakhomova, USSR	0	0	0	6	6
	= Aleksandr Zaitsev, USSR	0	0	6	0	6
9	= Dick Button, USA	5	0	0	0	5
	= Lawrence Demmy, GB	0	0	0	5	5
	= Carol Heiss, USA	0	5	0	0	5
	= Jean Westwood, UK	0	0	0	5	5

* Up to and including 2007

TOP 10 **MOST ALPINE SKIING OLYMPIC MEDALS***

	NAME / COUNTRY	M/F	YEARS	G	S	B	TOTAL
1	Kjetil André Aamodt, Norway	M	1992–2006	4	2	2	8
2	Janica Kostelic, Croatia	F	2002–2006	4	2	0	6
3	= Vreni Schneider, Switzerland	F	1988–94	3	1	1	5
	= Alberto Tomba, Italy	M	1988–94	3	2	0	5
	= Katja Seizinger, Germany	F	1992–98	3	0	2	5
	= Lasse Kjus, Norway	M	1994–2002	1	3	1	5
	= Anja Paerson, Sweden	F	2002–06	1	1	3	5
8	= Hanni Wenzel, Liechtenstein	F	1976–80	2	1	1	4
	= Deborah Compagnoni, Italy	F	1992–98	3	1	0	4
	= Stephan Eberharter, Austria	M	1998–2002	1	2	1	4
	= Hermann Maier, Austria	M	1998–2006	2	1	1	4

* Up to and including the 2006 Olympics

M/F—Male/Female; G—Gold; S—Silver; B—Bronze

Downhill racer
Croatia's Janica Kostelic won gold in the Alpine Combined event and silver in the Super-G at Turin in 2006. This took her medal tally to six, making her the second most successful Olympic Alpine skier.

Summer Olympics

TOP 10 **SUMMER OLYMPIC GOLD-MEDAL WINNERS (MEN)***

NAME / COUNTRY	SPORT	YEARS	GOLD MEDALS
1 = Paavo Nurmi, Finland	Athletics	1920–28	9
= Mark Spitz, USA	Swimming	1968–72	9
= Carl Lewis, USA	Athletics	1984–96	9
4 = Sawao Kato, Japan	Gymnastics	1968–76	8
= Matt Biondi, USA	Swimming	1984–92	8
= Ray Ewry, USA	Athletics	1900–08	8
7 = Nikolay Andrianov, USSR	Gymnastics	1972–80	7
= Boris Shakhlin, USSR	Gymnastics	1956–64	7
= Viktor Chukarin, USSR	Gymnastics	1952–56	7
= Aladàr Gerevich, Hungary	Fencing	1932–60	7

* Up to and including 2004

If his total from the 1906 Intercalated Games—the results from which are not recognized by the IOC—were included, Ray Ewry would have won a record 10 gold medals.

TOP 10 **SUMMER OLYMPIC GOLD-MEDAL WINNERS (WOMEN)***

NAME / COUNTRY	SPORT	YEARS	GOLD MEDALS
1 Larissa Latynina, USSR	Gymnastics	1956–64	9
2 = Birgit Fischer (née Schmidt) East Germany/Germany	Canoeing	1980–2004	8
= Jenny Thompson, USA	Swimming	1992–2000	8
4 Vera Casalavska, Czechoslovakia	Gymnastics	1964–68	7
5 = Kristin Otto, Germany	Swimming	1988	6
= Amy van Dyken, USA	Swimming	1996–2000	6
7 = Agnes Keleti, Hungary	Gymnastics	1952–56	5
= Nadia Comaneci, Romania	Gymnastics	1976–80	5
= Polina Astakhova, USSR	Gymnastics	1956–64	5
= Elisabeta Oleniuc–Lipa, Romania	Rowing	1984–2004	5
= Krisztina Egerszegi, Hungary	Swimming	1988–96	5
= Nelli Kim, USSR	Gymnastics	1976–80	5

* Up to and including 2004

Larissa Latynina holds the record for winning the most Olympic medals (18), and also for the most individual medals (15). She is also one of four athletes to win nine Olympic golds, and one of only three women to win the same individual event (floor exercises) at three consecutive Olympics. She coached the Soviet team from 1967 to 1977.

RAY EWRY

Born in Lafayette, Indiana in 1873, Ray Ewry contracted polio as a child and was confined to a wheelchair. He overcame his disabilities to win golds in the now-discontinued "standing" jumps: high jump, long jump, and triple jump, in which competitors had to jump without a run-up.

First held at the 1900 Paris Games, Ewry won all three gold medals on the same day, successfully defending his titles at St. Louis in 1904.

In London in 1908 he won both the high jump and long jump and at Athens in 1906 the high jump and long jump. The standing events were discontinued after the 1912 Olympics, and Ewry's world record of 3.476 meters for the standing long jump, set in 1904, was still standing at the time of his death in 1937.

TOP 10 **MEDAL-WINNING COUNTRIES AT THE SUMMER OLYMPICS, 1896–2004**

COUNTRY	GOLD	SILVER	BRONZE	TOTAL
1 USA	907	697	615	2,219
2 USSR/Unified Team/Russia	525	436	409	1,370
3 Germany/West Germany	229	258	298	785
4 UK	189	242	237	668
5 France	199	202	230	631
6 Italy	189	154	168	511
7 Sweden	140	157	179	476
8 Hungary	158	141	161	460
9 East Germany	159	150	136	445
10 Australia	119	126	154	399

THE 10 NEWEST SUMMER OLYMPIC SPORTS*

	SPORT	FIRST CONTESTED
1	= Taekwondo	2000
	= Triathlon	2000
3	Softball	1996
4	= Badminton	1992
	= Baseball	1992
6	Table tennis	1988
7	= Judo	1964
	= Volleyball	1964
9	= Canoeing	1936
	= Handball	1936

* By date they first became official Olympic sports

Beach volleyball was introduced at the 1996 Olympics, but the IOC recognizes it as volleyball rather than a separate sport.

Against the odds
Germany's Wojtek Czyz (born Poland) won the 100-meters gold in the T42 (leg amputees) class at the 2004 Athens Olympics. Czyz lost his lower left leg in a soccer accident in 2001. He has held world records at 100 meters, 200 meters, and long jump.

TOP 10 MEDAL-WINNING COUNTRIES AT THE SUMMER PARALYMPICS

The first international games for the disabled took place at Stoke Mandeville, UK, in 1952, when 130 athletes from the UK and the Netherlands competed. The first Paralympics to take place at the same venue as the Olympic Games was in Rome in 1960, since when they have been held every four years and, since Seoul in 1988, at the same venue as the Summer Olympics. Some 400 athletes from 23 countries took part in 1960, while at Athens in 2004 a total of 3,806 athletes from 136 nations competed. The USA won a record 131 gold medals in 1984.

	COUNTRY	GOLD	SILVER	BRONZE	TOTAL
1	USA	665	579	607	1,851
2	UK	470	468	454	1,392
3	Germany/West Germany	437	431	413	1,281
4	Canada	445	275	294	1,014
5	France	326	300	283	909
6	Australia	292	306	272	870
7	Holland	238	200	169	607
8	Poland	204	209	167	580
9	Sweden	206	203	145	554
10	Spain	176	166	182	524

Athletics

MARATHON CENTENARY

According to legend, Greek soldier Pheidippides ran from Marathon to Athens—a distance of approximately 25 miles (40.8 km)—to announce the defeat of the Persians in the Battle of Marathon—and promptly fell dead. The Marathon was included in the first Modern Olympics at Athens in 1896, with a distance of 24 miles 1,496 yd (40 km). It was slightly longer, at 25 miles 35 yd (40.26 km) in 1900, reverting to 40 km in 1904 and at the 1906 Intercalated Games revised to 26 miles (41.86 km). The Marathon at the 1908 London Olympics, starting at Windsor Castle and ending in the Olympic Stadium at Shepherd's Bush, was also scheduled for 26 miles (41.86 km). However, as the finishing line did not end in front of the Royal Box, it was moved forward by 385 yards so the royal party could get a good view. The next two Olympics saw the race run over 24 miles 1,725 yd (40.2 km) and 26 miles 986 yd (42.75 km), but in 1921 it was standardized by the International Amateur Athletic Federation (IAAF) at the 1908 London distance, and has remained so internationally ever since.

Dorando Pietri won the 1908 Olympic Marathon, but was disqualified.

TOP 10 ATHLETES WITH THE MOST OLYMPIC TRACK AND FIELD GOLD MEDALS*

	ATHLETE / COUNTRY	YEARS	GOLD MEDALS
1 =	Paavo Nurmi, Finland	1920–28	9
=	Carl Lewis, USA	1984–96	9
3	Ray Ewry#, USA	1900–08	8
4 =	Vilho Ritola, Finland	1924–28	5
=	Michael Johnson, USA	1992–2000	5
6 =	Alvin Kraenzlein, USA	1900	4
=	Melvin Sheppard, USA	1908–12	4
=	Hannes Kolehmainen, Finland	1912–20	4
=	Jesse Owens, USA	1936	4
=	Fanny Blankers-Koen, Netherlands	1948	4
=	Harrison Dillard, USA	1948–52	4
=	Emil Zátopek, Czechoslovakia	1948–52	4
=	Betty Cuthbert, Australia	1956–64	4
=	Al Oerter, USA	1956–68	4
=	Lasse Viren, Finland	1972–76	4
=	Bärbel Wöckel (née Eckert), East Germany	1976–80	4
=	Evelyn Ashford, USA	1984–92	4
=	Robert Korzeniowski, Poland	1996–2004	4

* Men 1896–2004, women 1928–2004
# Ewry also won two gold medals at the 1906 Intercalated Games

TOP 10 FASTEST WINNING TIMES IN THE NEW YORK CITY MARATHON

	RUNNER / COUNTRY	YEAR	TIME HR:MIN:SEC
1	Tesfaye Jifar, Ethiopia	2001	2:07:43
2	Juma Ikangaa, Tanzania	1989	2:08:01
3	Rodgers Rop, Kenya	2002	2:08:07
4	John Kagwe, Kenya	1997	2:08:12
5	Alberto Salazar, USA	1981	2:08:13
6	Steve Jones, UK	1988	2:08:20
7	John Kagwe, Kenya	1998	2:08:45
8	Rod Dixon, New Zealand	1983	2:08:59
9	Joseph Chebet, Kenya	1999	2:09:14
10 =	Salvador Garcia, Mexico	1991	2:09:28
=	Hendrik Ramaala, South Africa	2004	2:09:28

The first New York Marathon was held in 1970 around Central Park. To celebrate the US Bicentennial in 1976, it was moved to a street course, running through the five boroughs of New York City.

TOP 10 **MOST IAAF WORLD CHAMPIONSHIP MEDALS (MEN)**

	ATHLETE / COUNTRY	YEARS	GOLD	MEDALS SILVER	BRONZE	TOTAL
1	Carl Lewis, USA	1983–93	8	1	1	10
2	Michael Johnson, USA	1991–99	9	0	0	9
3	Haile Gebrselassie, Ethiopia	1993–2003	4	2	1	7
4	=Sergey Bubka, USSR/Ukraine	1983–97	6	0	0	6
	=Butch Reynolds, USA	1987–95	3	2	1	6
	=Lars Riedel, Germany	1991–2001	5	0	1	6
7	=Colin Jackson, UK	1987–99	2	2	1	5
	=Jan Zelezny, Czechoslovakia/ Czech Republic	1987–2001	3	0	2	5
	=Dennis Mitchell, USA	1991–2001	3	0	2	5
	=Antonio Pettigrew, USA	1991–2001	4	1	0	5
	=Jonathan Edwards, UK	1993–2001	2	1	2	5
	=Bruny Surin, Canada	1995–99	2	2	1	5
	=Allen Johnson, USA	1995–2003	4	0	1	5
	=Maurice Greene, USA	1997–2001	5	0	0	5
	=Hicham El Guerrouj, Morocco	1997–2003	4	1	0	5

First held at Helsinki in 1983, the IAAF (International Amateur Athletics Federation) World Championships in Athletics were originally held every four years, but since 1993 have been held every two years. Helsinki hosted the 10th anniversary championships in 2005. A record 1,882 athletes competed at Athens in 1997.

TOP 10 **MOST IAAF WORLD CHAMPIONSHIP MEDALS (WOMEN)**

	ATHLETE / COUNTRY	YEARS	GOLD	SILVER	MEDALS BRONZE	TOTAL
1	Merlene Ottey, Jamaica	1983–95	3	4	7	14
2	Jearl Miles-Clark, USA	1991–2003	4	3	2	9
3	=Gwen Torrence, USA	1991–95	3	4	1	8
	=Gail Devers, USA	1993–2001	5	3	0	8
5	Marion Jones, USA	1997–2001	5	1	1	7
6	=Heike Daute (née Dreschler), GDR/Germany	1983–93	2	2	2	6
	=Yuliya Pechonkina Nosova, Russia	2001–05	2	2	2	6
8	=Maria Lourdes Mutola, Mozambique	1993–2003	3	1	1	5
	=Inger Miller, USA	1997–2003	3	2	0	5
	=Eunice Barber, France	1999–2005	2	2	1	5

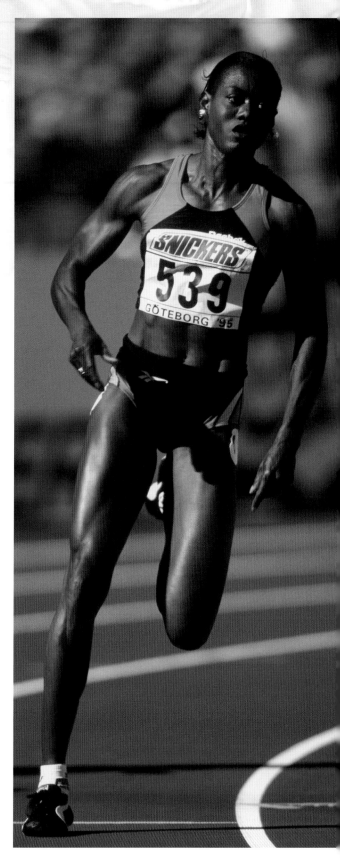

Age no barrier
In winning the 200 meters at the 1995 World Championships, Merlene Ottey became the oldest gold medallist at 35 years 92 days.

Boxing

THE 10 LATEST WBA HEAVYWEIGHT CHAMPIONS*

BOXER / COUNTRY	FROM	REIGN(S) TO
1 Nikolay Valuev, Russia	Dec 17, 2005	Present
2 John Ruiz, Puerto Rico	Feb 24, 2004	Dec 17, 2005
	Mar 2, 2001	Mar 1, 2003
3 Roy Jones Jr, USA	Mar 1, 2003	Feb 20, 2004
4 Evander Holyfield, USA	Aug 12, 2000	Mar 2, 2001
	Nov 9, 1996	Nov 13, 1999
	Nov 6, 1993	Apr 22, 1994
	Oct 25, 1990	Nov 13, 1992
5 Lennox Lewis, UK	Nov 13, 1999	Apr 29, 2000
6 Mike Tyson, USA	Sep 7, 1996	Nov 9, 1996
	Mar 7, 1987	Feb 11, 1990
7 Bruce Seldon, USA	Apr 8, 1995	Sep 7, 1996
8 George Foreman, USA	Nov 5, 1994	Mar 4, 1995
	Jan 22, 1973	Oct 30, 1974
9 Michael Moorer, USA	Apr 22, 1994	Nov 5, 1994
10 Riddick Bowe, USA	Nov 13, 1992	Nov 6, 1993

* Last 10 different men to hold the WBA title, as at January 1, 2007

The WBA (World Boxing Association) started life in 1921 as the NBA (National Boxing Association). It changed its name in 1962.

Long-reigning champ
Joe Calzaghe won all 42 of his professional fights up to 2007.

TOP 10 CURRENT WORLD CHAMPIONS WITH THE LONGEST CONTINUOUS REIGN*

BOXER / COUNTRY / WEIGHT	DATE TITLE WON
1 Joe Calzaghe, UK WBO Super-middleweight	Oct 11, 1997
2 Pongsaklek Wonjongkam, Thailand WBC Flyweight	Mar 2, 2001
3 Antonio Margarito, Mexico WBO Welterweight	Mar 16, 2002
4 Omar Andrés Narváez, Argentina WBO Flyweight	Jul 13, 2002
5 Rafael Márquez, Mexico IBF Bantamweight	Feb 15, 2003
6 Ivan Calderón, Puerto Rico WBO Strawweight	May 3, 2003
7 Lorenzo Parra, Venezuela WBA Flyweight	Dec 6, 2003
8 Zsolt Erdei, Hungary WBO Light-heavyweight	Jan 17, 2004
9 Yutaka Niida, Japan WBA Strawweight	Jul 3, 2004
10 Juan Díaz, USA WBA Lightweight	Jul 17, 2004

* As at January 1, 2007

THE 10 LATEST WBC HEAVYWEIGHT CHAMPIONS*

BOXER / COUNTRY	FROM	REIGN(S) TO
1 Oleg Maskaev, Kazakhstan	Aug 12, 2006	Present
2 Hasim Rahman, USA	Nov 9, 2005	Aug 12, 2006
	Apr 22, 2001	Nov 17, 2001
3 Vitali Klitschko, Ukraine	Apr 24, 2004	Nov 9, 2005
4 Lennox Lewis, UK	Nov 17, 2001	Feb 6, 2004
	Feb 7, 1997	Apr 22, 2001
	Dec 14, 1992	Sep 24, 1994
5 Mike Tyson, USA	Mar 16, 1996	Sep 24,1996
	Nov 22, 1986	Feb 11, 1990
6 Frank Bruno, UK	Sep 2, 1995	Mar 16, 1996
7 Oliver McCall, USA	Sep 24, 1994	Sep 2, 1995
8 Riddick Bowe, USA	Nov 13, 1992	Dec 14, 1992
9 Evander Holyfield, USA	Oct 25, 1990	Nov 13, 1992
10 James 'Buster' Douglas, USA	Feb 11, 1990	Oct 25, 1990

* Last 10 different men to hold the WBC title, as at January 1, 2007

The WBC (World Boxing Council) was formed in Mexico on February 14, 1963 in response to opposition from many bodies, including the British Boxing Board of Control, to the WBA's assuming "world" control of boxing.

100 Years Ago: Jack Johnson

On December 26, 1908, Jack Johnson became the heavyweight champion of the world, and the first black fighter to hold the title, gaining it from reigning champion Tommy Burns (Canada). A series of "Great White Hopes" challenged Johnson, but he held his title until 1915, when he was defeated by Jess Willard.

TOP 10 **LONGEST WORLD CHAMPIONSHIP FIGHTS**

	BOXERS (WINNERS FIRST)	WEIGHT	DATE	ROUNDS
1	Ike Weir v. Frank Murphy	Featherweight	Mar 31, 1889	80
2	Jack McAuliffe v. Jem Carney	Lightweight	Nov 16, 1887	74
3	Paddy Duffy v. Tom Meadows	Welterweight	Mar 29, 1889	45
4	Joe Gans v. Battling Nelson	Lightweight	Sep 3, 1906	42
5 =	George Dixon v. Johnny Murphy	Bantamweight	Oct 23, 1890	40
=	Ad Wolgast v. Battling Nelson	Lightweight	Feb 22, 1910	40
7 =	George LaBlanche v. Jack Dempsey	Middleweight	Aug 27, 1889	32
=	Stanley Ketchel v. Joe Thomas	Middleweight	Sep 2, 1907	32
9	Jack Dempsey v. Billy McCarthy	Middleweight	Feb 18, 1890	28
10	Jack Dempsey v. Jack Fogarty	Middleweight	Feb 3, 1886	27

All these were World Championship contests under the Marquess of Queensberry Rules (published in 1866), which stipulate the length of a round at three minutes. Prior to the Rules, a round ended when a fighter was knocked down, and consequently a great number of fights in the bare-knuckle days consisted of many rounds, the longest being the 276-round contest between Jack Jones and Patsy Tunney in Cheshire in 1825. The fight lasted 4 hours 30 minutes. The longest heavyweight contest under Queensberry Rules was the Jess Willard v. Jack Johnson contest on April 5, 1915, which lasted 26 rounds.

Joe Louis
Joe Louis held the world heavyweight title from June 22, 1937, after beating James J. Braddock, until his retirement in 1949.

TOP 10 **MOST WINS IN WORLD HEAVYWEIGHT TITLE FIGHTS***

	BOXER / COUNTRY#	BOUTS	WINS
1	Joe Louis	27	26
2	Muhammad Ali/ Cassius Clay	25	22
3	Larry Holmes	25	21
4	Lennox Lewis, UK	22	17
5 =	Tommy Burns, Canada	13	12
=	Mike Tyson	16	12
7 =	Joe Frazier	11	10
=	Evander Holyfield	16	10
=	Jack Johnson	11	10
10	Ezzard Charles	13	9

* As at January 1, 2007
\# USA unless otherwise stated

This list also represents the Top 10 most World Heavyweight title bouts, with the exception of Floyd Patterson (USA), who would be in 9th place with 12 fights. James J. Jeffries, with eight wins from eight fights, represents the best record of boxers undefeated in World Heavyweight Championship fights.

Basketball

TOP 10 BEST POINTS AVERAGES PER GAME IN THE NBA*

	PLAYER	YEARS	GAMES	POINTS	AVERAGE
1	=Michael Jordan	1984–2003	1,072	32,292	30.1
	=Wilt Chamberlain	1959–73	1,045	31,419	30.1
3	Allen Iverson	1996–2006	682	19,115	28.0
4	Elgin Baylor	1958–72	846	23,149	27.4
5	Jerry West	1960–74	932	25,192	27.0
6	Bob Pettit	1954–65	792	20,880	26.4
7	Shaquille O'Neal	1992–2006	941	24,764	26.3
8	George Gervin	1976–86	791	20,708	26.2
9	Oscar Robertson	1960–74	1,040	26,710	25.7
10	Karl Malone	1985–2004	1,476	36,928	25.0

* As at the end of the 2005–06 season

Source: NBA

TOP 10 ALL-TIME CAREER SCORING LEADERS IN THE NBA*

	PLAYER	YEARS	GAMES	POINTS
1	Kareem Abdul-Jabbar#	1969–89	1,560	38,387
2	Karl Malone	1985–2004	1,476	36,928
3	Michael Jordan	1984–2003	1,072	32,292
4	Wilt Chamberlain	1959–73	1,045	31,419
5	Moses Malone	1976–95	1,329	27,409
6	Elvin Hayes	1968–84	1,303	27,313
7	Hakeem Olajuwon	1984–2002	1,238	26,946
8	Oscar Robertson	1960–74	1,040	26,710
9	Dominique Wilkins	1982–99	1,074	26,668
10	John Havlicek	1962–78	1,270	26,395

* As at the end of the 2005–06 season
\# Lew Alcindor in 1971

Source: NBA

TOP 10 PLAYERS MOST FREQUENTLY LEADING THE ANNUAL SCORING LIST*

	PLAYER / TEAM(S)	YEARS	FREQUENCY
1	Michael Jordan, Chicago Bulls	1987–98	10
2	Wilt Chamberlain, San Francisco Warriors/Philadelphia Warriors	1960–66	7
3	=George Gervin, San Antonio Spurs	1978–82	4
	=Allen Iverson, Philadelphia 76ers	1999–2005	4
5	=George Mikan, Minneapolis Lakers	1949–51	3
	=Neil Johnston, Philadelphia Warriors	1953–55	3
	=Bob McAdoo, Buffalo Braves	1974–76	3
8	=Paul Arizin, Philadelphia Warriors	1952–57	2
	=Bob Pettit, St. Louis Hawks	1956–59	2
	=Kareem Abdul-Jabbar#, Milwaukee Bucks	1971–72	2
	=Adrian Dantley, Utah Jazz	1981–84	2
	=Shaquille O'Neal, Orlando Magic/ Los Angeles Lakers	1995–2000	2
	=Tracy McGrady, Orlando Magic	2003–04	2

* As at the end of the 2005–06 season
\# Lew Alcindor in 1971

Up to the 1969–70 season the scoring leader was based on the player scoring the most points, but since then it has been based on points average per game.

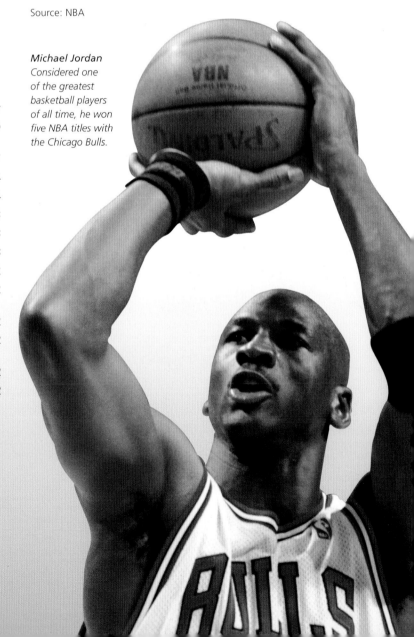

Michael Jordan
Considered one of the greatest basketball players of all time, he won five NBA titles with the Chicago Bulls.

Charlotte Bobcats
The Charlotte Bobcats joined the NBA in 2004, two years after Charlotte's other team, the Hornets, relocated to New Orleans. One of the Bobcats' co-owners is former player Michael Jordan.

THE 10 **TEAMS WITH THE LONGEST DROUGHT SINCE THEIR LAST APPEARANCE IN THE NBA FINAL***

	TEAM	LAST APPEARANCE IN NBA FINAL
1	Sacramento Kings	1951
2	Atlanta Hawks	1961
3	= Cleveland Cavaliers	1971#
	= Los Angeles Clippers	1971#
5	Milwaukee Bucks	1974
6	Golden State Warriors	1975
7	Denver Nuggets	1977#
8	Washington Wizards	1979
9	Boston Celtics	1987
10	New Orleans Hornets	1989#

* Up to and including the 2006 Final
# Team has never appeared in the Final—year shows the season they joined the NBA and hence eligible for Final

THE 10 **NEWEST CURRENT NBA TEAMS**

	TEAM	FIRST SEASON IN THE NBA
1	Charlotte Bobcats	2004–05
2	= Memphis Grizzlies	1995–96
	= Toronto Raptors	1995–96
4	= Minnesota Timberwolves	1989–90
	= Orlando Magic	1989–90
6	= Miami Heat	1988–89
	= New Orleans/Oklahoma City Hornets	1988–89
8	Dallas Mavericks	1980–81
9	Utah Jazz	1974–75
10	= Cleveland Cavaliers	1970–71
	= Los Angeles Clippers	1970–71
	= Portland Trail Blazers	1970–71

The Oklahoma City Hornets entered the League as the Charlotte Hornets in 1988 and moved to New Orleans in 2002. Because of Hurricane Katrina, they moved to Oklahoma City for the remainder of the 2005–06 season and also for the 2006–07 season, becoming known as the New Orleans/Oklahoma City Hornets.

TOP 10 **MEDAL-WINNING COUNTRIES IN THE BASKETBALL WORLD CHAMPIONSHIPS***

	COUNTRY	GOLD	SILVER	BRONZE	TOTAL
1	= USA	3	3	4	10
	= Yugoslavia	5	3	2	10
3	USSR/Russia	3	5	1	9
4	Brazil	2	2	1	5
5	= Argentina	1	1	0	2
	= Chile	0	0	2	2
7	= Croatia	0	0	1	1
	= Germany	0	0	1	1
	= Greece	0	1	0	1
	= Philippines	0	0	1	1
	= Spain	1	0	0	1

* Up to and including the 2006 Championships

Correctly known as the FIBA World Championship, the first Basketball World Championship was held at Buenos Aires, Argentina, in 1950. It is now held every four years and since 1967 the winning nation has received the Naismith Trophy. The Women's World Championship was first held at Santiago, Chile, in 1953.

Football

TOP 10 MOST POINTS IN AN NFL CAREER*

	PLAYER	YEARS	POINTS
1	Morten Andersen	1982–2006	2,445
2	Gary Anderson	1982–2004	2,434
3	George Blanda	1949–75	2,002
4	John Carney	1988–2006	1,749
5	Norm Johnson	1982–99	1,736
6	Matt Stover	1991–2006	1,715
7	Nick Lowery	1980–96	1,711
8	Jan Stenerud	1967–85	1,699
9	Jason Elam	1993–2006	1,672
10	Eddie Murray	1980–2000	1,594

* To the end of the 2006 regular season

TOP 10 MOST PASSING YARDS IN THE NFL*

	PLAYER	YEARS	YARDS
1	Dan Marino	1983–99	61,361
2	Brett Favre	1991–2006	57,500
3	John Elway	1983–98	51,475
4	Warren Moon	1984–2000	49,325
5	Fran Tarkenton	1961–78	47,003
6	Vinny Testaverde	1987–2006	45,281
7	Drew Bledsoe	1993–2006	44,611
8	Dan Fouts	1973–87	43,040
9	Joe Montana	1979–94	40,551
10	Johnny Unitas	1956–73	40,239

* To the end of the 2006 regular season

TOP 10 MOST POINTS IN A SUPER BOWL CAREER

	PLAYER / TEAM	GAMES	TD*	FG*	PAT*	POINTS
1	Jerry Rice, San Francisco 49ers/Oakland Raiders	4	8	0	0	48
2	Adam Vinatieri, New England Patriots, Indianapolis Colts	5	0	7	11	32
3	Emmitt Smith, Dallas Cowboys	3	5	0	0	30
4 =	Roger Craig, San Francisco 49ers	3	4	0	0	24
=	John Elway, Denver Broncos	5	4	0	0	24
=	Franco Harris, Pittsburgh Steelers	4	4	0	0	24
=	Thurman Thomas, Buffalo Bills	4	4	0	0	24
8	Ray Wersching, San Francisco 49ers	2	0	5	7	22
9	Don Chandler, Green Bay Packers	2	0	4	8	20
10 =	Cliff Branch, Los Angeles Raiders	3	3	0	0	18
=	Terrell Davis, Denver Broncos	2	3	0	0	18
=	Antonio Freeman, Green Bay Packers	2	3	0	0	18
=	John Stallworth, Pittsburgh Steelers	4	3	0	0	18
=	Lynn Swann, Pittsburgh Steelers	4	3	0	0	18
=	Ricky Watters, San Francisco 49ers	1	3	0	0	18

* TD—Touchdowns; FG—Field Goals; PAT—Point after touchdown

TOP 10 MOST CONFERENCE CHAMPIONSHIPS*

	TEAM	CURRENT CONFERENCE	FIRST WIN	LAST WIN	TOTAL
1	Green Bay Packers	NFC	1936	1997	10
2 =	Chicago Bears	NFC	1933	2006	8
=	Dallas Cowboys	NFC	1970	1995	8
4	Washington Redskins	NFC	1937	1991	7
5 =	Buffalo Bills	AFC	1964	1994	6
=	Denver Broncos	AFC	1977	1998	6
=	New York Giants	NFC	1934	2000	6
=	Pittsburgh Steelers	AFC	1974	2005	6
9 =	Miami Dolphins	AFC	1971	1984	5
=	San Francisco 49ers	NFC	1981	1994	5
=	Cleveland/LA/ St Louis Rams	NFC	1945	2001	5
=	Oakland/LA Raiders	AFC	1967	2002	5
=	Philadelphia Eagles	NFC	1948	2004	5
=	New England Patriots	AFC	1985	2004	5

* Up to and including the 2006 season

Championship games were introduced in 1933, when the National Football League (NFL) divided the teams into Eastern and Western Divisions. The Bears beat the Giants 23–21 in the first Championship game. The AFL (American Football League) was formed in 1960 and following the merger of the NFL and AFL in 1969, the two present Conferences, NFC (National Football Conference) and AFC (American Football Conference), were created. Each Conference is currently divided into four divisions—North, South, East, and West—each containing four teams. Unlike the National Hockey League, National Basketball Association, and Major League Baseball, there are no teams based in Canada.

TOP 10 LONGEST DROUGHTS SINCE A SUPER BOWL APPEARANCE*

	TEAM	LAST APPEARANCE
1	New York Jets	1969
2	Kansas City Chiefs	1970
3	Minnesota Vikings	1977
4	Miami Dolphins	1985
5	Cincinnati Bengals	1989
6	Washington Redskins	1992
7	Buffalo Bills	1994
8 =	San Diego Chargers	1995
=	San Francisco 49ers	1995
10	Dallas Cowboys	1996

* Of all current NFL teams who have appeared in the Super Bowl

Of current NFL teams, Arizona Cardinals, Cleveland Browns, Detroit Lions, Houston Texans, Jacksonville Jaguars, and New Orleans Saints have never appeared in the Super Bowl.

TOP 10 MOST SUPER BOWL APPEARANCES

	TEAM	WON	LOST	APPEARANCES
1	Dallas Cowboys	5	3	8
2 =	Denver Broncos	2	4	6
=	Pittsburgh Steelers	5	1	6
4 =	Miami Dolphins	2	3	5
=	New England Patriots	3	2	5
=	Oakland/LA Raiders	3	2	5
=	San Francisco 49ers	5	0	5
=	Washington Redskins	3	2	5
9 =	Buffalo Bills	0	4	4
=	Green Bay Packers	3	1	4
=	Minnesota Vikings	0	4	4

Dallas Cowboys, with 221, have also scored more points in the Super Bowl than any other team. Denver Broncos have conceded the most—206.

Special rice
Jerry Rice won three Super Bowl rings with the 49ers, and in winning the Super Bowl MVP in 1988 became only the third wide receiver to win the award.

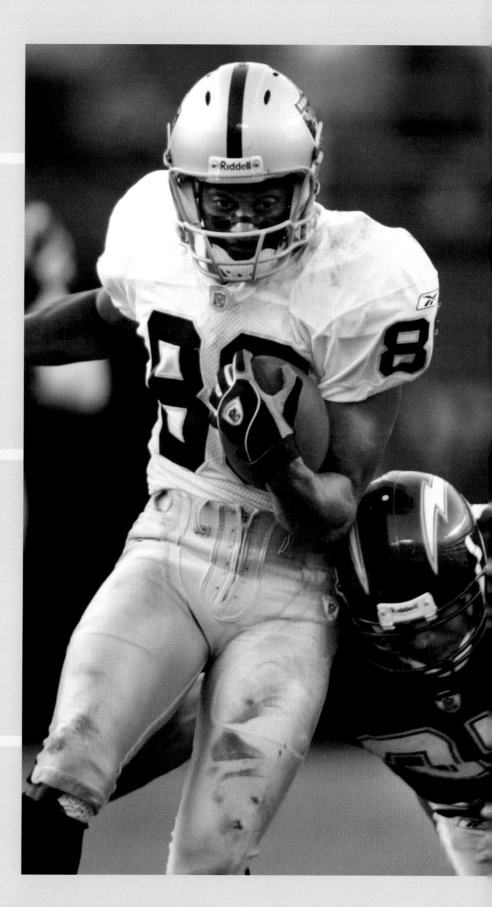

International Soccer

TOP 10 **GOALSCORERS IN THE UEFA EUROPEAN CHAMPIONSHIP***

	PLAYER / COUNTRY	YEARS	GOALS
1	Michel Platini, France	1984	9
2	Alan Shearer, England	1996–2000	7
3	Patrick Kluivert, Netherlands	1996–2000	6
4	=Marco van Basten, Netherlands	1988	5
	=Jürgen Klinsmann, West Germany/Germany	1988–96	5
	=Savo Milosevic, Yugoslavia	2000	5
	=Nuno Gomes, Portugal	2000–04	5
	=Thierry Henry, France	2000–04	5
	=Zinedine Zidane, France	2000–04	5
	=Milan Baros, Czech Republic	2004	5

* In the final stages, 1960–2004

Italian victory
Fabio Cannavaro holds aloft the World Cup after Italy's 2006 defeat of France on penalties.

TOP 10 **WORLD CUP GOALSCORERS***

	PLAYER / COUNTRY	YEARS	GOALS
1	Ronaldo, Brazil	1998–2006	15
2	Gerd Müller, West Germany	1970–74	14
3	Just Fontaine, France	1958	13
4	Pelé, Brazil	1958–70	12
5	=Sándor Kocsis, Hungary	1954	11
	=Jürgen Klinsmann, Germany	1990–98	11
7	=Helmut Rahn, West Germany	1954–58	10
	=Teófilo Cubillas, Peru	1970–78	10
	=Grzegorz Lato, Poland	1974–82	10
	=Gary Lineker, England	1986–90	10
	=Gabriel Batistuta, Argentina	1994–2002	10
	=Miroslav Klose, Germany	2002–2006	10

* In the final stages 1930–2006

Fontaine's 13 goals in the 1958 finals is a record for one tournament.

TOP 10 INTERNATIONAL GOALSCORERS*

	PLAYER / COUNTRY	YEARS	MATCHES	GOALS
1	Ali Daei, Iran	1993–2006	149	109
2	Ferenc Puskás, Hungary/Spain	1945–56	89	84
3	Pelé, Brazil	1957–71	92	77
4	Sándor Kocsis, Hungary	1948–56	68	75
5	Bashar Abdullah, Kuwait	1996–2005	132	74
6	Hossam Hassan, Egypt	1985–2006	170	69
7	Gerd Müller, West Germany	1966–74	62	68
8	= Majed Abdullah, Saudi Arabia	1978–94	139	67
	= Stern John, Trinidad & Tobago	1995–2006	100	67
10	Kiatisuk Senamuang, Thailand	1993–2006	121	65

* As at January 1, 2007

The most by a British Isles player is 49, Bobby Charlton (England) 1958–70. Vivian Woodward of England scored 73 goals in 53 matches between 1903 and 1914. However, 44 of them were in Amateur Internationals, which are not recognized as full international goals.

TOP 10 COUNTRIES IN THE FIFA WORLD CUP*

	COUNTRY	1ST	2ND	3RD	4TH	POINTS
1	= Brazil	5	2	2	1	31
	= West Germany/ Germany	3	4	3	1	31
3	Italy	4	2	1	1	25
4	Argentina	2	2	0	0	14
5	France	1	1	2	1	12
6	Uruguay	2	0	0	2	10
7	Sweden	0	1	2	1	8
8	Netherlands	0	2	0	1	7
9	= Czechoslovakia	0	2	0	0	6
	= Hungary	0	2	0	0	6

* In the FIFA World Cup 1930–2006, based on 4 points for winning the trophy, 3 points for finishing as runners-up, 2 points for finishing 3rd, and 1 point for finishing 4th

Source: FIFA

Up to the end of the 2006 tournament, a total of 708 matches had been played and 2,063 goals scored at an average of 2.91 per game. A total of 76 different teams have competed and 30,930,108 spectators have watched World Cup matches at an average of 43,687 per game.

TOP 10 COUNTRIES IN THE UEFA EUROPEAN CHAMPIONSHIP*

	COUNTRY	WINS	RUNNER-UP	SEMI-FINAL	POINTS
1	West Germany/ Germany	3	2	1	14
2	Soviet Union	1	3	1	10
3	= France	2	0	2	8
	= Czechoslovakia/ Czech Republic	1	1	3	8
5	= Italy	1	1	2	7
	= Netherlands	1	0	4	7
7	= Denmark	1	0	2	5
	= Spain	1	1	0	5
	= Yugoslavia	0	2	1	5
10	Portugal	0	1	2	4

* Based on 3 points for winning the tournament, 2 points for being the runner-up, and 1 point for being a losing semi-finalist, 1960–2004

The leading UK country is England, with two points from two semifinal appearances. The European Championship, then the European Nations' Cup, was inaugurated in 1958, with the first final being played two years later, when the Soviet Union beat Yugoslavia 2-1 after extra time in Paris.

TOP 10 INTERNATIONAL APPEARANCES*

	PLAYER / COUNTRY	YEARS	APPEARANCES
1	Mohamed Al-Deayea, Saudi Arabia	1990–2006	181
2	Claudio Suárez, Mexico	1992–2006	178
3	Hossam Hassan, Egypt	1985–2006	170
4	= Adnan Kh. Al-Talyani, UAE	1984–97	164
	= Cobi Jones, US	1992–2004	164
6	Sami Al-Jaber, Saudi Arabia	1992–2006	163
7	Lothar Matthäus, West Germany/Germany	1980–2000	150
8	Ali Daei, Iran	1993–2006	149
9	Martin Reim, Estonia	1992–2006	148
10	= Thomas Ravelli, Sweden	1981–97	143
	= Mohammed Al-Khilaiwi, Saudi Arabia	1990–2001	143
	= Marko Kristal, Estonia	1992–2005	143

* As at January 1, 2007

Mohamed Al-Deayea made his international debut in 1990 and in 1996 helped his country win the Asian Cup. He played in the 1994, 1998, and 2002 World Cups, and was a squad member in 2006.

Ice Hockey

Leading goaltender
Patrick Roy in action for Canada against the United States during the 1998 Winter Olympics at Nagano, Japan.

TOP 10 MOST WINS BY A GOALTENDER IN THE NHL*

	PLAYER	YEARS	GAMES	WINS
1	Patrick Roy	1984–2003	1,029	551
2	Martin Brodeur	1991–2007	891	494
3	Ed Belfour	1988–2007	963	484
4	Terry Sawchuk	1949–70	971	447
5	Curtis Joseph	1989–2007	912	445
6	Jacques Plante	1952–73	837	435
7	Tony Esposito	1968–84	886	423
8	Glenn Hall	1951–71	906	407
9	Grant Fuhr	1981–2000	868	405
10	Mike Vernon	1982–2002	781	385

* Regular season; as at end of the 2006–07 season

TOP 10 POINTSCORERS IN NHL PLAYOFF GAMES*

	PLAYER	YEARS	GAMES	POINTS
1	Wayne Gretzky	1980–97	208	382
2	Mark Messier	1980–97	236	295
3	Jari Kurri	1981–98	200	233
4	Glenn Anderson	1981–96	225	214
5	Paul Coffey	1981–99	194	196
6	Brett Hull	1986–2004	202	190
7	Doug Gilmour	1984–2002	182	188
8	Steve Yzerman	1984–2006	196	185
9	Bryan Trottier	1976–94	221	184
10	Raymond Bourque	1980–2001	214	180

* As at the end of 2005–06 playoffs

As at the end of the 2005–06 season, Wayne Gretzky either held, or jointly held, 61 official NHL records.

TOP 10 **MOST STANLEY CUP WINS***

	TEAM	FIRST WIN	LAST WIN	TOTAL WINS
1	Montreal Canadiens	1916	1993	24
2	Toronto Maple Leafs	1918	1967	13
3	Detroit Red Wings	1936	2002	10
4	= Boston Bruins	1929	1972	5
	= Edmonton Oilers	1984	1990	5
6	= New York Islanders	1980	1983	4
	= New York Rangers	1928	1994	4
	= Ottawa Senators	1920	1927	4
9	= Chicago Blackhawks	1934	1961	3
	= New Jersey Devils	1995	2003	3

* Since abolition of challenge match format in 1915

Source: NHL

TOP 10 **LEADING POINTSCORERS IN AN NHL CAREER***

	PLAYER	YEARS	GAMES	POINTS
1	Wayne Gretzky	1970–99	1,487	2,857
2	Mark Messier	1979–2004	1,756	1,887
3	Gordie Howe	1946–80	1,767	1,850
4	Ron Francis	1981–2004	1,731	1,798
5	Marcel Dionne	1971–89	1,348	1,771
6	Steve Yzerman	1983–2006	1,514	1,755
7	Mario Lemieux	1984–2006	915	1,723
8	Phil Esposito	1963–81	1,282	1,590
9	Joe Sakic	1988–2007	1,319	1,589
10	Raymond Bourque	1979–2001	1,612	1,579

* Regular season; as at end of 2006–07 season

Gordie Howe became the first player to achieve 1,000 points when he scored for Detroit in their 2-0 win over Toronto on November 27, 1960. When Wayne Gretzy achieved the same feat on December 19, 1984, he became the 18th to pass the milestone, and remains the only player to exceed 2,000.

TOP 10 **MEDAL-WINNING COUNTRIES IN THE ICE HOCKEY WORLD CHAMPIONSHIPS***

	COUNTRY	GOLD	SILVER	BRONZE	TOTAL
1	Canada	23	11	10	44
2	Czechoslovakia/Czech Republic	11	13	18	42
3	Sweden	8	18	14	40
4	USSR/Russia	23	8	6	37
5	USA	2	9	5	16
6	Switzerland	0	1	8	9
7	Finland	1	5	2	8
8	UK	1	2	2	5
9	Germany/West Germany	0	2	2	4
10	Slovakia	1	1	1	3

* Up to and including 2006

The Olympic ice hockey tournaments 1920–68 were also the world championships of those years. When they won the Olympic and World titles in 2006, Sweden became the first nation to win both titles in the same year. The leading tournament before the World Championships was the European Championships, which were first held in 1910 and won by Great Britain. The 1920 Olympic tournament also doubled as the inaugural World Championship and was won by Canada. The first World Championship to be held independently of the Olympics was in 1930 and, again, was won by Canada.

TOP 10 **COUNTRIES WITH THE MOST REGISTERED HOCKEY PLAYERS**

	COUNTRY	REGISTERED PLAYERS (2006)		COUNTRY	
1	Canada	574,125	6	Finland	52,597
2	USA	485,017	7	Germany	25,934
3	Russia	77,702	8	Slovakia	12,375
4	Czech Republic	72,075	9	Denmark	4,255
5	Sweden	65,613	10	Belarus	2,850

Baseball Teams

THE 10 **NEWEST MAJOR LEAGUE BASEBALL TEAMS**

	TEAM	FIRST SEASON
1	= Arizona Diamondbacks	1998
	= Tampa Bay Devil Rays	1998
3	= Colorado Rockies	1993
	= Florida Marlins	1993
5	= Seattle Mariners	1977
	= Toronto Blue Jays	1977
7	= Kansas City Royals	1969
	= Milwaukee Brewers*	1969
	= San Diego Padres	1969
	= Washington Nationals#	1969

* Known as Seattle Pilots in their first season
# Known as Montreal Expos 1969–2004

TOP 10 **MOST WINS IN MAJOR LEAGUE BASEBALL***

	TEAM	GAMES PLAYED	GAMES WON
1	San Francisco Giants	18,746	10,113
2	Chicago Cubs	19,282	9,900
3	Los Angeles Dodgers	18,686	9,794
4	St. Louis Cardinals	18,876	9,765
5	Atlanta Braves	19,251	9,612
6	Cincinnati Reds	18,886	9,600
7	Pittsburgh Pirates	18,847	9,556
8	New York Yankees	16,383	9,289
9	Philadelphia Phillies	18,720	8,764
10	Boston Red Sox	16,404	8,444

* Up to and including the 2006 season

The original Baltimore Orioles won more matches than any other former franchise. They won 1,133 of the 2,182 matches they played in the period 1882–99.

TOP 10 MOST WORLD SERIES WINS*

	TEAM	FIRST TITLE	LAST TITLE	TOTAL
1	New York Yankees	1923	2000	26
2	St. Louis Cardinals	1926	2006	10
3	Oakland Athletics (5 titles as Philadelphia Athletics)	1910	1989	9
4 =	Boston Red Sox	1903	2004	6
=	Los Angeles Dodgers (1 title as Brooklyn Dodgers)	1955	1988	6
6 =	Cincinatti Reds	1919	1990	5
=	Pittsburgh Pirates	1909	1979	5
=	San Francisco Giants (all titles as New York Giants)	1905	1954	5
9	Detroit Tigers	1935	1984	4
10 =	Chicago White Sox	1906	2005	3
=	Atlanta Braves (1 title as Boston Braves, 1 as Milwaukee Braves)	1914	1995	3
=	Minnesota Twins (1 title as Washington Senators)	1924	1991	3
=	Baltimore Orioles	1966	1983	3

* Up to and including the 2006 World Series

The Braves are the only team to win the World Series with three different franchises.

TOP 10 MOST NATIONAL LEAGUE TITLES*

	TEAM	FIRST TITLE	LAST TITLE	TOTAL
1	Los Angeles Dodgers	1916	1988	18
2 =	San Francisco Giants	1905	2002	17
=	St. Louis Cardinals	1926	2006	17
4	Chicago Cubs	1906	1945	10
5 =	Atlanta Braves	1914	1999	9
=	Cincinnati Reds	1919	1990	9
7	Pittsburgh Pirates	1903	1979	7
8	Philadelphia Phillies	1915	1993	5
9	New York Mets	1969	2000	4
10 =	San Diego Padres	1984	1998	2
=	Florida Marlins	1997	2003	2

* Up to and including the 2006 season

Since 1969, when the National League was expanded and split into two divisions, the Championship Pennant has gone to the Championship playoff winners. The original National League in 1876 consisted of eight teams, with Chicago claiming the first title, winning 52 of their 66 games. Ross Barnes of Chicago was the first National league player to hit a home run in the game at Cincinatti. Barnes topped the league with 126 runs but George Hall of Philadelphia hit the most homers – five.

TOP 10 BEST WIN PERCENTAGES IN MAJOR LEAGUE BASEBALL*

	TEAM	PLAYED	WON	WIN %
1	New York Yankees	16,383	9,289	0.567
2	San Francisco Giants	18,746	10,113	0.539
3	Los Angeles Dodgers	18,686	9,794	0.524
4	St. Louis Cardinals	18,876	9,765	0.517
5	Boston Red Sox	16,404	8,444	0.515
6	Chicago Cubs	19,282	9,900	0.513
7	Cleveland Indians	16,410	8,380	0.511
8	Cincinnati Reds	18,886	9,600	0.508
9	Pittsburgh Pirates	18,847	9,556	0.507
10 =	Detroit Tigers	16,433	8,316	0.506
=	Chicago White Sox	16,392	8,300	0.506

* Current teams, up to and including 2006 season

Amongst earlier franchises, Milwaukee Brewers have the best record, having won eight of their 12 matches in their only season in the League (1884). This represents a win percentage of 0.667. Boston Red Stockings (1871–75) had a 225–60 record, representing a win percentage of 0.789, but they played in the National Association, which is not regarded as Major League Baseball.

TOP 10 MOST AMERICAN LEAGUE TITLES*

	TEAM	FIRST TITLE	LAST TITLE	TOTAL
1	New York Yankees	1921	2003	39
2	Oakland Athletics	1905	1990	14
3 =	Boston Red Sox	1903	2004	10
=	Detroit Tigers	1907	2006	10
5	Baltimore Orioles	1944	1983	7
6	Minnesota Twins	1924	1991	6
7 =	Cleveland Indians	1920	1997	5
=	Chicago White Sox	1906	2005	5
9 =	Kansas City Royals	1980	1985	2
=	Toronto Blue Jays	1992	1993	2

* Up to and including 2006 season

Chicago, who were also the inaugural National League champions won the first American League title in 1901 with a .610 win percent average. They hosted the first-ever American league game in beating Cleveland 8-2. The legendary Cy Young won 33 games for Boston who finished second to Chicago.

Baseball Stars

TOP 10 **MOST HOME RUNS IN A CAREER***

	PLAYER	HOMERS
1	Hank Aaron	755
2	Babe Ruth	734
3	Barry Bonds#	714
4	Willie Mays	660
5	Sammy Sosa#	588
6	Frank Robinson	586
7	Mark McGwire	583
8	Harmon Killebrew	573
9	Rafael Palmeiro#	569
10 =	Ken Griffey#	563
=	Reggie Jackson	563

* Up to and including the 2006 season
# Active in 2006

TOP 10 **MOST RUNS IN A WORLD SERIES CAREER***

	PLAYER	RUNS
1	Mickey Mantle	42
2	Yogi Berra	41
3	Babe Ruth	37
4	Lou Gehrig	30
5 =	Joe DiMaggio	27
=	Derek Jeter#	27
7	Roger Maris	26
8	Elston Howard	25
9	Gil McDougald	23
10	Jackie Robinson	22

* Up to and including the 2006 season
# Active in 2006

TOP 10 **PITCHERS WITH THE MOST CAREER WINS***

	PLAYER	WINS
1	Cy Young	511
2	Walter Johnson	417
3 =	Grover Alexander	373
=	Christy Mathewson	373
5	Pud Galvin	364
6	Warren Spahn	363
7	Kid Nichols	361
8	Roger Clemens#	348
9	Tim Keefe	342
10	Greg Maddux#	333

* Up to and including the 2006 season
# Active in 2006

Warren Spahn is the only lefthanded pitcher on the list.

TOP 10 **PITCHERS WITH THE MOST STRIKEOUTS IN A CAREER***

	PLAYER	STRIKEOUTS
1	Nolan Ryan	5,714
2	Roger Clemens#	4,604
3	Randy Johnson#	4,544
4	Steve Carlton	4,136
5	Bert Blyleven	3,701
6	Tom Seaver	3,640
7	Don Sutton	3,574
8	Gaylord Perry	3,534
9	Walter Johnson	3,509
10	Phil Niekro	3,342

* Up to and including the 2006 season
# Active in 2006

Johnson and Carlton are the only lefthanded pitchers on the list.

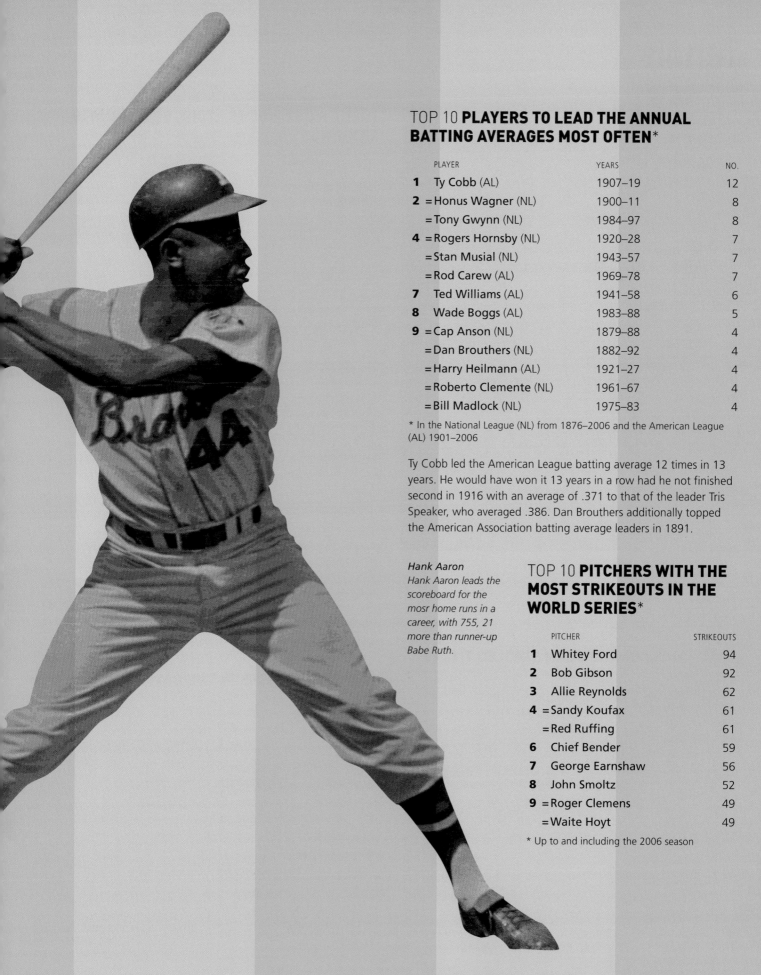

TOP 10 **PLAYERS TO LEAD THE ANNUAL BATTING AVERAGES MOST OFTEN***

	PLAYER	YEARS	NO.
1	Ty Cobb (AL)	1907–19	12
2	=Honus Wagner (NL)	1900–11	8
	=Tony Gwynn (NL)	1984–97	8
4	=Rogers Hornsby (NL)	1920–28	7
	=Stan Musial (NL)	1943–57	7
	=Rod Carew (AL)	1969–78	7
7	Ted Williams (AL)	1941–58	6
8	Wade Boggs (AL)	1983–88	5
9	=Cap Anson (NL)	1879–88	4
	=Dan Brouthers (NL)	1882–92	4
	=Harry Heilmann (AL)	1921–27	4
	=Roberto Clemente (NL)	1961–67	4
	=Bill Madlock (NL)	1975–83	4

* In the National League (NL) from 1876–2006 and the American League (AL) 1901–2006

Ty Cobb led the American League batting average 12 times in 13 years. He would have won it 13 years in a row had he not finished second in 1916 with an average of .371 to that of the leader Tris Speaker, who averaged .386. Dan Brouthers additionally topped the American Association batting average leaders in 1891.

Hank Aaron
Hank Aaron leads the scoreboard for the mosr home runs in a career, with 755, 21 more than runner-up Babe Ruth.

TOP 10 **PITCHERS WITH THE MOST STRIKEOUTS IN THE WORLD SERIES***

	PITCHER	STRIKEOUTS
1	Whitey Ford	94
2	Bob Gibson	92
3	Allie Reynolds	62
4	=Sandy Koufax	61
	=Red Ruffing	61
6	Chief Bender	59
7	George Earnshaw	56
8	John Smoltz	52
9	=Roger Clemens	49
	=Waite Hoyt	49

* Up to and including the 2006 season

Tennis

Top rank
Steffi Graf first topped the rankings on August 17, 1987. The following year she completed the Grand Slam and also won the women's singles title at the Olympic Games.

TOP 10 **MOST WEEKS AT NO. 1 ON THE WTA RANKINGS***

PLAYER / COUNTRY	YEARS	WEEKS	
Steffi Graf, Germany	1987–97	377	1
Martina Navratilova, Czechoslovakia/USA	1978–87	331	2
Chris Evert, USA	1975–85	262	3
Martina Hingis, Switzerland	1997–2001	209	4
Monica Seles, Yugoslavia/USA	1991–96	178	5
Lindsay Davenport, USA	1998–2006	98	6
Serena Williams, USA	2002–03	57	7
Justine Henin-Hardenne, Belgium	2003–06	46	8
Amélie Mauresmo, France	2004–06	39	9
Tracy Austin, USA	1980	22	10

* To January 1, 2007

Source: WTA (Women's Tennis Association)

TOP 10 **MOST GRAND SLAM SINGLES TITLES***

	PLAYER / COUNTRY	YEARS	A	F	W	US	TOTAL
1	Margaret Court (née Smith), Australia	1960–73	11	5	3	5	24
2	Steffi Graf, Germany	1987–99	4	6	7	5	22
3	Helen Wills-Moody, USA	1923–38	0	4	8	7	19
4	=Chris Evert-Lloyd, USA	1974–86	2	7	3	6	18
	=Martina Navratilova, Czechoslovakia/USA	1978–90	3	2	9	4	18
6	Pete Sampras, USA	1990–2002	2	0	7	5	14
7	=Roy Emerson, Australia	1961–67	6	2	2	2	12
	=Billie Jean King, USA	1966–75	1	1	6	4	12
9	=Björn Borg, Sweden	1974–81	0	6	5	0	11
	=Rod Laver, Australia	1960–69	3	2	4	2	11

* Up to and including 2006

A—Australian Open; F—French Open; W—Wimbledon; US—US Open

TOP 10 **MOST WINS IN THE DAVIS CUP***

	COUNTRY	YEARS	WINS
1	=Sweden	1975, 1984–85, 1987, 1994, 1997–98	7
	=USA	1978–79, 1981–82, 1990, 1992, 1995	7
3	Australia	1973, 1977, 1983, 1986, 1999, 2003	6
4	=Germany	1988–89, 1993	3
	=France	1991, 1996, 2001	3
6	Spain	2000, 2004	2
	=Russia	2002, 2006	2
8	=South Africa	1974	1
	=Italy	1976	1
	=Czechoslovakia	1980	1
	=Croatia	2005	1

* Since the abolition of the Challenge system in 1972

TOP 10 MOST WEEKS AT NO. 1 ON THE ATP RANKINGS*

	PLAYER / COUNTRY	YEARS	WEEKS
1	Pete Sampras, USA	1993–2000	286
2	Ivan Lendl, Czechoslovakia/USA	1983–90	270
3	Jimmy Connors, USA	1974–83	268
4	John McEnroe, USA	1980–85	170
5	Roger Federer, Switzerland	2004–06	152
6	Björn Borg, Sweden	1977–81	109
7	Andre Agassi, USA	1995–2003	101
8	Lleyton Hewitt, Australia	2001–03	80
9	Stefan Edberg, Sweden	1990–92	72
10	Jim Courier, USA	1992–93	58

* To January 1, 2007

Source: ATP (Association of Tennis Professionals)

Top of the first ATP rankings on August 23, 1973 was Ille Nastase (Romania). The most consecutive weeks at No. 1 is 160 by Jimmy Connors between July 29, 1974 and August 22, 1977.

Martina's Victories

Martina Navratilova won her last mixed doubles title at Flushing Meadow in 2006—at the remarkable age of 46. She had won her first Grand Slam title at the 1974 French Open, partnering Ivan Molina of Colombia. The first of her 30 women's doubles titles—21 of them with Pam Shriver—was with Chris Evert at the 1975 French Open. The first of her Wimbledon singles triumphs, over Chris Evert, was in 1978, and the last in 1990 when she beat Zina Garrison. She won 167 singles titles in her career, stretching from Orlando in 1974 to the Paris indoor title in 1994.

Grand master
Roger Federer came close to a fourth Grand Slam victory in 2006, losing out to Spain's Rafael Nadal in the French Open.

THE 10 LAST MEN TO WIN THREE OR MORE GRAND SLAM TITLES IN ONE YEAR

	PLAYER / COUNTRY	EVENTS WON	YEAR
1	Roger Federer, Switzerland	A, W, US	2006
2	Roger Federer, Switzerland	A, W, US	2004
3	Mats Wilander, Sweden	A, F, US	1988
4	Jimmy Connors, USA	A, W, US	1974
5	Rod Laver, Australia	A, F, W, US	1969
6	Roy Emerson, Australia	A, F, W	1964
7	Rod Laver, Australia	A, F, W, US	1962
8	Ashley Cooper, Australia	A, W, US	1958
9	Lew Hoad, Australia	A, F, W	1956
10	Tony Trabert, USA	F, W, US	1955

A—Australian Open; F—French Open; W—Wimbledon; US—US Open

The only other men to win three or more Grand Slam singles titles in the same year are Jack Crawford (Australia, 1933), Fred Perry (UK, 1934), and Donald Budge (USA, 1938)—who won all four titles.

Golf

TOP 10 MOST APPEARANCES FOR THE EUROPEAN TEAM IN THE RYDER CUP*

	PLAYER / COUNTRY	FIRST YEAR	LAST YEAR	APPEARANCES
1	Nick Faldo, England	1977	1997	11
2	= Christy O'Connor Snr, Ireland	1955	1973	10
	= Bernhard Langer, Germany	1981	2002	10
4	Dai Rees, Wales	1937	1961	9
5	= Peter Alliss, England	1953	1969	8
	= Bernard Hunt, England	1953	1969	8
	= Neil Coles, England	1961	1977	8
	= Bernard Gallacher, Scotland	1969	1983	8
	= Severiano Ballesteros, Spain	1979	1995	8
	= Sam Torrance, Scotland	1981	1995	8
	= Ian Woosnam, Wales	1983	1997	8
	= Colin Montgomerie, Scotland	1991	2006	8

* Great Britain—1921 to 1971; Great Britain & Ireland—1973 to 1977; Europe—1979 to 2006; up to and including 2006

Nick Faldo, with 25, has gained the most points for the Great Britain and Ireland/European teams.

TOP 10 MOST APPEARANCES FOR THE US TEAM IN THE RYDER CUP

	PLAYER	FIRST YEAR	LAST YEAR	APPEARANCES
1	= Billy Casper	1961	1975	8
	= Raymond Floyd	1969	1983	8
	= Lanny Wadkins	1977	1993	8
4	= Sam Snead	1937	1959	7
	= Gene Littler	1961	1975	7
	= Tom Kite	1979	1993	7
7	= Gene Sarazen	1927	1937	6
	= Arnold Palmer	1961	1973	6
	= Jack Nicklaus	1969	1981	6
	= Lee Trevino	1969	1981	6
	= Davis Love III	1993	2004	6
	= Phil Mickelson	1995	2006	6

* Up to and including 2006

Billy Casper holds the record for winning the most points for the USA—23.5, which is half a point more than Arnold Palmer. Casper also holds the record for appearing in the most matches, 37, and jointly holds the record for the most points won in singles, fourballs, and foursomes matches.

TOP 10 MOST WINS ON THE PGA EUROPEAN TOUR*

	PLAYER / COUNTRY	YEARS	WINS
1	Severiano Ballesteros, Spain	1976–95	49
2	Bernhard Langer, Germany	1980–2002	40
3	Colin Montgomerie, Scotland	1989–2005#	30
4	Ian Woosnam, Wales	1982–97	28
5	Nick Faldo, England	1977–94	27
6	= José Maria Olazábal, Spain	1986–2005	22
	= Ernie Els, South Africa	1994–2006	22
8	Sam Torrance, Scotland	1976–98	21
9	Mark James, England	1978–97	18
10	Sandy Lyle, Scotland	1979–92	17

* As at January 1, 2007
# Montgomerie won the Hong Kong Open in 2005, although it was part of the 2006 European PGA Tour of 2006

Ballesteros first enjoyed success in the 1976 Dutch Open. He went on to win five Majors in his career, his 49th and last European Tour success in the 1995 Peugeot Spanish Open at San Roque Golf Club, Andalucia.

TOP 10 MOST MEN'S MAJORS IN A CAREER*

	PLAYER / COUNTRY#	YEARS	MASTERS	US OPEN	BRITISH OPEN	PGA	TOTAL
1	Jack Nicklaus	1962–86	6	4	3	5	18
2	Tiger Woods	1997–2006	4	2	3	3	12
3	Walter Hagen	1914–29	0	2	4	5	11
4	= Ben Hogan	1946–53	2	4	1	2	9
	= Gary Player (South Africa)	1959–78	3	1	3	2	9
6	Tom Watson	1975–83	2	1	5	0	8
7	= Harry Vardon (England)	1896–1914	0	1	6	0	7
	= Gene Sarazen	1922–35	1	2	1	3	7
	= Bobby Jones	1923–30	0	4	3	0	7
	= Sam Snead	1942–54	3	0	1	3	7
	= Arnold Palmer	1958–64	4	1	2	0	7

* Professional Majors only, up to and including 2006
# All from the USA unless otherwise stated

In 1930, Bobby Jones achieved an unprecedented Grand Slam when he won the US and British Open and Amateur titles. Nicklaus, Woods, Hogan, Player, and Sarazen are the only golfers to have won all four Majors at least once, while Tiger Woods is the only player to hold all four Majors at the same time.

TOP 10 **MONEY WINNERS ON THE LPGA TOUR***

PLAYER / COUNTRY#	WINNINGS ($)
1 Annika Sörenstam, Sweden	20,304,562
2 Karrie Webb, Australia	12,826,995
3 Juli Inkster	11,255,669
4 Se Ri Pak, South Korea	8,966,948
5 Meg Mallon	8,818,462
6 Beth Daniel	8,755,733
7 Rosie Jones	8,355,068
8 Laura Davies, England	7,716,726
9 Betsy King	7,637,621
10 Dottie Pepper	6,827,284

* As at January 1, 2007
\# All from the USA unless otherwise stated

Kathy Whitworth (USA) holds the record for the most wins—88—on the LPGA Tour. Like her male counterpart, Sam Snead, she never won the US Open.

TOP 10 **MONEY WINNERS ON THE PGA CHAMPIONS TOUR***

PLAYER#	WINNINGS ($)
1 Hale Irwin	23,384,705
2 Gil Morgan	17,208,472
3 Bruce Fleisher	13,260,442
4 Dana Quigley	13,166,725
5 Larry Nelson	12,893,736
6 Allen Doyle	12,118,228
7 Jim Colbert	11,575,162
8 Jim Thorpe	11,429,823
9 Dave Stockton	10,840,231
10 Tom Jenkins	10,624,407

* As at January 1, 2007
\# All players from the USA

The Champions Tour was founded in 1980 as the Senior PGA Tour, and changed its name in 2002. Run by the PGA Tour, it is for professional golfers who have reached the age of 50 and many ex-stars of the regular Tour compete on the Champions Tour.

The "Golden Bear"
Jack Nicklaus is widely regarded as one of the greatest of all golfers.

Water Sports

TOP 10 OLYMPIC CANOEING COUNTRIES*

	COUNTRY	GOLD	SILVER	BRONZE	TOTAL
1	Germany/West Germany	29	23	20	72
2	Hungary	17	26	25	68
3	USSR/Unified Team/Russia	30	16	12	58
4	Romania	10	11	14	35
5	East Germany	14	7	9	30
6 =	France	6	6	17	29
=	Sweden	15	11	3	29
8	Czechoslovakia/Czech Republic	10	8	3	21
9	Canada	4	8	7	19
10	Bulgaria	4	5	8	17

* Up to and including the 2004 Olympics

A Kayak singles race was contested at the 1906 Intercalated Games in Athens, but it was not until 1936 that canoeing became a regular Olympic sport. Women first contested canoeing events at the 1948 London Olympics.

TOP 10 MOST GOLD MEDALS AT THE WORLD AQUATIC CHAMPIONSHIPS*

	SWIMMER / COUNTRY	YEARS	GOLD MEDALS
1	Grant Hackett, Australia	1998–2005	7
2 =	Ian Thorpe, Australia	1998–2003	6
=	Michael Phelps, USA	2001–05	6
4 =	Aleksandr Popov, Russia	1994–2003	5
=	Hannah Stockbauer, Germany	2001–03	5
=	Inge de Bruijn, Netherlands	2001–03	5
=	Aaron Peirsol, USA	2001–05	5
8 =	Kornelia Ender, East Germany	1973–75	4
=	Vladimir Salnikov, USSR	1978–82	4
=	Michael Gross, West Germany	1982–86	4
=	Tamas Darnyi, Hungary	1986–91	4
=	Yana Klochkova, Ukraine	2001–03	4
=	Xuejuan Luo, China	2001–03	4

* Individual medals at the FINA World Long Course Championships, 1973–2005

Wish granted
Grant Hackett celebrates winning a record seven golds at the World Aquatic Championships.

TOP 10 WATERSKIERS WITH THE MOST WORLD CUP WINS*

	SKIER / COUNTRY	M/F#	SLALOM	JUMP	TOTAL
1	Andy Mapple, UK	M	31	–	31
2 =	Emma Sheers, Australia	F	2	16	18
=	Jaret Llewellyn, Canada	M	–	18	18
4 =	Toni Neville, Australia	F	3	10	13
=	Kristi Johnson (née Overton), USA	F	13	–	13
6	Freddy Krueger, USA	M	–	12	12
7	Wade Cox, USA	M	10	-	10
8	Bruce Neville, Australia	M	–	9	9
9	Scot Ellis, USA	M	–	7	7
10 =	Susi Graham, Canada	F	6	–	6
=	Carl Roberge, USA	M	1	5	6

* Up to and including 2006
# Male/female

Waterskiing was invented in 1922 by 18-year-old Ralph W. Samuelson of Lake City, Minnesota, using two 8-ft (2.4-m) planks and 100 ft (30 m) of sash cord. It grew in popularity, and the first international governing body, the World Water Ski Union, was established in 1946 in Geneva, Switzerland. Its successor, the International Water Ski Federation, organized the Water Ski World Cup, which started in 1996. It ceased after the 2000 event but was revived in 2004.

Record-Breaking Spitz

Having won two golds, a silver, and a bronze medal at the Mexico City Olympics in 1968, at the 1972 Munich Games Mark Spitz (USA) not only won a record seven gold medals, but all, including the 100 and 200 meters freestyle and butterfly, were achieved in new world-record times.

THE 10 MOST OLYMPIC SWIMMING MEDALS BY A FEMALE SWIMMER*

	SWIMMER / NATIONALITY	YEARS	GOLD	SILVER	BRONZE	TOTAL
1	Jenny Thompson, USA	1992–2004	7	3	1	11
2	Franziska van Almsick, Germany	1992–2004	0	4	6	10
3 =	Inge de Bruin, Netherlands	2000–04	4	2	2	8
=	Shirley Babashoff, USA	1972–76	2	6	0	8
=	Kornelia Ender, East Germany	1972–76	4	4	0	8
=	Dawn Fraser, Australia	1956–64	4	4	0	8
=	Dagmar Hase, Germany	1992–96	2	5	1	8
=	Susie O'Neill, Australia	1996–2000	2	4	2	8
=	Dara Torres, USA	1984–2000	4	0	4	8
10 =	Krisztina Egerszegi, Hungary	1988–96	5	1	1	7
=	Amanda Beard, USA	1996–2004	2	4	1	7

* Up to and including the 2004 Olympics

TOP 10 OLYMPIC COUNTRIES ON AND IN WATER*

	COUNTRY	SWIMMING#	SAILING	ROWING	CANOEING	MOTOR BOATING†	TOTAL
1	USA	260	17	30	5	0	312
2	East Germany	40	2	33	14	0	89
3	Germany/ West Germany	22	6	27	28	0	83
4	USSR/Unified Team/Russia	32	4	13	30	0	79
5	Australia	54	5	8	1	0	68
6	UK	18	24	22	0	2	66
7	Hungary	32	0	0	17	0	49
8	Sweden	12	9	0	15	0	36
9	Italy	10	3	14	5	0	32
10	Romania	3	0	18	10	0	31

* Gold medals won at all games 1896 to 2004, including the Intercalated Games of 1906 and discontinued events
# Including water polo and diving but excluding triathlon
† Motor boating was part of the Olympic program only in 1908

Motor Sports

TOP 10 FASTEST WINNING SPEEDS OF THE INDIANAPOLIS 500*

	DRIVER / COUNTRY#	CAR	YEAR	MPH	KM/H
1	Arie Luyendyk, Netherlands	Lola-Chevrolet	1990	185.981	299.307
2	Rick Mears	Chevrolet-Lumina	1991	176.457	283.980
3	Bobby Rahal	March-Cosworth	1986	170.722	274.750
4	Juan Montoya, Colombia	G Force–Aurora	2000	167.607	269.730
5	Emerson Fittipaldi, Brazil	Penske-Chevrolet	1989	167.581	269.695
6	Helio Castroneves, Brazil	Dallara–Chevrolet	2002	166.499	267.954
7	Rick Mears	March-Cosworth	1984	163.612	263.308
8	Mark Donohue	McLaren-Offenhauser	1972	162.962	262.619
9	Al Unser	March-Cosworth	1987	162.175	260.995
10	Tom Sneva	March-Cosworth	1983	162.117	260.902

* Up to and including the 2006 race
# All from USA unless otherwise stated

TOP 10 MOST CAREER WINS IN CHAMP CAR RACES*

	DRIVER#	CAREER	WINS
1	A. J. Foyt	1960–81	67
2	Mario Andretti	1965–93	52
3	Michael Andretti	1986–2003	42
4	Al Unser	1967–87	39
5	Bobby Unser	1966–81	38
6	Al Unser, Jr.	1984–95	31
7	Paul Tracy, Canada	1993–2006	30
8	Rick Mears	1978–91	29
9	Johnny Rutherford	1965–86	27
10	Rodger Ward	1953–66	26

* Formerly CART (Championship Auto Racing Teams), Champ Car since 2004; as at the end of 2006 season
# All from USA unless otherwise stated

TOP 10 MOST RACE WINS IN A FORMULA ONE CAREER BY A DRIVER*

	DRIVER / COUNTRY	YEARS	WINS
1	Michael Schumacher, Germany	1992–2006	91
2	Alain Prost, France	1981–93	51
3	Ayrton Senna, Brazil	1985–93	41
4	Nigel Mansell, UK	1985–94	31
5	Jackie Stewart, UK	1965–73	27
6	=Jim Clark, UK	1962–68	25
	=Niki Lauda, Austria	1974–85	25
8	Juan-Manuel Fangio, Argentina	1950–57	24
9	Nelson Piquet, Brazil	1980–91	23
10	Damon Hill, UK	1993–98	22

* Up to and including 2006 season

Michael Schumacher's first Grand Prix was the Belgian GP in 1991 and his first win was in the same race the following year, driving a Benetton. He switched to Ferrari in 1996 and stayed with them until his retirement in 2006. His final win was in the 2006 Chinese GP.

TOP 10 MOST NEXTEL CUP WINS IN A SEASON*

	DRIVER#	CAR	YEAR	STARTS	WINS
1	Richard Petty	Plymouth Satellite	1967	48	27
2	Richard Petty	Plymouth Satellite	1971	46	21
3	Tim Flock	Chrysler 300	1955	39	18
4	David Pearson	Ford Torino	1968	48	16
5	David Pearson	Dodge Charger	1966	42	15
6	Buck Baker	Chrysler 300-B	1956	48	14
7	= Ned Jarrett	Ford Galaxie	1965	54	13
	= Richard Petty	Dodge Charger	1975	30	13
	= Jeff Gordon	Chevrolet Monte Carlo	1998	33	13
10	= Herb Thomas	Hudson Hornet	1953	37	12
	= Darrell Waltrip	Buick Regal	1981	31	12
	= Darrell Waltrip	Buick Regal	1982	30	12

* By the champion driver; up to and including 2006 season
# All drivers from the USA

The premier series in the NASCAR calendar, it was known as the Grand National from 1950 to 1971 and the Winston Cup 1973–2002.

TOP 10 **DISTANCES COVERED IN THE LE MANS 24-HOUR RACE***

	DRIVERS / NATIONALITY	CAR	YEAR	DISTANCE MILES	KM
1	Helmut Marko (Austria), Gijs van Lennep (Holland)	Porsche 917K	1971	3,315.20	5,335.31
2	Jan Lammers (Holland), Johnny Dumfries (UK), Andy Wallace (UK)	Jaguar XJR-9LM	1988	3,313.64	5,332.79
3	Jochen Mass (West Germany), Manuel Reuter (West Germany), Stanley Dickens (Sweden)	Sauber Mercedes C9	1989	3,271.59	5,265.12
4	Dan Gurney (USA), A. J. Foyt (USA)	Ford GT40 Mk IV	1967	3,251.57	5,232.90
5	Frank Biela (Germany), Emanuele Pirro (Italy), Marco Werner (Germany)	Audi R10	2006	3,223.05	5,187.00
6	Seiji Ara (Japan), Tom Kristensen (Denmark), Rinaldo Capello (Italy)	Audi R8	2004	3,212.46	5,169.97
7	Tom Kristensen (Denmark), Rinaldo Capello (Italy), Guy Smith (UK)	Bentley Speed 8	2003	3,196.28	5,143.93
8	Frank Biela (Germany), Tom Kristensen (Denmark), Emanuele Pirro (Italy)	Audi R8	2002	3,180.64	5,118.75
9	Gary Brabham (Australia), Christophe Bouchut (France), Eric Hélary (France)	Peugeot 905B	1993	3,168.99	5,100.00
10	Klaus Ludwig (West Germany), Paolo Barilla (Italy), "John Winter" (Louis Krages) (West Germany)	Porsche 956	1985	3,161.85	5,088.51

* Up to and including the 2006 race

Sebastian Loeb
Sebastian Loeb had the first of his victories in the Rally of Germany in 2002 in a Citroën Xsara.

TOP 10 **MOST WINS IN WORLD RALLY CHAMPIONSHIP RACES***

	DRIVER / COUNTRY	WINS
1	Sébastien Loeb, France	28
2	Carlos Sainz, Spain	26
3	= Marcus Grönholm, Finland	25
	= Colin McRae, UK	25
5	Tommi Mäkinen, Finland	24
6	Juha Kankkunen, Finland	23
7	= Markku Alén, Finland	20
	= Didier Auriol, France	20
9	Hannu Mikkola, Finland	18
10	Massimo Biasion, Italy	17

* Up to and including 2006 season

Motorcycling

TOP 10 MOST CONSECUTIVE WORLD MOTORCYCLING TITLES*

RIDER / COUNTRY	YEARS	CLASS	WINS
1 = Giacomo Agostini, Italy	1966–72	500cc	7
= Giacomo Agostini, Italy	1968–74	350cc	7
3 = Michael Doohan, Australia	1994–98	500cc	5
= Valentino Rossi, Italy	2001–05	Moto GP	5
5 = Mike Hailwood, UK	1962–65	500cc	4
= Jim Redman, Southern Rhodesia	1962–65	350cc	4
= Angel Nieto, Spain	1981–84	125cc	4
= Stefan Dörflinger, Switzerland	1982–85	50/80cc#	4
= Massimiliano "Max" Biaggi, Italy	1994–97	250cc	4
10 = Carlo Ubbiali, Italy	1958–60	125cc	3
= Hans Anscheidt, West Germany	1966–68	50cc	3
= Walter Villa, Italy	1974–76	250cc	3
= Angel Nieto, Spain	1975–77	50cc	3
= Jorge Aspar, Spain	1986–88	80cc	3

* In the same class; as at the end of the 2006 season
# The 50cc class was abandoned at the end of the 1983 season and replaced by 80cc in 1984

TOP 10 RIDERS WITH THE MOST WORLD ROAD RACE CHAMPIONSHIP WINS*

RIDER / COUNTRY	YEARS	WINS
1 Giacomo Agostini, Italy	1965–76	122
2 Angel Nieto, Spain	1969–85	90
3 Valentino Rossi, Italy	1996–2006	84
4 Mike Hailwood, UK	1959–67	76
5 Mick Doohan, Australia	1990–98	54
6 Phil Read, UK	1961–75	52
7 Jim Redman, Southern Rhodesia	1961–66	45
8 = Anton Mang, West Germany	1976–88	42
= Massimiliano "Max" Biaggi, Italy	1992–2004	42
10 Carlo Ubbiali, Italy	1950–60	39

* Solo classes only; as at end of 2006 season

Valentino Rossi
Italy's Valentino Rossi won seven world motorcycling titles between 1997 and 2005 and narrowly missed out on number eight in 2006.

TOP 10 **RIDERS WITH THE MOST SPEEDWAY WORLD TITLES***

	RIDER	NATIONALITY	YEARS	TITLES
1	Ivan Mauger	New Zealand	1968–79	6
=	Tony Rickardsson	Sweden	1994–2005	6
3	Ove Fundin	Sweden	1956–67	5
4 =	Barry Briggs	New Zealand	1957–66	4
=	Hans Nielsen	Denmark	1986–95	4
6 =	Ole Olsen	Denmark	1971–78	3
=	Erik Gundersen	Denmark	1984–88	3
8 =	Jack Young	Australia	1951–52	2
=	Fred Williams	UK	1950–53	2
=	Ronnie Moore	New Zealand	1954–59	2
=	Peter Craven	UK	1955–62	2
=	Bruce Penhall	USA	1981–82	2
=	Greg Hancock	USA	1992–97	2
=	Jason Crump	Australia	2004–06	2

* Individual titles; up to and including 2006

Up to 1995 the world title was decided by a series of qualifying heats with the final a single-night event. Since that year it has been a season-long series of Grand Prix events, with points tallied up ultimately to decide the champion.

Leader of the pack
AMA Motorcycle Hall of Famer Jeremy McGrath leading the field into the turn.

TOP 10 **RIDERS WITH THE MOST AMA SUPERCROSS RACE WINS***

	RIDER	250CC	125CC	TOTAL WINS
1	Jeremy McGrath	72	13	85
2	Ricky Carmichael	40	11	51
3	Chad Reed	24	6	30
4	James Stewart Jr	11	18	29
5	Ricky Johnson	28	–	28
6	Bob Hannah	27	–	27
7	Damon Bradshaw	19	6	25
8	Kevin Windham	12	11	23
9	Jeff Ward	20	–	20
10	Ezra Lusk	12	7	19

* 1974–2006; all riders from USA

Supercross racing was introduced in 1972, with the American Motorcyclist Association (AMA) staging its first championship in 1974, in which Pierre Karsmakers won the 250cc class and Gary Semics the 500cc class.

TOP 10 **MANUFACTURERS WITH THE MOST WORLD ROAD-RACE CHAMPIONSHIP WINS***

	MANUFACTURER / COUNTRY	YEAR OF FIRST WIN	TOTAL WINS
1	Honda (Japan)	1961	616
2	Yamaha (Japan)	1963	426
3	MV Agusta (Italy)	1952	275
4	Aprilia (Italy)	1987	209
5	Suzuki (Japan)	1962	154
6 =	Kawasaki (Japan)	1969	85
=	Derbi (Spain)	1968	85
8	Kreidler (Germany)	1962	65
9	Garelli (Italy)	1982	51
10	Gilera (Italy)	1949	47

* Solo classes only; as at the end of 2006 season

Honda's first World Championship win was at Montjuich, Barcelona on April 23, 1961, when Australia's Tom Phillis won the 125cc class. He was also Honda's first World Champion.

Two Wheels and Four

John Surtees from the UK remains the only man ever to win world titles on both two wheels and four wheels. He achieved seven world motor cycling titles between 1956 and 1960 before switching to driving cars in 1960. In 1964 he took the Formula One world title, driving a Ferrari.

Cycling

TOP 10 **MOST WINS IN THE THREE MAJOR TOURS***

	CYCLIST / COUNTRY	YEARS	TOUR	GIRO	VUELTA	TOTAL
1	Eddy Merckx, Belgium	1968–74	5	5	1	11
2	Bernard Hinault, France	1978–85	5	3	2	10
3	Jacques Anquetil, France	1957–64	5	2	1	8
4	=Fausto Coppi, Italy	1940–53	2	5	0	7
	=Miguel Induráin, Spain	1991–95	5	2	0	7
	=Lance Armstrong, USA	1999–2005	7	0	0	7
7	=Alfredo Binda, Italy	1925–33	0	5	0	5
	=Gino Bartali, Italy	1938–48	2	3	0	5
	=Felice Gimondi, Italy	1965–76	1	3	1	5
10	=Toni Rominger, Switzerland	1992–95	0	1	3	4
	=Roberto Heras, Spain	2000–05	0	0	4	4

* Up to and including 2006

The three major tours are the Tour de France, launched in 1903 and first won by Maurice Garin of France, the Tour of Italy (Giro d'Italia), first contested in 1909 and won by Luigi Ganna of Italy, and the Tour of Spain (Vuelta de España), first held in 1935 and won by Gustave Deloor of Belgium.

TOP 10 **MOST DAYS SPENT WEARING THE YELLOW JERSEY IN THE TOUR DE FRANCE***

	CYCLIST / COUNTRY	YEARS	TOTAL DAYS
1	Eddy Merckx, Belgium	1969–74	111
2	Lance Armstrong, USA	1999–2005	81
3	Bernard Hinault, France	1978–85	79
4	Miguel Induráin, Spain	1991–95	60
5	Jacques Anquetil, France	1957–64	52
6	Sylvère Maes, Belgium	1936–39	41
7	Antonin Magne, France	1931–34	39
8	Nicolas Frantz, Switzerland	1927–28	37
9	Louison Bobet, France	1953–55	36
10	André Leducq, France	1930–32	34

* Up to and including 2006

The leader of the Tour de France has been wearing the coveted yellow jersey since July 19, 1919, when Eugène Christophe (France) became the first rider to do so on the stage from Grenoble to Geneva. Journalists covering the race had asked the organizers if they could arrange for the race leader to wear a distinctively colored jersey so they could easily identify him. As the Tour director was Henri Desgrange, and the pages of his newspaper, *L'Auto*, were printed on yellow paper, he chose yellow.

PETIT-BRETON CENTENARY

Lucien Petit-Breton (1882–1917) holds the unique distinction of being the first man to win the Tour de France in consecutive years, 1907 and 1908. He moved to Argentina when he was six and started cycling as a child. His real name was Lucien Mazan; he was nicknamed Lucien Breton after his Brittany birthplace, but because there was another cyclist of that name, he changed it to Lucien Petit-Breton. He returned to France in 1902 and started competitive road racing in 1905, also setting a new one-hour distance record prior to his double Tour de France victories.

This achievement was later equaled by Guy Thys (Belgium) and others, but it took until 1955 for a rider —Louison Bobet (France)—to win three consecutive Tours. Jacques Anquetil (France) won his fourth consecutive Tour in 1961, a feat equaled by Eddy Merckx (Belgium). Miguel Induráin (Spain) won six years in a row (1991–95) and Lance Armstrong (USA) a remarkable seven in succession between 1999 and 2005.

TOP 10 **OLDEST CYCLING CLASSIC RACES AND TOURS**

	RACE	FIRST HELD
1	Liège–Bastogne–Liège	1892
2	Paris–Brussels	1893
3	Paris–Roubaix	1896
4	Paris–Tours	1896
5	Tour de France	1903
6	Tour of Lombardy	1905
7	Milan–San Remo	1907
8	Tour of Italy	1909
9	Tour of Flanders	1913
10	Championship of Zurich	1914

The Bordeaux–Paris race was the first major cycling race and was, until its demise in 1988, the oldest Classic. The race lasted for around 16 hours, starting in darkness in the early hours of the morning. The first race in 1891 was won by Britain's George Pilkington Mills.

Oldest race
Raced since 1892 in the Ardennes region of Belgium, the Liège–Bastogne–Liège takes place every April and is one of the races on professional cycling's UCI Pro Tour.

TOP 10 **COUNTRIES WITH THE MOST OLYMPIC CYCLING MEDALS***

	COUNTRY	GOLD	SILVER	BRONZE	TOTAL
1	France	39	15	26	80
2	Italy	36	13	7	56
3	Germany/West Germany	16	18	21	55
4	UK	12	23	19	54
5	Australia	13	14	13	40
6	USA	13	9	17	39
7	Netherlands	14	14	9	37
8	USSR/Russia	15	8	12	35
9	Belgium	6	7	11	24
10	Denmark	6	4	7	17

* All events (men and women) up to and including the 2004 Athens Games, including discontinued events and the 1906 Intercalated Games in Greece

TOP 10 **FASTEST TOURS DE FRANCE***

	YEAR	WINNER / COUNTRY	DISTANCE		AVERAGE SPEED	
			MILES	KM	MPH	KM/H
1	2005	Lance Armstrong, USA	2,234.8	3,596.5	25.904	41.689
2	2003	Lance Armstrong, USA	2,129.7	3,427.5	25.449	40.956
3	2006	Floyd Landis, USA#	2.272.4	3,657.1	25.341	40.784
4	2004	Lance Armstrong, USA	2,107.1	3,391.1	25.205	40.563
5	1999	Lance Armstrong, USA	2,290.9	3,686.8	25.026	40.276
6	2001	Lance Armstrong, USA	2,147.6	3,456.2	24.888	40.053
7	1998	Marco Pantani, Italy	2,306.6	3,712.1	24.847	39.988
8	2002	Lance Armstrong, USA	2.036.5	3,277.5	24.809	39.927
9	2000	Lance Armstrong, USA	2,275.8	3,662.5	24.589	39.572
10	1992	Miguel Induráin, Spain	2,474.9	3,983.0	24.547	39.504

* Based on average time of Tour winner
# At the time of going to print the outcome of the appeal against Floyd Landis' win in 2006 was still undecided

Horse Sports

TOP 10 **OLYMPIC EQUESTRIAN COUNTRIES***

	COUNTRY	GOLD	SILVER	BRONZE	TOTAL
1	Germany/West Germany	35	19	21	75
2	USA	9	19	18	46
3	Sweden	17	8	14	39
4	France	12	12	11	35
5	UK	6	9	10	25
6	Italy	7	9	7	23
7	Switzerland	4	10	7	21
8	Netherlands	9	9	2	20
9	USSR/Unified Team/Russia	6	5	4	15
10	Belgium	4	2	5	11

* Up to and including the 2004 Olympics

These figures include the medal totals for both individual and team disciplines: Showjumping, Three-Day Event, and Dressage.

Jumping to victory
Peter Wylde of the gold medal-winning US showjumping team on Fein Cera at the 2004 Olympic Games.

TOP 10 **US JOCKEYS WITH THE MOST CAREER WINS***

	JOCKEYS	WINS
1	Russell Baze#	9,565
2	Laffit Pincay, Jr.	9,530
3	Willie Shoemaker	8,833
4	Pat Day	8,803
5	David Gall	7,396
6	Chris McCarron	7,141
7	Angel Cordero, Jr.	7,057
8	Jorge Velasquez	6,795
9	Sandy Hawley	6,449
10	Earlie Fires	6,403

* As at January 1, 2007
# Active in 2006

Russell Baze broke Laffit Pincay's record in the 4th race at Bay Meadows, San Mateo, California on Friday December 1, 2006 when he came home first aboard Butterfly Belle. Baze started racing in 1974.

TOP 10 FASTEST WINNING TIMES OF THE EPSOM DERBY*

	HORSE	YEAR	TIME MINS:SECS
1	Lammtarra	1995	2:32.31
2	Galileo	2001	2:33.27
3	Kris Kin	2003	2:33.35
4	Royal Palace	1967	2:33.36
5	Northern Light	2004	2:33.72
6	Mahmoud	1936	2:33.80
7	Kahyasi	1988	2:33.84
8	High-Rise	1998	2:33.88
9	Reference Point	1987	2:33.90
10 =	Hyperion	1933	2:34.00
=	Windsor Lad	1934	2:34.00
=	Generous	1991	2:34.00

* Up to and including 2006, excluding wartime races run at Newmarket 1915–18 and 1940–45

Lammtarra also won the prestigious King George VI & Queen Elizabeth Diamond Stakes, and the Prix de l'Arc de Triomphe in 1995.

TOP 10 FASTEST WINNING TIMES OF THE KENTUCKY DERBY*

	HORSE	YEAR	TIME MINS:SECS
1	Secretariat	1973	1:59.40
2	Monarchos	2001	1:59.97
3	Northern Dancer	1964	2:00.00
4	Spend A Buck	1985	2:00.20
5	Decidedly	1962	2:00.40
6	Proud Clarion	1967	2:00.60
7 =	Grindstone	1996	2:01.00
=	Fusaichi Pegasus	2000	2:01.00
9	War Emblem	2002	2:01.13
10	Funny Cide	2003	2:01.19

* Up to and including 2006

The Kentucky Derby—which provided the name of the hat once popularly worn at the event—is held on the first Saturday in May at Churchill Downs, Louisville, Kentucky. It was first raced in 1875 over a distance of 1 mile 4 furlongs, but after 1896 was reduced to 1 mile 2 furlongs.

TOP 10 OLYMPIC EQUESTRIAN MEDALISTS*

	RIDER / COUNTRY	YEARS	GOLD	SILVER	BRONZE	TOTAL
1	Reiner Klimke, West Germany	1964–88	6	0	2	8
2	Hans-Günther Winkler, West Germany	1956–76	5	1	1	7
3 =	Piero d'Inzeo, Italy	1956–72	0	2	4	6
=	Raimondo d'Inzeo, Italy	1956–72	1	2	3	6
=	Josef Neckerman, West Germany	1960–72	2	2	2	6
=	Michael Plumb, USA	1964–84	2	4	0	6
=	Isabell Werth, Germany	1992–2000	4	2	0	6
=	Anky van Grunsven, Netherlands	1992–2004	2	4	0	6
9 =	Earl Thomson, USA	1932–48	2	3	0	5
=	André Jousseaumé, France	1932–52	2	2	1	5
=	Henri Chammartin, Switzerland	1952–68	1	2	2	5
=	Gustav Fischer, Switzerland	1952–68	0	3	2	5
=	Liselott Linsenhoff, West Germany	1956–72	2	2	1	5
=	Christine Stückelberger, Switzerland	1976–88	1	3	1	5
=	Mark Todd, New Zealand	1984–2000	2	1	2	5

* Up to and including 2004 Olympics

Born in Münster in 1936, Reiner Klimke's record haul of Olympic medals all came in the dressage event. He was a member of the German team that won five team golds.

Galileo triumph
Ridden by Mick Kinane in his second Epsom Derby win, favorite Galileo romps home.

Sport Miscellany

Bundesliga
As at the start of the 2006–07 season, SV Hamburg was the only team to play in every season of the Bundesliga.

TOP 10 LARGEST SPORTS STADIUMS*

	STADIUM / LOCATION / YEAR OPENED	CAPACITY
1	Rungnado May Day Stadium Pyöngyang, South Korea, 1989	150,000
2	Saltlake Stadium Calcutta, India, 1984	120,000
3	Estadio Azteca Mexico City, Mexico, 1966	114,465
4	Michigan Stadium Ann Arbor, USA, 1927	107,501
5	Beaver Stadium Penn State, USA, 1960	107,282
6	Neyland Stadium Knoxville, Tennessee, USA, 1921	104,079
7	Jornalista Mário Filho# Rio de Janeiro, Brazil, 1950	103,045
8	Ohio Stadium Colombus, USA, 1922	101,568
9	National Stadium Bukit Jalil Kuala Lumpur, Malaysia, 1998	100,200
10 =	Melbourne Cricket Ground Melbourne, Australia, 1853	100,000
=	Bung Karno Stadium Jakarta, Indonesia, 1962	100,000
=	Azadi Stadium Tehran, Iran, 1971	100,000
=	Jawaharlal Stadium New Delhi, India, 1982	100,000

* Based on official capacity 2006; excludes motor-racing and horseracing tracks
\# Formerly Maracanã Stadium

TOP 10 MOST-WATCHED SPORTS LEAGUES*

	LEAGUE	SPORT	COUNTRY	AVERAGE ATTENDANCE
1	National Football League (NFL)	American football	USA	66,453
2	Bundesliga	Soccer	Germany	40,775
3	Australian Football League (AFL)	Australian football	Australia	35,250
4	FA Premier League	Soccer	England	33,875
5	Major League Baseball (MLB)	Baseball	USA	31,423
6	Canadian Football League (CFL)	Canadian football	Canada	29,943
7	La Liga	Soccer	Spain	29,029
8	Mexican Football League	Soccer	Mexico	24,970
9	Nippon Professional Baseball (NPB)	Baseball	Japan	23,552
10	Serie A	Soccer	Italy	21,968

* Based on average attendance of last completed season, as at February 1, 2007

THE 10 LATEST WINNERS OF THE SPORTS ILLUSTRATED SPORTSPERSON OF THE YEAR AWARD

YEAR	WINNER / SPORT
2006	Dwyane Wade, basketball
2005	Tom Brady, football
2004	Boston Red Sox, baseball
2003	Tim Duncan and David Robinson, basketball
2002	Lance Armstrong, cycling
2001	Curt Schilling and Randy Johnson, baseball
2000	Tiger Woods, golf
1999	US Women's World Cup Squad, soccer
1998	Mark McGwire and Sammy Sosa, baseball
1997	Dean Smith, college basketball

First presented in 1954, when it was won by British athlete Roger Bannister, this annual award honors the sportsman or sportswoman who in that year, in the opinion of the editors of *Sports Illustrated*, most "symbolizes in character and performance the ideals of sportsmanship." Tiger Woods made history not only on the golf course in 2000, when he became the first sportsman to win this award twice.

THE 10 WORST DISASTERS AT SPORTS VENUES

	LOCATION / DISASTER	DATE	NO. KILLED
1	Hong Kong Jockey Club, Stand collapse and fire	Feb 26, 1918	604
2	Lenin Stadium, Moscow, Crush in football stadium	Oct 20, 1982	340
3	Lima, Peru Football stadium riot	May 24, 1964	320
4	Sinceljo, Colombia, Bullring stand collapse	Jan 20, 1980	222
5	Accra, Ghana, Riot and stampede in football stadium	May 9, 2001	127
6	Hillsborough, Sheffield, UK, Crush in football stadium	Apr 15, 1989	96
7	Mateo Flores National Stadium, Guatemala City, Guatemala, Stampede during World Cup soccer qualifying match, Guatemala vs. Costa Rica, with 147 injured	Oct 16, 1996	84
8	Le Mans, France, Racecar crash	Jun 11, 1955	82
9	Katmandu, Nepal, Stampede in soccer stadium	Mar 12, 1988	80
10 =	Buenos Aires, Argentina, Riot in soccer stadium	May 23, 1968	74
=	PhilSports Arena, Manila, Philippines, Stampede (related to TV show, not sporting event)	Feb 4, 2006	74

TOP 10 HIGHEST-EARNING SPORTSMEN

	SPORTSMAN / COUNTRY*	SPORT	EARNINGS $#
1	Tiger Woods	Golf	90,000,000
2	Michael Schumacher (Germany)	Motor racing	58,000,000
3	Muhammad Ali	Boxing (ex)	55,000,000
4	Phil Mickelson	Golf	47,000,000
5	Michael Jordan	Basketball	32,000,000
6	Kobe Bryant	Basketball	31,000,000
7 =	Shaquille O'Neal	Basketball	30,000,000
=	Valentino Rossi (Italy)	Motorcycling	30,000,000
9 =	Tom Brady	American football	29,000,000
=	Alex Rodriguez	Baseball	29,000,000

* USA unless otherwise stated
\# Estimated June 2005–June 2006

Source: Forbes

Soccer player David Beckham's $27 million makes him the highest-earning British sportsman, while Russian tennis player Maria Sharapova's $19 million establishes her at the top of the earnings league among sportswomen.

Tiger Woods
The world's greatest golfer, Tiger Woods is now fast approaching Jack Nicklaus' alltime record of 18 wins in professional Majors.

Leisure Activities

TOP 10 PARTICIPATION SPORTS IN THE USA

	SPORT	TOTAL*
1	Exercise walking	86,000,000
2	Swimming	58,000,000
3	Exercising with equipment	54,200,000
4	Camping (vacation/overnight)	46,000,000
5	Bowling	45,400,000
6	Fishing	43,300,000
7	Bicycle riding	43,100,000
8	Billiards/pool	37,300,000
9	Weightlifting	35,500,000
10	Workout at club	34,700,000

* Seven years of age and older who participated more than once during 2005

Source: National Sporting Goods Association

TOP 10 CASINO MARKETS IN THE USA

	CASINO	REVENUE 2005 ($)
1	Las Vegas Strip, NV	6,031,000,000
2	Atlantic City, NJ	5,018,000,000
3	Chicagoland, IN/IL	2,441,000,000
4	Detroit, MS	1,229,000,000
5	Tunica/Lula, MS	1,187,000,000
6	Connecticut	982,650,000
7	St Louis, MO/IL	959,600,000
8	Reno/Sparks, NV	920,220,000
9	Boulder Strip, NV	885,990,000
10	Shreveport, LA	814,230,000

Source: The Innovation Group/American Gaming Association

TOP 10 TRADITIONAL TOY AND GAME-BUYING COUNTRIES

COUNTRY / TRADITIONAL TOY AND GAME SALES 2008 ($)*

1 USA 36,460,116,000

2 China 9,083,485,000

3 Japan 4,498,450,000

4 UK 8,896,088,000

5 France 6,194,771,000

6 Germany 4,685,498,000

7 Mexico 3,998,685,000

8 Italy 3,790,901,000

9 Spain 3,001,306,000

10 South Korea 2,879,576,000

Traditional toys encompass toys other than video games. The category leader is preschool toys but also includes model vehicles, construction toys, dolls and action figures, soft toys, and teddy bears.

* Forecast

Source: Euromonitor

TOP 10 **VIDEO GAME-BUYING COUNTRIES**

COUNTRY / VIDEO GAME SALES PER CAPITA 2008 ($)*

1 UK 73.09

2 Australia 61.38

3 South Korea 52.24

4 USA 46.15

5 France 42.37

6 Netherlands 39.64

7 Spain 34.08

8 Canada 32.04

9 Belgium 30.01

10 Japan 28.54

* Forecast

Source: Euromonitor

TOP 10 **LEISURE ACTIVITIES IN THE USA**

	ACTIVITY	NO.*
1	Dining out	104,113,000
2	Entertaining friends or relatives at home	80,860,000
3	Reading books	76,455,000
4	Barbecuing	74,050,000
5	Surfing the net	60,162,000
6	Playing cards	54,140,000
7	Going to the beach	40,114,000
8	Going to bars/night clubs	40,114,000
9	Baking	39,599,000
10	Board games	38,124,000

* Participated during previous 12 months, from sample interviewed in 2005

Source: Mediamark Research, Inc.

Further Information

THE UNIVERSE & THE EARTH

Astronautics
http://www.astronautix.com/
Spaceflight news and reference

Caves
http://www.caverbob.com/home.htm
List of long and deep caves

Comets
http://www.cometography.com/
Comet catalog and descriptions

Islands
http://islands.unep.ch/isldir.htm
Information on the world's islands

Mountains
http://peaklist.org/
Lists of the world's tallest mountains

NASA
http://www.nasa.gov/home/index.html
The main website for the US space program

Oceans
http://www.oceansatlas.org/index.jsp
The UN's resource on oceanographic issues

Planets
http://www.nineplanets.org/
A multimedia tour of the Solar System

Space
http://www.space.com/
Reports on events in space exploration

Waterfalls
http://www.world-waterfalls.com/
Data on the world's tallest and largest waterfalls

LIFE ON EARTH

Animals
http://animaldiversity.ummz.umich.edu/site/index.html
A wealth of animal data

Birds
http://www.bsc-eoc.org/avibase/avibase.jsp
A database on the world's birds

Conservation
http://iucn.org/
The leading nature conservation site

Endangered
http://www.cites.org/
Lists of endangered species of flora and fauna

Environment
http://www.unep.ch/
The UN's Earthwatch and other programs

Fish
http://www.fishbase.org/
Global information on fishes

Food and Agriculture Organization
http://www.fao.org/
Statistics from the UN's FAO website

Forests
http://www.americanforests.org/
Information on the nation's trees and forests

Insects
http://ufbir.ifas.ufl.edu/
The University of Florida Book of Insect Records

North American mammals
http://www.mnh.si.edu/mna/
The Smithsonian Institution's comprehensive site

THE HUMAN WORLD

Death penalty
http://www.deathpenaltyinfo.org/
Facts and statistics from the Death Penalty Information Center

Health
http://www.cdc.gov/nchs
Information and links on health for US citizens

Leaders
http://www.terra.es/personal2/monolith/home.htm
Facts about world leaders since 1945

Military
http://www.globalfirepower.com/
World military statistics and rankings

Names
http://www.ssa.gov/OACT/babynames/index.html
Most common names from the Social Security Administration

Presidents
http://www.whitehouse.gov/history/presidents/
Biographies, facts, and figures from the White House

Prisons
http://www.bop.gov
Public information on all aspects of the US prison system

Religions
http://www.worldchristiandatabase.org/wcd/
World religion data

Rulers
http://rulers.org/
A database of the world's rulers and political leaders

World Health Organization
http://www.who.int/en/
World health information and advice

TOWN & COUNTRY

Bridges and tunnels
http://en.structurae.de/
Facts and figures on the world's buildings, tunnels, and other structures

Countries
http://www.theodora.com/wfb/
Country data, rankings, etc.

Country and city populations
http://www.citypopulation.de/cities.html
A searchable guide to the world's countries and major cities

Country data
https://www.cia.gov/cia/publications/factbook/index.html
The CIA World Factbook

Country populations
http://www.un.org/esa/population/unpop.htm
The UN's worldwide data on population issues

Development
http://www.worldbank.org/
Development and other statistics from around the world

Population
http://www.census.gov/ipc/www/
International population statistics

Population issues
http://www.un.org/esa/population/unpop.htm
The UN's Population Division

Skyscrapers
http://www.emporis.com/en/bu/sk/
The Emporis database of high-rise buildings

Tunnels
http://home.no.net/lotsberg/
A database of the longest rail, road, and canal tunnels

CULTURE

The Art Newspaper
http://www.theartnewspaper.com/
News and views on the art world

Books
http://publishersweekly.com
Publishers Weekly, the trade journal of American publishers

Education
http://nces.ed.gov
The home of federal education data

Languages of the world
http://www.ethnologue.com/
Online reference work on the world's 6,912 living languages

Languages online
http://global-reach.biz/globstats/index.php3
Facts and figures on online languages

Libraries
http://www.ala.org
US library information and book awards from the American Library Association

The Library of Congress
http://www.loc.gov
An online gateway to one of the world's greatest collections of words and pictures

The New York Public Library
http://www.nypl.org/
One of the country's foremost libraries, with an online catalog

The Pulitzer Prizes
http://www.pulitzer.org
A searchable guide to the prestigious US literary prize

UNESCO
http://www.unesco.org/
Comparative international statistics on education and culture

MUSIC

All Music Guide
http://www.allmusic.com/
A comprehensive guide to all genres of music

American Society of Composers, Authors, and Publishers
http://www.ascap.com
ASCAP songwriter and other awards

Billboard
http://www.billboard.com/
US music news and charts data

Classical music
http://classicalusa.com
An online guide to classical music in the US

Country Music Hall of Fame
http://www.countrymusichalloffame.com/site/
The history of and information about country music

Grammy Awards
http://www.naras.org/
The official site for the famous US music awards

MTV
http://www.mtv.com
The online site for the TV music channel

Recording Industry Association of America
http://www.riaa.org
Searchable data on gold and platinum disk award winners

Rock and Roll Hall of Fame
http://www.rockhall.com
The museum of the history of rock

Rolling Stone magazine
http://www.rollingstone.com
Features on popular music since 1967

STAGE & SCREEN

Academy Awards
http://www.oscars.org/
The official "Oscars" website

Emmy Awards
http://www.emmyonline.org/
Emmy TV awards from the National Television Academy site

Golden Globe Awards
http://www.hfpa.org/
Hollywood Foreign Press Association's Golden Globes site

Hollywood
http://www.hollywood.com/
A US cinema site with details on all the new releases

Internet Movie Database
http://www.imdb.com/
The best of the publicly accessible film websites; IMDbPro is available to subscribers

Internet Broadway Database
http://www.ibdb.com/default.asp
Broadway theater information

Internet Theatre Database
http://www.theatredb.com/
A Broadway-focused searchable stage site

Tony Awards
http://www.tonyawards.com/en_US/index.html
Official website of the American Theatre Wing's Tonys

Variety
http://www.variety.com/
Extensive entertainment information (extra features available to subscribers)

Yahoo! Movies
http://uk.movies.yahoo.com/
Charts plus features and links to the latest film releases

THE COMMERCIAL WORLD

The Economist
http://www.economist.com/
Global economic and political news

Energy
http://www.eia.doe.gov/
Official US energy statistics

Environmental Sustainability Index
http://sedac.ciesin.columbia.edu/es/esi/
Data on the planet's future

Gold
http://www.gold.org/
The website of the World Gold Council

Internet
http://www.internetworldstats.com/
Internet World Stats

Organisation for Economic Co-operation and Development
http://www.oecd.org/home/
World economic and social statistics

Rich lists
http://www.forbes.com/
Forbes magazine's celebrated lists of the world's wealthiest people

Telecommunications
http://www.itu.int
Worldwide telecommunications statistics

United Nations Development Programme
http://www.undp.org/
Country GDPs and other development data

The World Bank
http://www.worldbank.org/
World development, trade, and labor statistics

TRANSPORT & TOURISM

Air disasters
http://www.airdisaster.com/
Reports on aviation disasters

Air speed records
http://www.fai.org/records
The website of the official air speed record governing body

Amusement parks
http://napha.org/nnn/
Historical facts and links to amusement parks, rollercoasters, etc.

Aviation
http://www.aerofiles.com/
Information on a century of American aviation

Car manufacture
http://www.oica.net/
The International Organization of Motor Vehicle Manufacturers' website

Railroads
http://www.railwaygazette.com/
The world's railroad business in depth

Shipwrecks
http://www.shipwreckregistry.com/
A huge database of the world's wrecked and lost ships

Tourism Offices Worldwide Directory
http://www.towd.com/
Contact details for tourism offices around the world

Travel industry
http://www.tia.org
Stats on travel to and within the USA

World Tourism Organisation
http://www.world-tourism.org/
The world's principal travel and tourism organization

SPORT

Baseball
http://www.mlb.com
The official website of Major League Baseball

Basketball
http://www.nba.com
The official website of the NBA

Cycling
http://www.uci.ch/
The Union Cycliste Internationale, the competitive cycling governing body

Football
http://www.nfl.com
The official website of the NFL

Golf
http://www.pgatour.com
The Professional Golfers' Association (PGA) Tour

Hockey
http://www.nhl.com
The official website of the NHL

Olympics
http://www.olympic.org
The official website of the International Olympic Committee, with a searchable database

Skiing
http://www.fis-ski.com/
Fédèration Internationale de Ski, the world governing body of skiing and snowboarding

Sports Illustrated
http://sportsillustrated.cnn.com/
Sports Illustrated's comprehensive coverage of all major sports

Track & Field
http://www.iaaf.org
The IAAF's statistics and rankings of the world's top athletes

Index

C

canoeing
Olympic countries 232
Capitals of Culture
first European 106
latest Arab 106
carbon dioxide
countries emitting most 182
cars
bestselling 192
countries producing most 192
countries with the highest theft rates 78
manufacturers 192
most common makes stolen 78
cats
pet populations 45
cattle
countries with the most 46
caves
deepest 21
longest 20
cereal
countries producing the most 48
crops 48
charities
in the USA 74
China
ethnic groups 95
exports from 94
patent categories 94
sunniest major cities 95
tallest buildings 95
types of book published 94
churches
tallest 101
cinema
admissions in the USA 143
countries with the most screens 142
cities
countries with the most million plus 98
first with populations of more than one
million 98
largest 99
largest capital 99
most skyscrapers 101
most visited in the USA 205
sunniest in China 95
with highest proportion of population 98
coal
countries consuming most 180
countries producing most 180
countries with greatest reserves 180
comedies
Broadway, longest-running 139
comedy road-trip films 148
Emmy award-winning television series,
last 167
comets
coming closest to Earth 11
most frequently seen 12
comics
films adapted from 148

computers
countries with the most 188
corruption
countries most and least 61
cosmetic surgery
procedures performed in USA 57
countries
air quality
best 182
worst 182
amphibian species, most 39
animal species, most threatened 33
armed forces
largest 84
World War I, largest 82
armour 84
astronauts or cosmonauts in orbit, first 14
beehives, most 46
birth rates, highest 58
birth rates, lowest 58
births, most 58
borders
longest 89
shortest 89
box-office revenue, highest 143
broadband users, most 189
Buddhists, most 69
carbon dioxide-emitting 182
car-producing 192
car-theft rates, highest 78
cattle, most 46
cellphones, most 188
cereal-producing 48
Champagne consumers 179
cinema screens, most 142
coal reserves 180
coal-consuming 180
coal-producing 180
coffee drinkers 178
cola-drink consumers 179
computers, most 188
corruption
least 61
most 61
crime rates, highest reported 79
death rates, lowest 67
deaths, most 67
deforesting 50
dentists, most 56
diamond production 175
divorce rates
highest 65
lowest 65
doctors, most 56
dollar billionaires, most 172
egg consumers 176
elevations, lowest 21
Environmental Performance Index
best 182
worst 183
exporters 170
FIFA World Cup winners 221
fish consumers 177

fish species, most 41
forests
largest areas 50
most 51
fruit-producing 49
Girl-Guide and Girl-Scout membership,
highest 75
goats, most 47
gold production 175
high-technology exports 186
Hindus, most 69
horses, most 47
ice hockey
registered players, most 223
World Championship medals, most 223
importers 170
in which men most outnumber women
91
in which women most outnumber men
91
industrial robots, most 186
inland water, greatest areas 19
Internet users, most 189
Jews, most 69
largest 88
life expectancy
highest 59
lowest 59
livable
least 60
most 60
mammal species, most 35
military aircraft, most 85
military expenditure 84
milk consumers 179
million-plus cities, most 98
missile defense systems 85
motor vehicle-owning 192
movie-producing 143
murder rates, highest 80
Muslims, most 68
natural gas reserves 180
natural gas-consumers 181
naval ships, most 85
neighbors, most 89
nurses most 56
nut-producing 49
obesity, highest levels of 57
oil reserves, greatest 181
oil-consuming 181
oil-producing 181
Olympic canoeing 232
Olympic cycling medals, most 239
Olympic on and in water 233
ozone concentration
highest 183
lowest 183
Paralympic medal winners, most 211
patents 186
pet-owning 44
pigs, most 46
platinum production 174
population

Acknowledgments

Special research: Ian Morrison (sport);
Dafydd Rees (music)

Roland Bert
Peter Bond
Richard Braddish
Thomas Brinkhoff
Philip Eden
Christopher Forbes
Russell E. Gough
Robert Grant
Benjamin Lucas
Aylla Macphail
Chris Mead
Sylvia Morris
Roberto Ortiz de Zarate
Robert Senior
Lucy T. Verma

Academy of Motion Picture Arts and Sciences
 – Oscar® statuette is the registered
 trademark and copyrighted property of the
 Academy of Motion Picture Arts and Sciences
Advertising Age
American Film Institute
American Society for Aesthetic Plastic Surgery
Animated Film Society (Annie Awards)
The Art Newspaper
Association of Tennis Professionals
American Forests
Audit Bureau of Circulations Ltd
The Barth Report 2005/2006
Beverage Marketing Corporation
Billboard
Box Office Mojo
BP Statistical Review of World Energy 2006
British Council
British Library
British Museum
British National Corpus
Bureau of Federal Prisons
Bureau of Justice Statistics
Business Week
Central Institute of Indian Languages
Central Intelligence Agency
China Statistical Yearbook 2006
Christie's
Computer Industry Almanac
CRC Handbook of Chemistry and Physics
Crime in the United States 2005
Department of Trade and Industry (UK)
Diamond Facts
Drama Desk Awards
Earth Impact Database
EarthTrends
The Economist
EM-DAT, CRED, University of Louvain
Emporis
Energy Information Administration
Essential Science Indicators
Ethnologue
Euromonitor
FBI Uniform Crime Reports

Fédération Internationale de Football
 Association
Fédération Internationale de Motorcyclisme
Fédération International de Ski
Food and Agriculture Organization of the
 United Nations
Forbes
Global Education Digest (UNESCO)
GlobalFirePower.com
Global Forest Resources Assessment (FAO)
Golden Raspberry Awards
Gold Fields Mineral Services Ltd.
Hollywood Foreign Press Association (Golden
 Globe Awards)
Human Development Report (United Nations)
Imperial War Museum
Interbrand
International Association of Athletics
 Federations
International Centre for Prison Studies (UK)
International Commission on Large Dams
International Federation of Audit Bureaux of
 Circulations
International Federation of Robotics
The International Institute for Strategic
 Studies, *The Military Balance 2006–2007*
International Intellectual Property Alliance
International Iron & Steel Institute
International Obesity Task Force
International Olympic Committee
International Organization of Motor Vehicle
 Manufacturers
International Telecommunication Union
International Union for Conservation of
 Nature and Natural Resources
Internet Movie Database
Internet World Stats
Interpol
Kentucky Derby
Ladies Professional Golf Association
League of American Theaters and Producers
Library of Congress
Lipmann Walton
Magazine Publishers of America
Major League Baseball
Mediamark Research, Inc.
Metropolitan Opera
Morgan Quitno Press, *State Rankings 2006*
Motion Picture Association of America
Music Information Database
National Academy of Recording Arts and
 Sciences (Grammy Awards)
National Academy of Television Arts &
 Sciences (Emmy Awards)
National Aeronautics and Space
 Administration (NASA)
National Amusement Park Historical
 Association
National Basketball Association
National Center for Education Statistics
National Center for Health Statistics
National Climatic Data Center
National Football League

National Hockey League
National Sporting Goods Association
Newspaper Association of America
Niagara Falls Museum
AC Nielsen
Nielsen Media Research
Nobel Foundation
NonProfit Times
Northwest Territories
Official Museums Directory
Organisation for Economic Co-operation and
 Development (OECD)
Organisation Internationale des Constructeurs
 d'Automobiles
Pilot 2006 Environmental Performance Index
Point Topic
Population Reference Bureau
Professional Golfers' Association
Railway Gazette International
Recording Industry Association of America
 (RIAA)
River Systems of the World
Royal Astronomical Society (UK)
Screen Digest
Screen International
The Silver Institute, *World Silver Survey 2006*
Social Security Administration
Sotheby's
Sports Illustrated
Statistical Abstract of the United States
Stores
Tony Awards
Tour de France
Transparency International
United Nations
United Nations Educational, Scientific and
 Cultural Organization (UNESCO)
United Nations Population Division
US Census Bureau, International Database
US Department of Agriculture, Economic
 Research Service
US Department of Commerce
US Geological Survey
Variety
Video Business
Ward's Motor Vehicle Facts & Figures 2006
Women's Tennis Association
World Association of Girl Guides and Girl
 Scouts
World Association of Newspapers
World Bank
World Christian Database
World Conservation Monitoring Centre
World Development Indicators (World Bank)
The World Factbook 2007 (CIA)
World Gold Council
World Health Report (World Health
 Organization)
World Intellectual Property Organization
World of Learning
World Organization of the Scout Movement
World Tennis Association
World Tourism Organization

Picture Credits

The publisher would like to thank the following sources for their kind permission to reproduce the photographs and illustrations in this book.

(Abbreviations key: t = top, b = bottom, r = right, l = left, c = centre)

Big Blu Picture Library: 34-35 Jonathan Bonnick

Christie's Images Ltd: 118

Corbis: 10b Charles & Josette Lenars, 16-17 Digital Art, 17 STScI/NASA, 19 Layne Kennedy, 20 Alison Wright, 20-21, 23 Sharna Balfour/Gallo Images, 25 Lawson Wood, 26 Dean Conger, 28-29, 32 Visuals Unlimited, 33 Stapleton Collection, 34tr Frank Krahmer, 35tr DLILLC, 36b Jeff Vanuga, 37b Royalty Free, 38b Joe McDonald, 39 Kennan Ward, 42t Volkmar Brockhaus/zefa, 43r Anthony Bannister/Gallo, 44t Flavio Pagani/Sygma, 47 Michel Setboun, 48 Keren Su, 50 Ricky Rogers/Reuters, 51 Catherine Karnow, 55 Bettmann, 58 Norbert Schaefer, 59 Christophe Boisvieux, 60tl Uli Wiesmeier/zefa, 60r Ann Johansson, 61 Amet Jean Pierre/Sygma, 64 Farahnaz Karimy/epa, 66 Kim Ludbrook/epa, 67r Nevada Wier, 68b David Pollack, 69r Thierry Roge/Reuters, 70t Archivo Iconografico, SA, 71 Webistan, 73l&r Bettmann, 77t Eric Preau/Sygma, 78 John-Francis Bourke/zefa, 79r Paul A. Souders, 81r Sygma, 82t, 83r Nik Wheeler, 83b Hulton-Deutsch, 85 Philip Wallick, 88 Bob Krist, 89 Frank Lukasseck/zefa, 90 Peter Adams/zefa, 90-91 Michael Hagedorn/zefa, 92 Bo Zaunders, 95 Christophe Boisvieux, 96-97 Remi Benali, 99 Jose Fuste Raga, 100, 101 Macduff Everton, 102 Murat Taner/zefa, 106-107 Ladislav Janicek/zefa, 108t Earl & Nazima Kowall, 110 Randy Faris, 111 Leonard de Selva, 112 Rune Hellestad, 114-115 Tom Grill, 116-117 & 117 Archivo Iconografico, SA, 119 Hulton-Deutsch, 122r & 123t Bettmann, 124l Reuters, 125t Denis O'Regan, 126 Jacqueline Sallow, 127t, 128t Cardinale Stephane/Sygma, 129 Reuters, 131 Steffen Schmidt/epa, 135 Suzanne Tenner/20th Century Fox/Bureau L.A. Collection, 138 Robbie Jack, 139 Seth Wenig/Reuters, 141 Reuters, 143t Arko Datta/Reuters, 144 Bureau L.A. Collection, 146 Bettmann, 150 Blue Sky Studios/20th Century Fox/Bureau L.A. Collection, 151 DreamWorks Animation/Zuma, 155t Melissa Moseley/Sony Pictures/ Bureau L.A. Collection, 156l Bettmann, 158t Sunset Boulevard, 160 John Springer Collection, 165 DreamWorks SKG/Zuma, 166 Sergei Ilnitsky/epa, 171 Frank May/dpa, 173t Kevin P. Casey, 174b Michael S. Yamashita, 177 Adam Woolfitt, 180l Shepard Sherbell, 182-183 Lester Lefkowitz, 185 H. Sung Hyok/Sygma, 187 Oliver Berg/dpa, 188-189 Yang Liu, 192l Toyota Motor Corp/Handout/Reuters, 195b Bryan F. Peterson, 196l The Mariners' Museum, 197b Neil Rabinowitz, 198l Museum of Flight, 199 George Hall, 200 Reuters, 201 Kapoor Balder/Sygma, 203l Pablo Corral V, 203b Jon Hicks, 204-205 Kelly-Mooney Photography, 208t Troy Wayrynen/NewSport, 209b Karl-Josef Hildenbrand/epa, 211t Alexandros Vlachos/epa, 212b Hulton-Deutsch Collection, 213r Dimitri Lundt/TempSport, 212-213 Robert Ghement/epa, 215 Bettmann, 216b Duomo, 217 Bob Leverone/TSN/Zuma, 219 Reuters, 220-221 Alan Schein Photography, 220b Kay Nietfeld/epa, 222 Wally McNamee, 224 Justin Lane/epa, 226-227 Bettmann, 228l Le Segretain/Sygma, 229r Christian Liewig/Liewig Media Sports, 231r Tony Roberts, 232b Jim Young/Reuters, 235b Nikos Mitsouras/epa, 236-237 Tolga Bozoglu/epa, 237r Rick Rickman/NewSport, 239r Gero Breloer/DPA/epa, 240b Mike Finn-Kelcey/Reuters, 241 Michael Crabtree/Reuters, 242t Kay Nietfeld/epa, 243 Charles W Luzier/Reuters, 245 Ken Kaminesky/Take 2 Productions.

Getty Images: 28, 41 National Geographic, 46 Don Farrall, 76, 132, 175r, 193r, 194t&b, 210r, 214t, 222bl, 238r Roger Viollet.

Ivan Hissey: 21r, 32-33, 37t, 44r, 45r, 49l&r, 72b, 98, 157b, 158-159, 181t&c, 208b, 210b.

iStockphoto: 18, 22, 24, 24-25, 26t&b, 27t&r, 34-35, 35tr, 36t, 38t, 40, 42b, 43t&l, 45l&b, 49t&l, 50b, 54t, 56 all, 57r, 58t, 64-65, 65l&r, 67l, 68t, 69l, 72t, 75r&b, 77b, 79t&b, 80 all, 81, 82b, 84t&b, 88b, 93t, 94t&b, 96t, 100-101, 103, 106l, 107r, 108b, 109r&b, 110t, 111l, 112-113, 113b, 119t&b, 122b, 123b, 125l&b, 127b, 128b, 130, 133t&b, 134-135, 138-139t&b, 140, 141b, 143b, 147b, 155b, 163l, 167, 170, 173b, 175t&b, 176t&b, 178, 179, 180t, 181b, 183r, 184t&b, 186, 192t, 192b all, 193t&b, 195t, 196-197, 198t, 202 all, 203t, 209t, 210t, 211b, 214b, 216t, 222l&b, 228t,r&b, 229l, 230-231, 232-233, 234, 235t, 238t, 240-241, 242b, 243t, 244r&b, 247.

Kobal Collection: 134 20th Century Fox, 142 Warner Bros/DC Comics, 145 Lucas Film/20th Century Fox, 147t Universal, 148 20th Century Fox, 149t MGM/United Artists/Sony/Maidment, Jay, 152 Walt Disney, 153 20th Century Fox, 154 Miramax/James, David, 156r Universal, 157t Warner Bros., 159t Fox Searchlight, 161 Miramax/Sparham, Laurie, 162 Oil Flick/UK Film Council/16 Films/Element/Barratt, Joss, 163t Sony/Buitendijk, Jaap, 164 New Line/Saw Zaentz/Wing Nut/Vinet, Pierre, 172 Universal/Amblin/James, David.

Mary Evans Picture Library: 29, 74, 77c, 114.

NASA: 10-11, 11l, 12tr, 13 Jet Propulsion Laboratory, 14, 15, 15r Kennedy Space Center, 15l Johnson Space Center, 15br Marshall Space Flight Center, 37t.

Science Photo Library: 12tl David Nunuk, 54r John Daugherty, 57 Adam Gault.

Publisher's Acknowledgements
Cover design: Ron Callow

Packager's Acknowledgements
Palazzo Editions would like to thank Richard Constable and Robert Walster for their design contributions.